REMEMBERING ESPERANZA

REMEMBERING ESPERANZA

A Cultural-Political Theology for North American Praxis

Mark Kline Taylor

ORBIS BOOKS

Maryknoll, New York 10545

The Catholic Foreign Mission Society of America (Maryknoll) recruits and trains people for overseas missionary service. Through Orbis Books, Maryknoll aims to foster the international dialogue that is essential to mission. The books published, however, reflect the opinions of their authors and are not meant to represent the official position of the society.

Library of Congress Cataloguing-in-Publication Data

Taylor, Mark Kline, 1951-
  Remembering Esperanza : a cultural-political theology for North
American praxis / Mark Kline Taylor.
      p.   cm.
  Includes bibliographical references.
  ISBN 0-88344-642-1
  1. Theology—Methodology.   2. Postmodernism—Religious aspects—
Christianity.   3. Christianity and politics.   4. Christianity and
culture.   5. Christianity and justice.   6. Jesus Christ—Person and
offices.   I. Title.
BR118.T39 1989
261.8'097—dc20   90-30183
                                                          CIP

To A. S. K.

Thru the wild cathedral evening the rain unraveled tales
For the disrobed faceless forms of no position
Tolling for the tongues with no place to bring their
thoughts
All down in taken for granted situations
Tolling for the deaf an' blind, tolling for the mute,
Tolling for the mistreated, mateless mother, the mistitled
prostitute,
For the misdemeanor outlaw chased an' cheated by pursuit
An' we gazed upon the chimes of freedom flashing. . . .
Tolling for the aching ones whose wounds cannot be
nursed
For the countless confused, accused, misused, strung out
ones an' worse
An' for every hung up person in the whole wide universe
An' we gazed upon the chimes of freedom flashing.

from "Chimes of Freedom"
Words and music by Bob Dylan, 1964

CONTENTS

PREFACE

This book is an attempt to trace one of the lifelines of my theological work. It begins with some of my earliest memories as a five-year-old boy in a Zapotec village in southern Mexico, where I first encountered Esperanza and her world. The book moves from those memories into proposals for theological method, which is now awash in the turbulent currents of "postmodern" society in North America. It extends to drawing the main lines of a christology that addresses the contemporary challenges of cultural pluralism and political oppression.

The argument at the heart of this book is that present North American social and institutional practices feature a thoroughgoing, albeit often well disguised, "abstraction" from material conditions, an abstraction that wreaks abuse and oppression on humanity and on nature; an abstraction that is a turning away from, often an abhorrence and fear of, concrete existence. The fault is not abstract thinking; rather, it is thinking and practice turned away from the sources of human and natural life: matter, bodies, mothers, darkness. The christology of *Christus Mater* with which I experiment in the closing two chapters emerges as a way for us to think and practice in response to this abstraction that drives so many of the political oppressions from which we suffer and by which we cause suffering to others.

This central argument is situated, however, within a larger argument that suffuses the entire volume. This more pervasive argument holds that any position should attempt to show how it is entangled in particular social locations and intellectual biases. Accordingly, the book works slowly toward its central argument, which is developed across chapters 3 and 4, enveloping it with thoughts (personal, cultural, philosophical, theological) that are elaborated from memories I have of the world of the young Zapotec woman Esperanza. So it is that this book in its entirety is an exercise in *Remembering Esperanza*.

Writing a book of this sort makes me ever more aware of the large number of friends, scholars, and students who form the matrix within which this book was written. I am happy to acknowledge, therefore, the valuable criticism that I have received from them and the significant support given me by so many.

Michael Welker, Cleo McNelly Kearns, and Daniel L. Migliore were teaching colleagues here at Princeton Theological Seminary who, during the past year, found time to read this book's manuscript or portions of it and offer me their criticisms of it. I am also appreciative of the readings and criticisms offered by Paul Knitter, Sharon Welch, and Catherine Keller. Certainly none of these should be taken to task for my failing to follow all their good advice. The faults of the book remain my own, as were the pleasure and challenges of writing it.

I owe a special debt of gratitude to Terrence N. Tice, not only for offering his substantive criticism of my theological project, but also for his caring and meticulous attention to details of grammar and syntax. He especially will note just how significant his contribution has been and how far short I still am from the ideals of scholarship embodied in his thought and practice.

I am also pleased to thank those who have hosted me and educated me in Central America over the last three years as they reacquainted me with the language, nations, cultures, and political struggles of churches and other groups in that region. Both Central Americans and the North Americans working there, often at considerable personal risk, have taught me much about the struggles for liberation by people of Christian faith there and here. Acknowledging them by name in this all-too-academic a book would no doubt endanger them little; but to be sure, I will leave them unnamed while underscoring my profound gratitude for their contributions to this work. Given the title of this volume I especially acknowledge my indebtedness to the witness of those laboring in one of Guatemala City's largest barrio settlements, named "Esperanza." The compassion, wisdom and human labor evident in the Esperanza barrio, among some of the world's poorest people, is striking testimony to what I understand to be "life in Christ."

Students in both Masters and Ph.D. programs at Princeton Theological Seminary have provided a constant source of challenge and productive conversation. Several of these were able to take time to read an early draft of the book, and I therefore happily acknowledge the contributions of Kimberly P. Chastain, John W. Webster, Carol Jean Cook, Donald R. Schweitzer, David M. Joint, and Stephen Stell. Portions of the draft were also helpfully read by Linda L. Kinch Wass and Kenneth S. Willian.

Further, it is a pleasure to acknowledge the support of two special communities.

Princeton Theological Seminary not only provided major funding for my research trips in Central America, but also made possible a research leave that allowed time for part of the research going into this book.

The Workgroup on Constructive Theology meeting at Vanderbilt University Divinity School in 1987 and at the Candler School of Theology at Emory University in 1988 provided occasions for me to present two papers on some of the seminal ideas of this book. I thank the theologians of this workgroup for patiently giving me a hearing and their vigorous criticism.

Joe Herman provided the secretarial labor for this book. I note gratefully his patience while rendering this manuscript into typed form. The editorial staff at Orbis Books has been helpful at every step. I thank Paul Knitter for his early support and Robert Ellsberg's and Eve Drogin's editorial interest. Special thanks to William R. Burrows, who provided editorial oversight for this particular book. He brought both intellectual acumen and an editor's patience into conversation with me about this text.

Life with my family is always such a source of challenge and creativity that it seems inadequate to thank them here. However, given the contents of this book, I happily name and thank Anita Kline, Nadia Kline-Taylor, and Laura Kline-Taylor.

Especially I thank my mother and father, Floris B. Taylor and Robert B. Taylor, who included their children in their adventures of anthropological fieldwork, thus enabling me to live with the memories from which this book begins.

ACKNOWLEDGMENTS

Grateful acknowledgment is made to the following authors and their publishers for the use of copyright materials appearing in *Remembering Esperanza.*

To Frances Croake Frank for the poem appearing on pages 244-45. These verses were taken from *Celebrating Women,* which appeared in *The National Catholic Reporter,* 21 December 1979.

To Bruce Springsteen for the verse of his song, "Factory" appearing on page 96, taken from his album *Darkness on the Edge of Town,* © Columbia Broadcasting System, 1978.

To Gwendolyn Brooks for segments from her poem, "Primer for Blacks," Brooks Press, Chicago IL, © 1980.

To Julia Esquivel for lines from the poem, "They Have Threatened Us with Resurrection," appearing on page 244. They were taken from her *Threatened with Resurrection: Prayers and Poems from an Exiled Guatemalan* (Elgin, Ill.: The Brethren Press, 1982), © Brethren Press, 1982.

To Margaret Walker Alexander, for lines from the poem, "THIS IS MY CENTURY ... Black Synthesis of Time," appearing on page 229. They were taken from Baraka, eds., *Confirmation,* © University of Georgia Press, 1989.

To Bob Dylan for lyrics from "Chimes of Freedom," appearing on page vi, © 1964 by Warner Bros Inc., all rights reserved.

Prologue

AUTOBIOGRAPHY, RE-MEMBERING, THEOLOGY

Esperanza used to pick me up, hold me tight, and tickle me. She was a fourteen-year-old girl of the Zapotec village of Teotitlan del Valle, in southern Mexico's province of Oaxaca. She lived just down the street on which my anthropologist father and family lived for a year when I was five.

I both dreaded and loved the attentions of Esperanza. Even today, preserved as she is on anthropologist's film, this Zapotec girl's image can prompt in me two unfortunate postures toward "the other" that we Euro-Americans have often assumed: dread, and for me the more usual temptation, romanticizing. One may recall the North Atlantic images of "the noble savage."[1] Usually my tendencies toward these postures are checked when I remember that in all her difference, Esperanza and I shared a world —not one primarily of values, language, or culture, but one formed by the dusty street we shared, by our houses connected by walls of cactus, or by the playful touch that somehow happened between us without a negotiating of common ground.

In the encounter with Esperanza and in my memories of her, more is going on than I am able (or probably willing!) to probe here. Playing in that encounter are dynamics involving my gender, sexuality, race, class, and culture. Boy and girl, the joy of touch and desire in children's play, being, along with my sister (just one year younger than me), the only light-skinned children among the browner-skinned Zapotecs, never really shedding the middle-class privileges of North American life during our year-long dwelling in Teotitlan's adobe structures—all these realities existed between Esperanza and me.

There may be much for me to celebrate here as a valuable encounter with cultural difference at an early age. There may also be much to engender suspicion. Indeed, anthropologists and their families doing fieldwork have often been situated in the context of Euro-American conquest and oppression of colonized and third-world regions.[2] As between Esperanza and me, so in this book's attention to "others," there lies the risk that talking about some persons as other reflects their subordinate position.

1

AUTOBIOGRAPHY

I have begun with my memories of Esperanza not to initiate a tortuous, pointless self-reflexivity on my own subjectivity, as if through some willful self-scrutiny I could yield knowledge of myself that somehow facilitates theological knowledge. I neither propose nor am able to write my autobiography here, but I do wish to show that autobiographical elements can have an important place in contemporary theology.

Putting autobiographical elements into theology ·is one way to redress the often-lamented distance of theology from peoples' religious, cultural, and political experiences. What Johann Baptist Metz has written about Roman Catholic theology applies to a wide range of theological writings produced by North Atlantic academics: "dogmatic theology . . . became an increasingly atrophied form of teaching and often functioned as a systematized fear of contagion from life that was not understood."[3]

The flood of current writings from so-called third-world regions and from oppressed and marginalized peoples within North Atlantic societies, among its other contributions, dramatizes the importance of interweaving theological reflection not only with cultural-political contexts but also with the writer's own story.

These are lessons that many of us North American theologians have learned in dramatic form from writings like those of Gustavo Gutiérrez, who has spoken of theology as a "second act," an act of reflection on praxis as a historical struggle of churches for the freedom and sustenance rights of their people. This second-order character of theology is consonant with the Augustinian view of theology as "faith seeking understanding." Preeminently, today's liberation theologies are critical reflections born of a faith that is seeking understanding. The special drama and significance of this faith search, however, is that it is done by theologians with and for those struggling for their very survival. Among many other theologians who have been carrying out this effort are José Míguez-Bonino, Jon Sobrino, Clodovis Boff, Leonardo Boff, Hugo Assmann, Allan Boesak, Desmond Tutu, Mercy Ambah Oduyoye, Tissa Balasuriya, and others. To them must be added the thousands of Christians whose names are not well known at all, but whose participation in ecclesial struggles for liberation from political subjugation is a striking witness to vital Christian practice and forms the base of those liberation theologies that have sharply challenged both North American and European theological academies.

While these theologies tend to interweave dramatically their theological reflections with their churches' dynamic cultural and political contexts, they do not frequently display their connectedness to praxis through autobiographical reflection. Perhaps some of the North American liberation theologies that have put their autobiographies into play to a greater degree may eventually help intensify the concreteness found in other liberation theologies as well. African American theologian James Cone, for example, has not only written a short autobiographical work, he has also integrated autobiographical elements into his other theological texts. His *God of the Oppressed* begins with the line: "I was born in Fordyce, Arkansas."

Within North American academies, perhaps Christian feminists most noticeably place the element of story at the heart of theological method and writing.[4] This provides feminist theological writing much of its power to connect with and address contemporary readers. As some of these same feminist writers acknowledge, however, the story, when related to religious experience, can easily become an individualistic narrative, a pious fabrication of one's spiritual life journey akin to what is called a "testimony" in fundamentalism. A feminist's "story" can easily become the radicalized obverse of the fundamentalist individual's testimony. The story in theology may be especially prone to this distortion in North American settings, where individualistic currents flow quite forcefully through our commitments and practices.[5]

Autobiographical elements need not be jettisoned for fear of individualism or subjectivism. The individual and the subject can be introduced into theology without those distortions. For this to occur best, we need to articulate our personal stories in relationship to cultural and political dynamics. Theology without self-reference may become lifeless, but self-reference without specifying one's entailment in cultural and political contexts allows an exaggerated individualism.

The more valuable kind of self-reference, or integration of one's story into reflection, is given helpful technical treatment by Calvin Schrag in his book, *Communicative Praxis and the Space of Subjectivity*.[6] Throughout the North Atlantic academies of the 1980s, much has been said about the "twilight of subjectivity" or the "end of the subject." In conversation with these themes, Schrag argues persuasively for a resituating of the subject within a space that he calls a "communicative praxis." This position offers anything but an individualistic notion of the subject. Herein, the "space" of the subject is an "actional route" that includes *both* our concrete individual stories *and* the social practices of other agents, actors, and forces that issue from them. As Schrag puts it, "The space of subjectivity of the acting subject is that of a field of projects, incorporating an agenda of action that has both its precedents and its new business to be enacted."[7]

The act of specifying this subject is a way of addressing the "who" of discourse. Schrag terms this act of specifying "hermeneutical self-implicature." A given discourse — speaking, writing and/or acting — is that of a situated subject. Discourse is not reduced to such a situated subject, nor is the subject the "foundation" of the discourse. Rather, the subject is an essential implicate of the discourse. Thus, a "hermeneutical self-implicature" that tracks the who of discourse is necessary for understanding that discourse and dramatizing its relatedness to diverse life processes.

If I begin with my memories of Esperanza, then, I do so not just to tell "my story" but to signal and affirm the kind of communicative praxis or "actional route" in which I find myself moving. It is a way to signal "the who" of this written discourse as one also connected with others in particular ways. The ability of these particular memories of Esperanza to signal my own or others' spaces of communicative praxis needs testing in the writing and readings to follow, but memory, as a subterranean, critical, and imaginative reflection on one's past, is what best initially reveals the specificities of my communicative action and historical frame of reference.[8]

As a theologian, my academic training did not prepare me for the integration of autobiography into theology, even for the more academic-sounding "hermeneutical self-implicature" that I have just sketched. Theologians in North American divinity schools, universities, and colleges labor hard to clothe their theology with a kind of critical rigor and technical language that earn it a place in the academy. I do not at all resist the need for theology to be an academic, critically rigorous practice. Critical disciplines need their own technical jargons, but often these lead to the neglect of self-involving elements of discourse. Even when theology turns to critical reflection on experience, the turn is often to phenomenology, ontology, perhaps to the social sciences, but rarely to the messy world in which dynamics of class, gender, race, and culture interplay and condition the analyst's reflections. Still more rare is a self-locating consciousness operative in the various philosophical-theological studies of experience.

Theologians located in the seminaries often claim to be better in this respect, but the act of self-implicature there is mainly in terms of "faith" experience or "ecclesial" confession and heritage. These theologians often invoke the "faith seeking understanding" formula of Anselm and others to stress the ways in which the "second order" character of theological knowledge emerges from faith. This is hardly a sufficient mode of self-implicature and location, however. Generally, faith and religious experience are indeed determinants of human identity, but these are far from being the major demarcators that locate situated subjects. Faith practices and religious experiences are refracted by a variety of political factors, such as gender, class, sexual orientation, and ethnicity, in their diverse cultural forms. Exposure of theologians' self-implicature is thus inadequate if it invokes only "faith" or "ecclesial" tradition as the experiential settings.

RE-MEMBERING

If it is true that a critical weaving of autobiographical elements into theological reflection—what Metz calls "theological biography"[9]—plays a crucial role in mitigating theology's slide into objectively atrophied forms of teaching, then we need to ask how we can best present those autobiographical elements for theological use.

I suggest that the move through autobiographical elements to theological reflection occurs not by attending to the specific plot or trajectory of events that make up one's story as it may be told to a friend, in a citizens' movement meeting, in a women's or men's support group, or in a Christian ecclesial community. More significant is disciplined probing of one's experience of remembering. Remembering is, of course, what empowers the telling of a story or the construction of an autobiography.[10]

Anyone who has attempted to write or tell his or her story discerns how its pattern or plot changes from one telling to the next as it is offered to first this group and then another. Because of this tendency, it is better to focus on autobiographical elements less as a linear sequence of events and more as a recurring set of emphases or themes that come to light through reflection on the shape and nature of remembering. Remembering is reconstituting, restoring to connection what is often fragmented. When emphasizing the memory's power to restore connections, I will write of *re-membering*.

Below, I will present my own remembering in terms of four major traits of remembering that I identify from some phenomenological explorations of memory and remembering.[11] Each of these traits will allow me to put into play some of my own particularly salient autobiographical elements, thus attempting to present what Calvin Schrag has termed "the who" of this book's discourse.

Visions of Esperanza's World

The first trait highlights *the predominantly visual character*. Some writers, when reflecting on the power of memory, note the lesser function of the memory's "hearing" and the predominance of its "seeing." "The overall effect is of a moving montage of visual contrasts."[12]

This is certainly true concerning my own remembering of Esperanza and the scenes of our encounter. Primary is a montage that includes visions of the layout of my family's large one-room dwelling in Teotitlan, the dirt courtyard in which my sister and I played cars (sometimes with our Zapotec friends). One quadrant of the courtyard included the deep well from which we drew water to boil for cooking and washing ("Stay away from the well. Don't fall in."). Further out to the corner of the same quadrant was the outhouse, which somehow let in a few rays of light from the riverbed area that ran behind our courtyard. From that perch I could hear the Zapotec women at the riverside talking while washing garments.

Included in my visual montage are the colors of the *serapes*, the well-known blankets produced by the male weavers of Teotitlan. There remains in my memory the dim candlelight of late-night religious processions through village streets, to which my father would take me—rendered all the more magical by the multicolored, feathered headdresses reflecting that light among the portable shrines the Zapotecs carried.

There are also the grays and browns of the village street, of adobe walls and the nearby rugged, stony foothills that we climbed or hiked to find other dwellings. I can still see the noiseless, swift movement of my family from our adobe structure to the open courtyard during earthquake tremors.

The memory's "hearing" should not be underestimated. In my case, I retain the sounds, perhaps especially the smells, of early mornings in Teotitlan: *burros* braying, roosters crowing, Zapotec women grinding their corn on their stone *matates*, our mother and father rattling pots in our make-do kitchen. With me, too, are the sounds of our fear-laden voices when our mother lay very ill with typhoid fever and malaria, from which she recovered. This latter "heard" memory interplays with "seeing" her lying on the bed my father built and the sight of my father caring for her.

Concerning Esperanza in particular, the visual is clearly dominant. There lingers the coloring of her Zapotec blouse and wraparound skirt. Though several years older than me, she was close to my height. Her browner skin and dusty and callused feet (especially the feet), unshod in contrast to mine, also left their impressions. Sight and touch predominate over hearing, not only because the lack of a shared language prevented verbal exchange between us, but also because of the overwhelming power of the visual and sensory in memory.

Esperanza's World as Elusive

A second trait of memory concerns a special kind of contrast: *a contrast between the clarity and the indefiniteness of the memory*. Elements of memory often have a certain clarity and unabated impact, but there is also indefiniteness concerning the place, time, objects, and names in the remembered scenes. There is a strong sense of the self's own place and role, but this is diminished in memory by the self's "curiously diluted or dispersed form: faceless and almost bodiless."[13] Other persons are present in the memory, but they are attenuated, indefinite.

This is the case with my memories of encountering Esperanza. The indefiniteness of my memories is signaled by recent discussions with my father, that revealed his surprise that I remembered the encounter with Esperanza with pleasure as well as discomfort. He remembers mainly my discomfort. Dressed in traditional Zapotec costume, a little loud and coarse in her behavior, even by Zapotec standards, always intoning my name, hugging and aiming slobbery kisses — all this was part of Esperanza's persona toward me and my sister. Fear and discomfort? Surely. Often I ran. But my memory has left Esperanza clothed with an aura that mixes both desire and fear.

Nor should it be surprising that my sense of self, as of other persons' presence, are tenuous in my memories of scenes with Esperanza. I have a vivid sense of my own, my family's, and Esperanza's presence in the memory, but my own status as an onlooker on the past makes them seem like onlookers, almost passive in their movements relating to me and to one another. All this makes the sense of self and others indefinite. There is little sense that these figures in my memory are actors. Movements between

Esperanza, my family, me, and others are something like a shadow play. To start with memories of Esperanza, then, is to begin with vivid and powerful determinative images that I cannot save from an overall indefiniteness.

Esperanza as Pleasure and Threat

Perhaps it is this play of clarity and indefiniteness that leads to a third trait: a distinctive *emotional tonality*. This trait addresses more directly the feelings of both pleasure and dread linked to my remembering of Esperanza. Casey describes the emotional tone of his memory of waterfalls at Yosemite Park as one of "muted exaltation." Although encounter with Esperanza is of a very different type, that phrase captures the tone of my memories, too. There was exhilaration in the presence of someone I knew who was so different in language, custom, dress and appearance. My sister and I loved anticipating going to Teotitlan and liked many features of being there.

The memory's exhilaration is also muted, however, not only because even a vivid memory is muted by its distance from the past but also because the exhilaration was muted at the time. Although other North Americans might experience more radical forms of cultural difference, in Teotitlan the experience of difference was sufficient to cause my five-year-old sensibilities to feel the very repulsion that is so intrinsic to ethnocentric responses in the face of cultural difference.[14] Then there was also the comparative hardship of life there, that even at age five I could contrast with the comforts of North American life in Oregon or Illinois. The exhilaration, therefore, was muted by an always-present unease. Excitement and pleasure remain primary to the memory, but unsettling difference and perceived hardship contributed to a muting of the pleasure, yielding for me a subtle mixture of longing and pleasure, discomfort and a will to avoid.

Esperanza and Intersecting Memories

A fourth trait of memory, one very significant in my own case, is *the way this primary memory intersects with others*. I have already said just how full and heterogeneous are my memories of Esperanza, loaded with colors, sounds, smells, family hardship, diverse cultural practices, and the like. With this trait, however, I want to note how memories of Esperanza intersect with other major clusters of memories that relate to other major themes or to other locations and persons. I will note just three of these intersecting memories.

1. *A Family's Practice of Christian Faith*. First, there intersects with Esperanza memories my earliest memories of our family's practice of Christianity. The most powerful first memories of this occur on the same scene on which Esperanza was encountered. Given the longstanding tensions between pro-

fessional anthropologists and practicing Christians,[15] it was somewhat unusual for me to be exposed to the family practice of Christianity in connection with a professional anthropologist's fieldwork. In my father's case the practice of Christianity was not allowed to interfere with the practice of fieldwork, though of course there could not help but be significant mutual conditioning of the two practices, if only within the person of the anthropologist.

Our Christian worship experience took place in the neighboring village of Mitla, in association with area Wycliffe missionaries carrying on translation work, people who had played a role in situating our family in Teotitlan. It is not unusual for anthropologists to receive this kind of aid from missionaries, even though many an anthropologist has found it necessary to critique both past and continuing forms of missionary ethnocentrism and cultural imperialism. However, the blanket antimissionary polemic of many anthropologists overlooks the mutually supportive relationship that often existed between them.[16]

In the context of this distinctive Christian practice, I recall sensing that Esperanza and I were not only culturally different but also religiously different. I knew almost nothing about her religious practice, other than the mystique of her Zapotec people's nighttime processions and strange shrines. My Christian faith was "other" to her, and her practice was "other" to me.

This realization permeated my encountering Esperanza with a religious puzzlement signaled to me in subtle ways. Within the milieu of a Protestant evangelical Christian community like the Wycliffe translators, this puzzlement could be intense. On the one hand, the Wycliffe appreciation for cultural, anthropological, and linguistic approaches to the peoples with whom they worked imparted a sense of the intrinsic worth of Esperanza and the Zapotecs. Their unsettling magnificence was simply there, to be accepted, learned, and even seen as source of my own instruction. It was a Christian virtue to adapt to the ways of the other's culture, language, and social location.

On the other hand, Wycliffe missionary zeal ("spreading the gospel of Christ") suggested that something was lacking in the Zapotec world. Indeed a deficiency was signaled in Esperanza and her world, however many sophisticated techniques might be employed to study and affirm her world's cultural distinctiveness. Later in life I would again encounter this mix of saying a sophisticated Yes to the culturally others and of saying a No to them. This occurred in subsequent encounters with Wycliffe missionaries in the United States: through association with friends of my parents, attending "jungle camps" for youth led by Wycliffe missionaries to impart survival skills (hammock and machete use, hiking skills and so forth) and, of course, also to teach their Protestant evangelical vision.

I have long since lost touch with the Wycliffe people. As a Christian and a theologian, I find their Protestant evangelical thought impossible to accept, often seeing it as misguided and even superstitious. Moreover, while I still appreciate their cultural and language translation skills, I believe that, with some exceptions, Wycliffe political consciousness in third-world contexts is so unformed (at best) or imperialistically constructed (at worst) that the typical damage done to many societies by North American efforts is only reinforced by them.[17]

I suspect that my early exposure to Protestant evangelicalism laced my early intercultural encounter in Teotitlan with religious and theological import and kept two major problems on my agenda.

The first problem concerns the sheer fact of my early experience of both professional anthropological practice *and* a remarkably serious Christian practice. As I grew, my wonder at this mix also grew, especially as I learned more about the frequent alienation of these two practices, particularly in North American academies. Both kinds of practice were put on my agenda of existential and theoretical interests, and of paramount concern was my felt need to articulate some relationship between the two practices that would not violate the distinctive character of each. Years later my Ph.D. dissertation and first book comprised one such attempt, there exploring (as is customary, without divulging the reasons for my interest!) religious dimensions *in* cultural anthropology. Prior to the dissertation, during my college and seminary years, almost all my intellectual and personal quests had to be both anthropological and Christian, whether finding expression in a college research paper, a seminary polity exam, or a dorm-room bull session.

The second major problem has been the more properly theological one. It focuses on the meanings of Christian practice *for* intercultural experience. Christian practice and thought need the criticism emerging from anthropological practice, severe as it often may be, but this does not mean that Christian practice and thought are without their own contribution to intercultural dialogue. Through some strong recasting of the Christian tradition (in ways many Christians probably would not accept), I have tried to portray Christian practice and thought as nurturing vigorous affirmation of cultural difference, together with sustained resistance to the oppression and exploitation found in any culture.[18]

This is all, in large part, a working out of constantly developing memories of Esperanza and Teotitlan, especially as they intersect with the memories of the intense Christian practice present there. With that intersection, my received Christian tradition — always undergoing rapid revisioning — could not be thought or lived apart from exploration of its meanings for cultural difference.

2. Suffering and Oppression in Today's Guatemala. A set of more recent adult memories also intersects with the early ones of Esperanza. These are of travel and life in Central America for short trips, never more than six weeks long. I have not returned to Teotitlan. Nicaragua, and especially Guatemala, have been the scenes of these most recent memories. While I was working to improve my Spanish in these Central American settings, especially among the Amerindian areas of Guatemala, my memories of Esperanza were freshly awakened. As might be said about intersecting memories generally, so it is with mine: These more recent ones, by intersecting, confirm and fix the primary remembrance, contributing to the survival of my Esperanza memories.[19]

The feature of the Guatemalan context that works the survival of the primary remembrance, keeping it fresh, is one that explicitly highlights what often only lay implicit in my memories of Esperanza: a heightened awareness of Native Americans' situation of oppression and suffering. Above, I noted memories of my family's "hardship" in Teotitlan. Now, as real as those memories still are, more salient are the hardships of the Central Americans, borne by Guatemalans of the towns of Chimaltenango, Santiago Atitlan, Nebaj, Panzos, Chajul, and elsewhere. The hardships in question include not only the grinding poverty of everyday life but also the massacres of Guatemalan counterinsurgency campaigns in the 1980s. Memories focused on those salient hardships have broadened my remembering Esperanza beyond being a cultural-personal affair to being one that is also cultural-political. From the beginning of my encounter with her, Esperanza's hardship was always known to me on some level. My family had food that hers did not; we had a doctor in another town and medical services that her family could not afford. I had shoes, she did not.

This latter memory, especially, signaled not only her hardship but her impressive strength. It displayed both vulnerability and resilience. There was something about bare feet (not only Esperanza's, but those of the other Zapotecs) daily working their way through the rituals of work and play that impressed upon me how material hardship and survival often dwell together. I am in danger of romanticizing here, almost valuing a barefoot life, but pity for the hardship would not be appropriate either. Somehow, abiding concern and respect for survival under adverse material conditions must be melded to avoid both pity and romanticizing.

Central American hardship and survival are the experiences that present themselves in Guatemala. That is one reason, perhaps, that memories of Esperanza always come cascading back into mind when I travel or live in today's Guatemala. Many others have documented the nature of hardship and survival there. I must here summarize some major problems in that situation in order to indicate the politicized dimension of my memories of Esperanza.

Through adult memories of my experiences in Guatemala, remembering Esperanza also becomes a matter of remembering the dead — those killed in Amerindian villages in the course of one of the most ruthless counterinsurgency campaigns ever conducted in Latin America. Some sources estimate the number of deaths at 50,000 to 75,000 between 1978 and 1984. Visits to church services, resonant with the plaintive voices of orphan choirs, or to various orphanages in Guatemala, display the reality of 100,000 children who lost one or both of their parents in the early 1980s. Some 35,000 people have been "disappeared" by government security forces over the past two decades.[20]

Remembering Esperanza in Guatemala becomes further politicized in light of my own government's refusal to acknowledge the Guatemalan Amerindians' plight. These Native Americans—like the others already chased, massacred, and confined over the last century on North American terrain—are burdened on Central and South American soil by North American political and economic power and practice.[21] While touting Guatemala as a "model democracy," United States officials propose development projects that do little to improve the Amerindians' lot. Most notably, cash-crop programs have been started that have so far been of little benefit to the native growers. Moreover, the crops do not provide the food that is the substance of Amerindian life. "Any damn fool can grow corn and beans," complained an economic officer at the United States embassy when he spoke glowingly to us visitors about the virtues of starting cash crops for export. That lament displays a gross ignorance of these contemporary Mayans' dependence and reverence for *maize* in daily practice and mythic tradition.

The United States' dominance works exploitation in Guatemala, part of the fabric of relations between the United States and Central American countries, in which that dominance constantly asserts itself. The United States sponsored military aggression against Nicaragua is one more recent example of that hegemony—one maintained by an extraordinary degree of deviance and deceit.[22] Meanwhile, the losers are the dying poor of Central America.

The complicity of United States government and business practice in the suffering of today's Central America is not difficult to trace, but it is such a complex task that I cannot do it here. I am now simply pointing to the contemporary Guatemalan struggle, bound up with United States policy, as it functions to maintain the politicization of my Esperanza memories.

As theologian, then, I am one whose memories, already constituted by the intersection of *cultural* difference and Christian practice, also now include the intersection of ongoing, disturbing memories of *political* domination. To be sure, the Amerindians display a striking strength, poise, will to resist, and even joy that should chasten any North American's tendency to paternalistic pity. But this resilience dwells amid an ongoing experience of quieted, searing pain. In Guatemala, Esperanza's world is a land of "eternal spring and eternal tyranny."[23]

With the development of the memory of Esperanza into its political significance, the fuller shape of my own North American theological program comes into view. It is one that seeks to appropriate a tradition of Christian practice, that exists not only in relation to and for the realities of cultural difference, but also for those suffering political domination.

Memories of tyranny and domination in Guatemala do not, of course, stimulate an exclusive focus on the Guatemalans' plight. Quite to the contrary, the Guatemalan context prompts focus on a whole infrastructure of oppression—not only that existent between North American and Central American societies, but also that found *within* North America. Hence, remembering Esperanza is bound up with a consciousness of the United States oppression of North America's own Native Americans, of racism, classism, and sexism.

Even before my adult experiences in Central America, there had been awareness of North America's own social distortions, though this awareness has become intensified through my Central American encounters. My college years in Seattle involved living for a summer in its skid row community, experimenting as best I could with some urban anthropology techniques for studying lives of displaced men. In southside Chicago during my work on a Ph.D. dissertation, I helped found a local church's program for victims of crime, attempting also to assist community offenders who were identified in the process of working with victims. The involvements were sometimes successful and sometimes not. I often interpreted them, and still would, as opportunities for faithfulness in Christian practice. On another level, however, I am sure that I valued these involvements because they somehow enabled me to stay close to lives where both hardship and survival were salient concerns. Among these concerns, I also found the visions and emotional tone of desire and threat that pervade my memories of Esperanza. I might prefer to cite more altruistic motivations for these involvements (and maybe there were some), but whether urban nomad, crime victim or criminal offender, all were "oppressed others." My being with them was a way of remembering Esperanza.

Remembering Esperanza, however, bears yet another intersecting set of memories, which in large part perhaps accounts for the important, indeed almost privileged, place I will give in this book to analyses of sexism and a theology of resistance to it.

3. *My Memory's Sexual Code: Esperanza and Women.* This third set of intersecting memories I will simply identify as remembered ways of my relating to women. This subject is of course anticipated by a memory that centers on fourteen-year-old Esperanza. My memories of Esperanza, although variously structured, are marked by a definite gender or sexual code. Cultural difference, political domination, and a tradition of Christian practice are integrally bound up with one another, but ultimately, in different ways, they concern *her*. Although their connections to Esperanza run deep and are in some respects still quite shrouded in mystery for me, it should not surprise us that another set of memories intersecting the remembering of Esperanza are those that concern my relating to women—not just to Esperanza but also to my mother, sisters, spouse, daughters, friends, students and professional colleagues.

So the amalgam of religious Christian practice, cultural difference, and political domination that I have already discussed is now made more complex by an added dimension of gender and sexuality. I say sexuality because the dynamics of embodiment are operative in the remembering of Esperanza. The playful touch, the play of color (of dress and skin), all against the background of the physical dynamics of town, nature and culture in Teotitlan, together with the nascent sexuality of my five-year-old body — all give the memory a sensuous quality that makes it all the more vivid. I describe this dimension also as one of gender (a matter of sociocultural formation of sexual identities) because sexuality and sensuousness are mediated by social, cultural and political factors.[24]

Gender and sexuality involve a "code" in the memory of Esperanza, because I can identify certain patterns in my relating to women. The word *pattern* perhaps connotes too much a sense of repetition. But there are what I will call some recurrent emotional-practical postures experienced in relation to women that I will try to name by invoking several pairs of terms: dread/attraction, fear/desire, mystery/mundane. I see the third pair as most persistent and comprehensive, subsuming the other two, which name more occasional tensions.

Viewed and experienced as both mysterious and mundane, women have seemed unknown and known, both other and same. In the uniqueness of a given relationship, it is easy to privilege one posture in the pair over the other, and to that extent a relationship of mutuality is undermined. Typically, women seem and need to be neither the mysterious, unknown other, nor the ordinary, fully known same. The first distortion has led and can lead to the romanticization, fear, and dread of women as "other" that has often fueled the fires of witch-hunting and other forms of containment. The second distortion glosses women's particularity, subsumes their difference within male visions of the ordinary. Both distortions seem the stuff of interpersonal conflict between individual men and women and of social and political alienation between the sexes on more systemic levels. When I experience relationships with women that work, usually there is a co-occurrence of both the mysterious and the mundane in my emotional-practical posture toward them. I am not speaking of some idealized, intellectualist mode of relating, whereby an overly intentional approach seeks to combine awe and sense of the common. I am acknowledging, retrospectively, that in the process of seeking to do justice to the particularity of a woman colleague, spouse, or friend and to her respective journey, I note in myself an emotional posture that combines both awe and a sense of shared commonness.

To be sure, this tension persists in almost all relationships. It is true of my relationships with other men and to myself. In both cases the mysterious and the mundane interplay and separate in varying ways. But the play and the struggle are most intense vis-à-vis women. With memories of Esperanza this is strikingly true, but also with my mother, with whom, for all our closeness, the sense of unknowing is always as intense as that of knowing.

A similar play of emotional-practical postures, of the mysterious and the mundane, touches other relationships: with a sister just a year younger, with whom an everyday commonality was long shared but whose growth — bodily, emotionally, and intellectually — became and remain so different; with my spouse, with whom a fifteen-year period of sharing routines of eating, fighting, sleeping, playing, loving, and child raising is intertwined with a sense of mystery, a wonderful knowing that not all is known; with our daughters whose enthusiasm and struggle for growth invite me to share a commonness across the gender gap but also remind me that in the father-daughter relationship the difference of gender puts some real limits on experienced commonality; with women friends, students, and colleagues, with whom I usually always anticipate a full mutuality and shared freedom in friendship, classroom and work places, but whose differences — of body, maybe of psychological development and language, surely of cultural experience — I cannot forget and remain a source of continual wonder.

I hope I am saying more than what men often say about women amid their living with them: "Women! Who can understand them?" Perhaps I am closer to this ordinary observation than I like to admit, but I am also aware how that lament usually functions as misogyny. I am not free from my own forms of misogynist lament, but I value the whole tense interplay between the mystery and the mundane that seems to abide in concrete encounters with women. Remembering Esperanza, her being at once other and same, has come to mean that I acknowledge, affirm, and value both the threatening anxiety and the assuring strength that at times emanate from this tense interplay of the mysterious and the mundane in women.

Remembering Esperanza, as I have developed it in this section, may seem to yield a view of women as other. As Simone de Beauvoir long ago argued persuasively, that posture is fraught with difficulties. When woman is simply "the other," man becomes "the same," the standard by which women are made other. Women easily become objects of dread and are then often wrongfully restricted, becoming "the expendable others."

Viewing women as other, however, need not entail dominating them. In fact, as some of the new French feminisms argue (as well as some North American feminisms), the valuing of women's differences, in ways contrary to the stereotypical differences, is a component of women's freedom.[25] As I will suggest later in this volume, it is actually the full dialectical play between a view of woman as other and a view of woman as same that is necessary for a practice and thought consonant with women's liberation.

A large part of my interest and commitment to contemporary feminism (and for men I believe this is always an imperfect commitment)[26] can be traced to the fact that in feminism I encounter women claiming both a common humanity with men and a valuable female difference, one that is not just the culture's established way of specifying women's differences. It is a struggle where once again the lure of the mysterious and the mundane is extremely intense. I have foundered before, in both thought and action, in my attempts to embrace fully both the otherness and sameness of women, sometimes making too much of their difference and too little of their common humanity, at other times making too much of their sameness and too little of their valued difference. As I have already suggested, in my case there may be a tendency to romanticize women's liberating difference. Contemporary feminist theorists themselves seem divided on the issue of how to hold this dialectic in unity, some arguing for women's freedom by insisting on basic rights issuing from a common humanity (an Enlightenment liberal feminism) while others argue for this freedom out of a sense of women's valuable difference flourishing in women's culture (a cultural theory of feminism).[27] I do not explore these theoretical conflicts at this point. My concern now is primarily to indicate the presence of this dialectic of the otherness/sameness of women, with which I continue to wrestle, as interwoven with my remembering Esperanza and my valuing of feminist claims.

As I stressed when remembering Esperanza as *culturally* different, so I claim when remembering her as *sexually* different: She is at once other and not other. Affirming this complexity seems necessary in order to do justice not only to my own experience of remembering Esperanza and other women to whom I have related, but also to certain theoretical problems discussed in contemporary studies of women's difference.

In sum, memories of my early Christian practice, of political domination, and of the attracting play of the mysterious and the mundane in relating to women, constitute three major memory complexes that intersect with the primary one of remembering Esperanza.

RE-MEMBERING ESPERANZA AS TROPE

In this prologue so far, I have collected autobiographical elements, ordering them by reference to particular traits of the phenomenon of remembering. Discussing these traits has enabled me to identify additional autobiographical elements and then to explore various relationships between them. I have suggested that it is this reflection on the character of remembering in relation to elements of one's own autobiography that shapes those elements into a meaningful whole — re-members them. Such a whole, with its distinctive set of issues and dynamics, facilitates the move into theological reflection. Before turning to theology in this context, however, it will be helpful to summarize how the phrase *Re-membering Esperanza* is functioning in this text.

Reflecting on the character of remembering as I have, and through the autobiographical elements ordered by such reflection, I am able to take *Re-membering Esperanza* as a trope. In the field of rhetoric, a trope is any literary or rhetorical device that consists in the use of words in more than their literal sense. Re-membering Esperanza functions as a trope in that it invokes awareness and reflection on a set of problems connected to, but ranging beyond, my own specific memories of the Zapotec young woman,

Esperanza. The phrase, then, is a trope in the following senses.

First, it is a trope for the complex set of dynamics and encounters that make up my own self, "the who" generating this book. It is a kind of naming that, in Calvin Schrag's words, constitutes the necessary and intersubjective act of hermeneutical self-implicature — necessary because no longer can we write books, in this view, without attending to the located selves entailed in the writing, and intersubjective because selves (contrary to much North American popular culture) are not just individual, discrete egos, but distinctive beings produced at the centers of various intersubjective dynamics.[28]

The "who" of this discourse is a North American with a particularly meaningful set of memories. These situate my thought and practice in an area of intersection between cultures — between particular ones of North America and Central America. I do not doubt that many others may have dwelled in this sort of encounter with greater intensity, longevity and perhaps sophistication than I have. Given the way I have probed that intersection so far, however, it should be clear that much is involved in that intercultural encounter. Re-membering Esperanza is a trope for my pilgrimage, a journey that has not only an intercultural dimension, but religious, theological, political, and sexual dimensions as well.

Re-membering Esperanza, then, enables me to present myself not just in terms of well-known categories: white, male, relatively affluent. It also enables me to be presented in the particular ways these categories pertain. I seek to write from a space that resists a stereotypical misreading of myself. Yes, white, middle class, straight male are terms that apply to my social location, and these are necessary terms that specify my access to some privileges that are denied others in a systematically distorted North American society. But I write from a space that is also a particular kind of dislocation, or at least disorientation. Esperanza and I as children were both marginal to the adult worlds in which we found ourselves. Further, as a result of my exposure to Esperanza's world, and of all that Re-membering Esperanza means, I am left with a valuable dissonance that interrupts and keeps unsettled my sense of place as a North American. That dissonance resulting from exposure to cultural, political, sexual, or religious difference I experience not as license for "play" or disembodied suspension between worlds, but as a call to be myself where I am, always in relation to others, where they are. This place of dissonance, with its consonant set of concrete practices, tends to place me at the margins of my own official social placement and of other social structures. This is the space which I value, from which I write, and where my own suffering and identity are forged.

Re-membering Esperanza is also a trope for the closely related problems that I see facing today's North American theologians more generally. Unless we sequester ourselves behind our walls of privilege, we are confronted with new voices and new texts. Re-membering Esperanza is not only me staying in touch with an initial wonder and challenge emanating from my personal memories of Esperanza and ongoing experiences of others. It is also North American theologians turning toward and responding to the new voices and texts of peoples who for so long have been denied both voice and text. In North America, feminist, womanist, and black liberation theologies are just three of the powerful currents producing new texts and voices. Add to these the explosion of theologies from other groups—gays and lesbians seeking liberation within the hetero-reality of North American life, Native Americans, North American Hispanics and Chicanos, and various cultures throughout the world that can be heard in North America—and we then find Christian theological and ethical visions refracted into a whole prism of perspectives. Re-membering Esperanza is also a trope for the professional reality of the North American theologian's thought and practice being challenged by these voices.

I would only be repristinating North Atlantic theologians' evasive intellectualism, if I were to imply that Re-membering Esperanza is a trope only for personal or professional problematics. In a third sense, it is also a trope for a certain kind of pain: the pain of a North American who is not only not Zapotec (causing a relatively painless kind of cultural disorientation), but who is also neither poor nor discriminated against because of skin color, gender, or sexual orientation. The pain lies not just in a loss of privilege that goes with acknowledging the oppression made by predominantly white, straight, affluent males in North Atlantic cultures, among whom I am numbered. It more significantly abides in the necessary and appropriate exposure to constant self-critique in which I, and many like me, have been led to work in the hearing of theology's new voices. Living in that self-critique without capitulating to unproductive guilt is also part of the challenge.

There is also the pain of not knowing what *our* particular voice is, now that we affluent, white male Euro-Americans have ceased to speak for all. What does it mean to speak and write for and from my own particularity as a non-poor, male, affluent member of North American society? That kind of painful questioning is not similar in degree or kind to the suffering borne by victims of classism, racism, sexism, or heterosexism, but it does need to be acknowledged and appropriated by me on the way to any real thinking with and acting for those who struggle against more systemic distortions. Re-membering Esperanza is a trope for this kind of pain, and the intellectual struggles and proposals of this book are forged from within it.

The fact that I still struggle and propose is indicative of another sense in which Re-membering Esperanza is a trope. There survives a hope that in spite of the self-critique from which traditionally privileged academics must learn, there can still come a discourse in North American theology that is a genuine contribution to the theological conversation emerging from new contexts: "third-world" cultures, women's experience, the struggles of the materially disenfranchised and disinherited. Re-membering Esperanza, as trope for this hoping, suggests a conviction that somehow the re-membering is one contribution to the reconstituting of new life for those most "dis-membered" by oppressive forces.

The English meaning of Esperanza's name, hope, enables the phrase to be a trope for the hopefulness that I still retain concerning theological work by North American scholars. We must strive within a situation in which North Atlantic intellectual enterprises in theology are appropriately stripped of their traditional privileges, mindful of the fact that there is still much labor demanded of us all.

Alice Jardine addressed "male feminists" who claim solidarity with women feminists with some crucial words. I quote them because I also hear them from women theologians to their male colleagues and from the burgeoning set of the world's new voices to their would-be colleagues in first-world, North Atlantic worlds.

> If you will forgive me my directness, we do not want you to *mimic* us, to become the same as us; we don't want your pathos or your guilt; and we don't even want your admiration (even if it's nice to get it once in awhile). What we want, I would even say what we need, is your *work*. We need you to get down to serious work. And like all serious work, that involves struggle and pain.[29]

Re-membering Esperanza is a work carried on in hope not only of finding one's own contribution but of contributing to the lives of those who demand of us a new mode of relating to and working with them. Re-membering Esperanza is an affirmation in hope of work that ought and can be done by North Atlantic theologians. Thanks in large part to Esperanza (in my case) and to the challenging dissonance created by her world today (for all of us), a culturally, politically, and personally situated North American theology can be crafted that will have something to say and do in the present period. To remember without hope, to remember and then only take up a North American posture of silence and self-doubt—this only reinforces the patterns of dismemberment operative in Esperanza's worlds.

It remains to anticipate the kind of theological *work* that this book will undertake.

THEOLOGY AND PLAN OF THE BOOK

What do I mean by *theology* and what kind of theological work do I offer here? Ultimately, the best response to these questions comes in the exercise of the work which this book represents. A few guiding claims, however, may be helpful.

Within Christian religious contexts, theology takes rise from and occurs within what I call *christopraxis*. It emerges from the acting and thinking that coalesce around lives of commitment to Christ.

It is true, as its parts indicate, that the term theology may be termed discourse (*logos*) about or relating to God (*theos*). God may be variously interpreted as the one who (or that which) ultimately matters to humans in the world; provides the furthest horizons circumscribing our being, action and thought; or nurtures all that is. In Christian contexts, however, this language about the notion of God, and various doctrines of God, rarely avoid the need to talk more particularly of Jesus and the Christ, the one who manifests for Christians what ultimately matters. Christian theology is not just *logos* about God; it is this as a reflective response to a practice of commitment to the Christ. Theology, thus, begins in *christopraxis.*

Both halves of the term *christopraxis*, as denoting contexts and practices in which Christian theology occurs, warrant further comment. As *praxis*, christopraxis entails components of action, decision and reflection.[30] A key question in discussions of praxis — and this pertains to christopraxis as a form of praxis — revolves around how to order the components of action and reflection in praxis.

In this book I am indebted to those theorists who give primacy to communal action over theory *without* reducing theory to a mere reflex of action's determinative forces. Theory and reflection may be necessary and indispensable, but they are not seen to be primary. It is action that gives rise — through symbols, images, and concepts — to theory; but it is theory that, among other things, reflects on that action, clarifies it, and considers certain actions in relation to alternative ones.

To say that Christian theology emerges from praxis, then, is to point to a complex mélange of thinking and doing. In this mélange, action has primacy, but is not antithought. The components of theory make a contribution to action.[31] To accent praxis as I do here is also to highlight the socially and politically conditioned character of theology. This commentary on re-membering Esperanza has been a way to signal not only the complex entanglement of my thoughts and actions, but their social and political contexts. Praxis, then, is surely not only a sense of interiority or spirituality, though that is included. Praxis is also not just individual or personal acting and doing, though again, those are included. Praxis is primarily all this as a communal or intersubjective process laden with social and political freight.

Because theology works within such a complex praxis, it is necessary for it to collaborate with other disciplines.[32] Readers who read on in this book will, in subsequent chapters, find me drawing from writers not only in philosophy, but also in political theory, the social sciences (especially cultural anthropology), and literary criticism. None of us — surely not I — claims mastery in these areas. Nevertheless, collaborating with scholars in those fields is necessary for theologians to understand their own theological task, rooted as it always is in praxis.

This book's theology, however, does not grow out of just any praxis, but a *christo*praxis. The general setting shaped by praxis is necessary and determinative for theology, but for generating Christian theology, there must also be some christic configuration in that praxis.

As *christic* the praxis within which theology occurs is centered around and substantively concerned with the Christ as symbol. This symbol is available to theologians through specific historical configurations of narrative scripture, creeds, doctrinal traditions, and present, living sociocultural instantiations of these configurations.

The autobiographical elements in my re-membering Esperanza, especially those concerning my family's Christian practice and my subsequent development and criticism of this Christian faith, signal part of my own way of experiencing the Christ symbol. Although variously mediated to Christians, the Christ symbol is structured by a fundamental act of association: associating ultimacy, meaning, and transformative power (implied by the very title *Christ*) with Jesus of Nazareth or with the early Christian movements that bore witness to the ministry of Jesus. Clarifying this "association" of Christ with Jesus will be essential for the contemporary christology I will suggest below.

The placement of theology in christopraxis accounts for what may be viewed as the christocentric character of this book. I conclude this volume with two chapters on christology, both of which set the book's major cultural and political concerns in relation to the figure of Christ. I justify this move to christology not out of a belief that doctrines of God, ecclesiology, or anthropology can be reduced to christology, but because within Christian religious praxis it is talk about Christ that gives it its distinctiveness in a religiously plural world. It is from the vantage point of christology, as always inscribed in worlds of praxis, that understandings of God and God's actions in history, society and church can be understood. As readers will sense, in my final two chapters my interpretations of Christ stretch that term so that it moves in and out of regions often considered those of other doctrines.

Here Christian theology is understood as a necessary moment of reflection within christopraxis, my own christopraxis and that of others with whom I come in contact and know. This orientation to concrete christopraxis not only accounts in large part for this prologue but also requires a distinctive subsequent approach.

In chapter 1, I offer an interpretation of the present situation within which much of North American theology is currently implicated. It is a situation that gives distinctive shape to the christopraxis from which what I term a *cultural-political theology* may arise. The tensions implicit in my re-membering Esperanza will affect that interpretation, but I will offer a wider interpretation that engages other literatures in contemporary theology. In this chapter I will propose that the North American situation can be interpreted as featuring a *postmodern trilemma*. This trilemma involves the struggle to appropriate a Christian tradition, to celebrate plurality, and to critique political domination—all in ways that are at once intelligible and morally justifiable.

In chapter 2, I sketch the main lines of a hermeneutical approach to tradition that might be practiced in response to this trilemma. What I propose is a *cultural-political hermeneutics of tradition*: a set of interpretive strategies enabling a renewed sense of Christian tradition while enabling a critical assessment of the diverse political and cultural forces that constitute and mediate that tradition to us. As "political," this hermeneutics gives primary theoretical attention to patterns of domination that operate in our practice of tradition. As "cultural," this hermeneutics insists that the specific patterns of domination be identified, studied and resisted as culturally variable patterns. Although racism, for example, is a pattern of domination operating in the practice of tradition, a *cultural*-political hermeneutics will focus on not just white supremacy in North America but on this in interaction with other oppressions and forms of racism. This sense of cultural difference is necessary to a cultural-political hermeneutics, but I will close this chapter by arguing for the primacy of giving hermeneutical attention to patterns of political domination and to the voices of the oppressed.

Chapter 2 provides a basic orientation, a hermeneutical "understanding" of a cultural-political theology. The hermeneutics of this theology, however, cannot do without explanatory theories, i.e., political and cultural analyses of the political dominations and cultural plurality that challenge us. Both chapters 3 and 4, therefore, offer a presentation of the explanatory theory and analysis that I see to be necessary for beginning a cultural-political theology that addresses the challenges of the North American context. Chapter 3 does this through extensive focus on the political domination we name sexism; chapter 4 connects analysis of this form of domination to other interlocking forms: heterosexism, classism, and racism.

Some readers may find these two chapters on theories of oppressions to be far from the worlds of theological discourse. But as I have already begun to argue, and will continue to show, Christian theology—as emergent from praxis—is implicated in and needs to address these oppressions. A theoretical treatment of them is necessary for theology's own essential task.

In chapter 5, I take the distinctively theological turn. There I revision christology from certain strands of Christian tradition in order to respond to the postmodern trilemma. Oriented by the hermeneutical understanding developed in chapter 2 and further shaped by the explanatory theories outlined in chapters 3 and 4, I propose a christology in which *Christ* names a sociohistorical dynamic of reconciliatory emancipation. This dynamic is one in which primacy is given to *emancipation* from patterns of domination, while insisting that christic emancipation also entails *reconciliatory* postures that seek out, study, and celebrate difference and plurality. To emancipate *and* to reconcile, while maintaining the urgent primacy of emancipation for oppressed groups—is the challenge and the hope of experience "in Christ."

Chapter 6 then experiments with some additional refiguring of christology, so that reconciliatory emancipation is more specifically crafted to the needs of North American praxis. I here return to the four basic patterns of domination identified in chapter 3 and articulate my christology in response to each. In this way, a christology of reconciliatory emancipation can be articulated further as a fourfold process of emancipation in resistance to sexism, heterosexism, classism and racism.

What results is far from a theology that exhausts all that needs to be said theologically, even about these systemic distortions. But I offer this as one way for Christians to address the interlocking oppressions in which North American praxis is implicated, oppressions that I believe a responsible theology must address. For me, it is a way to re-member, theologically, the many fragments of memories and experiences associated with Esperanza. It is one way for Christians to re-member hope (*esperanza*) amid a world that so often works to dis-member victims of sexism, heterosexism, racism, and classism.

1

A POSTMODERN TRILEMMA

The point of departure of the theology of liberation is not only different from that of the progressivist theology, it is in contradiction with it. The contradiction can be grasped only in the real world of history. To speak of "the postmodern world" is a superficial response and of little help.

Gustavo Gutiérrez
The Power of the Poor in History

Gutiérrez claims that referring to a "postmodern" era or world is not much help to contemporary theology. Yet we North Americans read daily that we are "hip-deep in post-modernism."[1] Our music (popular and classical), graphic arts, life-styles, and academic discourses are increasingly being described and assessed as "postmodern."[2] Gutiérrez is right in the sense that any facile labeling of our context as postmodern is insufficient, but we cannot avoid asking what changes and tensions are implicated in our invocations of that term. A cultural-political theology in and for North American praxis does well to give serious attention to North American societies' alleged postmodern traits, while developing a critical relation to them.

In this chapter, I do not simply list traits of North Atlantic postmodern society; rather, I group them so that a "postmodern trilemma" comes to the fore. I suggest that contemporary North American theologians are both entangled in and need to respond to a situation that features a trilemmic tension. The trilemma is manifest in three demands that we often wish to respect simultaneously: to acknowledge some sense of tradition, to celebrate plurality, and to resist domination. As compelling as each of these demands seems to be, pursuing any one of them makes highly problematic the realization of the other two. The various kinds of tension experienced in this trilemma provide an important way to view the situation in which contemporary theologians work.

Before I present the specifics of this trilemma, it is necessary to comment on the general problem of how theology is to engage its situation. While almost no theologian denies that his or her theology should and does engage its situations, the manner in which the engagement occurs is often controversial. In my own presentation of a postmodern trilemma I will be using extraecclesial and extrascriptural categories (political, social, philosophical), even while acknowledging that my own ecclesially and scripturally shaped interests affect my presentation. Not all theologians are willing to allow extrascriptural categories to have the force they do in my presentation.[3] My cultural-political theology, like any theology, has a very complex relationship to its situations, and it is important to discuss the nature of that relationship.

In the next section, therefore, I comment on this relationship by discussing the various theoretical practices of cultural-political theology in contrast to "methods of correlation" in recent and contemporary theology. Readers less interested in this methodological controversy among contemporary theologians may wish to move immediately to my presentation of the trilemma, which begins with the section "Postmodern Traits in Theology."

CULTURAL-POLITICAL THEOLOGY: ITS THEORETICAL PRACTICES

The very use of the word *situation* in relation to theology may suggest that the theological method practiced here is one of correlation. If theological methods of correlation are generally characterized by a correlation of Christian revelation or tradition on the one hand, with the experiences, cognitive insights, and moral claims of the contemporary world on the other, then my approach may be viewed as similar to these methods.

The similarity lies in the banal observation that the theological method developed in this book addresses and is conditioned by contemporary experiences and reflection. In other words, I will offer here a reading of contemporary situations, which reading not only structures the theology I develop but is also something that a Christian theology needs to address and structurally challenge. As a theology both shaped by and responding to North American situations, the method of this theology may be one of correlation.

I prefer, however, to call this a "cultural-political theology," the hermeneutical approach and doctrinal content of which departs significantly from theologies using a method of correlation. I am able to differentiate a cultural-political theology's engagement of situations from that of correlational theology by briefly discussing four critiques of theological methods of correlation.

First, there is the general but emphatic critique of Francis Schüssler Fiorenza in his 1984 work, *Foundational Theology: Jesus and the Church*. Fiorenza's critique is that methods of correlation, practiced especially by Paul Tillich, David Tracy, and others, risk making one of the two factors (tradition *or* contemporary situation) foundational and the other only epiphenomenal. "Either the Christian revelation would be reduced to the criterion of modern world or the biblical form of revelation would be the criterion of contemporary experience."[4] On the basis of a diverse philosophical literature, Fiorenza challenges correlationists' confidence that tradition and situation can constitute two poles that are subject to correlation. Fiorenza then proposes his own method of "wide reflective equilibrium," which highlights the diverse ways tradition and experience are already interrelated.

A second critique comes from feminist theology. In 1979, it was clearly directed at Roman Catholic correlationist theologians Hans Küng, Eduard Schillebeeckx, and David Tracy by Rosemary Radford Ruether. She challenged not so much the method of correlation as its preoccupation with experiences of a bourgeois intelligentsia: secularity, scientific rationality, meaninglessness, disorder. Ruether laments the neglect of "those whose contemporary experience is primarily that of life-and-death struggle of the poor of the world for survival."[5] When Ruether formulates her own feminist method of correlation, the crucial correlation is between contemporary feminist critiques of sexism and all oppression, with "that critical principle by which biblical thought critiques itself and renews its vision as the authentic word of God."[6]

Ruether's own critical version of a method of correlation was then challenged by Elisabeth Schüssler Fiorenza. In a 1984 work, Schüssler Fiorenza argues that a critical principle of biblical thought cannot be abstracted from the biblical materials. Feminist thought must begin, she argues, with a critical assessment of that biblical material, since any of the Bible's critical principles are always intertwined with androcentrism.[7] Although the differences between Ruether and Schüssler Fiorenza are marked, the two are similar in their critiques of correlational theology as wrongfully silent about the experiences of oppression borne by women and others.

A third, very different critique is offered by George Lindbeck in his 1984 book, *The Nature of Doctrine*. There Lindbeck develops one of the primary concerns noted by Francis Schüssler Fiorenza: that correlation methods risk reducing the traditional and biblical forms of revelation to criteria of contemporary thought and practice. Lindbeck's particular concern is to defend the integrity of the Christian tradition's communal interpretation of scripture. He argues not for a correlation of scripture interpretation with "extrascriptural realities" but for the vigilant practice of a particular "direction of interpretation"—from the text to the world. For Lindbeck it is not true that "believers find *their* stories in the Bible, but that they make the story of the *Bible* their story."[8] Lindbeck's critique is thus twofold: First, that correlational theologies fail to guard the distinctive identity of Christian tradition's narratives, allowing them to be absorbed or lost into the world; and second, that correlational strategies overlook the significant one-way interpretation that moves *from* text *to* world.[9]

A final and vigorous critique of the method of correlation is offered by Rebecca S. Chopp in her 1986 and 1987 writings. She pulls together many of the concerns already voiced by Francis Schüssler Fiorenza, Rosemary Radford Ruether, and Elisabeth Schüssler Fiorenza, and she does so on the basis of arguments for the primacy of *political* analyses of both experience and tradition. Such political analyses would situate theological reflection among the concrete practices and suffering of the victims of oppression. While not proposing that liberation theologies alone are fully adequate in every respect, she acknowledges their method as more adequate than the correlational method of liberal-revisionists, because liberation theologians (North American feminist, African American, Latin American) have shown themselves better at avoiding notions like *"common* human experience" or "the tradition." Chopp argues for what has not yet really been done by the correlationist theologians: thinking theologically with a notion of praxis as a "web of social interactions" within which experience and tradition are always embedded. Practitioners of the method of correlation, she argues, have insufficiently embraced political analyses of the praxis web of social relations. Chopp also sees this deficiency as of a piece with the correlationists' at best only tentative embracing of "the option for the victims of history."[10] The lack of political analysis in their exercising preference for hermeneutical or phenomenological explorations of "human subjectivity" or "being-in-the-world" obscures the distinctive plight of those victimized by special patterns of political domination.

With these four critiques of the method of correlation before us, I want to indicate how this book's cultural-political theology, while clearly an intentional engagement of contemporary situations, is not a method of correlation—at least not one bearing features like those criticized above.

Although there is an obvious and banal similarity between a cultural-political theology and methods of correlation in that they both seek to engage current situations, the differences are striking. I can highlight these differences best by focusing on three theoretical practices of a cultural-political theology. As "theoretical practices," these are movements of theory and reflection in theology, but they are strategically formulated for engaging our present situations.[11]

Reflexive Analysis

First, a particular theoretical practice markedly differentiates cultural-political theology from the method of correlation: *reflexive analysis.* By analysis that is reflexive, I mean theologians' explicit attention to their own locations. Chopp especially has commented on tendencies among practitioners of correlational method to neglect focusing on "the who" of correlational theology. Rarely has there been much "hermeneutical self-implicature" in strategies of correlation. Typically, "experience" and "tradition" are discussed in generalizable terms, without attending to the location of the theologians as phenomenologists of experience or as appropriators of tradition. This cultural-political theology, in contrast, seeks to be reflexive in three senses. First, in the very attempt to write a theology as a North American, I display one distinctively reflexive move. This is not theology for everyone. Even the term *North American* is too ambitious a designation for these pages. Other cultural and political tools must be used in order to locate this North American contribution: tools pertaining to gender, class, sexual orientation, and ethnic tradition.

Second, it is reflexive in its starting point—in particular, in my situating the book's problematics in relation to my own "remembering Esperanza." This hermeneutical self-implicature should be instructive to readers who not only want to know why the themes of this book are interrelated as they are but also wish to anticipate the book's limitations.

Third, the mix of substantive themes in the complex of memories about Esperanza (cultural difference, Christian practice, and political oppression) is an element of my reflexivity that sets the agenda for the entire work. In a sense, the whole project is an outworking of those memories, without being reducible to them. I allow the images of Esperanza's world, as I know it, to haunt my presentation of the situation that theology seeks to engage.

Portraiture

A second theoretical practice is added: *portraiture*. In 1982, Edward Farley proposed this term for the theologian's deriving a portrait of "ecclesial existence," which for Farley is the matrix out of which theology emerges. The portrait of ecclesial existence shows it to be a "total corporate historical phenomenon."[12]

I use the word *portraiture* for a somewhat broader concern than Farley, who tends to see tradition as the subject matter of portraiture. He writes, ". . . we can say that theological portraiture is a theology of tradition."[13] I will be using portraiture to name cultural-political theology's act of portraying not only the complexities of tradition, but also other kinds of complexity as well, elements that are nevertheless bound up with tradition.

In portraying the situation, a cultural-political theology offers a portrait not just of ecclesial tradition, but also of the forces of cultural diversity and political power that are never separable from that tradition. The theoretical practice of portraiture seeks to provide some picture of how elements of ecclesial tradition, cultural practice, and political power interplay in the situations with which theologians work. It is this kind of picture that I begin to provide in this chapter's discussion of a postmodern trilemma.

In providing this interpretation or portrait of the situation, there is, of course, a marked similarity to the methods of correlation. This cultural-political theology significantly departs from those methods, however, in that it never identifies tradition and experience as two poles.

As I will also argue, a cultural-political theology develops a hermeneutics within its trilemmic consciousness that grants a significant privilege to the interpretive stance of the victims of political oppression. A critical embrace of an option for the oppressed implies a further differentiation from the method of correlation. Moreover, in a way that at least tries to hear the critiques of Rosemary Ruether and Elisabeth Schüssler Fiorenza I hope to write of "the poor" not in general, but as sufferers of particular kinds of oppression: sexism, heterosexism, classism, and racism.

Address

A final theoretical practice I term *address*. Although a cultural-political theology can never legitimately write of tradition in the singular and can never separate traditions from their cultural and political matrices, I will suggest that a cultural-political theology can marshal senses of tradition (involving communal practices and texts) that are distinguishable within their cultural-political matrices. In the fifth and sixth chapters, especially, I will comment on possibilities within cultural-political theology for forming a Christian message and practice that addresses its cultural and political matrix with a new word.

Crucial to a cultural-political theology's mode of address is its capacity to identify and mine the richness of distinctively Christian narratives and Christian communal practices. A cultural-political theology not only engages situations through portraiture and is engaged in them, as its own reflexive analyses should show, but it also engages its situations with words and actions that address those situations. In doing so, it produces in and for those situations challenges to reigning understandings and practices, and it generates critical resistance to dominative movements and ideas, as well as affirmation of alternative ones. All of these possibilities may issue from theological address.

Its theoretical practice of address is what gives cultural-political theology a position mindful of the kinds of concerns raised by Lindbeck. Cultural-political theology is not just a thematizing of elements already present in situations. To use the terms of Lindbeck's concerns, it is not only an "expression of" the "experience" pervading current situations. It *may* at times legitimately be that, and here I depart from Lindbeck's proposals; but the cultural-political theology I am proposing here also works out of a disciplined attention to specific Christian narratives and communal practices, and this attention prohibits their reduction to the status of simply being expressions of cultural-political experience.

Granting this integrity to Christian narratives and communal practices, through this theoretical practice of address, can be achieved without isolating Christian narrative and practice from the cultural and political concerns that Elisabeth Schüssler Fiorenza, Rosemary Radford Ruether, Rebecca S. Chopp, and Francis Schüssler Fiorenza all emphasize. In order to heed those political concerns, however, it is important not to neglect the other two theoretical practices of portraiture and reflexive analysis.

In summary, this cultural-political theology is a deliberate theological engagement of its situations, as are the methods of correlation, but it moves beyond those methods by pursuing a strategy of engagement that gives disciplined attention to the "theoretical practices" of reflexivity, portraiture, and address.

The prologue began with my theoretical practice of reflexivity. The remainder of this chapter is an exercise in portraiture, an attempt to discern the major lines of the conditions within which North American theologies labor.

POSTMODERNISM AND NORTH AMERICAN CONTEXTS

The theological task of portraying a current situation is always a complex one. This is especially true in the North American context today. Many attempts have been made to describe and interpret the complexity of social segmentation and cultural dynamics in the United States. In the human sciences alone, studies such as Robert Lynd's on *Middletown* and American culture were important for identifying a whole set of elements of American culture, including casual processes of patterning, individual competitive aggressiveness, extreme differences in power, high individual mobility, population masses determined by individual ties to jobs, a primary orientation to the future, emphasis on youth, linkage of values to processes of material advancement, and others.[14] Studies of United States society have centered on its industrial mode of production,[15] on its unique kinship and family structures,[16] or on the way its major cultural forms seek to hold together "centrist values and challenges from its border."[17]

In whatever way North American theologians may borrow from such works to emphasize various traits, it is virtually impossible to characterize any North American situation accurately by identifying just one trait or even a few traits. Increasingly among academics in North America, the sheer multiplicity of factors that need attention itself becomes a major trait of North American life. This is especially apparent among many teachers, students, and administrators who refer to this multiplicity, and to related factors of pluralism and fluidity, as the key mark of our time, a central element of our postmodernism.

The term *postmodernism* is hardly one that is prevalent only in North American contexts. Its first usages, in fact, were apparently in texts pertaining to Latin American poetry,[18] and today some of the key formulators of postmodernism are continental writers: Jacques Derrida, Jacque Lacan, Gilles DeLeuze, and others. By now, however, the term has gained a strong North American pedigree among scholars who employ the term to interpret major currents of thought and practice, currents identifiable in the newly formulated pragmatism of Richard Rorty,[19] in sculpture, architecture, and dance,[20] and even in the world of rock-and-roll video, where lyrics, musical scores and visual images coalesce in short segments on the twenty-four-hour a day television network of MTV.[21]

A definition of postmodernism has become notoriously elusive. Numerous North American dissertations and scholarly papers want to invoke it, often without even a limning of its various meanings. The term is so tied to pervasive, major shifts of thought in our recent history that we probably do better to avoid defining it too exactly. Recall Nietzsche's warning: "Only that which has no history is definable."[22] Even Ihab Hassan, who has offered a "catena" or "paratactic list" of postmodern features, acknowledges the problem: "At worst, postmodernism appears to be a mysterious, if ubiquitous, ingredient like raspberry vinegar, which instantly turns any recipe into *nouvelle cuisine.*"[23]

Admitting the voguish character of the term's invocation, exploring meanings of the term can still aid in understanding North American settings. A simple listing of Hassan's features of postmodernism, as they extend across a wide array of disciplines, evokes for us some sense of the postmodern ethos. That ethos tends to affirm "indeterminacy, fragmentation, decanonization, self-less-ness/depth-less-ness, the unpresentable/ unrepresentable, irony, hybridization, carnivalization, performance/participation, constructionism, immanence."[24] Any theologian who has tasted of the postmodern set of writings, perhaps especially in Mark C. Taylor's 1984 "a-theological" book,[25] will recognize at least some of these as characterizing the postmodern ethos.

In a manner less playful than Hassan's, though perhaps more helpful, theologian Peter C. Hodgson has recently identified five dimensions within which the postmodern temper can be articulated and felt by North Atlantic scholars generally and United States scholars in particular: cognitive, historical, political, socioeconomic and religious. In each of these areas there is a crisis or fundamental shift: a sense of limitation or deconstruction of technical rationality and subjectivity (the cognitive dimension); a decrease in the power and influence of North Atlantic cultures (the political); the crises of capitalist and socialist state systems (socioeconomic); and new challenges to Christianity's and all world religion's truth-claims (religious).[26]

Each of the shifts or crises noted by Hodgson—indeed each of the listed terms and oppositions collected by Hassan—could in themselves serve as the complex subject matter for a single volume. Such texts are increasingly being written in the academic worlds of North American postmodernism.

In this chapter I choose to accent three major traits of North American postmodernist discussion that not only have a certain salience outside theological circles but which, not surprisingly, are integrally related to theological controversies in our present. That is, the three traits are not just traits of a postmodern situation; they are also features intrinsic to theological discourse.

Before discussing these features, a qualification is in order. As my comments on the trendiness of the word *postmodern* suggest, I am not claiming that the definitive characterization of our age is provided by the term, *postmodern.* Nor am I claiming that there is now operative in North American contexts something as all-encompassing as a pervasive, postmodern "paradigm." Some significant voices in philosophy and history of culture, such as that of Stanley Rosen, admit the new and distinct emphases in postmodernism but argue that these are really developments occurring within modernist problematics, already envisioned by the Enlightenment.[27] Jürgen Habermas sees postmodern projects as a cultural heir to the Enlightenment, and he calls not for new postmodern sensibilities but for "a critical reappropriation of the modern project."[28] Fredric Jameson, a noted Marxian analyst of narrative, laments postmodernism's penchants for pastiche and its reluctance or refusal to think historically.

Therefore, I know that there are persuasive challenges to the adequacy of characterizing North American culture as postmodernist and equally persuasive critiques of postmodernist discourse. I do claim, however, that focus on the major traits of discourses using the term postmodern is an essential first step in coming to terms with the spirit of the North American context within which theologians work.

POSTMODERN TRAITS IN THEOLOGY

I now turn to a discussion of the traits that constitute a postmodern trilemma. Again, this is no mere list of traits, but a presentation and development of them, showing how they intersect with one another to create a trilemma. I will develop these traits, drawing from literature beyond the field of theology, with specific references, however, to the impact of these postmodern emphases on recent theology.

A Sense of Tradition

A first feature of postmodernism is surely not unique to it, but the feature is central: a need to acknowledge one's tradition. This may seem a strange point in the face of postmodernist demands. Above all, do we not now face persuasive testimonies from philosophy, the humanities, and a host of wise personal pilgrimages, that there can only be a "decanonization" of all conventional authorities, a "delegitimization of the mastercodes in society?"[29] In many senses, this is true. But a sense of tradition remains, in a minimal but significant sense. Exposures of the bankruptcy of conventional authorities, whether through postmodernist psychoanalysis, Marxism, feminist theories, or deconstructionist tools, reveal that no thinking is free from the mediations and limitations of traditioning. There is always limitation to place, time, style, and more. The critical delegitimating of authority pivots on exposing authority's lack of any privilege to claim freedom from location. If I can somewhat crudely derive a lesson from this feature of the postmodernist ethos, it is this: Own up to where you are, whoever you are and however complex your located self and group identities may be. In this sense, our postmodernist ethos suggests the need to acknowledge one's tradition.

With this feature, postmodernism shows its similarity to modernist critiques and their challenges to tradition. Modernity, too, sought to delegitimize the authorities. However, the critiques of authority by postmodernists are not only more intense, they also often deliver the critic to a valuation and nurturing, even celebration, of one's place and time. This of course is not tradition in the sense of the "liberal tradition," surely not as in the "Christian tradition." The postmodern minimalist tradition is something more aptly described as a social location. I call this "tradition," however, because our specific social locations often feature historical legacies and fragments of myth, ritual practice, and communal solidarity.

Among the North American academic subcultures, perhaps none is more well-known for this trait than proponents of so-called communitarian ethics. Alasdair MacIntyre's *After Virtue*, a prime example of that approach, is a work rich in texture and arguments, and its contributions to contemporary moral philosophy are significant.[30] Two tendencies of that text make it exemplary of postmodernists' tendency to affirm tradition.

First, much of his narrative is a lament of the fragmented character of contemporary visions of the good. MacIntyre himself, like a good postmodernist, offers arguments showing how difficult it is for contemporary philosophers to achieve agreement. Incommensurability seems the order of the day.[31] MacIntyre discerns an earlier time when, within an Aristotelian framework that provided a commonly agreed-upon telos, such incommensurability of initial premises and moral arguments did not cripple a society's capacity for securing moral agreement as it does today. This retrospective glance amid a fragmented present then sets the conditions for the second major tendency of *After Virtue*, a championing of "local forms of community within which civility and the intellectual and moral life can be sustained through the new dark ages which are already upon us."[32]

I wish to characterize McIntyre's project as a particular kind of post-modern appropriation of tradition—a "postmodernism of reaction," a phrase formulated by Hal Foster in his studies of postmodern culture.[33] This kind of postmodernism faults the project of modernity and liberalist culture for its disorder and fragmentation. This is clearly a theme in MacIntyre's *After Virtue*, wherein the moral quandaries are described as in "grave disorder," prompting in MacIntyre a profound disquietude, indeed a sense of catastrophe. Here MacIntyre's postmodernism becomes a therapeutic discourse suggesting a return to tradition. In contrast to what Foster calls a "postmodernism of resistance," where modernity is criticized in order to formulate strategies that are both subversive of and resistant to the status quo, this postmodernism retreats from the status quo and so fails really to challenge it.

Granted, MacIntyre at times writes as if the constructing of local communities that provide settings for traditions of virtue and character can be a strategy for resistance—a resistance even in hope.[34] Still, this hope is announced without articulating how local communities could engage institutions and their surrounding culture so that they might indeed become "Aristotelian traditions" that restore "intelligibility and rationality to our moral and social attitudes and commitments."[35]

This postmodernism of reaction is also alive and well in North American Protestant theology. It is self-titled a "postliberal theology"[36] and is best exemplified in George Lindbeck's *The Nature of Doctrine.* This work, which I have already cited for its critique of methods of correlation, is worth our attention if for no other reason than its strong and continuing influence on academics and in the general religious press of North America, in both Roman Catholic and Protestant contexts.[37] As postliberal, it is critical of modern liberalism for its alleged individualism, rootlessness, and deficient sense of tradition. Theologians live in times, writes Lindbeck, when "the exigencies of communicating their messages in a privatistic cultural and social milieu lead them to commend public and communal traditions as only optional aids in individual self-realization rather than as bearers of normative realities to be interiorized."[38] Theologians, he continues, are under the sway of tendencies of "experiential expressivism," viewing their theological reflections as little more than expressions of reigning, deep-running, universal experience.

In order to reorient theologians' discourse, Lindbeck draws from Ludwig Wittgenstein, Clifford Geertz, and others to attempt to instill a healthier respect for the communal and the linguistic. Lindbeck proposes a cultural-linguistic theory of religious traditions, and he seeks to orient Christian theological doctrine toward its cultural-linguistic specificities. Theology, according to this view, must own up to its cultural-linguistic specificity, its location. In particular, this means that theology must eschew its liberal and modern propensities to generalize about humanity or religion and must instead develop the particularity of its ecclesial communal rules and, especially, of its narrative texts.[39] Hans Frei's studies of narrative and scripture made this point a decade earlier and continued to make it during the debates about Lindbeck's book.[40] Several theologians influenced by Lindbeck, and especially Frei, use his claims to restore notions of "scriptural authority."[41]

How are we to interpret this theological postliberalism? In general, it can be appreciated as a healthy reminder to theologians who, in their tendencies to address human situations, often speak too easily about "common human experience" or other allegedly universal traits of experience. Lindbeck's proposals call one to explore the distinct narrative texts of tradition. Theological postliberalism is postmodern in its attempt to heighten the sense of tradition and in its caution against generalist and foundationalist claims.

Like MacIntyre's postmodernism, however, this theological postliberalism tends to be a "postmodernism of reaction." Lindbeck hopes that the theological program he develops may increase a "tribe of theologians" who rely on "the culture-forming power of the biblical outlook in its intratextual, untranslatable specificity," which will renew "the ancient practice of absorbing the universe into the biblical world."[42] In the opening pages of his volume, Lindbeck ably explores this biblical world's entailment in cultural-linguistic contexts of practice, suggesting ways that his theological program might engage the so-called predominant liberalism of North American society. By his book's conclusion, however, a utopian textualism, one at points reactionary (in Foster's sense), sets in. Lindbeck turns increasingly to the biblical text or narrative, a move particularly evident in his frequent emphases on "*intra*textuality."

Also gone by the end of his work is any serious attention to the ways diverse cultural-linguistic settings make difficult the very task of identifying a text or a narrative. Lindbeck's footnotes show him to be aware of other approaches, such as deconstructionism, which would make intratextuality problematic, but he contents himself with providing contrasts of his proposals with these other theories, and he does not enter into their critiques of what a "text" is.[43] Nor does he discuss other theories that would entangle texts in the complex worlds of readers, such as reader-response criticism, social symbolic theories of narrative, or feminist and African American literary criticism,[44] all of which give integrity to a narrative but within a more intricate matrix of interpretation than Lindbeck seems willing to explore.

Because of the failure to take up this exploration and because of his resort to a narrative posited against a liberal "experiential-expressionist" age, Lindbeck's theology is to be termed a postmodernism of reaction. It is postmodern in its healthy sense of limitation and particularity; but it is largely reactive because it exploits the postmodernist sense of tradition for a retreat into and defense of a narrative tradition which, in utopian fashion, aims to "absorb the world."

While Lindbeck helpfully exhibits a first trait of the postmodernist milieu in theology—the need to acknowledge one's tradition—the two other traits of postmodernism are neglected by him, and to these we must now turn.

Celebrations of Plurality

Senses of relativity and plurality (of institutional practices, ethnic heritages, religious customs, intellectual premises) have long been intrinsic to North American contexts. Indeed, a certain affirming of plurality and diversity has been an essential feature of North American liberal traditions, nurturing their rhetoric of tolerance as virtue and the often overstated and even misguided belief that United States society is a scene wherein diversity is nurtured and freedom of expression fully valued.

This longstanding embrace of plurality is both intensified and challenged by postmodernism. Its celebration of plurality is a second trait of postmodernism. In this celebration, almost all normative judgments are rendered problematic because of their linguistic, cultural, social, economic, political, and sexual specificities.[45] The liberal rhetoric that affirms plurality usually sees the plurality as diverse expressions of some foundational truths; the postmodern critique splits the foundations, noting their own variability, often dissolving them. The foundations are exposed to a critique showing that they too are often distinctive sets of premises among many others. In postmodernism, longstanding affirmations of plurality become a veritable celebration to the point of preferring the montage, the collage, pastiche, and related indeterminacies. As I will suggest, this celebration becomes problematic even for the celebrants; it becomes "the irritable condition of postmodern discourse."[46] So frequent are the references to "pluralism" in contemporary North American theologies that it seems almost too ordinary to identify it as a major trait. So pervasive are references to the term that careful reflection on pluralism itself and its various meanings does not always accompany its invocation. Identifying pluralism as a trait is a necessary step, however, if it is to be related to other features of postmodern discourse.

In theology, the ways that senses of difference and specificity have nurtured pluralist sensibilities emerge from many sources. Developments in the more recent periods have had a role in building this awareness of plurality.

The sense of historical consciousness emerging from the Enlightenment touched biblical interpretation, Christian faith, and constructive theology with a sense of relativity, even if in the first instance (and often still for many), problems of relativity and plurality focused merely on *temporal* relativity—on the fact of that "ugly ditch" between the past world of biblical characters and salvific events on the one side, and the present world of lived faith. In addition, however, theology, steeped in the problems of historical consciousness, was thereby prepared for affirming difference and relativity in other senses as well.

The "history of religions" provides another example. This area of inquiry soon quickened Christian theologians to think not only about the temporal relativity of Christian religious phenomena but also about a kind of spatial relativity: the relativity of different religions in any given present. History of religions taught theologians to think about plurality and relativity synchronically as well as diachronically. Ethnographic reports of other societies' lifeways, setting conditions for the formation of ethnology and cultural or social anthropology, prepared the way for a socio-cultural consciousness that further complicated the issues of historical consciousness in theology.

While historical consciousness and the history of religions were for Christian theologians perhaps the nearest nurturers of pluralist sensibilities, current theological reflection is often confirmed in its pluralist convictions by more recent developments in the natural and social sciences. Both clusters of sciences display the impact of a relativizing affirmation of different forms of life, particularly in the debates about the incommensurability of competing paradigms or research programs. In the natural sciences, the discussion is exemplified by debates between Thomas Kuhn, Paul Feyerabend, and Stephen Toulmin.[47] In the social sciences, the discussion is perhaps best represented as occurring between Peter Winch and Alasdair MacIntyre.[48] Wittgenstein's reflections on the different "language games" inquirers play, together with the relativizing impacts of cultural anthropology and the sociology of knowledge, also make it difficult for theologians to live, at least with intellectual integrity, anywhere other than in a pluralistic universe.

Add to these discussions current developments in hermeneutics, literary criticism, and feminist theory, and the challenge of difference and plurality can hardly be dodged.

The hermeneutical theorist Hans-Georg Gadamer, whose influence has affected North American academies in almost all the humanities, social sciences, and even the natural sciences to a small extent,[49] has contributed to this sense of difference. Although Gadamer is, for many postmoderns, too prone to accept tradition unquestioningly,[50] he still emphatically reminds us that any subject matter (text, law, gospel) "must be understood at every moment in every particular situation, in a new and different way."[51] As John Caputo has said about Gadamer's rehabilitation of tradition, he "offers us the most liberal possible version of a fundamentally conservative idea."[52] Gadamer, and theologians influenced by him, build difference into the very notion of tradition and so bring the sense of tradition into relation with the realities of plurality.

While recent trends in literary criticism have yet to leave their mark on biblical and theological interpretation, this area is yielding a more marked sense of difference and plurality in theology. In this area, theorists have pushed well beyond the "new literary criticism," with its notions of the "world of the text," to locate textual meaning more in a region wherein may be found a dynamic play of meanings between texts and interpreters, and then in the whole world of readers who "are played" in relation to texts.[53]

Another source of difference and plurality is feminist theory, a set of perspectives that emerges in relation to almost all other fields.[54] Now, though, the specificities of discourse are relative to modes of gender difference, whether this difference be understood biologically/sexually, psychologically, developmentally, linguistically, or culturally. Hence, another factor of difference is added, due especially to the explosion of literature regarding gender and feminist theory. As I will suggest below, confronting this kind of difference and specificity is particularly important because the issue of domination is intrinsic to this difference. At present, I simply highlight gender theory, particularly that formulated by feminist scholars, as another source of current relativizing, pluralist consciousness, one that has a special impact because the difference explored concerns the male-female dyad.

One way to summarize the impact on thought and action in the pluralist mode is to say that theologians must now, like their colleagues in other fields, work without foundations, i.e., without a touchstone located outside the play of relativizing forces. In theology, Francis Schüssler Fiorenza's claim is clear: "No external standard, be it history or human experience, exists independent of cultural traditions and social interpretation that can provide an independent foundation for either faith or theology."[55] As philosopher Richard Bernstein reminds us, however, this does *not* mean that we are simply locked within our own frameworks and are unable to get out of them to achieve a critical distance.[56] It is a distinctively postmodern trait, however, to locate theological criteria within the play of diverse perspectives rather than outside them. David Tracy's attempts to formulate Christian theology amid our culture of pluralism is perhaps the clearest theological example of the search for criteria *within* the celebration of plurality.[57]

Precisely how might we emerge from a specific framework to achieve a critical distance without creating a new foundationalism? Numerous proposals have been offered in response to this ordeal of postmodernism. It is a question to which I do not wish to respond theologically here, before setting in place a third feature of our postmodern ethos.

Resistance to Domination

As should be clear by this point, the theme of domination is not treated in isolation here, but as complexly interwoven with the other two features of postmodern discourse already presented. Because of this complex interweaving, and because the logics of domination display their own distinctive complexities, great care needs to be taken concerning the often loose invocation of terms pertaining to oppression and domination.

I here understand oppression, generally, as the systemic exercise of authority and power in a burdensome, cruel, and unjust manner. In order to reflect on this oppression, it is necessary to employ some other distinctions. To do this I follow Cornel West's suggestion that we distinguish among "modes of oppression."[58] West identifies four modes that are important for understanding the travail of postmodern discourse: domination, subjugation, exploitation, repression.

The first two, domination and subjugation, are largely discursive modes. To say they are discursive is not to say they are theoretical rather than practical. In fact, Michel Foucault, and West following him, rightly stress that discourses are themselves a kind of practice. However, discursive elements are unique in that they include ideas, texts, theories, and uses of language, all of which are both theoretical and practical. There is always something more in these elements of discourse that makes their use an exercise of power. Hence, they are termed discursive *practices*.[59]

When I write of resistance to domination as a trait of postmodernity I do so in explicit reference to the discursive practices of thinkers and writers who deal with ideas, texts, theories and uses of language. Examples of the discursive practice called domination include the systematic imposition of supremacist logics in terms of racial, sexual, ethnic or national identities.[60] "Subjugation" is West's distinctive term for the process of producing subjects and subjectivities consonant with the dominating supremacist logics. These subjugating processes, I might add, include both the subjectivities of agents benefitting from the supremacy and those of agents suffering domination. Without blaming the victim, it can be observed that those who suffer from domination are often themselves forced to participate in the process of subjugation that keeps them dominated.[61]

These two strands of discursive practices can be distinguished, though never separated, from the "extradiscursive affairs" of exploitation and repression. This second pair pertains to a configuration of social systems, class divisions, economic needs, and institutions, in the context of which the discursive practices of domination and subjugation are maintained.

Postmodernism often includes awareness of the suffering entailed in the extradiscursive affairs of exploitation and repression. More, its adherents often seek to formulate their discourse as a resistance to domination, i.e., as a resistance to the dominant supremacist logics that permeate interpretation regarding exploitation and repression. What Hal Foster terms a "postmodernism of resistance" especially acknowledges this view of discourse as resistance.

The marshaling of a discursive practice that resists domination is extremely difficult to achieve, especially given what often seems to postmodernists to be the equally important need to affirm plurality. The pluralist's affirmation seems to accelerate the impetus toward a *danse macabre* which — though perhaps a wonderful antidote for ethnocentrisms, foundationalisms, and absolutisms of all sorts — does not in itself render us capable of discerning or resisting domination in our time.

Often postmodern thinkers will claim that current problems of domination are largely functions of a refusal to acknowledge difference, and that by affirming difference, saying Yes to pluralism and to play amongst differences, we will thereby dissolve the "economies of domination."[62] Mutual acknowledgment of one another by subjects in "the play" yields an almost sanguine hope for the dissolution of domination. Accordingly, Mark C. Taylor writes, referring to Hegel:

> With the realization of the total reciprocity of subjects, the entire foundation of the economy of domination crumbles. No longer conceiving themselves as self-equal by virtue of the exclusion of all difference, each self "is for the other the mean [*Mitte*] through which each mediates itself with itself and unites with itself." In this play,

which is interplay, subjects *recognize* themselves as mutually *recogniz-ing* one another.[63]

Philosopher John D. Caputo, in his book *Radical Hermeneutics*, makes a similar point, seeing postmodern play, or its surfing on the seas of relativity, as possessing an "ethics of dissemination."

And so I envisage, as the moral upshot of this, a "community of mortals" bound together by their common fears and lack of meta-physical grounds, sharing a common fate at the hands of the flux sent by a *Geschick* [fate or destiny] which will not disclose its name.[64]

Such a community within the flux so celebrates difference and plurality that it develops a moral force to challenge "constellations of power, centers of control and manipulation, which systematically dominate, regulate, exclude."[65]

To the extent that these dominant systems pivot around the exclusion of difference, the celebration of difference does seem to be a posture of critique. Whether it can move beyond that critical posture to real strategies or sustained discursive and extradiscursive practices of resistance is another question. Caputo's own critical posture, evident in his "ethics of dissemi-nation," seems to lose much of its potential for resistance, especially when, toward the end of his discussion of ethics, he settles for what seems to be a *laissez faire*, almost liberal, trust in a marketplace of positions, when he says, "In a radical ethics our own concern is to keep the conversation moving, mobile, and to trust the dynamics of the *agora*."[66] Or again:

Socio-ethical discourse does not require a transcendental rationality which transcends local interests — if it does we are finished — but sim-ply the keeping of competing interests in play in a fair game, letting the dynamics of the *agora* play itself out in a fair competition.[67]

Caputo, though, admits that this ethics, in order to do justice to the special suffering known by the victims of systems, needs to "take its stand" with "women, children, the mad, the ill, the poor, blacks, the religious and moral minorities."[68] Caputo does not say *how* this "taking a stand" is con-sonant with the celebration and valuation of the flux. Indeed, he acknowl-edges the puzzle at the very end of his book, modestly wondering if it is not the special role of religion to stake limits to play in order to work for and to resist the suffering of victims.

Caputo does not write as a theologian, but his taking up religious ques-tions in relation to the problem of domination and given affirmations of the flux signals a contemporary theological problematic exemplary of the general postmodern struggle for a critical pluralism. Some names, taken from here and there, display scholars who are also engaged in theological search for a critical pluralism: John Cobb, Francis Schüssler Fiorenza, Gordon Kaufman, Sallie McFague, Langdon Gilkey, and Rosemary Radford Ruether. Each of these has spun a distinctive theological program, but all display in their own ways the penchant of the postmodern critical pluralist for affirming plurality as enriching while also striving to formulate a critique that enables resistance to the kind of "disseminating" play that leads directly or indirectly to the dis-membering of dominated peoples' lives and bodies.

Hassan points out the pathos of this postmodern condition when he says that the various "cognitive, political and affective restraints remain only partial." They finally fail to delimit pluralism without sliding into a new monism or into a new relativism. Surely there is not a consensus, in theory or practice, about how to formulate a "critical pluralism."[69] But the need for critique, a persistent identification and resistance to the destruction of life we already see and the global destruction that threatens — all this results in the effort to check sheer celebration of the flux. The "postmodernism of resistance" identified by Hal Foster is by no means an easily maintained posture; it is a struggle, given the accompanying affirmations of plurality. As Langdon Gilkey put it for theology, the pluralism so dear to North American academics "is toothless if one faces oppression."[70]

A TRILEMMA

The three traits of postmodernism addressed in the previous section comprise no mere list of features; each possesses special problematics that interweave with the other two. In this section I want to develop more explicitly these problematics as a trilemma in postmodern thought, one within which a cultural-political theology inescapably works and which it must address.

A trilemma, in the strictest sense, is a situation requiring a choice among three equally undesirable choices. In the case of postmodernism's three traits, each presents a demand that invites attention and development: to acknowledge tradition, to celebrate plurality, and to resist domination — all three together. The problem is that in attending to and developing any one of the three traits, postmodernists often find themselves unable to attend to and develop the others.

The necessity to affirm all three together emerges from reflection on the deleterious effects of nurturing only one, or even only two, of these three traits.

The disadvantages of developing our theological discourse in terms of just one of postmodernism's concerns are clear.

A singular attention to *tradition alone* issues in a traditionalism that involves not only a provinciality unaware of other traditions but also a shallow understanding of the plurality of forms within one's own tradition. When traditionalists also fail to attend to domination and the needs for thoroughgoing critical resistance, they risk an uncritical support of traditions and often reinforce domination.

Likewise, a singular attention to *plurality* alone can issue in the kind of pluralism that celebrates "the flux" and the "play" of relative forms. But as my discussion of Caputo's "ethics of dissemination" showed, then the failure to marshal resistance to dis-membering nihilism easily emerges. A singular focus on plurality, without a sense of some tradition, often blinds the would-be celebrant of plurality to a knowledge of how traditions, despite all their imperialist postures and practices, have also nurtured, and might yet help create, a sense of play and appreciation of difference. Taylor's deconstructionist celebration of plurality, dissemination (and erring), for example, is a critique of Christian theology's ontotheological tradition. While his critique is both eloquent and needed at many points, it overlooks substantive ways in which the tradition (for example, some figurations of trinitarian thought or the Silesian mystics)[71] actually nurtures affirmations of difference and flux.[72]

Giving singular attention to *domination* alone can also entail unfavorable consequences. First, a program of resisting domination, without the other two postmodern emphases, easily fails to actualize its own envisioned strategies for achieving justice and freedom from oppression. Without developing a sense of plurality, the struggle to be free from domination can founder on the divisiveness that springs up among agents for change who work with different visions of "the just" and from different experiences of oppression. Moreover, without a sense of tradition (*some* tradition of myth and ritual, at least, not necessarily the established Traditions), the struggle is impoverished, lacking the resources of communal memory and symbolic heritage that often provide some minimal dialogical consensus for marshalling critique and action.

It is also the case that attending to only two traits while excluding either of the three others results in lamentable consequences, some of which I have already identified.

Correlations of only *tradition and plurality*, leaving untreated the need to resist domination, easily become a Christian liberalism centering on tolerance, one which is repressive through its lack of a specific critique of oppression. Such repressive tolerance finds it difficult to stop the "grand conversation" among many voices in order to point out wrong, to envision a just future, or to take a stand.

This Christian liberalism, present within many North American mainline denominations, is often, as Carter Heyward argues, "morally bankrupt" regarding response to the specific voices of women and gay/lesbian persons, and others, because the specific advocacy needed for responding to those voices sits uncomfortably with the liberals' claimed allegiance to an ethic of tolerance for all, without special interests and particular claims.[73]

Correlating only a sense of *tradition and resistance to domination* often undermines the Christian struggle for justice by ignoring the need to orchestrate differences among the communities defining and working for justice. Present-day Guatemala is one of several possible examples of how a Christian tradition nurturing struggles against oppression also needs to affirm plurality within that struggle. Mayan peoples in Guatemala experience exploitation and repression under one of the most ruthless of military powers. There in a number of instances Christian tradition is being reshaped to mobilize resistance to this oppression and to supremacist logics that serve subjugation of the Mayan peoples. However, to be effective, a mobilization for this struggle cannot afford to neglect differences that exist among those who are engaged in the struggle. Not only must the differences between Mayans and poor ladinos (non-Indian) be dealt with; the differences existing within the Maya-Quiche peoples must also be orchestrated—between Mam, Quiche, Cakchiquel, Tzutujil, Kekchi and others. Because struggles for justice are often relative to diverse cultural meanings and practices, it is intrinsic to the struggle for justice to navigate those differences.

No wonder that one Mayan leader in the Presbyterian church of Guatemala, during one of my visits there, named the "problem of differences" (among Amerindian groups) as his major one to tackle, even though it was understood that the major challenge was posed by the systemic repression worked by Guatemala's military rule. The struggle for justice requires both the identification and the management of difference and plurality. Guatemala's high number of cultural-linguistic Amerindian groups (about twenty-two in all) certainly poses the challenge of plurality within the struggle for justice in an unusually acute manner.[74] At the same time the lesson it brings is also instructive for other contexts; attending to difference cannot be neglected in the course of nurturing a unified resistance against oppression.

Finally, to correlate affirmations of *plurality and resistance to domination* without articulating of a sense of tradition is to forge a link between the greatly valued virtue of tolerance and the need for freedom as the priceless conditions for a full humanity. Tolerance and freedom, however, can be sustained on their own terms and by means of their own rhetoric only for a short, unstable time. The forging of tolerance and the struggle for freedom (no easy link to make) often require the resources of myth, ritual, memory—in short, tradition. Without these resources of tradition, the rhetorics of tolerance and freedom may often retain their appeal and inspiration, even their power to affect social-political practice, but their appeal and power to nurture the common good is likely to be short, like the life and beauty of a cut flower. Because of this need, I continue seeking traditions that can sustain freedom and affirmations of plurality.

Such traditions are by no means easy for me to find. For scholars committed to thinking within the trilemma, many traditions just need to be let go. This may suggest a theological work that is always alienated from every tradition. That is one possibility. I continue to see another alternative, one that retains a sense of tradition crafted from those shreds and patches of life where hope seems to glow, however faintly, amid certain peoples' struggles to affirm an authentic plurality or to resist trenchant oppressions. To many observers, such a patchwork tradition—made up, for example, of a Christian base community here, a community-organizing effort there, now an important friendship, and then a link to a church or non-church institution—may not seem like much of a tradition. Often from my own perspective, too, it does not seem enough to provide the nurture, sense of belonging and mutual challenge that a traditional community often seems to give. Compared to distortions operative in many a traditional community, however, a tradition of such shreds and patches can also seem a great gift.

This is the lot of those who live and think within the trilemma. It is also the complex plight of one who lives and works "re-membering Esperanza." Part of my effort is to craft a theology within this plight that creates new kinds of connection between Christian tradition, the celebration of difference, and the struggle against oppression.

THEOLOGICAL INTERPRETATION IN LIGHT OF THE TRILEMMA

In light of the postmodern trilemma, the kind of theology needed may, at first glance, seem to be some *via media*, some well-balanced theological method that has a distinctive sense of tradition, a reasonable amount of openness toward the plurality of others, and, of course, abiding "concern for the poor." This kind of theological response, however, simply will not do, primarily because it overlooks the travail and pathos that the trilemma holds and the demands that this travail puts on reflection.

If the trilemmic character of the three traits means anything, it is that taking seriously the demands of each trait requires radical revisioning, not just a modest balancing act among all three. The Christian theologians who take seriously both plurality and the problems of domination, for example, may very well need to recast the tradition in ways that are unfamiliar to their traditional communities. In this recasting, they risk alienation from their communities. Van A. Harvey has referred to this alienation as "the pathos of the liberal theologian."[75]

Without ever quite saying so, Harvey implies that because of this pathos, theologians should either relinquish their program of interpreting Christian tradition in and for contemporary situations or confine themselves to ever-more-refined presentations of the tradition's own resources, trusting to its own authority of revelation. Harvey does not explicitly consider the possibility that precisely in and through the pathos might come alternative renderings of Christian traditional commitments that both express and critically challenge thinking and practice in the theologian's present. This book is one theologian's exploration of the possibility that trusting the Christ of the tradition may mean working toward a vision of Christian traditions unanticipated and even viewed as improper by many adherents to the Tradition. This is at least part of what it means to take seriously the theologian's own interpretive pathos as a resource in constructive theology.

Many other examples can be given of the travail of theological thought and practice in the light of this postmodern trilemma, which helps us see that something more demanding than a simple mixing of tradition, openness to plurality, and critique of domination is being asked of the theologian. Two more examples will serve to make the point.

First, those who insist on the need to affirm plurality are steeped in the travail not only of trying to discern what thinking and reason are within our shifting, pluralized context, but also of continually suffering the critique of those who think that amid the celebration of difference there can be no normativity or no critique of injustice. Whether this critique comes from defenders of established normative traditions or from liberation theologians devoted to an uncompromising critique of injustice, the implication often is, unfortunately, that celebration of plurality is only leisurely play for a theological elite. In response, I would say that such celebration is, indeed, often simply an affirmation of all others, one that can marshal neither dialogical agreement nor critical resistance to systematically imposed suffering. For those of us who work within a pluralist paradigm, based on the intense presentation of differences in our contemporary contexts, the discomforting heat of this critique, like the pathos of theologians alienated from their traditions, must be accepted as a challenge to formulate the celebration of difference in terms that create both meaningful senses of tradition and powerful critical resistance against particular oppressions.

As a final example, there also is a travail regarding reflection and practice that accompanies any clear advocacy of the need to resist domination. Especially when theologians address the operative supremacist logics in North America—racism, sexism, heterosexism, classism, or our current government's amalgam of nationalism and militarism—theological advocates of the need to resist domination are sure to experience a particular travail. Both theological defenders of tradition and theological celebrants of plurality direct a critique at theologians of critical resistance, claiming or implying that the latter are subjecting the theological task to a set of special interests that somehow compromises the essence of theological scholarship.

Rarely does this charge come out explicitly, but it is evident in an exchange reported by African American theologian James Cone that occurred between him and Paul Holmer at Yale.[76] As this exchange shows, we North American academics have too long carried the implicit view that specific theological challenges to supremacist logics (such as that of racism) are somehow not of universal concern and hence are not at the heart of theological labor. Again, it is a major task of this book to propose that resistance to domination, in the form of specific critiques of operative supremacist logics in North America, is not only essential to Christian theology but also can be undertaken in a way consonant with a sense of Christian tradition and with a celebration of difference.

These examples are perhaps enough to indicate the travail characteristic of the postmodern trilemma, a travail that demands labor in theory and practice exceeding any mere mixing of the traits of postmodernity.

In my discussion of the travail, readers may discern that I am weary of certain features of the theological conflict and disagreement characterizing North American academies, the religious press, and the churches. I am not tired of theological conflict as such; conflict and disagreement are the stuff of theological creativity and that from which fresh, meaningful discourse may emerge. But the terms of the conflict are troubling—terms that often neglect the full set of challenges emerging from serious response to all three traits of the postmodernist ethos.

I am weary of the theological postliberals (a "postmodernism of reaction") who in the course of defending Christian tradition and narrative are virtually silent about the needs to celebrate and study the plurality of traditions and their interpretations and perhaps even more silent about the tradition's complicity in reinforcing the supremacist logics of oppression. I find myself increasingly less long-suffering with the proponents of plurality and difference who, defending the need to "keep the conversation going," seem unable to articulate the relation of Christian tradition to the goal of conversation and are often even more unwilling to say when, how and why the conversation should ever be closed to those who would undermine others' rights to be present in the conversation.[77] I also find it continually unfortunate that our theological reflections about liberation and the urgent matters intrinsic to liberation so often imply that critical examination of plurality, and a theological response to it, is only leisurely play, without its own kind of passion for justice.

I do not claim that the portrait of North American contexts for theological discussion that I have offered in this chapter is the definitive one. Surely, it does not claim to be a purely objective description. Readings of one's own settings are especially difficult to separate from the ways one is entangled in them. Concerning the traits and the trilemma that I have portrayed as constituting postmodernity, I have no qualms in admitting that my discernment of these signs of the times is conditioned by my own complex place in North American society. Readers may note, for example, how each trait of the postmodern trilemma has its correlate with a major theme in my re-membering Esperanza: plurality, with my memories of cultural difference; domination, with memories of Central American suffering; tradition, with my remembered Christian practice in Esperanza's Teotitlan. I have presented the traits of the trilemma, however, in conversation with major texts of our period, hoping to evoke some sense that these are indeed traits of a situation that is more than my own set of thematic interests.

2

A CULTURAL-POLITICAL HERMENEUTICS OF TRADITION

There is no intellectual, cultural, political, or religious tradition that does not ultimately live by the quality of its conversation; there is also no tradition that does not eventually have to acknowledge its own plurality and ambiguity.

David Tracy
Plurality and Ambiguity

In this chapter I turn more directly to what theological interpretation is to become in light of the trilemma. Reading and rereading traditional texts has often been viewed as central to theological reflection. Surely now, however, given the complexity of the trilemma, there can be no easy readings and rereadings of the Christian traditions' classic sources, especially of the Bible. There are no easy readings of the Bible, I say, because biblical writings are not only difficult in their literary forms, but also by reason of their complex historical contexts. Further, and perhaps most important, biblical texts and studies of their historical contexts are approached by present-day interpreters who have radically different cultural and political viewpoints.

Present-day social locations, shaped by diverse cultural practices and different degrees of access to political power, shape readings of the tradition's texts. Consider, for example, readings of the Markan passage about the possessed man of Gadara, in which "unclean spirits" come out of the Gadarene man and enter two thousand swine who then rush to their drowning in the sea.[1] According to the summaries of Ernesto Cardenal in *The Gospel in Solentiname*, today's landless *campesinos* in Central America approach this passage as a judgment on inordinate wealth and as a signal of how Jesus' life was unsettling for the rich wanting to hold onto their wealth in the form of "about two thousand pigs."[2] Rarely do today's North Atlantic interpreters, with different cultural views and political or economic opportunities, even see this dimension of the passage.

One way of discussing this kind of difference among interpreters is to say that the *campesino* and North Atlantic interpreters live and think differently "in front of" the text that they both interpret.[3] We cannot adjudicate the different readings by the *campesino* and the North Atlantic scholar simply by attending rigorously to details "in the text." Nor would it be sufficient simply to apply exacting historical analyses to the historical worlds "behind the text," within which this passage about Jesus and the Gadarene was formed. No, careful attention also needs to be given to the different contemporary social locations that these interpreters occupy "in front of" the text, from which they move to encounter and are encountered by it. Here is the region where a cultural-political hermeneutics does its work: exploring the dynamics occurring between different interpreters "in front of" the texts.

This is not to deny the necessity of disciplined reading "in the text" and of critical historical analyses of factors and settings "behind the text."[4] In fact, later in this book I will draw from some important studies of scripture's literary themes and historical settings. However, this cultural-political theology works toward such studies by exploring what happens in that difficult contemporary area "in front of" texts, or between texts and their different readers.

The cultural-political hermeneutics that follows in this chapter focuses on the "quality of conversation" (to recall Tracy's term) occurring in this area. The focus appropriately falls here because it is in front of our texts that we most directly confront the current trilemmic situation wherein tradition, plurality, and resistance to oppression all demand response. The region in front of the text is a complex, intersubjective territory involving, for example, *campesinos* and their relationship to one another, North American Christians and their relationships to one another, as well as the intricate interconnections in the political, economic, and social systems that unite the worlds of *campesinos* and North American citizens.

Such worlds in front of texts have not always been the concern of discourses called hermeneutics. There are, however, some salient features of what academics have referred to as hermeneutics that draw attention to the importance of analyzing these worlds. It is the aim of this chapter to identify those salient concerns and then press hermeneutical reflection toward a more serious analysis of the social locations that make up the region in front of texts. When this is done, hermeneutics becomes much more than a professor's playground; it is transformed into a way of thinking about our texts and traditions that has a strategic value for worlds in crisis.[5] In particular, hermeneutics, as a cultural-political hermeneutics of worlds in front of texts, can become a way to address the quandaries of thinking and living in the trilemma. It remains for us to show in more detail why something called hermeneutics can be a resource for such a crisis. To do this, we first need to address the issue of what hermeneutics is.

WHAT IS HERMENEUTICS?

Invoking the term *hermeneutics* has become so prevalent in theology, as in other fields, that one wonders if it has a specificity that warrants its being preserved. One has only to note the frequency of its use in academic conferences, and the variety of its usage, to suspect that we are dealing with a popular term that may be detached from any valuable, discrete meaning.

Even Hans-Georg Gadamer, perhaps the figure most recently known for consistent advocacy of a philosophical hermeneutics, laments that "hermeneutics has become fashionable and every interpretation wants to call itself hermeneutical."[6] Although he is suspicious of the merely fashionable uses of the term, Gadamer does not retreat from using it to refer to an important intellectual and cultural movement.

The Problem of Definition

No easy definition of hermeneutics is attainable for any purpose. Kurt Mueller-Vollmer writes in his *The Hermeneutics Reader* that the problem of definition is that "hermeneutics is both a historical concept and the name of an ongoing concern" in various human and social sciences.[7]

Because hermeneutics is a historical concept, it has a complex history that renders definition problematic. To delineate what hermeneutics is, Mueller-Vollmer himself has to tell a story beginning with the eighteenth-century biblical interpretation of Johann Martin Chladenius, which then continues into the nineteenth-century works of Friedrich Schleiermacher, Wilhelm von Humboldt, Johann Gustav Droysen, Philip August Boeckh, Wilhelm Dilthey, and into the twentieth-century works of Edmund Husserl, Roman Ingarden, Martin Heidegger, Rudolf Bultmann, Gadamer, Jürgen Habermas, and Karl Otto Apel.

This is a long story, one with many different plots and subplots. On the most general level, it is the story of how rules for interpreting scripture have become the occasion for studies of philosophical understanding, and of how these philosophical studies in turn have led scholars to revise or enrich interpretation of biblical and other texts and events significant for Western cultures. Hermeneutics as a historical concept, then, refers to a striking, perhaps surprising, journey of thought from biblical interpretation to a set of philosophical and literary concerns that often have little to do with the Bible and sometimes little to do with any text at all. In fact, if "deconstruction" can be viewed as a critical development among hermeneutical approaches, a kind of radical hermeneutics, then hermeneutics involves inscribing texts in ever-larger matrices.[8]

Especially since the English translation of Gadamer's *Truth and Method* appeared in 1975, this predominantly German tradition of thought has left its mark almost everywhere among the human sciences (notably in sociology, law, literary theory, history, theology) and in the philosophy of natural science.[9] With Gadamer, one might say, a German continental tradition has spread throughout a variety of discourses, not only in continental but also in Anglo-American academies.

If it seemed that hermeneutics was taking the place of what had usually been called epistemology, this was confirmed in the widely read 1979 philosophical treatise, *Philosophy and the Mirror of Nature*, penned by North American philosopher Richard Rorty. Marshaling the many tools of analytic philosophy, Rorty draws insights from Wittgenstein, the later Heidegger, and the later Dewey in an attempt to lead philosophers from epistemology to hermeneutics.[10] Hermeneutics, in contrast to most epistemology, does not seek to lay foundations for correct knowledge. Rather, according to Rorty, it edifies by the continuous posing of questions, keeping alive a conversation through a discourse that is "supposed to be abnormal, to take us out of ourselves by the power of strangeness, to aid us in becoming new beings."[11]

The words just cited from Rorty's work, however, indicate how elusive is the subject matter of hermeneutics. What is hermeneutics *about*? What is it—not just as a historical concept but, in Mueller-Vollmer's terms—as an ongoing concern? This is a question I cannot attempt to answer for every region of academic study that registers the impact of hermeneutics, but I can reasonably comment on some relations to theological studies.

As an ongoing concern, I wish to characterize hermeneutics as a configuration of six salient concerns. Contemporary theological approaches that are hermeneutical tend to display these salient issues and relate them one to another.

The Focus on Texts

A first salient concern for hermeneutical reflection is its focus on *texts*. Whatever else hermeneutics is, it has been a set of disciplined studies about the nature of texts, whether texts can be said to have a nature, and their interpretation. This has been the case historically and continues to be so. Although contemporary reflections termed hermeneutical may obscure this concern with texts by probing other salient issues that I note below, there are still those working in theology who would link hermeneutics most closely with the rules and principles governing the exegesis of written texts.

The emphasis on texts can take different forms, ranging from the almost complete identification of hermeneutics with interpreting texts to the use of textual interpretation as a model for interpreting other things. Within this range three forms of this salient concern with texts can be identified.

1. First, the full-scale identification of hermeneutics with textual interpretation is evident when scholars invoke the term as simply referring to procedures for exegeting a text. In theology, Hans Frei's understanding of hermeneutics has been exemplary of this approach: "Hermeneutics I define in the old-fashioned, rather narrow, and low-keyed manner as the rules and principles for determining the sense of written texts, or the rules and principles governing exegesis."[12]

In theology, hermeneutics thus becomes a set of strategies for displaying the contours and structures of religious texts, particularly the sacred scriptures. This view has served to show the text as a whole to be an integral world, while enabling scholars to focus on various functions of its parts: its words, sentences, paragraphs, chapters, books; its images, metaphors, symbols, narratives, concepts; its composition, genre, style. Hermeneutics is *about* these things. It has to do with the stuff of texts. It is a way to cultivate one's sense of the "textuality" of the sacred classics that are important not only to scholars who work with scriptures directly but also to doctrinal theologians and other interpreters.

2. The salient issue of texts is also apparent when the activity of interpreting a text becomes linked by hermeneutes to reflections on the general nature of human understanding. Understanding is often taken to be *like* the interpretation of a text. On the one hand, this has meant the extension of textual interpretation to a philosophy of understanding; on the other hand, it has meant a certain tendency to view the interpretation of texts as one important case of human understanding. The positions and problems are many, and there is no need to attempt any summary of them here. The point to be emphasized is that the text remains a salient concern of hermeneutical reflection when hermeneutics takes the form of a general philosophical exploration of human understanding. In all his discussion of literature and texts, Hans-Georg Gadamer never lets go of the connection of those concerns to the larger issues that he calls hermeneutical. "I have therefore preserved the term 'hermeneutics,' which the early Heidegger used, not in the sense of a methodical art, but as a theory of the real experience that thinking is."[13] David Tracy's work on the experience of a classic may be the clearest example of the extension of issues in textual interpretation to a philosophy of understanding for religious and theological understanding.[14]

3. For some, hermeneutical reflection displays its salient concern with texts in studies of human action. Human actions and social forms are taken to be textlike.[15] This has been suggested by one philosopher of hermeneutics (Paul Ricoeur)[16] as well as by a few theological scholars such as Gibson Winter in social ethics and Donald Capps in pastoral care.[17] Controversy and the play of position and counterposition also attend this kind of hermeneutical reflection.

Roles of Language

A second salient concern of hermeneutics is *language*. Hermeneutics, as a contemporary movement of thought, is seen to be largely a result of the so-called "linguistic turn" in philosophy. Language has been termed the great preoccupation of twentieth-century philosophy, and it is also a distinctive preoccupation of hermeneutics.[18]

The hermeneutical concern with language opens out in several directions. Three of these can be briefly mentioned.

1. The study of language is a way to deepen and extend the salient

interests of hermeneutics in texts. Religious texts, as language, invite study that utilizes all the tools of contemporary analyses of language. The so-called textuality of the text is not decipherable without an understanding of the text as comprising configurations of language.

2. The study of language in hermeneutics has meant the study not only of language systems and structures (codes, grammars) that one might find in texts but also of speech, the use of language in particular instances, subject to the arbitrary and contingent flow of life. Paul Ricoeur's hermeneutical thought is characterized by an attempt to develop a view of discourse that unites these two major domains in the study of language.[19]

3. Then, too, the concern with language opens the way for an acute consciousness of the particularity of every human interpretation. As Wittgenstein's work indicated, the inescapable reality of language in human interpretation means that our knowledge and understanding are constituted by a striking plurality of "language games." Language is not just a trait of texts and speech. It is constitutive of all understanding; "language games are where we as learners—and when we do we cease to be that?—rise to the understanding of the world."[20]

Embracing the significance of language in these ways, hermeneutics is very much a part of philosophy's linguistic turn. The concern with texts reaching back to classic seventeenth-century texts and earlier is now also fed by the vast tributary of thought that is frequently called analytic philosophy. This "analytic wing" features adherents who "find their geography of preference in a belt that runs from Scandinavia, across England, Canada, and the United States, and into Australia and New Zealand,"[21] though it can be found elsewhere as well.

Awareness of Pre-Understanding

A third salient concern is that of *pre-understanding*, focusing on the significance and function of prejudgments.[22] With this issue we come closer to concerns relating to the region in front of texts—a region wherein readers interact with texts. In studies of texts and language, hermeneutical approaches stress that all interpretation involves, in different ways, the preunderstanding of interpreters. In contrast to all "positivisms," hermeneutics has been emphatic about the need to acknowledge the interpreter's prejudgments and prejudices in acts of interpretation and understanding. Hermeneutics has sometimes been portrayed as so greatly taken up with empathic, intuitive, meditative aspects of the presuppositional dimensions of understanding that it is to be branded subjective or relativistic. Accordingly, in the academy hermeneutics is sometimes referred to as mere intuitionism, a sophisticated kind of alchemy that violates the standards of critical science.

Some uses of hermeneutical reflection may indeed move toward such subjectivism, but more typically hermeneutical thinkers seek to understand the subjective and intersubjective dimensions of all inquiry in ways that allow for rigorous and disciplined methods of exegesis, social science inquiry, literary critical analysis, or scientific experimentation and technique. Among the more prominent early advocates, the articulation of such explanatory methods in relation to hermeneutical understanding is more clearly present in the work of Ricoeur than in that of Gadamer.[23] In the cultural-political hermeneutics of this project, I will likewise be insisting that hermeneutical understanding be strengthened and challenged by analyses of explanation.

Sometimes the pre-understanding of interpreters is understood existentially, as constituted by the kinds of positive and negative boundary experiences identified by the early Heidegger or by Karl Jaspers. More typically, contemporary hermeneutics insists that all these experiences are integrally bound up with linguistic and communal forms of life. Ultimately, an interpreter's pre-understanding is not so much subjective as it is intersubjective, representing a configuration of language and social interaction. Again, it is this view of interpreters' pre-understandings which in part leads me to develop a cultural-political hermeneutics in this book.

Pre-understanding, viewed as linguistic and communal and not as simply existential, brings this salient concern near to the concerns of the analytic wing of hermeneutics. But the notion of pre-understanding is lodged in current hermeneutical reflection largely as the result of another tributary of nineteenth- and twentieth-century thought: a phenomenological one. This tributary flows most freely through a geography of preference that comprises West Germany, the Netherlands, France, Belgium, and Italy,[24] though the United States is now a major area as well.

This phenomenological wing may present interpreters' pre-understandings in terms of language and tradition (Gadamer's largely later-Heidegger version) or in terms of language and social interest (Habermas' largely Freudian and Marxian version).[25] Gadamer's and Habermas' ways of viewing interpreters' preunderstandings are distinctively combined and assessed in the works of French hermeneutic philosopher Paul Ricoeur, in whose writings the phenomenological tributary is explicitly joined with the analytic one.

Emancipatory Interests

There is also the salient concern for what I shall term *emancipation*. Although hermeneutics can indeed be spoken of as an obfuscating, even repressive academic language, those indebted to hermeneutics often view it as emancipatory. Gadamer's well-known attempts to rehabilitate tradition have led many to see hermeneutics as almost a tradition-bound, text-centered mode of inquiry. This claim may be partly true, but it is not unambiguously true of Gadamer's contributions, and it is certainly not true of many other scholars who turn to hermeneutics for an inquiry that nurtures their emancipatory interests. In what senses does hermeneutics feature an emancipatory interest? Responding to this question is important, because below I will develop emancipation as a crucial interest and theme of a cultural-political theology.

It may be helpful to refer to a 1986 conference bringing together a number of North American theologians and religion scholars, all interested in hermeneutics, who met at Princeton Theological Seminary.[26] These scholars represented Jewish, Christian, and Islamic traditions, and included African American, feminist, and other perspectives. An emancipatory dimension of hermeneutics was identified in different ways. Several scholars identified the role of hermeneutics as freeing academics, especially in the area of theology, from authoritarian and dogmatic conceptions of truth. Others stressed that it brought a freedom from the "positivisms" and "objectivisms" attending the explanatory methods of many of the human sciences in North American academies. Still others saw hermeneutics as a releasing of intellectual criticism into a conversational world where diverse perspectives, often marginalized, are encouraged and affirmed. Feminists in the discussion found the issue of the emancipatory function of hermeneutics to be salient but claimed that the record did not show hermeneutical discourse to have had emancipatory impact for women. They insisted that the emancipatory function for women comes more from specific appropriations of women's experience. These feminists echoed the punning claim of feminist literary critic Elaine Showalter that hermeneutics is more a "hismeneutics."[27]

Although at times ambiguous when discussed by scholars of hermeneutics, the salience of the emancipatory theme is also clearly evident in the literature. It is important to recall that when two of the leading formulators of contemporary hermeneutics (Gadamer and Rorty) risked definition-like statements of what hermeneutics is, a strong emancipative motif was heard. In a collection of writings since *Truth and Method*, Gadamer states that hermeneutics is "the theory and also the practice of understanding and bringing to language the alien, the strange, and whatever has become alien." He then adds, "this *may help us to gain freedom* in relation to everything that has taken us in unquestioningly, and so with respect to our own capabilities."[28] Rorty's view of hermeneutics as an expression of hope for agreement is meant to open up a conversational and "edifying philosophy" that envisions a *societas* — persons whose paths through life have fallen together, united by civility rather than by a common goal, much less by a common ground.[29] Hermeneutics is for Rorty a way to resist "the freezing-over of culture" and the "dehumanization of human beings."[30] Some Latin American and liberation theologians also use elements of the Euro-American discourse of hermeneutics to articulate their own liberative concerns.[31] Latin American scholars, especially, have found hermeneutics to be an important resource for revaluing Christian texts and experiences in an emancipatory mode — outside the constraints of North Atlantic canons of scholarship.[32] In short, an emancipative interest runs deep in much hermeneutical reflection, and I will give it a key place in the cultural-political hermeneutics presented in this chapter and in the theology of subsequent chapters.

Encountering Plurality

A fifth salient concern of hermeneutics is *plurality*. Texts are themselves a plurality of subtexts, of parts and wholes in interaction, of many literary devices. Language manifests a plurality of forms, not only because there are many languages, but also because languages are always changing. Moreover, interpreters' pre-understandings, when viewed as linguistic and communal, display the radical plurality of language games and forms of life.

The plurality with which hermeneutics is concerned is itself plural,[33] but we can identify two kinds of plurality that are frequently affirmed and discussed: historical and cultural.

First, especially in dealing with ancient texts, hermeneutics is concerned with a plurality of interpretations generated by the distance between the horizon of those texts and that of a contemporary interpreter. Between text and interpreter is a historical distance that is traversed by a whole history of interpretation, wherein earlier interpretations are effective in later ones. Hermeneutical theorists' concern with relativity and plurality is most often united to this historical consciousness.[34] Indeed, our contemporary interpretation of ancient texts is possible largely because of this stream of interpretation and its effects upon us. Hermeneutics focuses on how interpretation of a text entails standing among, and in conversation with, an often conflicting plurality of historical interpretations, distinguishable by the stretches of time that distance them one from another.

There is a second mode of plurality that is especially crucial for a cultural-political hermeneutics. Historical consciousness is compounded by a sociocultural consciousness. The interpretation of an ancient text is not merely the conflictual play of many past interpretations; it is also the play of many social and cultural forms of life in the present—again, in front of the text. The interpretation of texts is a problem not only because we interpreters are historically distant from them but also because we are culturally distant from one another and so often engage that history in conflicting ways, socially and culturally.[35]

The Problematic of Truth

A final salient concern is that of attaining *truth*. Hermeneutics' affirmation of historical and cultural plurality renders the notion of truth problematic. In the face of radical plurality, the various coherence and correspondence theories of truth, though often necessary, are insufficient. For many hermeneutes, truth is not identifiable when thought only some-

how "corresponds to" experience or when thoughts feature "coherence."
Instead, truth for the hermeneute has an event character. It has something of the miraculous about it.[36] It is a disclosure of agreement in intersubjective community that one hopes for amid a conversation between the plurality of positions. Truth is a disclosure that is always more than what our criteria of coherence or correspondence lead us to expect; it is an event laden with surprise. Gadamer put it this way: "In understanding we are drawn into an event of truth and arrive, as it were, too late, if we want to know what we ought to believe."[37]

A similar notion of truth is operative in the revised pragmatism of Richard Rorty's writing. In his work, too, the focus shifts away "from the relation between human beings and the objects of their inquiry to the relation between alternative standards of justification, and from there to the actual changes in those standards which make up intellectual history."[38] Truth becomes a matter of keeping a conversation going—a conversation in which the hope for agreement is never lost.[39]

It is fair to say that theologians and religionists are both attracted to and troubled by these views of truth as an event disclosed in the life of conversation. This ambivalence was manifest at the 1986 Princeton hermeneutics conference of theologians and religious scholars. On the one hand, this approach may be lauded for its openness and nonauthoritarian approaches to truth. On the other hand, several thinkers voiced frustration about truth of this sort. When does the hermeneute's valuation of open conversation need to be checked by a courage to close the conversation? When does the hermeneute take a stand? Does not hermeneutics' salient concern with emancipation itself require a notion of truth carrying a greater sense of certitude? Such questions born of this ambivalence constitute a salient concern regarding truth for hermeneutical reflection.

The diversity of these salient concerns and of the many complex issues contained within them keeps hermeneutics a type of intellectual discourse that is difficult to focus clearly. But I suggest that these six salient concerns typify hermeneutical approaches, whether they be distinctly related to one another by a hermeneutical phenomenologist like Gadamer, or in yet another way by the analytic philosopher Richard Rorty, or by the increasing numbers of African American, feminist, and womanist scholars who discuss hermeneutics.[40] Perhaps the best overall description of what hermeneutics is, which can be appreciated if we keep in mind all the salient concerns I have discussed, is given by philosopher John D. Caputo:

Hermeneutics is thus for the hardy. It is a radical thinking which is suspicious of the easy way out, which is especially suspicious that philosophy, which is meta-physics, is always doing just that. ... For hermeneutics always has to do with *keeping the difficulty of life alive* and with keeping its distance from the easy assurances of metaphysics and the consolations of philosophy.[41]

The salient concerns I have discussed here, each variously "keeping the difficulty of life alive," enable hermeneutics to be a resource for theology as it responds to the postmodern trilemma within which it must work.

As a set of studies pertaining to texts, language, and preunderstanding, hermeneutics of course facilitates a sense of tradition. It offers resources for studying the contours and forms of texts and linguistic traditions. Some versions of hermeneutics, as many critics have pointed out, seem to be little more than conservative attempts to hold up the bulwarks of tradition. More positively, as I will try to show, hermeneutics can articulate a sense of the integrity of texts and language in relation to cultural and political critique. The first three salient concerns of hermeneutics—focusing on texts, language, and preunderstanding—can equip theologians more authentically for response to the first trait of the postmodern trilemma: the need to acknowledge tradition.

It is the presence of the salient concerns of emancipation and plurality that especially signal the importance of hermeneutics for Christian theology within the postmodern trilemma. In a variety of hermeneutical projects, emancipation and plurality are not taken up as separate topics; rather, they are intimately related to and render problematic the sense of tradition. In other words, the set of salient concerns displayed in hermeneutics (text, language, preunderstanding, *plus* emancipation and plurality) enables theologians to work toward an approach that is responsive to the postmodern trilemma.

But how are the concerns of emancipation and plurality to be related to a hermeneutics of tradition? How is it possible to marshal resistance to domination (thus valuing emancipation) while also celebrating a multiplicity of interpretations (thus valuing plurality)? In the section that follows, I will argue for a celebration of plurality that is possible only through limiting that celebration by commitment to the emancipation of dominated groups.

A HERMENEUTICAL "UNDERSTANDING" OF PLURALITY AND EMANCIPATION

Hermeneutical approaches generally, and this cultural-political hermeneutics in particular, are made up of an orienting "understanding" and a body of "theories of explanation" that develop, analyze, and even challenge that understanding. Later in this chapter I will discuss this dialectic of understanding and explanation. In this section, I present the orienting understanding of a cultural-political hermeneutics. In presenting it, I am laying out the major features of the encompassing vision that guides a cultural-political approach. This vision, or understanding, entails an important way of relating emancipation to plurality.

The hermeneutical theory of Hans-Georg Gadamer will be my starting point. Although it is important for the understanding of a cultural-political hermeneutics to move beyond and radically critique Gadamer's views, his influence in the United States and elsewhere makes his work unavoidable. A preparatory word on his importance in the North American context is therefore necessary.

By 1985, Gadamer had already spent more than ten years teaching at Boston College. From there he made numerous trips to other North American colleges, universities, and divinity schools to provide lectures and so diffuse among academics of many sorts the insights of his hermeneutics. Although Gadamer was an established scholar in the 1930s in Germany, he was not part of the great sea change of that period which, according to Robert Sullivan, brought German academics to the United States. However, alongside the critical theorist Jürgen Habermas and Paul Ricoeur, "Gadamer has paved the way for the reception in the United States of a revised German intellectual life." He is frequently referred to as "the doyen and prime example of a new generation of international professors who, with the help of the airplane, have brought about a second sea change in the German-American intellectual relationship."[42]

The sea change has been dramatic, leaving a residue of hermeneutical categories (preunderstanding, tradition, effective-history, "hermeneutical circle") in many of North America's academic subcultures. A quarter of a century has elapsed since the appearance of Gadamer's *Wahrheit und Methode* in 1960, and over a decade since its translation as *Truth and Method* in 1975. This text is now internationally recognized as the most important contribution to philosophical hermeneutics since Heidegger's *Being and Time*.[43] Hardly any area of study has been free from its influence, whether theology, sociology, literary theory, law, or natural science. His impact on these areas in the North American context has been greatly aided by his being taken up and even critically endorsed by major North American pragmatic traditions, as evident in the case of Richard Rorty.

Tradition and Plurality in Gadamer

It may seem puzzling that in developing a hermeneutical understanding for the postmodern trilemma, I would begin with a figure like Gadamer, whose attempts to rehabilitate tradition allow him to appear quite conservative.[44] How can attempts like his help navigate the postmodernist concerns with plurality and domination? But the label *conservative* fits Gadamer only in a very ambiguous manner in the postmodern milieu.

Gadamer's notion of tradition, in fact, opens out into the issues of plurality and domination. In this section, I note how Gadamer's view of tradition entails an affirmation of plurality, thus stretching his notion of a rehabilitated tradition toward the breaking point.

Three notions in his hermeneutical theory have rather explosive potential in this regard: "prejudice," "application," and his modeling interpretation after the experience of "conversation." These deserve brief comment, because each facilitates my own critique of Gadamer and my move beyond him to a cultural-political hermeneutics.

The first notion, that of prejudice or prejudgment, is important because he grants prejudice a role in the very movement of tradition. The movement of tradition is not just *from* the past of ancient texts *to* the present horizon of interpreters. Tradition, it is more accurate to say in Gadamer's terms, is a play of movements, a to-and-fro motion involving movements on the part of both tradition (with its classic texts and history of interpretation) and of interpreters in the present. The notion of prejudices is crucial here. Through the prejudices of interpreters, they enter the play, taking with them their particularities and interests. Again, Gadamer does not explore these prejudices with detailed analyses, yet he gives them place in a way that challenges any traditionalist assumptions that would accent only the march, or handing on of tradition, moving in one direction, from past to present. Gadamer states specifically, when describing the hermeneutical circle of understanding, that what is involved here is something more complex: "the interplay of the movement of tradition and the movement of the interpreter."[45] True, Gadamer insists on the texts and tradition as "other," as making a claim on interpreters, but he is also emphatic about interpreters needing to acknowledge their prejudices and to give them "full play" as "the only way through which the other's claim to the truth can be experienced."[46] Into the very notion of tradition, therefore, is etched the dynamic historicality of interpreters, with all their plurality of prejudices, interests, and contexts.

The second notion, that of application, intensifies the possibilities of linking tradition to the problem of plurality. For Gadamer, application of a tradition's text is not something that happens after one understands it; rather, application of the text to the present situation of interpreters is integral to the act of understanding itself. Here again, Gadamer continues to write about "the superior claim of the text," but this does not prevent him from developing arguments from legal and homiletic practices for the role of application in understanding itself. "All reading involves application, so that [persons] reading a text [are themselves] part of the meaning [they apprehend]. They belong to the text that they are reading."[47] If application is "the central problem of hermeneutics," as Gadamer claims,[48] then at the heart of his hermeneutics of tradition is an indeterminacy and a valuation of difference that requires attention. Gadamer's summary is clear: ". . . the text, whether law or gospel, if it is to be understood properly, i.e., according to the claim it makes, must be understood at every moment, in every particular situation, *in a new and different way*. Understanding here is always application."[49]

Gadamer does not explore concretely the present worlds of interpreters within which the necessary "application" occurs. He does not explore "the who" of discourse in a way that introduces into hermeneutics the rich details of social location, which are to my mind so essential to the complexities of interpretation in front of texts. Nevertheless, the notion is there, inviting exploration—inviting even a kind of dismantling of Gadamer's talk elsewhere in *Truth and Method* about the superiority of tradition's claims.

The final notion in Gadamer's hermeneutics that can be developed beyond Gadamer's own position is that of conversation. Conversation, as "a process of two people understanding each other," is employed by Gadamer as a model for clarifying the process of understanding occurring between present interpreters and the tradition. For him, I-Thou, conversational dynamics—both their virtues and their vices—constitute a kind of paradigm presenting the "highest kind of hermeneutical experience" between interpreters and their texts.[50] The conversational model may seem to enable Gadamer only to write about the interplay between past and present in another way. He tends to view the diachronic, historical relationships playing between present and past as analogous to the synchronic, present relationships playing between "I" and "Thou." For Gadamer, the present is to the past as an "I" is to a "Thou."[51] This analogy has significant limitations because it lays upon the complex dynamics of historical interaction what appears to be a two-person encounter (I with Thou) in conversation.

Actually, however, by taking up the conversational model for understanding experiences of interpretation, Gadamer opens the door to a host of challenges and problems that his own project does not always address. In particular, the interpreter as an "I," as a person engaged in conversation, becomes much more complex and dynamic. Although Gadamer usually presents tradition as the "Thou" with whom a contemporary "I" must converse, the "I" now becomes identifiable as a contemporary interpreter who is at the same time conversing with a set of other contemporaries who are also "Thou." This renders the experience of interpretation much more complex. Now interpretation is not just conversation with a past "Thou," but also conversation with "Thou(s)" in the present. In other words, to interpret that Markan passage about the man from Gadara, I need not only converse with that passage as Thou, I also need to converse with others who are its interpreters in my present.

Taking up the conversational model, therefore, shifts our attention to a synchronic dimension, wherein a dynamic interplay takes place between interpreters in the present. The emphasis on conversation grants Gadamer's readers a respite from his preoccupation with the diachronic dimension, in which past texts interplay with a present reader. The shift into the synchronic realm raises a whole set of issues not addressed by Gadamer. Among them are the following questions: How does the dynamic interplay between different interpreters in a given present affect the interplay with past texts? How do the realities of force and subjugation expressed in interpreters' prejudices and operative in the social locations of interpreters' applications constrain the meanings they derive from past texts? In short, the turn to conversation puts the complexities of an interpreter's intersubjectivity on the hermeneutical agenda. Not only are these complexities left unexplored by Gadamer; they demand a hermeneutics of a different sort.

That Gadamer brings us to this point of critique and transcendence of his own project by way of a hermeneutics claiming to rehabilitate tradition and authority in large part testifies to the accuracy of John D. Caputo's claim that Gadamer "offers us the most liberal possible version of a fundamentally conservative idea."[52] A cultural-political hermeneutics will move beyond both the conservative idea of tradition and the liberal version of this idea that sanguinely presupposes, as Gadamer seems to, that difference and plurality dwell more or less comfortably with tradition.

In Conversation: A Hermeneutical "Privilege of the Oppressed"

The distinctive vision for the kind of understanding I propose for a cultural-political hermeneutics can be set forth through a more careful study and critique of Gadamer's notion of conversation. In short, I will be highlighting elements of critique in Gadamer's notion of conversation — elements that are conditions for more cultural and political readings, even to the point of clarifying the senses in which interpreters might speak of a "hermeneutical privilege of the oppressed." This critical development of Gadamer's logic of conversation does not yield the complete set of strategies that would make up a cultural-political hermeneutics. For that to occur, it is necessary to identify the place of critical theories of explanation, as I will in my next section. Here I present the general structure of an understanding that unites a valuation of difference with critique, defined as resistance to domination marshaled by acknowledging the privilege of oppressed voices in the conversation. This critique is essential if a cultural-political hermeneutics is to engage the issue of emancipation that is so central to the trilemma's concern with resisting domination.

I now return to provide a closer examination and critique of Gadamer's notion of conversation. I agree with him that it can serve as a model of interpretive experience; but the model, as I have already suggested, needs challenging and extensive revising. This enables us to talk not only of conversation among a plurality of interpreters, but also of a hermeneutical privilege of the oppressed. Five dynamics of conversational experience need to be identified in order to identify this hermeneutical privilege. Three of these are present in Gadamer's discussions; the other two emerge as necessary in light of issues raised by Gadamer but not fully treated by him.

1. A first dynamic, and perhaps the one most discussed by Gadamer, is the *movement of question and answer in conversation between two or more different parties*. This dynamic includes the many kinds of interchanges that can occur within an openness between conversation partners — an openness to questioning and being questioned. Among the interchanges included are those of the partners' first encounters, false starts, assumed agreements, and breakdowns. This movement is at the heart of this first dynamic: the

sheer initial struggle of each partner to understand the other. Whether I am conversing in remembrance of Esperanza, in the villages of Guatemala with Ladinos or the Cakchiquel, or with my spouse, the dynamic first necessary to achieve authentic conversation is an openness to exploratory questioning and answering.

2. It must also be noted, as a second dynamic, that *authentic conversation highlights the particularity of the other*. Conversation partners are not really accepted, heard, or included if they are not released from the interlocutors' first impressions and freed from stereotypical and classifying approaches to each other. In authentic conversation, there is a highlighting of the otherness or distinctiveness of conversation partners. Gadamer himself does not explore what it would mean to highlight otherness, but taking his own call seriously would mean allowing the partner in conversation to come forth in all her or his specificity, as determined not only by special events of individual life history but also by different modes of contextuality: class, race/ethnicity, gender, and so forth.

For a North American taking seriously this component of conversation — whether in conversation with Esperanza's world of Zapotec society, contemporary Guatemalan groups, or the many distinctive groups and heritages on our own North American terrain — the interchange must move beyond the intrigue and vicissitudes of general interaction into an intentional focusing upon each other's differences. Pertinent to the conversation would be the deliberate description of each other's heritages, cultural contexts, political power, language, and other differences. A genuine conversation heightens these differences with respect to each party in the conversation. Not just one party or partner is "the other." Each must come forward embodied as distinctive other.

What is often criticized as the "liberal project" often ends here, with this delighting in the ever-more-refined presentation of these differences, this celebrating of diversity, this working to preserve an "enriching plurality." Critics of this liberal spirit, of this easy plurality, rightly point out the tendency of the mere delight in difference to issue in forms of repressive tolerance, and they rightly indicate its toothlessness, especially in the face of oppression. Also, an unqualified delight in difference can obscure the fact that different parties in a given conversation do not possess equal resources of power. It is possible (and often happens) that North Americans delight in differences of the kind manifested in Mexico's Zapotec Amerindians or in Guatemala's Mayan groups but fail to note that the Amerindian's difference is not merely a matter of cultural variation from North American customs. It is also one of their domination by a North American society's practice in which "delighting" North American tourists are implicated.[53] This liberal, often repressive, "tourists' delight," I suggest, is not the necessary result of a hermeneutics of conversation. It is a distortion. It is a failure of conversation partners to allow their interlocutors to break free from the stereotypes and first impressions brought to them. This distortion amounts to a failure to see conversation as containing more than the first dynamic I identified. It is a distortion because it fails to play out fully the second dynamic of highlighting difference. To play out that dynamic fully would mean developing the differences of each party, in their own contexts and their relation to each other.

3. A third dynamic of conversation, if allowed to be present, also helps guard the integrity of difference or otherness between partners. It is also crucial for identifying the role of critique in hermeneutical conversation. This is another dynamic that Gadamer identifies as intrinsic to conversation but does not fully develop. Against those who would assume that conversation is only an irenic exchange of viewpoints, a "gentlemanly art," Gadamer notes that *real conversation that highlights difference entails clash and conflict.*

A conversation in which difference is indeed highlighted will lead to parties' hearing and marshaling claims against each other. In Gadamer's words, "openness to the other" demands not just liberal inclusion of the other but "the acknowledgment that I must accept some things that are against myself."[54] Openness to others is not real openness if it does not mean vulnerability as a source of valuable and new insights coming through conversation. There is a "fundamental negativity that emerges between experience and insight."[55] This negativity may include challenging points made by a conversation partner that challenge the whole structure of the modes of interaction in a given conversation. The critiques of liberation theologians directed toward North Atlantic theologies feature this radical challenge to the very structure of theological conversation.

In the Guatemalan case, taking differences between North Americans and Central Americans seriously would imply that North Americans would move well beyond any liberal's delight in difference—surely beyond the tourists' delight. It would mean their being exposed to critique from the ones discerned as different, especially to critique against themselves, generated by Central Americans who experience their own lives as in subordination to powerful North American societal and business practice.[56] Authentic conversation would not exclude the appropriateness of North American critique of the Central American interlocutors, but there is a certain privilege attaching to the critiques of the subjugated. However privileged they are, for us to take both their otherness and our own otherness seriously means risking criticism of them as well as our accepting their critique of us.

Although Gadamer makes the experience of negative critique intrinsic to conversation, he blunts the effect of this dynamic of critique by discussing conversation as mainly an interplay of individual interpreter with the tradition. That is to say, for him, the other who must be allowed to say something against the interpreter is largely a given tradition. The past "other" is what Gadamer posits as possessing creative negativity for an interpreter. He reflects insufficiently on how interpreters in any given present need to allow other present interpreters to be against them. Gadamer does not bring sufficient disciplined attention to the conversation occurring between contemporary, different, and often rival readers and the ways those conversations constrain or reinforce certain conversations with tradition.

To further clarify the way critique is generated by conversation, it is necessary to navigate the world of rival claims among interpreters in any given present. For such a navigation we need to leave Gadamer and draw more from the analytic tributary of hermeneutics, though it, too, will need correction by taking another step in the logic of the interplay in conversation between affirming difference and generating critique.

4. This analytic tributary enables us to acknowledge a fourth dynamic of conversation: what I term *the nurturing of breadth in conversation*. The analytic tributary has given itself explicitly to reflection on how conversational interplay among different and often seemingly incommensurable perspectives or contexts can be navigated such that we can still speak of reason, truth, or intercontextual agreement. To try to summarize this large, complex body of philosophical literature is risky business, but one may fairly indicate the following: Reasoning in a conversational setting attains its truths not by opting out of the heightening of difference by fixing on some fulcrum outside differences or on some foundation below them. Rather, those truths are attained by maximizing "the breadth" of the conversation, so that truths are disclosed in the conversation playing between different perspectives emerging within the widest possible fields.[57] The conversation in which difference is really valued, then, will feature not only the vulnerability that goes with openness generally but also those experiences of difference and negativity that may be had in encounters with the most multifarious, widely arrayed "others." This nurturing of breadth is a feature of the conversational valuation of difference. Conversation attains its truth by striving for and maintaining what some of the analytical thinkers have termed a "wide reflective equilibrium."[58] This requires, in Charles S. Peirce's words, a trusting to "the multitude and variety of arguments rather than to the conclusiveness of any one. Its reasoning should not form a chain which is no stronger than its weakest link, but a cable whose fiber may be ever so slender, provided they are sufficiently numerous and intimately connected."[59]

North American theologians' engagement with others, especially those of distant culture and language as well as those who may be nearby and alienated, can be viewed, then, as a pursuit of wide-reflective equilibrium. As these groups are often absent from, or marginal to, North American conversations, adverting to their lives and perspectives is necessary to appropriate reasoning in the North American setting. What is operative in this nurturing of breadth in conversation is neither just travel, nor the garnering of new cultural exposure, nor the mere extension of truths already known. Rather, it is the constituting of a dialogical community, without which "the truth" of North American reasoning and practice cannot come to pass. This can be achieved without reducing distant or alienated ones to the status of people who merely serve our own quests for truth. That would simply be one more imperialist move—one more attempt to make others' backs our bridges to truth and wholeness.[60] The previously noted dynamics of conversation remind us that exploration of *our own otherness* is also crucial to the whole breadth of conversation.

5. The insight from the analytic tributary concerning the necessity of breadth, of achieving a wide reflective equilibrium between diverse perspectives, leaves unaddressed the question of precisely what constitutes the widest parameters of a conversation. These parameters will always be changing and will themselves become a matter of conversation. I therefore propose a fifth feature of conversation: *the acknowledgment of a privilege for those excluded or absent from the conversation.* Recognizing the voices of those absent from conversation—often voiceless because of death, persistent hunger, or systematic distortion of their social and political life—is the crucial way by which the fullest breadth of conversation can occur, a breadth needed for the truth of reasoning to occur and be sustained. I suggest quite intentionally that we acknowledge that privilege, because it is not something for us to grant. It is something seen and claimed by oppressed groups themselves and which has been articulated in Latin American and other theologies of liberation. What follows is my attempt to acknowledge the legitimacy of claims for the preferential option for the poor and to allow that acknowledgment a determinative place in a cultural-political hermeneutics.

When I say that these excluded ones have a privilege, this is not in the preposterous sense that *only* the excluded ones have the truth or that they *always* speak the truth. These are not even the claims of those liberation theologians who have urged our recognizing the preferential option.[61] Accordingly, I suggest the following meanings of the hermeneutical privilege of the oppressed.

First, those marginalized and absent from a given conversation constitute the outer reaches of conversation, where the width and breadth of the conversation is intensified. Those excluded and marginalized from our conversations constitute the far limits of the width that is necessary to the experience of truth in conversation. Those who are excluded thus both constitute and intensify the quality of width in a way that those "expert in," long accustomed to, or at the center of the conversation, cannot. Their status as the nonincluded ones—the ones absent from conversation by reason of their being politically "disappeared," malnourished, or dead—makes their presence the orienting boundary of conversation.

Second, this privilege lies in the excluded or oppressed ones' greater experiences of negativity. All parties to a conversation have negative experiences, suffer, and draw insight from them, but in addition to the negativity and suffering borne by all, other systemic distortions are imposed on only some. Victims of the oppressions of racism, classism, sexism, heterosexism, vicious forms of ethnocentrism—these not only occupy a privileged position that intensifies the width of a conversation, they also have a distinctive insight born out of sustained, radical suffering. Common parlance occasionally gives lip service to the role of suffering in seasoning one's knowledge and generating insight. The relationship of negativity to insight needs to be affirmed, however, in such a way that those forced to cope with sustaining life and joy under the conditions of imposed, systemic injustice are affirmed as possessing distinctive insights—possessing a privilege in the sense of an insight born of radical negativity not experienced by more elite, centrist groups.[62]

Third, there is a certain privilege lying in the expanded vision of social and political life that marginalized, oppressed groups have in ways that those at the center of social political systems usually do not have. As Janice E. Perlman shows in her 1976 study of the poor in Rio's slums, those marginalized and oppressed are not so cut off from structures of power that they lack familiarity with them. Rather, their marginality is a thoroughgoing integration into the world of the powerful, even though their opportunities and benefits are unequally restrained.[63] Not only in Rio, but also in places like Washington, D.C., Houston, and Princeton, subordinated groups have not only learned how to survive in the powerless spaces of a system but have also learned more about the culture of the powerful than the powerful know about those they subjugate. Thus they tend to know not only the dynamics of their own muted group but also much of the dynamics operative in the groups that dominate them.[64] Thus, Bell Hooks has written with respect to African American women:

Living as we did—on the edge—we developed a particular way of seeing reality. We looked both from the outside in and from the inside out. We focused our attention on the center as well as on the margin. We understood both. This mode of seeing reminded us of the existence of a whole universe, a main body made up of both margin and center.[65]

In such greater wholeness of vision, we can acknowledge another privilege of marginalized and oppressed groups.

A conversational hermeneutics, especially as it culminates in this fifth dynamic, is far from being an urbane mode of speech or an easy tolerance. Through its heightening of difference, it accentuates particularities, involves exposure to mutual critique, and acknowledges a primacy for voices emerging from politically subjugated groups.

In sum, a cultural-political theology is marked by a kind of hermeneutical understanding of plurality and emancipation. It dwells in a world in front of its tradition's texts, i.e., between those texts and their diverse readers. This world is constituted by a conversation, the basic traits of which are the focusing of difference (plurality) and the privileging of the critical voices of oppressed groups (emancipation). In this hermeneutical understanding, difference and the critiques by the oppressed are always thought together. They are inseparably so. Although inseparable, however, they are not equal. The fact that there is a primacy or privilege for the voices of the oppressed in the senses I have indicated above means that the problematics of plurality and emancipation do not have an equal standing. Quite to the contrary, in the hermeneutics of a cultural-political theology, the problematic of the oppressed's domination plays the leading role. The nature of the conversation and its navigation and play amid differences are constrained by the voices that come from the boundaries of the conversation. This means that the voices of the oppressed are not only those that "are heard first"[66]; they are also heard constantly. Further, the function of this constant hearing is not to claim that voices of the oppressed are the only voices heard, but they orient the hearing and evaluation of all other voices.

A shape that we might envision to illustrate a conversation that connects difference to critique by the oppressed is that suggested by a web. The web, always being spun and respun, features its many intersections, its outermost strands, and also the gaps and interstices throughout the web. I suggest that the manifold connections and intersections portray the conversational penchant of this hermeneutics, indeed of all interpretation. Interpretation involves making connections in conversation, the continual intersecting of different persons, groups, perspectives, and practices. All of these, however, go on within the limits of a breadth set by the web's outermost strands. These are like the limiting function that oppressed groups can play in a truly wide-ranging, diverse conversation. Those who are excluded from conversation — by having their voices silenced, their bodies taken away, their everyday practice shackled — count as the most radically different ones within a conversational process that values difference. As the penchant for nurturing difference in conversation seeks its fullest breadth, the excluded and subjugated ones, standing at the margins of the conversation, set the limits of the conversation and so give it its shape. The shape of the web, as a way to picture the logic that intensifies conversational play among differences to a point where the subjugated groups attain privileges for orienting the whole, provides an image of the understanding that envelops and pervades the interpretive strategies making up a cultural-political hermeneutics. Insofar as this understanding entails a tendency to privilege the politically subjugated, the hermeneutics is *political*. Insofar as this understanding also always holds this privilege to be intrinsic to the full play among differences, this hermeneutics is also *cultural*, since, as I will argue below, once the political differences are grasped, cultural ones are the most necessary to use for articulating the fullest play among differences.

The privileging of the political problematics of emancipation, though never apart from focusing the cultural differences that refract those problematics, is the key trait of the understanding or orienting vision, that envelops and pervades this book's cultural-political hermeneutics.

THEORIES OF "EXPLANATION": STRENGTHENING THE VISION

What does the development of a hermeneutical "understanding" yield us? Gadamer would be the first to say it hardly leaves us with a method. All along, his intentions were focused on providing a portrait or a vision (an "understanding") of what is the event of interpretation or thinking.[67] His is a phenomenological work that prescinds from particular methods of explanation, for the time being at least.

A cultural-political hermeneutics is hardly adequate, however, if it only articulates its general, orienting understanding of the tradition in which one stands. The way I have critically moved through and beyond Gadamer's conversational understanding to stress cultural and especially political differences implies the need for still more methodical study of those differences. This methodical study cannot be provided by phenomenological or general study of conversational understanding, but by diverse theories of explanation.

In making this claim, I am assuming that the critiques of Gadamer formulated by Jürgen Habermas must be heeded. I will not discuss here the complexities of the debate between these two hermeneutical theorists.[68] The crucial point in the debate, made in diverse ways by Habermas, is that Gadamer's hermeneutics lacks a serious ratification and practice of the need for critical theory and method.[69] This fault would certainly accrue to my own cultural-political hermeneutics, if that hermeneutics was limited to the understanding that I developed in the previous section. A hermeneutical understanding operating in conversation, in front of a tradition's texts, which I developed toward inclusion of a critical privilege for the oppressed, serves as a critical orienting vision; but it must be strengthened by means of methods and theories of explanation.[70]

Although I heed this critique by Habermas, I believe that explanatory theories and methods are never fully practiced outside an orienting understanding that suffuses them. Consequently, although I devote the following two chapters to explanatory theories, I do not claim for these theories a hard certainty forged apart from the orienting understanding I have crafted in this chapter, which is to a large degree a function of my own history, social location, and experience of a postmodern trilemma. In this I am in agreement with Gadamer, who has insisted that the language and traditions we experience can never be set aside when utilizing explanatory theory.[71] In affirming this response by Gadamer to Habermas's criticism, I can nevertheless inject the stronger dose of critical theory and method that Habermas prescribes for hermeneutics. A cultural-political hermeneutics, while beginning and enveloped in an understanding gives greater care than Gadamer to theories of explanation. These theories strengthen the orienting vision of a cultural-political hermeneutics.

Explanatory Theories for a Cultural-Political Hermeneutics

Which explanatory theories, then, are needed to strengthen the understanding that orients cultural-political hermeneutics? The possibilities are legion. To the theologian wishing to respond to the complexities of multiple systems of contemporary societies and their interaction, the great number of theories can be daunting, perhaps discouraging any use at all.

The number and kind of theories I propose here for theological use will be limited by what I see required by the hermeneutical understanding already explored through critical development of Gadamer and in relation to the postmodern trilemma.

In considering the many theories available to cultural-political hermeneutics, we may distinguish two major classes. The first class is a group of theories pertaining to "Christian discourse." A second class pertains to "extradiscursive affairs." Theories of the first class, pertaining to Christian discourse, have as their primary subject matter for analysis the following elements: linguistic texts, symbols, ritual practices, creeds, and doctrines of the Christian tradition. Accordingly, explanatory theories that have these elements as subject matter to be explained pertain to Christian discourse. These theories "explain" the dynamics and functions of each of those elements of Christian discourse in relation to the other elements and, insofar as possible, in relation to the extradiscursive affairs that variously intersect Christian discourse.

Theories of the second class, pertaining to what I am terming extradiscursive affairs, have as their primary subject matter for analysis: social systems, political processes, class divisions, economic needs, institutional orders and practices, and various configurations of these elements' interaction with one another. The elements of this second class pertain to the larger contexts within which Christian discourse is maintained and within which it labors. These theories "explain" the dynamics and functions of these extradiscursive affairs and contribute to analyses of how they relate to the discursive elements that concern the first class of theories.

The distinction drawn between these two classes can by no means be a real separation. The distinction is made only in order to facilitate thinking about the various ways of relating the elements involved. The distinction of the two classes is necessary not only formally but in order to acknowledge the particularity of Christian discourse, a particularity that cannot be reduced to extradiscursive dynamics. Not only do Christian discourses (their language, narratives, myths, communal practices) feature their own nonreducible dynamics. Those dynamics can also affect and be affected by extradiscursive dynamics appearing in society and culture. Theories pertaining to Christian discourse (theories of narrative, myth, and ritual practice) are needed to articulate what these powers within Christian discourse are.

The more we give ourselves to these studies of the integral dynamics within Christian discourse, the more we will also discern the ways they are also implicated in and conditioned by extradiscursive processes. This discernment calls forth the other class of theories needed to analyze those complex processes. We need theories, then, that enable us to analyze both how discursive powers such as biblical text and church practice function in themselves and how extradiscursive affairs such as industrial modes of production or a culture's socialization practices condition and often alter the impact of discursive dynamics.

So which theories qualify? I do not pretend to answer for all theology, but here I will identify several specific theories. In the next chapter I will employ those theories in a way that moves in the direction of forming a particular christology.

The specific theories that I identify here must meet three criteria that have emerged as crucial in this work. First, the theories selected must enable critical analyses of each feature of the postmodern trilemma: tradition, difference and plurality, and domination and oppression.

Second, these theories must facilitate analyses of both discursive elements and extradiscursive affairs. In other words, the theories selected should be drawn from both of the classes of theories I discussed above, enabling critical reflection on the distinctions and relations between the discursive elements and the extradiscursive affairs.

As a final criterion, my selection of theories is guided by the need to strengthen the major dimensions of the hermeneutical understanding that I developed in relation to Gadamer's position on conversation. The strengthening needed pertains to Gadamer's study of tradition, to his affirmation of difference, and to the privileges of oppressed voices in the conversation. These three dimensions of hermeneutical understanding parallel the three features of the postmodern trilemma. Hence, what is required of critical theories by hermeneutical understanding is the same as that required by the postmodern trilemma.

There are three groups of theories that meet these criteria. Again, at this point, I am simply identifying the theories, not developing them as I will over the chapters to follow.

1. Making up a first group are *literary-critical theories*. Included here are theories of narrative, "new literary criticism," structuralism, reader-response criticism, as well as deconstructionist criticism. These theories and others are ways of studying the discursive elements of traditions. Literary critical studies of classic texts and their ongoing interpretation are crucial for understanding the distinctive dynamics of tradition, the first feature of a postmodern trilemma. Historical criticism, as practiced for example in biblical studies, belongs within this group, since even its explicit focus on historical processes and structures is often prompted by clues found in classic texts and by perspectives gained from other texts bearing on the historical world that the critic wishes to reconstruct. In addition, the his-

torian's reconstruction is almost always an interpretation expressed in literary form.

To be sure, the tradition studied by literary criticism and the discursive elements to which critics primarily attend are always more than just texts. Moreover, it is the relation of textual dynamics to extradiscursive affairs, a relation often signaled by literary critical theories, that prompts the need for still other explanatory theories.

Several relatively recent developments in literary criticism especially dramatize the way texts and interpretations of texts intertwine with extradiscursive affairs. Among these we may include African American literary criticism,[72] new feminist criticism,[73] Marxist literary criticism,[74] and gay/lesbian literary theories.[75] These not only explore forms integral to the texts and attempts to interpret them; they also accent the way textual matters are bonded to extratextual processes, particularly to processes that involve disproportionate distribution and systematic abuse of power. These recent literary critics signal the need for another group of critical theories. I will draw from literary critical theories of Christian tradition in the last two chapters of this book.

2. The second group, then, is constituted by *political theories*. By this I mean critical theories pertaining to the ordering of power and force in communal life. Examples of such theories include Habermas's theories of communicative action,[76] Foucault's "archaeologies" of power/knowledge,[77] Jameson's studies of the political unconscious in narrative,[78] and Antonio Gramsci's studies of cultural hegemony.[79]

Also included here are an increasing number of often neglected new voices whose political theories about the arrangement of power are formulated from the perspective of those who have been abused by power. While the general political theories of scholars like Foucault, Gramsci, Habermas and others are important, especially for study of systemic and intersystemic political affairs, greater specificity and insight into the mechanisms of power abuse are available from political theories on racism and white supremacy,[80] sexism,[81] classism[82] and heterosexism.[83]

Political theories about these systemic distortions, especially in the United States context, have a special priority for a cultural-political hermeneutics. Not only do such political theories relate generally to the postmodern need to resist domination, they also enable special strengthening of the critical perspectives of the oppressed's voices—voices for which I have claimed certain privileges. If the voices of the oppressed have the privileged perspectives I have articulated, and if they are as crucial to an experience of truth in any event of "understanding," as I have claimed, the political theories allow us to know better who these privileged voices are, what the mechanisms of their oppression are, and what we might expect of a more substantive nature from the distinctive perspectives contributed by their groups.

What does a "hermeneutical privilege of the oppressed" mean, for example, regarding African American perspectives in theology? To answer that kind of question requires careful attention to how black cultural practices are formed, how they are exercised in relation to white supremacist logics and institutions, and how these have all developed over time. To attend to this closely requires a body of theoretical reflection, specifically in the form of theories concerning racism. In this way political theories give critical depth to, and so strengthen, the hermeneutically privileged margins of conversation, from which the oppressed are so often forced to speak.

Given the privilege I have articulated for oppressed voices, theories of political oppression lead the way in the next two chapters, wherein I discuss theories of sexism, heterosexism, racism, and classism. Those political oppressions, in fact, form the major structure for the rest of the volume.

3. Finally, a cultural-political hermeneutics requires *anthropological theories of culture*. Like the political theories discussed above, these, too, primarily concern extradiscursive affairs, while also not reducing discursive elements to the status of mere reflections or functions of extradiscursive dynamics. Anthropological theories of culture especially enable our response to the postmodern demand to attend to the realities of plurality. Regarding plurality, anthropological theories provide two kinds of insights.

First, they enable a cultural-political hermeneutics to locate its explanatory theories, and hence the "understanding" developed by those theories, within a cross-cultural perspective. This by no means assures a "universalist" vision as some early, all-too-sanguine anthropological theorists reckoned, but it does enable cultural-political hermeneutics to work in a wider, more diverse field of theorization about human life and thought.[84] Use of anthropological theories of culture, therefore, enables a cultural-political hermeneutics to engage the postmodern pressure to do one's thinking in relation to plurality.

Anthropological theories offer a second kind of insight, this one involving the notion of "culture" that anthropologists have employed as their key for organizing the plurality of ethnographic materials in cross-cultural studies. Just which theory or theories of culture should be used to cope with the plurality of communal life-forms studied by anthropologists is a matter of dispute among cultural anthropologists themselves. Functionalist, structuralist, materialist, symbolic, and still other approaches to theories of culture are current.[85]

One trait of the notion of culture often persists, regardless of the particular theory developed. This trait has been called the "holism" of anthropology's culture concept. In common North American parlance, the word *culture* often names or connotes a realm of mass-media arts or refined sensibilities (as in "popular culture" or "high culture," respectively). Sometimes it is used to refer to the set of values a given society may share. These usages, however, do not do justice to the holistic concept of culture in anthropology.

The holistic concept works to check any quick moves to one part of society as being the cultural part. Culture, as I use the term here, refers to a configuration that relates, in a holistic dynamic process, factors of a spoken and/or written language, habitat, techno-environmental practice, kinship system, political organization, religious ritual and belief. This holistic view of culture serves to guide anthropological approaches to human difference. Within the broad scope of anthropology's cross-cultural views, human behavior and communal identity bear internal variations, to be examined in terms of specific differences delineated within such cultural configurations. It is the special contribution of anthropology to foster study of the plurality of communal forms with regard to these configurations.

True, people also live in other kinds of communal contexts, in nation-states, or in racially stereotyped groupings, and political theories are needed to uncover the impact of those communal identities on particular groups. Nonetheless, doing justice to the full plurality of life-forms in our world requires attending to the actual cultures, the lived configurations of factors whereby people conduct their daily practices. Perhaps the need for respecting cultural specificity and plurality is nowhere more dramatically represented than in Africa. There, cultural differences have been largely ignored by the colonialists' drawing of national boundaries. This is not to say that nation-state boundaries should never be drawn, only that they need to be drawn in ways that make for both unity and justice among cultural groups. The failure of this kind of orchestration of cultural difference results in the production of systems that are either so fluid as to be ungovernable (democratically or otherwise) or so pervaded by oppression that they become international symbols of infamy (as with the apartheid system in South Africa).

Anthropological theories of culture, then, provide a heuristic notion, that of "culture," that is both holistic with respect to the factors making up a group's communal practice as well as open to a cross-cultural panorama of cultural identities. Anthropological culture theory is a way to study the world's diversity of communal life-forms (the plurality *of* cultures) and to study the diversity within those communal life-forms (the plurality *within* a culture).

The cultural theories provide an important qualifying perspective on political theories of oppression. First, the anthropological theories of culture situate the theorization of political power in a broad intercultural context. Drawing on these cultural theories means, for example, that no easy generalizations about a political oppression such as racism can be made without attending to its different forms. The broad perspective of cultural theories reminds us that the political distortion of racism takes different forms, depending on whether we are thinking of white racism in North America or in South Africa, of the oppression of blacks in Brazil or England, or of oppressions worked against others on the basis of other physiological or ethnic traits. Cultural theories keep the fact of the plurality *of* cultures within the political theorists' horizons.

Second, cultural theories enable political theorizations of oppression to explore the many complex dynamics playing in a given scene of oppression. The holistic orientation of cultural theories, especially, enables one to study how distortions of political power touch the other dimensions of people's lives: kinship practice, domestic life, religious custom, academic traditions, occupational style. For example, political theories about the powerful impact of transnational corporate structures on third-world peoples are not complete without cultural theories which, with a "thicker description," trace those power dynamics within all the cultural dynamics they touch in both local and international scenes.[86] Cultural theories, therefore, keep the fact of plurality *within* given cultures on the political theorist's agenda by providing resources for studying how power interlaces the many dimensions of a cultural configuration.

The issue of plurality can therefore be richly developed by anthropological culture theories. Consequently, in the following two chapters, while I allow the politically theorized oppressions to form the basic structure, I draw considerably from cultural theories to clarify the oppression being discussed. For example, when discussing sexism, I will discuss theories of sexism as a distortion of power between the sexes, but I will also give a key place to cultural anthropology's study of gender systems. This way of mixing cultural and political theories of sexism enables my formulating a particular kind of approach to sexism. This is one of the ways that I seek to develop the claims of the privileged voices of those suffering oppression, without violating the need to respect diversity and plurality.

Understanding and Explanation

My frequent invoking of the terms *strengthening* and *disciplining* to characterize the contributions that these explanatory theories make to the general understanding achieved in a cultural-political hermeneutics of tradition again raises the issue of how "explanation" is related to "understanding." My relating of these two terms is indebted to discussions in Paul Ricoeur's hermeneutics of the dialectic of "understanding and explanation." Both resemblances and significant differences between this cultural-political hermeneutics and Ricoeur's hermeneutics need to be noted.

For Ricoeur, understanding (*Verstehen*) is a more intuitive, nonmethodic moment of a scholar's work of interpretation. This understanding, however, is not antithetical to the more disciplined, methodic formulation and testing of theories called "explanation" (*Erklären*). Quite to the contrary, he sees understanding to be a kind of "expansive thinking" implicit in operations of explanatory method.[87]

The "understanding" of the cultural-political hermeneutics presented in this book is one that relates tradition, difference, and critical resistance in an overall vision, as I did in discussing Gadamer's thought. It is that kind of understanding which, placed in Ricoeur's terms, is an expansive thinking implicit in explanatory theory—in literary-critical, political, and anthropological theories.

Just how this book's understanding, or any other, is implicit in explanation and just what the relationships are between understanding and explanation are the major questions addressed by Ricoeur's studies of the understanding/explanation dialectic. Here I cannot do justice to the full complexity of Ricoeur's treatment of the dialectic,[88] but a brief comment on his studies of it will help clarify how the explanatory theories that I have proposed for a cultural-political hermeneutics relate to the notion of understanding that I formulated earlier.

The major resemblance of my cultural-political hermeneutics to Ricoeur's lies in my tendency to subsume critical explanatory theory within the concept of understanding. As critical as my proposed theories may be, they still remain informed by an understanding that is given to me and envisioned in a complex amalgam of tradition, affirmation of difference and will to critical resistance. This understanding, like the understandings suffusing all explanatory exercises, is on the order of a pervasive orienting and expansive thinking, one that is admittedly intuitive and nonmethodic. It is not only a result of my place as a scholar living within a North American postmodern academic milieu, it is also a result of the complex set of personal, social and ecclesial experiences I have cited in re-membering Esperanza.

Like Ricoeur, too, I insist that the critical theories *subsumed* within understanding should not be *eclipsed* by it. To say that understanding "precedes, accompanies, closes and so *envelops* explanation,"[89] is not to say that the critical theories are weakened, viewed as optional or considered of less significance. Quite to the contrary. Again with Ricoeur and in his words, I would insist that the literary-critical, political, and anthropological theories constitute a necessary task of explanation that *"develops* understanding analytically."[90]

So the major resemblance to Ricoeur's views is that I am calling for a hermeneutics that insists on critical methods but also acknowledges that these always do their work subsumed within understanding. Having noted the resemblance, three important differences must be noted.

First, the enveloping understanding in this book has been given a more specific, personal, and intersubjective twist. In Ricoeur's writing, enveloping understanding tends to involve matters of existential wonder or anguish, as well as general awareness and intuition. I have tried to give greater specificity to the understanding of this cultural-political hermeneutics by tracing its connections to some quandaries of a postmodern North American trilemma and to some of the major autobiographical elements of my own life. Current emphases on particularity suggest the need for giving a finer-grained portrait of that understanding which Ricoeur claims envelops all scholarly work.

Second, I would like to adopt a revision of Ricoeur's studies of understanding and explanation suggested by David Tracy. Tracy suggests that Ricoeur's proposed role for explanation is insufficiently critical. It is not enough to say that explanation *develops* understanding analytically. Explanatory methods, notes Tracy, also have the capacity to "challenge and correct" understanding.[91] This does mean that explanation escapes its envelopment within understanding, but its analytic categories and reflection are distinctive and powerful enough both to challenge and correct understanding. For example, cultural and political theories of explanation can be focused on the conditions that give rise to a scholar's use of a conversational approach to hermeneutical understanding and so challenge that very understanding itself. Such theories may show a given understanding to have cultural, political, or theoretical implications unwanted by even its adherents, but of which they were not conscious prior to challenge by the theorists.[92]

Finally, a cultural-political hermeneutics significantly departs from Ricoeur's in that it makes an intentional effort to nurture explanatory critique by way of theories of both discursive elements and extradiscursive affairs. Even when responding to the calls by Habermas for critical political theories, Ricoeur has a tendency to point to texts, and a semiotic or structuralist analysis of texts, as the sources and the explanatory methods sufficient to generate whatever critique is needed. His preference is for explanatory methods that treat texts and other discursive elements. He grants less importance to theories of extradiscursive affairs than may be necessary. Rarely does one find in Ricoeur's writing the incorporation into his hermeneutics, even in "explanation," of political or anthropological themes, for example, as they might pertain to the matrices within which readers encounter or are encountered by texts.[93] More directly, a cultural-political hermeneutics attends, by way of carefully selected explanatory theories, to those extradiscursive affairs. It is time, then, to develop those explanatory theories that are so important to a cultural-political hermeneutics and theology.

3

THEORIES OF SEXISM

A Cultural-Political Approach

*Male consciousness turns . . . to a world-fleeing spirituality as the domi-
nant focus of energy. All that sustains physical life — sex, eating, reproduction, even sleep — comes to be seen as sustaining the realm of "death,"
against which a mental realm of consciousness has been abstracted as
the realm of "true life." Women, as representatives of sexual reproduction
and motherhood, are the bearers of death from which male spirit must
flee to "light and life."*

Rosemary Radford Ruether
Sexism and God-Talk

As I acknowledged in my Prologue, remembering Esperanza has a gender or sexual dimension, with its memories sparked by the figure of Esperanza.[1] It is appropriate, therefore, to begin the theorizing of political
oppression with analyses of the distortion occurring between men and
women, even though I will ultimately be relating this distortion to other
forms of political domination.

In this and the following chapter I will argue that practices of domination
entail continuous and elaborate exercises in abstraction. This abstraction,
from realms of women and reproduction, as Ruether has summarized it
here, is a central feature of sexism. According to Sara Shute's helpful definition, *sexism* is the name for systems in which "there are some people
whose actions, practices and use of laws, rules and customs limit certain
activities of one sex, but do not limit those same activities of people of the
other sex."[2] In later sections of this chapter I will develop this definition,
discussing the nature of the limits put on women's activities, the domination
experienced by women, and the pain that women and men know as a result.

In order to relate sexism to other systemic forms of political oppression,
however, it is important not simply to define sexism but to develop it in
ways that allow us to see its character as an abstraction from material
connections. When this is done, as I will try to show in chapter 4, we then

76

develop a perspective enabling identification of some key links between sexism, heterosexism, racism, and classism.

In order to achieve this perspective, explanatory theories pertaining to these forms of oppression are essential. Although it was crucial in the previous chapter to articulate this book's "understanding" of plurality in relation to the privileged needs of oppressed groups, we cannot move directly from that understanding to theological advocacy of oppressed groups and resistance to domination. The responding theologies must come only after a theorization of particular oppressed groups. Further, such a theorization must keep the political problematics to the fore while preserving respect for cultural difference. Cultural-political theories of explanation are thus essential to the resistance of domination. When this resistance works only out of a vision of understanding or only out of a corresponding advocacy, it often rides only the waves of emotion.

I do not demean emotion. In fact, I cannot imagine, nor would I want, a resistance to domination that was not begun in and sustained by an affective abhorrence of oppression on behalf of oneself or others. But without critical theories about the oppressions that call forth our abhorrence, the emotion rarely sustains struggle over the long haul.

Would that we could move directly *from* a vision of understanding that privileges the voices of the oppressed in theological conversation *to* advocacy in the form of song and to a transformative practice of resistance. Songs and other art forms have been crucial in the linking of visions of understanding and transformation. The history of United States labor movements illustrates this.[3] Since recently shaking his lyrics free from the co-opting efforts of United States superpatriots, Bruce Springsteen's music also sustains many who seek resources for struggle and celebration toward justice and peace.[4] For others, alternative artists and their music may play that role more powerfully: Bob Marley, whose reggae reaches from the plight of Jamaica's "Trenchtown" to around the world; Sweet Honey in the Rock, whose members lay tone on tone to remember past migrant workers, needs for peace, and women's strength; Sting, whose "They Dance Alone" is sung for and with the "mothers of the disappeared" at his Latin American concerts; Tracy Chapman, always "Talkin' About a Revolution." These songs and other art forms can enrich one's vision and understanding and enable their communication to others.

The systemic and complex character of political domination, however, also demands critical theory and explanation. As I have claimed, explanation cannot do without understanding; nor should it seek to supplant enveloping and pervasive roles of understanding. So, yes, resistance to political denomination and a real hearing of the cries of the oppressed do require a sustained vision of hermeneutical understanding, and they require a pervasively felt affective engagement; but without explanatory theory, the needed resistance is often erratic at best, neglected at worst.

In North American theological education, resistance to political dominations and supremacist logics (whether of racism, classism, militarism, heterosexism, or sexism) is often left to ride the somewhat unpredictable waves of group or individual sentiments about suffering. Hunger, for example, might become a major issue on scenes of theological education if North American media choose, for whatever reasons, to convey images of famine from world regions where radical suffering always occurs. These essential issues, however, are often left without ongoing theoretical analysis in the curricula and structures of theological education. Without a theoretical formulation that is carved into the very interpretive structure of theology, these essential issues of human survival and liberation are often subordinated to less important concerns or are neglected outright.[5]

It is the aim of this chapter, therefore, not only to formulate theories of explanation needed for strengthening the understanding of a theology's cultural-political hermeneutics but also to provide the critical resources that our lived struggle, both affective and political, requires.

As I move into explicit discussion of the explanatory theories that are essential to a cultural-political hermeneutics, it should be no surprise that, in the following two chapters, I am privileging political theories. These chapters organize theories available to theology in a way that gives the political theorizations of domination primacy over both the literary-critical theorizations of tradition and the anthropological theorizations of cultural difference. This is consonant with, and a way to strengthen, the logic I explored in the previous chapter that privileged the voices and insights of the exploited and marginalized in the complex process of interpreting a tradition.

The primacy of the problematic of dominance is given full play in these chapters, in that I am organizing theology's explanatory theories in accord with specific categories of political domination in which theory construction occurs. In particular, I will be looking at four forms of political domination that are a special concern in North American contexts, but not only there. After exploring sexism in this chapter, I will in the next chapter seek theoretical connections to heterosexism, racism, and classism. I do not stop at allowing these organizers to provide a fourfold discussion of the theories most relevant to a cultural-political hermeneutics; they will also provide a fourfold structure for the christology and christopraxis that I will propose in the final chapters.

WHY SEXISM, HETEROSEXISM, RACISM, CLASSISM?

Before turning directly to sexism, a brief comment is necessary concerning the reasons for my privileging sexism, heterosexism, racism, and classism as the distortions to be theoretically treated. I am aware of the possibility of starting with other abuses of political power. Such other distortions include nationalism, militarism, ethnocentrism, ageism, and others. I offer three major reasons for this book's selection of these four systemic distortions. The first two pertain to developments in academic settings; the third is more ecclesial and personal.

First, there are increasing indications in academic literature that each of these forces of exploitation so structures life that writing, reading, and interpretation are shaped by them. If theologians are concerned with connections between their discursive exercises (in writing, reading, and interpretation) and extradiscursive affairs, then this literature is of enormous importance, for it shows diverse ways in which those systemic distortions of political power shape and leave traces in the writing, reading and interpretations with which theologians and other academics deal.

Below, I will draw from the theories suggesting the presence of a literary aesthetic that in one way or another can be traced to one or more of the exploitative forces of sexism, heterosexism, racism, or classism. My exploration of such an aesthetic will be most extensive in relation to sexism and the discussions of a "female aesthetic." But there is a literature in all four of these areas suggesting the possibility of making connections from a literary aesthetic to exploitative forces.[6]

Second, there is a growing literature on the nature of these forms of systemic distortions. Here the focus is not on possible connections of exploitative forces to a literary aesthetic but on the exploitative forces themselves. The literature suggests that, although these forces are complexly interrelated with one another and often with other dynamics, they do have their own integral character as systemic exploitations. Especially in North America, as Joel Kovell shows for white racism, this integral character features a particular organization of political power, of social institution, with a reinforcing symbolic matrix.[7] This literature, grouped in terms of racism, sexism, heterosexism, classism, is important for clarifying the complex ways a literary aesthetic might be traceable to exploitative forces. The literature is crucial, especially if we are to avoid the temptation to see the literary aesthetic as simple reflections of political forces to which we might reduce them. Whether the works in question are on racism, as with Kovell's *White Racism: A Psychohistory*; on sexism, as analyzed historically in Gerda Lerner's *The Creation of Patriarchy*; on heterosexism, as historically and philosophically treated in Janice G. Raymond's *A Passion for Friends: Toward a Philosophy of Female Affection*—in all these, the distinctive character of one of the four named systemic distortions is presented. The tendency of our literature to be specific to these groupings, then, provides a second reason for my selection of the four. Almost all of the more traditional fields of study—history, philosophy, political science, sociology—increasingly feature a literature that names and focuses on these four distortions. This is especially true in cultural anthropology. I will draw especially from anthropology's cultural perspectives on these political distortions in order to give nuance to any theorizing about how the political exploitation impacts literary work and interpretation.

Finally, I invoke the more ecclesial or personal reason. I find it impossible to engage in Christian worship and communal practice without engaging persons who speak out of a sense of experiencing one or more of these four named exploitative systems. Whether these Christian colleagues are women, African Americans, gay men, lesbians, or those living in poverty (whether in Trenton, New Jersey, or the barrios of Guatemala City), they each as a group keep presenting to me, and to all the church, the urgency of their plights—plights worked by these four exploitative systems and their corresponding supremacist logics that explicitly and implicitly privilege maleness, heterosexuality, whiteness, and wealth. To be sure, my ecclesial and personal concerns cannot be reduced to these four problems, but in terms of a theological response to forms of systemic exploitation in North American life, these four have primacy.

I grant that selecting these four gives my analysis of oppression a kind of societal and political cast that at first may seem unrelated to militarism, ageism, the global imperialism of large states, or to the technological damage done to our nature system. Nonetheless, I seek to develop the selected distortions in a way that not only enables relating the four to one another but also facilitates insight about the other important challenges of our day. In addressing the four I have selected, it will not be possible to avoid at least some commentary on the other issues. But now, we move explicitly to sexism.

BEGINNING WITH SEXISM

Given the complex interaction of the four forces of systemic distortion, their tendency to forge interlocking systems or an infrastructure of oppressions,[8] we must acknowledge that there remains something impressionistic about any sequence in analyzing oppressing systems. Wherever one starts, say with a man's or woman's awareness of sexism or racism, one can think backward and forward, in and out of one kind of systemic distortion and into others. Indeed, eventually attending to this kind of networking among systemic distortions is far more important than the matter of how one begins.

In this chapter, however, I not only begin with sexism, I tend also to privilege insights drawn from feminist critiques of sexism over those who critique other distortions, even though the other distortions must retain their uniqueness, should not be collapsed into the structure of sexism, and must not be assumed to share an identical structure or problematic. Why, then, my tendency to privilege sexism? Why not begin with critiques of heterosexism, racism, or classism? I offer two responses.

The first pertains to the kind of person writing these essays. There is something inauthentic for me, a white, heterosexual, relatively affluent male in North America, to reflect on systemic distortion, or a theology of liberation from it, out of someone else's situation of pain. For me to craft a theology primarily out of and for the pain of African Americans, for gay and lesbian communities, or for the materially disenfranchised, would be (in spite of all my empathy) at best to tap a resource that really is not mine. At worst, it would be a voyeurism with regard to other's pain.

My sense is that white, heterosexual, affluent males best begin to unravel the whole fabric of domination and distortion by reference to regions of pain attending their own relatedness to mothers, wives, sisters, women friends and colleagues within their own kin, social, and professional groups. I am not suggesting that men begin by doing theology *for* women's experience. That would still be the way of the voyeur and co-opt their own task. Rather, we can begin to think theologically out of the pain caused by sexism, primarily to women but also to men. I increasingly sense that the pain men know in their various relationships is a pain borne out of pressures generated by the forces of still-reigning dominance of men over women — forces that persist in even the seemingly most egalitarian arrangements between the sexes.[9] Feminist critiques of sexism generally are more accessible to the pain of white, heterosexual, affluent men than are other critiques (of racism, classism, and so forth).

In support of this generalization is Elaine Showalter's account, backed by that of Gayatri Chakravorty Spivak, of the phenomenon of "male feminism." Pointing to the social location of male academics, Showalter and Spivak suggest that "unlike the race and class situations, where academic people are not likely to get much of a hearing, the women's struggle is one that they can support 'from the inside.' "[10] The negative outcome of this has often been that men, under the cloak of solidarity with women's struggle, simply seek one more arena within which to correct and guide women or within which to demonstrate (usually to other men with whom they are in competition) their own courage in frontier seeking. Given the pervasiveness of sexism and the extent to which all of us men are trained in both the blatant and subtle logics of dominance, I cannot claim that my own privileging of the sexist distortion and my own stands against sexism are free from such sexist posturing. Showalter and Spivak ably challenge any male confidence in the virtuousness of their studies or of their resistance to sexism.

Nonetheless, at the heart of the male feminists' admittedly ambiguous plight (Stephen Heath calls it "necessary but impossible"[11]), there is an insight relevant to the male scholar's ongoing practice and thinking of resistance to sexism. Spivak and Showalter do not question the tendency that, given the places in Western social systems that we academic males occupy, we have greater accessibility to authentic struggle within the worlds we share with women than we do in whatever worlds we share with those of, say, another ethnic or class group. For us "to look to join other politico-economic struggles is to toe the line between hubris and bathos."[12] I take this insight not as cause for ignoring our participation in political-economic struggles against racism and classism. Quite to the contrary, the lesson I derive is that these other struggles, if authentically borne, must come through our resistance to sexism (our own sexism and "the metasexism of our systems"). It is surely the case that seeking a raised consciousness about racism or classist domination while ignoring our own proximate and daily sexist domination is, at the very least, a highly dubious kind of solidarity. North American theologians writing about "the poor of Latin America" while silent about their own roles within the sexism of their own terrain will hardly understand the dynamics of classism, either. My confidence that a resistance to sexism can pull even the white academic male into resistance to the other systemic distortions anticipates my second response to the question: Why begin with sexism?

This second response emerges from the observation that the situation of dominance between men and women that we name sexism has a certain ubiquity demanding immediate and constant, if not first, attention. We need not agree with Daniel Maguire's characterization of sexism as the "elementary sin" or as original sin, but he is right to note that with the distortion of the male/female dyad "nothing will be spared the fallout from so radical a corruption": "The most fundamental form of otherness is male/female otherness. If this otherness is marked by opposition and disdain, it will be easier to oppose other others—be they black, Jewish, foreign or poor."[13]

Not only is men's domination of women related to oppression of other groups, it has often provided a historical paradigm for other oppressions as well. The low legal status of women and children, for example, provided guidelines for dealing with blacks imported to North America in the seventeenth century,[14] and general domination of women was developed into a discrimination against Jews in Germany.[15] Gerda Lerner has suggested that men's exploitation of women's reproductive powers and sexuality historically preceded class and racial oppression—indeed, that this practice of dominating women was a *practice* for incorporating other subordinate groups.[16] Sexism, then, may be seen as a paradigmatic form of oppression, reflection upon which can begin exploration of the whole tangle of oppression's infrastructural oppressions.

The two sets of reasons I have given here for beginning with sexism and for giving sexism the priority I do throughout this book do not mean that critiques of sexism have to be the starting point for everyone. Note that I have suggested sexism as starting point predominantly for North American white males. Even this group is heterogeneous enough, however, that some of its members conceivably could theorize out of an experience of pain closely conjoined to one or more of the other oppressions, and then formulate a theology from and for that experience. Generally, though, it is much more difficult to say that there exists a shareable pain across the divides of class and race that would enable a white North American male to undertake theological work that is authentically for others *and* for oneself. Further, if white, heterosexual, relatively affluent males are to undertake theological construction in a way that is reflexive, it must not just be for others, but also for oneself.

In this chapter, therefore, I will consider the politics of domination in interpretation by discussing sexism; in the next chapter I will seek connections between sexism and heterosexism, racism and classism. I cannot pretend to possess a mastery of all the literatures involved. The works in literary criticism, political and anthropological theories on these systemic distortions, and their impact on interpretation, are growing faster than I can keep up with while still forging a theological response. I admit, therefore, the selective nature of my treatment. While I hope this and the next chapters are especially cautious ones, they must also appear sometimes reckless, journeying across vast and changing literary terrains. It is like "dancing through a minefield."[17]

CULTURAL-POLITICAL THEORIES OF A LITERARY AESTHETIC

Movement of Cultural-Political Theories

The particular journey through the minefield that I will follow in the case of the systematic distortion of sexism is one that begins with the notion of a literary aesthetic. This involves beginning on the level of interpreted texts, with literary-critical theory's study of particular codes, styles, themes and interpretive approaches associated with written texts. A *literary aesthetic* is a particular set of these codes, styles, themes, and interpretive approaches.

In the course of displaying this literary aesthetic, in particular a *female aesthetic*, I will make two other moves that constitute the cultural-political approach to the aesthetic. The first move involves political theory. Here exploration of the literary aesthetic is undertaken in connection with analyses of the political situations of the writer or interpreter. For example, a "black aesthetic," identifiable in, say, the works of Richard Wright, involves study of that aesthetic not only in literature but also in relation to North American racism. The difference that gives a text's black literary aesthetic its uniqueness is linked to experiences of racism, as suffered by that text's writers, readers and interpreters. This first move involves thinking about the literary text in connection with a configuration of oppressive power. Concerning a female aesthetic, then, it will be necessary to provide political theories of sexism.

A second move will be necessary, however. Those who have formulated the notions of a literary aesthetic corresponding to the systemic distortions I have selected stress that theories pertaining to configurations of power, though necessary, are hardly sufficient; for they neither describe the dynamics playing between the systemic distortion and the literary aesthetic nor identify the diversity of forms the systematic distortion may take. The notion of a black aesthetic may again serve as our example. Especially in its most recent reformulation, the black aesthetic is linked not just to a sense of "blackness" in artistic expression, nor simply to a political theory of racism, but also to cultural theories of black people's lives. The cultural approach to the political exploitation borne by North American blacks, as exemplified by Houston Baker's use of anthropologists Victor Turner and Marshall Sahlins,[18] is what is necessary to complete an understanding of the connections between the systemic distortion of racism and a black literary aesthetic and to uncover the diverse racisms and their different literary aesthetics. Cultural approaches tend to keep discussions of racism and black literature connected to the vernacular level of African American experience. As Baker especially argues, this keeps the understanding of black experience and practice from being approached only through the techniques of professional critics (usually white) or professional theorists of power.

Given the functions of anthropological theories of culture, as I presented them in the previous chapter, it is not surprising that the African American poet and literary critic Baker should use anthropological culture theory in order to stay close to his people's vernacular experience.[19] Anthropological cultural theory is holistic in its study of the factors playing in systems of power, and its working within a cross-cultural field keeps its theories exposed to varieties of power forms. Furthermore, it approaches all this through a method of participant observation that keeps theorization close to the viewpoint and experiences of those studied. In this chapter, anthropologists' cultural theories of women's subordination will be crucial in accounting for a female aesthetic.

A cultural approach to the political domination of sexism, associated with the notion of a female aesthetic, will enable us to discern other elements of particular importance to theologians: the symbols and myths that reinforce sexism as a political power. The identification of those symbols and myths provides the essential clues for a cultural-political theology, presented in the final two chapters, that can marshal resistance to the distortions of our time.

"Cool" and "Hot" Theorizing

The phenomenon of men theorizing about sexism and female difference as one expression of our resistance against sexism is fraught with ambiguity. Stephen Heath has written that "men's relation to feminism is an impossible one ... My desire to be a subject there too [with women] in feminism—to be a feminist—is then only also the last feint in the long history of their colonization ... I am not where they are ... cannot pretend to be (though men do, colonizing, as they always have done), which is the impossibility of my men's relation."[20] Heath acknowledges that even this commentary on the limits of men's feminism can be a kind of posturing.[21]

Our theories about sexism, as Heath suggests, can become a co-optation of women's task to theorize out of the insights borne of their acute suffering. So pervasive are the patterns of dominance in which we men are steeped that I see no warrants for claiming freedom from them. But this acknowledgment should not lead to crippling senses of guilt, overwhelming sadness, and anger (though all of these, at times, may be appropriate expressions along the way of men's journeys against sexism). The acknowledgment is more a political one, a taking stock of one's social location in the process of theorizing. The work we academic males do—and we should both begin and continue the work of theorizing about and in resistance to sexism—must be carried on within the shadow of this acknowledgment. To fail to make this political acknowledgment is to allow one's theorizing to become the colonizing and controlling, supremacist logic it has been so often in the past. That kind of theorizing is not consonant with resistance to sexism.

Moving in the wake of this acknowledgment, we theorize as within a shadow—not as a place of evil darkness (as the West's color and light/dark symbolism often suggest[22]) but as a place of coolness, indeed of refreshment. This kind of theorizing does well, it seems to me, to find a "cool" rhetoric, in contrast to a "hot" one. A theory characterized by a hot rhetoric seeks a radiance for the theorists' positions untainted by the problematics they study, and is intoxicated by the drive for clarity that exposes every dynamic to "the light of day." A cooler rhetoric in theorizing works in the shadows, but it can be just as committed to theoretical description and analysis, even to the tracing out of the shapes and forces making up the oppressions about which we theorize. It is in such a shadow, indeed with shadows, that I here proceed to theorize about sexism, better, to theorize with other theorists about the systemic forces that shape us.

The Female Aesthetic

The recent emergence in North America of feminist theologies, which often invoke women's experience as a norm in theological interpretation, invites careful consideration of the difference entailed in women's experience and of how that experience makes theological writing different. Study of the notion of a female aesthetic can assist us in discerning this difference.

The notion of a female aesthetic has been given its clearest formulation by literary critic Elaine Showalter.[23] This notion, however, certainly did not originate with Showalter or from any other one literary critic, but rather through a long process of feminist literary criticism.

Showalter refers to this aesthetic as marking a third phase in the development of feminist criticism. In a first phase, the primary concerns were to uncover the misogynous dimensions of literary practice and create a new, more questioning posture in readers concerning the way women are depicted in our culture's texts: "the stereotyped images of women in literature as angels or masters, the literary abuse of textual harassment of women in classic and popular male literature and the exclusion of women from literary history."[24]

Showalter is writing about a major current throughout the study of literature, but we can see this phase at work also in theological studies. Perhaps this is nowhere more evident than in the questioning of the way women are portrayed in biblical texts. The stories about women and portraits of them are questioned and challenged. In this light, the Bible is increasingly acknowledged as "androcentric"; for women especially, the sacred books become "texts of terror."[25]

The second phase identified by Showalter involved a large-scale turning of women critics to the study of the uniqueness and coherence of women's writing. The works by these critics sought to present the contours of female creativity and the narrative sequencing of women's texts.[26] Many attempts were made to rediscover women's literary contributions, often obscured by centuries of filtering through patterns of male dominance. This is an exercise in recovering of women's texts that Showalter sees ongoing in literary criticism generally, but again it has its analogue in biblical studies, perhaps most notably in Elisabeth Schüssler Fiorenza's work, among whose tasks is a "hermeneutics of remembrance," keeping alive "the *memoria passionis* of biblical women" by reconstructing their suppressed texts and voices.[27]

The complexities of this phase warrant whole works to do justice to them. Here I want simply to highlight the fruit of studies in this phase, studies which set the conditions for identifying a female aesthetic. Showalter's summary is best for indicating how the work of this second phase delivered feminist criticism into a third phase studying the female aesthetic. She states:

> Since 1979, these insights have been tested, supplemented, and extended so that we now have a coherent, if still incomplete, narrative of female literary history, which describes the evolutionary stages of women's writing during the last 250 years from imitation through protest to self-definition, and defines and traces the connections throughout history and across national boundaries of the recurring images, themes, and plots *that emerge from women's social, psychological, and aesthetic experience in male-dominated cultures.*
>
> The concept of a female aesthetic logically emerged from the recognition of such connections in women's writing. As the black aesthetic of the 1970s celebrated a black consciousness in literature, so too the female aesthetic celebrated a uniquely literary consciousness.[28]

The most significant effect of the emergence of the female aesthetic in literary-critical theory is that it enables us to connect the realm of literature to the realms of power in politics and culture. That there can be a female aesthetic, regardless of what we take its precise nature to be, suggests that literature needs to be thought of in relation to power. Literary-critical theories of the female aesthetic provide theologians an occasion for reflecting on the gender-specific character of their writing, of their writing's connection to distributions of power that often vary with respect to gender.

If there is a limitation to Showalter's approach to the female aesthetic, it may lie in her tendency to relate it almost solely to the experience of writing. It can more generally be applied to women's reading as well, and hence, more generally, to interpretation. Patrocinio Schweickart raises this issue by putting the important question to Showalter:

> But why should the activity of the woman writer be more conducive to theory than the activity of the woman reader is? If it is possible to formulate a basic conceptual framework for disclosing the "difference" of women's writing, surely it is no less possible to do so for women's reading.[29]

Nowhere do I read Showalter making claims that would deny Schweickart's insight. The latter may be taken as developing what is intrinsic to Showalter's position, i.e., that we may theorize about women's difference, as the concept of a female aesthetic in literature enables us to do, in relation to both women's writing and reading—all this yielding a difference attaching to women's entire literary interpretation or literary practice.

What precisely is the difference manifest in a female aesthetic? Is it defined by a particular literary style, by tendencies to address particular problems, by the recurrence of certain themes? Many clues are available from the literary texts, but scholars of the female aesthetic themselves suggest that extradiscursive affairs need theorization in order to account for the phenomenon of the female aesthetic. Actually, political and cultural theorizations of extradiscursive affairs have been integral to the literary critics' identification of the aesthetic in literature. The aesthetic—seen as comprising recurring images, themes, and plots—"logically emerged," says Showalter, from studying the occurrence of women's literary practice in different historical and national contexts. However, these diverse contexts shared a distinct trait: male dominance. The literary-critical theorization of a female aesthetic entailed, for the very identifying of the aesthetic, a theorization about the abuse of political power between genders, i.e., sexism. That fact signals our need to look at the main elements in political theories of sexism.

NORTH AMERICA'S FAMILY WAGE SYSTEM: POLITICAL THEORIES

The literature here is again vast, but a few features of it need highlighting to enable the formulation of a theological response. In order to specify the meanings of sexism, I will draw from a variety of political theories to provide a working definition of sexism, an overview of the kind of systemic distortion that sexism is, and then a suggestion of the kind of pain borne by women and, to a lesser degree, by men within sexism. I will then draw from anthropological theories of culture to suggest ways in which cross-cultural perspectives can clarify how the political distortion we name sexism creates a particular kind of female aesthetic.

Identifying Sexism

For a working definition of sexism, we can recall the one provided by Sara Shute. She argues that sexism is the name for a system in which "there are some people whose actions, practices, and use of laws, rules and customs limit certain activities of one sex, *but* do not limit those same activities of other people of the other sex."[30]

This definition, as Shute recognizes, leaves open the question of whether or not the limited sex is negatively affected, and it also leaves open to whose advantage it is that the limitation is made.[31] The advantage of leaving these questions open, in the formulation of a definition at least, is that one can allow for study of a wide array of sexist practices in diverse cultural practices. Some of the limitations could work on women's behalf, some not.

In North Atlantic societies, however, the studies of sexism show that these limitations placed on women but not on men have disadvantageous, oppressive and exploitative consequences for women. I would argue also, on the basis of anthropological studies of women's place in diverse cultures, that this oppressive effect is quite evident.[32] Staying for now within the North American context, what precisely are the limitations placed on women and not on men that constitute oppression? There are many instances and realms within which we could identify these, and there are many theoretical entry points into their discussion. I choose here to begin with commentary on political studies of the family wage system in recent North American history. It entails a set of limitations placed on women but not on men that force oppressing pain on both women and, indirectly, men. The family wage system features four mutually interlocking components: (1) a presupposed sexual division of labor, (2) an economic principle, (3) a female-dominated child-care arrangement and (4) a male-dominated breadwinner role. All of these components have undergone recent and rapid change, but they still function in a powerful way; and diverse political studies, theories of the *polis* within which men and women interact, help us identify them.

A Sexual Division of Labor

The essential presupposition of the family wage system is a sexual division of labor. Human societies generally work out ways to divide duties among family members. In the United States' two hundred-year history, the division has taken different forms and is still in flux. Therefore, it is hard to generalize about the North American experience. But there is a fundamental expectation of how work is to be divided among the sexes, and even if we know exceptions, we have to deal with the force of expected patterns.

In colonial America, women had greater occupational freedom than in later periods. Colonial women were "butchers and gunsmiths, running mills and shipyards, working as midwives and sextons, journalists and printers. They often learned a trade, as did men, through apprenticeship."[33]

By the mid-1890s, however, occupational opportunities narrowed for women. Variety of work was perhaps possible before marriage, but once these occupations were appropriated by men, the women were, as Alexis de Tocqueville noted, "subjected to stricter obligations" than were women in Europe. The important cause of this restriction was the growth of industrialization in America, which of course was not just a North American development but was centered in Britain, involved all of Europe, and indeed affected the entire world economy.[34]

During industrialization, the home became divorced from the workplace, femininity becoming identified with home, masculinity with work. Even though there was some sexual role division of labor before the industrial revolution, there was not the same split between home and work. Without romanticizing the life of colonial women, it can be noted that they were more involved in the work that supported the family; men were more involved in child rearing. After the industrial revolution, as Amaury de Riencourt concludes, "the wife as the husband's productive partner and fellow worker, disappeared."[35] When men went away to jobs, as industrialization prompted, their sons and daughters could not follow, and child raising more often was directed to women.

This transition was neither immediate nor simple. I am providing here a shortened story about a complex development. Nonetheless, the industrial revolution profoundly affected the setting up of a sexual division of labor in North America, which in turn encouraged ideals of femininity and masculinity. The husband-wife relationship was a union of opposites.[36] SHE was family oriented, HE was success/work oriented. SHE was pure, HE worldly. SHE emotional, HE rational. SHE delicate, HE tough. SHE weak, HE strong. Many of these contrasts can be found in preindustrial contexts and, as I will indicate below, in other cultural settings. For present North Americans' experience, the industrial developments intensified these contrasts and gave to them a new sense of legitimacy. Mark Gerzon, in *A Choice of Heroes*, summarizes and questions the profound impact of this ideology in contemporary North American popular cultural life:

> By splitting the national character in half, one feminine and the other masculine, the nineteenth century family engaged in a holding action against the tumult of history. Women would embody tradition; men would embody change.
>
> Feminist historians have every reason to question this unwritten patriarchal contract that governed the American family. One does not

need a lawyer to realize that some of its clauses make it a dangerous document for women to sign.[37]

The sexual division of labor in the last two centuries of North American life, together with the cults of femininity and masculinity that often go with it, may from the perspective of grander historical views be traceable to a fundamental misogyny or exploitation of women's reproductive powers. Lerner, in fact, argues this in her *The Creation of Patriarchy*.[38] Here, however, I must keep the question of origins in abeyance for now, and proceed to lay out the other components of the family wage system.

The Principle of the "Family Wage"

The economic principle is that from which the system takes its name: the "family wage." Feminist economists, with many nonfeminist economists, have noted that the North American economy by the early twentieth century was based on the principle of the family wage, i.e., that "a male worker should be paid enough to support a family." It is important to emphasize that this principle was an ideal. In actuality, relatively few men earned the family wage. Nevertheless, as Louise Kapp Howe stresses, the principle applied to everyone: as a goal for an individual's upward mobility (a man took pride in the fact that his wife didn't "have" to work) as well as a widely shared social ideal.[39]

Interestingly, at the turn of the century, socialists and capitalists, feminists and trade unionists, all acquiesced to or fought for the family wage (as one way to mitigate harsh labor existence of women and children in industrial America, for example). The cost of bestowing this family wage on the male, however, was high. As Heidi Hartmann argues, the family wage helped establish our present gender-based occupational hierarchy, wherein men have more of the higher paying and most powerful jobs.[40] Barbara Ehrenreich sums up the problem for women, suggesting that not only were women often denied enough to support a family, "the other side of the [family wage] principle that a 'man should earn enough to support a family' has been that a woman doesn't need enough to support even herself."[41]

There are various ways to identify the present economic dependency of women on men that the family wage system generates and reinforces. On the average, men earn 40 percent more than women do.[42] Two-thirds of full-time working women earn less than $10,000 a year and less than 7 percent of all working women are managers.[43] One might think that today, with women entering the work force (labor and the professions) in greater numbers, this dependency and disadvantage would be decreasing. Not necessarily. Recent studies[44] indicate just how recalcitrant the ideologically reinforced sex barrier still is: "The majority of women live in low-level administrative and clerical jobs. In addition, the number of poor women is growing. Whether the new respectability of work for women will generate respectable jobs for them is a pressing question for feminists. So far, the dual labor market has survived changes in attitude on which it was based."[45]

Within this unequal situation, the one thing that has often salvaged women's dignity has been the fact that women "work too" — at domestic labor in the home — but this kind of labor bears an awkward, uncertain status in our culture. It is largely without significant public acknowledgment and is unrecompensed in a cultural economy that tends to recompense what it does value. Officially, men often extol the hard work of homemaking and child raising but seldom direct public funds for it. Teddy Roosevelt, for example, once declared homemaking a "career ... more worthy of honor and ... more useful to the community than the career of any man, no matter how successful." Still, neither he nor his successors have offered women any financial recognition for their efforts, and what public relief became available was far below the amount by which a man would have been judged successful. Ehrenreich summarizes: "Whether homemaking is an essential career as Roosevelt claimed, or merely a 'pseudo-occupation' as sociologist Talcott Parsons later concluded, it has been left to the sponsorship of individual men."[46]

Ehrenreich is especially helpful in showing how the cultural and economic conditions set by the sexual division of labor and the family wage principle also introduce a structural instability at the heart of North American marriage. Women's economic dependence in marriage tends to threaten the structures of reciprocity that make for sustainable and satisfying relationships. Although there may be mutuality of friendship, sexual desire, emotional support, even in the "good marriages," cultural conditions promoting economic dependency of women on men take their toll on both. Ehrenreich again: "The family wage system guarantees that, at least for economic reasons, women will have a greater interest in marrying and in marrying well," and a "greater financial stake in their marriages than men do."[47] No wonder, then, that when marriages are or grow bad, or when love is fickle, it is women who usually bear the severer economic hardships.

Female-Dominated Child Care

The sexual division of labor, together with a family wage principle, tend to perpetuate a female-dominated child-care arrangement. Young husbands today may be "helping," may be more involved in child raising than before, but as numerous writers and studies show, women are still those whose presence dominates the care of young children.[48] Our daughters are still mother-raised daughters. Our sons are still predominantly mother-raised sons. Adrienne Rich, in *Of Woman Born* (1976), laments that sons — again, because most men's work takes them away from regions of child-care — in essence grow up fatherless.[49] Because we know exceptions to Rich's statement, and because many of us men, in some sense, value our relation to our fathers, her observation can seem overstated. Rich's point is that our fathers have rarely "fathered" in the sense of providing regular, long-term sharing of child care during their sons' upbringing. It is this that she laments.

But why would Rich and others lament sons' mother-raisedness or daughters' mother-raisedness? Clearly, none advocate the end of the mother's important presence in raising children. Psychologist Dinnerstein is, for me, the most sobering analyst who portrays the psychological, cultural, and political drawbacks of the female-dominated child care dimension of our family wage system.

Dinnerstein's book, *The Mermaid and the Minotaur* (1976), is a complex one, but is well worth careful study. Her fundamental claim is that in almost all dimensions of our lives, there are forms of suffering traceable to the fact that our sons and daughters tend to be predominantly mother-raised. Again, Dinnerstein does not devalue one bit the experience and importance of committed mothering, and her arguments give no credence to a "blame the mother" perspective. But she does question (as did Adrienne Rich in *Of Woman Born*) an "institution of motherhood" that tends to expect from the mother the role of primary (if not exclusive) emotional nurturer. The result of such an institutional arrangement is not simply that the mother is valued and praised for the primal nurture rendered; she also becomes the primal human parent against whom we sons and daughters often unconsciously mobilize our rage.

Men are harder to bring into focus as primal targets for unconscious, primal rage, because they have not by and large been the ones whose hands rocked the cradle. Dinnerstein calls for a thoroughgoing involvement of men in the earliest of children's development, so that as children and adults grow their primal rage will be directed at both the mother and father alike, rather than primarily at the mother. Dinnerstein shows, through a booklong argument I am summarizing here, that mother/female dominated child care can be linked to the double standard in male/female sexual opportunity,[50] to the muting of female erotic expression,[51] to our nation's evident nervousness about women holding positions of authority,[52] and even to the threat of nuclear holocaust.[53] Again, her arguments are not simple or quick, but they are profound. They indicate just how high a cost is paid by a family institutional arrangement that presupposes the sexual division of labor that is reinforced by the family wage principle.[54]

There are complexities of parenting and family relationships that would demand of Dinnerstein's account more nuances than they have in her book, and certainly more than I have been able to provide in my cursory summary of her position. In particular, we can ask an important question—one that Catherine Keller has helpfully asked of Dinnerstein's position in her 1986 work, *From a Broken Web*:

But is it yet evident that even under the most liberated of circumstances, men *can* make a precisely equal initial impact on children?

Prenatal bonding and breast-feeding may work a certain inevitable imbalance in favor of maternal influence. If the literal equality of early influence is the only key to liberation, the door may not be open.[55]

Keller's commentary calls into question Dinnerstein's confidence that men's participation in child care would significantly mitigate the primal rage directed at women as primary nursery care givers. We may, however, appreciate, as does Keller, the value of Dinnerstein's work in calling attention to female-dominated child care as a problematic dimension of the sexual division of labor. Conceivably, we could even argue that child care should be dominated by women, and still recognize Dinnerstein's valuable insight that this comes at a high cost to women's lives and even to the culture that defends such an arrangement. While I do not think it can be shown that men's participation in child care alleviates the problems, as Dinnerstein seems to suggest, other literature does show that the primary burdens for child care create an inordinate and unacceptable pain for women.[56]

In this book's final chapter, wherein I attempt a mythic revaluation of the maternal in Christian theology, I will certainly argue for more equal sharing between men and women, emotionally and practically, in the nurturing of children than current patriarchal arrangements foster. I will also argue, however, that a significant part of the problem is that the culture (and much long-standing Christian imagery) does not value the maternal presence. Concerning the mother's presence to the infant as a kind of "global, inchoate, and all-embracing presence,"[57] members of our culture not only hold ambiguous feelings, but also hostile ones. Any effective response to the problems of female-dominated child care must not only release women from inordinate responsibility for it but also deal with the matriphobia that so often devalues the inevitably powerful maternal presence that needs to be preserved.

Male-Dominated Breadwinner Roles

It is of special importance to reflect on the male-dominated breadwinner role. Being a "breadwinner" in our culture is now a somewhat anachronistic term for male self-understanding—at least among males who live and work with women who expect and want to share the financial burdens of supporting family units of diverse sorts. Yet, in many contexts today, as in the past, *breadwinner* refers not only to a prevalent male role; it also functions as an implied ethic for North American male maturation. It has long functioned as the centerpiece of an ideology according to which men's masculinity was judged. It has also been the key ideology against which men have often revolted, most notably in a period beginning in the 1970s and 1980s and continuing today.

That the man should be breadwinner for a family was supported by an enormous weight of "expert opinion," moral sentiment and public expectation, both within popular culture and within the elite centers of academic wisdom. This put the *un*married male on the fringe of the respectable. From the turn of the century to well past mid-century, these opinions, sentiments and expectations have held sway. As late as 1966, American psychoanalyst Dr. Hendrik Ruitenbeek wrote:

> Contemporary America seems to have no room for the mature bachelor. As a colleague of mine once remarked, a single man over thirty is now regarded as a pervert, a person with severe emotional problems, or a poor creature fettered to mother.[58]

By the 1950s and 1960s, psychiatry had developed a massive weight of theory "establishing that marriage, and, within that, the breadwinner role, was the only normal state for the adult male. Outside lay only a range of diagnoses, all unflattering."

Some argued that men had an instinctive drive to be breadwinner/provider.[59] If they did not invoke our male instincts, experts touted an ideal of manly maturity. Supposedly a man would be less than grown-up if he shirked the breadwinner role.

> A man is immature if he regards the support of a family as a kind of trap in which he, an unsuspecting male, has somehow been caught. Again, the person who cannot settle down, who remains a vocational drifter, or the persons who want the prestige of a certain type of work but resent the routines that go with it, are immature in their sense of function.[60]

One "expert," psychologist R. J. Havighurst, taught that there were "eight developmental tasks of early adulthood," prerequisites for mature adulthood. This list is significant because it was repeated for nearly three decades in developmental psychology textbooks and in social work manuals, illustrating the pervasive hegemonic control of the breadwinner expectation. The eight steps were: selecting a mate, learning to live with a marriage partner, starting a family, rearing children, managing a home, getting started in an occupation, accepting civic responsibilities, finding a congenial social group. These prerequisites were, of course, distributed in accord with one's gender, so that rearing children and managing a home were primarily domains of women's mature development, while men's region of growth was getting started in an occupation and accepting civic responsibilities. The key for men was marrying and breadwinning. That was to achieve maturity, to exercise one's masculinity. The man who failed in these roles was not fully adult and not fully masculine.[61]

Not surprisingly, then, when men cracked under the pressure of breadwinning, as they often did and do, clinicians were unsympathetic. Men who broke, in some form, under the pressure were diagnosed as suffering from some "adaptive failure" to meet the standards of masculine conformity, *and*, as the experts often told it, had begun a subconscious slide toward a homosexual identity.[62]

Here we begin to see the connection to the issue of homosexuality. Note the sequence of the sometimes subtle, sometimes blatant message lodged in cultural expectation: To fail as a breadwinner was to fail as a man, was to be poorly adjusted, was to be a failed heterosexual, was to be a homosexual. Although there is much antipathy in the rhetoric of straight, macho breadwinners toward the homosexual community, the fact remains that the cultural messages about male maturity that create stress on the straight male breadwinner are a part of the same pressure that works more damaging effects for the marginalization of gay men.

In order to reinforce further the ideology that presses upon both straight and gay men, we men have often mobilized (sometimes with women's help) a diverse set of archetypal images to sustain us along the hard road of successful breadwinning. As Mark Gerzon discusses at length in *A Choice of Heroes* (1982), we image ourselves as heroic frontiersmen exploring our new land, as soldier, expert, lord. It is no accident that American men, when asked, will name John Wayne more often than any other figure as primary hero, especially in his roles as frontier cowboy or as soldier. The roles of the breadwinner are cast in heroic proportions, and they are sustained by myths of various heroes' journeys.

Sexism as Pain

It only remains to point out what is most significant: the pain borne by the sufferers of the family wage system I have outlined. The pain involves, first, outright and pervasive violence against women's bodies (direct and indirect forms), and second, a lesser but nevertheless real pain carried by the men, who of course are integrally related to the women they dominate. Here I call attention to each in turn.

Collette Dowling's book, *The Cinderella Complex* (1981), popularized a phrase that is frequently invoked to portray women as brought up in the family wage system, brought up to depend on a man and to feel naked and frightened without one. The general pain alluded to here is a loss of self-worth, of responsibility for self. Dowling writes: "to avoid hardships and indignities of working for a living, such women cling to men. Even if the relationship is not emotionally fulfilling, at least these wives have a source of security for protecting them from economic woes."[63] However, aside from the general pain of loss of self-worth that is bred by this dependency, being dependent on a man is rarely the safest place to be.

Breadwinning men, in search of control and success, often work out their need to be in control — especially when they are under stress — by turning to domestic violence. Wife battery and child abuse are often the result. Several songs of our popular culture bear witness to the lived reality.

> End of the day, factory whistle cries,
> Men walk through these gates with death
>   in their eyes;
> And you just better believe, boy,
> somebody's gonna get hurt tonight,
> It's the working, the working, just the
>   working life.[64]

Although statistics vary, the most responsible estimates are that one out of six marriages involves wife abuse.[65] When Congresswoman Barbara Ann Mikulski, now United States senator, introduced the Family Violence and Treatment Act in 1977, she claimed that one-fourth of American couples engage in violence during their relationship. Gerzon's address to us men makes the point very clearly:

Anyone who thinks that [the abused woman's plight] is rare should read the literature on wife beating. Read it not for its statistics, which vary widely, but for its case studies of countless frightened, helpless, sometimes crippled women. Observe how a man can talk about his wife's "cute baby face" and minutes later beat her across the face with his belt. Ponder how easily these men redirect their frustrations toward their wives. Recall every man you have known who beats his wife, every movie you have watched in which men beat women. Consider the fact that, in the time it takes to read this page, another woman will be beaten in her home.[66]

Maybe we do not need to consider that fact. Maybe we know it within our family or our extended families. The pain of women's bodies is real.

Mental anguish is another region of women's pain. As interpreted by many feminists and others, the institution of marriage is especially hard on women. Married women are at least more inclined to report suffering from mental anguish. Dr. Jesse Bernard: "More wives than men consider their marriages unhappy, have considered divorce or separation, have regretted their marriages."[67]

Male pain is also evident. Some of this I have already indicated in my discussions of the male-dominated breadwinner role as a component of the family wage system, especially as it places stress on males generally and also marginalizes and stigmatizes gay men more particularly. A number of studies have attempted to further focus this pain. Some studies focus men's higher mortality rates and average earlier death and then link this stress to the pressures of the breadwinning role. Herb Goldberg, a male-liberation proponent and a primary architect of the new psychology's self-actualization movement of the seventies, even considers men to be the major sufferers in a patriarchal society. Goldberg's claims are overstated, but he signals the need to attend to the reality of male pain generated by a sexist family wage system. Gerzon, as well as Goldberg, relates this pain to men's being out of touch with their emotions while also trying to live up to others' expectations that they bear the load of providing and succeeding. Gerzon states: "They suppress their feelings, until their gut, their back, their lungs, or their heart betrays them. The breadwinner's ethic often does not permit a man to openly acknowledge them and then deal with his distress."[68]

There is also the emotional pain imposed on men through their alienation from their families, through their abstraction from the household. The very structure of a breadwinner's day is often a built-in barrier to intimacy between father and child.

Not only do most of us not share equally with our wives the responsibilities of child care; we barely have time to help. After our nine-to-twelve hour absence, not much time is left. And if we have time, we lack energy or patience. When we are at home, we are either dressing, eating, and rushing out the door or dashing in tired, needing to relax and unwind.[69]

Perhaps if I had lived a generation earlier, I could have seen the commuter train that I rode every weekday for more than three years as a symbol of my worldly success. But times have changed. My wife expected to see her husband and expected me to see my children. And I expected it too. Therein was the dilemma. No matter how I stretched myself, I could not be a father and a breadwinner.

I would leave the office between five and six, while many of my colleagues were still at work. An hour would pass before I was home. My sons, then both under five, would already have eaten dinner by the time I arrived.

I wanted to be with them, and they wanted to be with me. But it was the end of their day and time for bed. "They're tired," my wife would say to me. "Better let them sleep." Of course, she was right. And yet my day with them, and theirs with me, was just beginning.

I was also tired, quick to lose my temper, and hungry. After several years of this shuttlecock schedule, I was confused too. I was making a living, my wife was taking care of the kids (and teaching part time), and the children were growing up. We were all doing what we were supposed to do, but it was not working—not for me, not for my wife, and not for our children.[70]

The pain? Gerzon states the all-too-predictable outcome: "Confronted by [this], we do what human beings do so well: adapt. Children stifle their feelings for their fathers; fathers numb themselves to their capacity for nurturance; and both lose themselves in other things."

OUR MATRICIDAL ETHOS AND MYTHOS: CULTURAL THEORIES

If we now turn to some of anthropology's cultural theories, we do so to effect two insights. First, we gain a sense that male dominance is much more than only a feature of the North American sexist structures I have described. Second, anthropological studies on the cultural situation of women can help us see the relationship between their cultural-political location and the basic structure of a female aesthetic.

The Pervasiveness of Male Dominance

The pervasiveness of male dominance throughout human cultures has been a frequent theme of anthropological studies of female power and status. One presentation is offered in Michelle Zimbalist Rosaldo's and Louise Lamphere's *Woman, Culture and Society* (1974). Neither cross-cultural nor historical studies yield convincing evidence of the existence of matriarchal cultures that eliminate male dominance. Whatever the benefits of the paradisal dreams of matriarchy, and these dreams may be valuable ones, anthropological research indicates that regardless of modes of kinship patterning and production, most contemporary societies feature some degree of male dominance. In 1974, Rosaldo summed up this viewpoint, even suggesting the universality of this dominance:

> Everywhere we find that women are excluded from certain crucial or political activities, that their roles as wives and mothers are associated with fewer powers and prerogatives than are the roles of men. *It seems fair to say then, that all contemporary societies are to some extent male-dominated, and although the degree and expression of female subordination vary greatly, sexual asymmetry is presently a universal fact of human social life.*[71]

There is a diversity of opinion about how and why the male dominance occurs. Rosaldo herself highlights the fact that women's maternal role leads to a "universal opposition" of domestic to public roles. Through socio-cultural definitions that script women for maternal tasks, women are then consigned to domestic spheres, largely (though with exceptions) cut off from centers of power, authority, and control over systems of material production. Nancy Chodorow, taking a developmental as well as socio-cultural view, traces ongoing practices of women's subordination to women's primary role in raising children of both sexes.[72] Anthropologist Sherry Ortner also begins with women's particular role in child care and reproduction. She emphasizes that women's bodily functions tend to define them as closer to nature than men. Because of this, women are associated more with pervasive, often untameable powers of nature, requiring control and manipulation to serve culture's ends—hence, women's subordination. Ortner emphasizes that this logic linking women to nature is not, in her view, necessary; it is, rather, a widely prevalent cultural construction.[73]

None of these theorists would endorse the epithet that for women, "biology is destiny." Perhaps a more complex epithet is required: "biology plus cultural construction and exploitation is destiny." Biology does, for most of the world's women, provide capacities for lactation and the bearing of children, and cultural definitions of role and sphere for the two genders have also been implemented to limit women to activities so they are subordinate to men.

More recently, other anthropologists, such as Peggy Reeves Sanday in her 1981 book, *Female Power and Male Dominance*, have cautioned that claims about the universality of male dominance are overdrawn. From her perspective male dominance is, indeed, a widely prevalent practice, especially in North Atlantic cultures. Sanday, however, draws extensively from ethnographic materials to show many experiences of female power and authority. She also summarizes the literature, indicating that women are by no means universally identified with nature and men with culture. In some cultures it is men who are identified with nature.[74] The most important question for Sanday, therefore, is not whether there is a universal asymmetry of power favoring men, but rather: What are the conditions favoring male dominance, and what are those favoring a more symmetrical disbursement of power between men and women?[75]

Having registered this demurral about the universality of male dominance, it is noteworthy that Sanday does *not* refer, conversely, to female dominance. There are numerous instances of female power that should not be glossed in the study of male dominance, but this does not enable us to identify socio-cultural systems featuring thoroughgoing female dominance.[76] Moreover, her cultural analyses of Western, North Atlantic societies clearly present the reality of male dominance and its oppressive costs as borne by women and by the ecological environment of Western industrial societies.[77] She recognizes not only the accuracy of describing Western societies as "male dominated" but also the need to analyze the religious ideologies and theologies that provide the guiding and reinforcing symbols for social systems of male domination.[78]

Universality is a term, then, that we cannot use for speaking of male dominance and sexist structural practices. *Pervasive* is the word I prefer, suggesting the widespread nature of its practice but allowing for the exceptions. These exceptions, while not comprising full-fledged matriarchies, do show practices of female power and sexual equality of power. These exceptions are helpful for forging alternatives to the pervasive, even systemic arrangements of male dominance in Western societies.

But why the pervasive cultural exploitation of women's mothering and nurturing capacities? While Sanday would urge us to recall that not all power relations between genders entail this exploitation, when male dominance is practiced it usually involves the demeaning and exploitation of women's fertility and reproduction. Gerda Lerner, drawing from anthropological and historical studies, develops a similar theory. She focuses first on the almost magical power women seem to have by reason of their birthing of infants. This has not only encouraged veneration of the early, great Mother-Goddesses, it has also involved an important male response. Men venerated the Goddess along with women, but they also sought modes of institutional power designed to compensate for the birthing power so visible in women and absent in them. Lerner summarizes:

> The ego formation of the individual male, which must have taken place in a context of fear, awe, and possibly dread of the female, must have led men to create social institutions to bolster their egos, strengthen their self-confidence and validate their sense of worth.[79]

Moving beyond this mode of argument, Lerner goes on to develop her more extensive set of claims, arguing that the cultural exploitation of women's reproductive power was a strategy for tribal groups in the Neolithic period to assure their survival in intertribal warfare. Subordinating women's reproductive power to male warriors enabled male control over the exchange of women.[80] A woman could be captured from, or traded to, other tribes, in the knowledge that her bonds to her offspring would keep her supportive of the tribe in which she resided. Lerner accounts for the pervasiveness of male dominance and of "women's world-historic defeat" by tracing in her book, *The Creation of Patriarchy*, the development of this early practice of exchanging women into later agricultural and state systems. The basic working hypothesis is revealed in the following quotation which I provide in full:

> Women's reproductive capacity is first recognized as a tribal resource, then, as ruling elites develop, it is acquired as the property of a particular kin group.
>
> In the fully developed society based on plow agriculture, women and children are indispensable to the production process, which is cyclical and labor intensive. Children have now become an economic asset. At this stage tribes seek to acquire the reproductive potential of women, rather than women themselves. Men do not produce babies directly; thus it is women, not men, who are exchanged. This practice becomes institutionalized in incest taboos and patrilocal marriage patterns. Elder males, who provide continuity in the knowledge pertaining to production, now mystify these "secrets" and wield power over the young men by controlling food, knowledge, and women. They control the exchange of women, enforce restrictions on their sexual behavior, and acquire private property in women. The young men must offer labor services to the old men for the privilege of gaining

access to women. Under such circumstances women also become the spoil for the warriors, which encourages and reinforces the dominance of older men over the community. Finally, "women's world historic defeat" through the overthrow of matriliny and matrilocality is made possible, and it proves advantageous to the tribes who achieve it.[81]

Lerner admits that this scenario is, even at its best, a hypothesis. The archaeological evidence does not provide *any* theorist with materials to support unquestionable conclusions. Lerner, however, develops her hypothesis in conversation with the archaeological materials available and with other previous and contemporary theorists who have proposed interpretations of the earliest rise of patriarchy.[82]

In twentieth-century North America, sexist structures, of course, have a complex form that is markedly different from that of the Neolithic period explored by Lerner or of diverse groups studied by anthropologists. Nonetheless, we North Americans also manifest the structures of "women's world-historic defeat." The societies of North America still feature a sexual division of labor based not only on women's biology but also on sociocultural exploitation. This exploitation is most pervasively seen in the family wage system, the subordinating effects and pain of which I already have summarized.

A Cultural Theory of Women's Double Consciousness

In order to understand how this world-historic defeat is evident in interpretation, yielding a female aesthetic, operative in many disciplines including theology, still more material from anthropology proves helpful.

Women's experience as one of male dominance is a very complex affair. The forms of dominance themselves vary in accordance with cultural context, and the very situation of dominance generates a kind of vision, or way of seeing, that is complexly structured. In a cultural situation of dominance, the vision of both the dominated and the dominating bear a complexity that is crucial for understanding male dominance, and the production of a female literary aesthetic depends on this achievement. Here is where cultural-political theory moves into the terrain of hermeneutics. A female aesthetic is not primarily the result of women's biology, of a unique gender-specific way of developing, or of a "women's language."[83] Rather, it is the result of a unique *cultural* situation that involves distinctive constellations of all three factors: biological, developmental, and linguistic.

This cultural situation of women is suggestively explored in the writings of anthropologists Shirley and Edwin Ardener. These are two of several anthropologists who early on addressed themselves to their discipline's neglect of the study of women's cultural situations.[84] The Ardeners work within an anthropological perspective that nurtures awareness of the cross-cultural phenomenon of male dominance. Edwin Ardener therefore characterizes women as a "muted group." The word *muted* is a fruitful one, suggesting not only a denial of voice (oral and literary) but also of political power. Most helpful, however, is Ardener's study of the way the life and vision of women as a muted group overlaps with the dominant male group. Ardener offers the following diagram:[85]

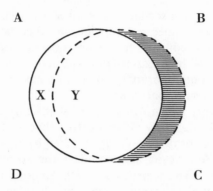

A   B

X   Y

D   C

The dominant male group (x) is represented by the unbroken circle. Women are the muted group, represented here by the broken-line circle (y). Note that the muted group's circle overlaps in such a way that most of it is included within the dominant circle, but the muted group also possesses a sector outside the dominant male group. This is the crescent of women's cultural experience and vision, which is uniquely theirs, though the dominant male group may seek to control it. Ardener refers to this crescent as women's "wild-zone," opening out as it does into the whole wild terrain depicted in the diagram as the field ABCD.

This diagram is particularly helpful for describing the difference between the ranges of vision held by men and women in their respective cultural situations. At first glance it may seem that there is a fundamental parity of vision and cultural experience. After all, both men and women share the central overlapping area, and both have their own distinctive crescent. Yet, there is a marked difference between the two crescents.

Because the women's crescent lies outside the dominant male cultural patterns and values, the distinctive crescent insights and experiences of women are not available to men. It is thus, from man's perspective, unviewable, inchoate, wild. For the Cameroon peoples studied by Edwin Ardener, this crescent outside dominant culture is wild in the sense of being outside the tameable contours of Bakweri culture in the Cameroon, and also in the sense of being closer to the wildness of nature (the forest and the sea). "Although the men bound off 'mankind' from nature, the women persist in overlapping into nature again." The problem for Bakweri men is that women "insist on living in what is for them the wild."[86] And once again, as other anthropologists have stressed, this linkage of women to the wild or to nature, in men's minds, is clearly prompted by women's reproductive powers.[87]

The male crescent, while representing the unique male traits of the culture (perhaps a unique language, biological and psychological development), is more accessible to women's vision than the women's crescent is to men's vision. The primary reason for this is that the male crescent, although unique to men, lies within the dominant group culture in which women significantly share. The values and knowledge of that unique experience tend to be celebrated in the pervasive mythology, knowledge, and ritual practice of the culture. To be sure, men guard their own space, have their own secrets that are taboo to women. This simply means that the male crescent is not exhaustively known by women. Nevertheless, because men's crescent is part of the dominant and celebrated cultural sphere in a way that the women's crescent is not, women tend to have a greater knowledge of the male crescent than men do of women's.

A unique dual stance, then, characterizes women's cultural situation. They speak, work, and see both as participants in dominant male culture (the central overlapping area) and also as participants in the realm of the women's crescent. Noting this dual stance is crucial for identifying links between women's cultural-political subordination, on the one hand, and their modes of writing and reading (interpretation), on the other.

In fact, literary critic Showalter draws on Ardener's studies in order to identify the conditions giving rise to a female aesthetic. In other words, there is such a thing as a female aesthetic not just because of biology, of a woman's language, or of psychological traits, but quite distinctively because of the dual stance characterizing women's cultural-political situation. The distinctive feature of the female aesthetic is that it is a "double-voiced discourse" that "always embodies the social, literary and cultural heritages of both the muted and the dominant."[88]

Women writers, but perhaps especially feminists in the academy, feature this double-voiced discourse, or what Showalter terms elsewhere a "divided consciousness." She writes:

> We are both the daughters of the male tradition of our teachers, our professors, our dissertation advisors, and our publishers — a tradition which asks us to be rational, marginal and grateful; and sisters in a new women's movement which engenders another kind of awareness and commitment, which demands that we renounce the pseudo-success of token womanhood and the ironic masks of academic debate.[89]

Three very important books in recent feminist theological interpretation display the double-consciousness noted by Showalter: Sallie McFague's *Metaphorical Theology* (1982), Elisabeth Schüssler Fiorenza's *In Memory of Her* (1983), and Rosemary Radford Ruether's *Sexism and God-Talk* (1983). Each text clearly displays each aspect of the double-consciousness. In all three there is, for example, a distinctive feminist commitment to insights derived from the cultural experiences of women as a muted group — from the "wild crescent" in Ardener's diagram. This is exemplified in the serious attention given by McFague to the science fiction writings of Ursula K. LeGuin for imaginatively reversing habitual ways of thinking,[90] in the reconstructive imagination affirmed by Schüssler Fiorenza as resource for interpreters,[91] or in Ruether's turn to women's experience and poetry for insight into the suffering of women and others.[92]

In each there is also a sustained use of resources that have had a place in the dominant, predominantly male tradition. This is evident in McFague's use of categories from Ricoeur, Gadamer, Habermas, from literary criticism, and from theories of models in philosophy and science. It is evident in Schüssler Fiorenza's use of historical-critical methods to reconstruct the institutional and social fabric in which New Testament texts and canon were produced, and in Ruether's release of her own writing, *Sexism and God-Talk*, in a form quite closely following long-reigning modes of ordering theological *loci*: method, creation, anthropology, christology, church, eschatology. Feminist usage of the dominant language games is not done as a compromise that mitigates insights from the wild zone, rendering them palatable. Quite to the contrary, they use these reigning discourses critically, and in qualified ways, so that distinctive insights of women's cultural and religious experience are conveyed more forcefully.

A Matricidal Mythos

Although elements of dominant male discourse may be utilized, the mythic content of that discourse is subjected to different kinds of critique by feminist theologians. This critique is perhaps most significant for any "re-visioned theology" that looks for a more emancipatory mythos. The mythos and knowledge of the dominant discourse is such that the insights and experience of the wild crescent are devalued in a host of ways. The special pathos of the *Christian* feminist theologian lies in the tension between this critique of the woman-denying mythos of Western culture and Christianity, on the one hand, and some appropriation of that mythos, on the other. Perhaps this tension is most clearly displayed in a chapter title formulated by Ruether: "Can a Male Savior Save Women?" In this book's concluding two chapters I will attempt a reconstituted understanding of Christ that can be related to emancipatory processes (for women and others). This reconstitution cannot occur apart from awareness of the ways Western mythos and knowledge have reinforced the subordination of women.

The very linking of women to the wild or to nature, as we noted in Ardener's study, is itself a dominative act, even though women's reproductive functioning may signal that connection. Still in debt to Ardener's diagram, we can reflect further on the notion of women's being of the wild, and there find a fundamental dialectic of women's oppression. This dialectic of male oppression involves, first, making a woman monstrous, then muting her. Her perceived monstrousness sets the conditions for her need to be conquered or muted; her being muted then can be viewed as a kind of "mutation" calling forth continuing characterizations of women's strangeness, reinforcing continual efforts to keep women timid wild game, as it were, ever wary of the hunter.

For Bakweri men, the women's wildness consists in the fact that their reproductive powers link them to nature, to the wild forest and to the sea, all beyond the village fence. To be fitted for marriage to men or for exchange in systems of alliance, a girl must be "rescued from the wild" through Bakweri *liengu* rites, though even afterward she bears a water-spirit name through which she communicates with other women in a mermaid language.[93] From the dominant male perspective, the rite seeks to work and reinforce the muting of women who otherwise would be a (monstrous) threat to Bakweri culture.

In the West, the dialectic of making women monsters and muting them is far more dramatic, vicious and deep running than among the Bakweri. It can be seen especially in the mythologies that have oriented our civilizations. The major gender myths that orient Euro-American civilizations primarily emerge from Mesopotamian and later Hebrew contexts.[94] The subordination of women appears natural because of the way these myths pervade our lives. They help set in place a symbolic matrix of subordination. As Sanday notes, "Collective sentiments centering on maleness and masculine symbols acquire coercive power by defining females as the 'other' and feminine symbols as evil."[95] The Christian mythos, dependent as it is on these great Mesopotamian and Hebrew resources, reinforces and perpetuates that subordination. I will argue in the closing chapters, however, that it also resists that subordination and hence that a Christian mythos can be crafted for contemporary strategies of emancipation.

The oppressing dialectic wherein women are both made monstrous and also muted is dramatically presented in the myth of Tiamat, the First Mother of the Babylonian creation epic. Catherine Keller, in her book, *From a Broken Web: Separation, Sexism, and Self* (1986), has summarized the major features of this myth as it occurs in the epic, the *Enuma Elish*, dating from the time of Babylon's ascendancy to military power (2057-1758 B.C.E.):

> The divine hero Marduk, of the rising warrior class of rulers, annihilates Tiamat in a mighty combat and, by dismembering her carcass, creates his cosmos of her pieces. *Tiamat* means "the primeval waters, the precreation chaos, the salt waters, the ocean"; she embodies that space-time "when there was no heaven, no earth, no height, no depth, no name," "when there were no gods." She is no-thing, and in her all things exist potentially. She symbolizes something like the state of

immanence, yet surely not as stagnation but as an all-encompassing inwardness. And by the time Marduk, the Babylonian culture hero, slays his (Great-Great-Grand-) Mother, she appears as a huge serpentine monster and breeder of monsters of all kinds. Observing how the demotion of this cosmic creatrix into "the old Hag, the first mother" takes place may lend us the needed "deep background" of the heroic pattern of monster-making/monster-slaying. His defiant masculinity now inaugurates an unprecedented misogyny: "I will accomplish what you long for most in your heart . . . *Only a female thing*, only Tiamat flies at you with all her contrivance. You shall soon straddle Tiamat's neck [Keller's emphasis]. A classic moment: we see the collective matriphobia converted to matricidal aggression.[96]

The dark, warm, and watery source of life and life relations, this Great Mother Tiamat, is not only that from which the warrior must separate, it is something he must slay, and this is also seen to be the occasion of world creation.

Phenomenologists of the creation symbol such as Paul Ricoeur may have noted connections between creation and violence generally,[97] but more recently it has been the feminist theorists who have turned out the matricidal dimensions of our creation mythos for all to see. In this mythology, the Mother is the primal threat, generating in men, it seems, a matriphobia, a terror of maternal power. This matriphobia is not just in the myth, viewable in the speeches of Marduk; it is a lesson conveyed to the hearers and to ritual participants in that myth.

Both Jewish and Christian commentators tend to differentiate the Genesis creation accounts in the Hebrew scriptures from the Babylonian epic,[98] and indeed there are marked differences. "No primeval intercourse and oedipal rivalry, no monsters, combat and crushed she-carcass litter the cosmic scene."[99] Perhaps the Hebrew scriptures are free of the mythology of matricide and matriphobia. Not quite. That mythology is still present, though in a subtler form. There are several indicators that the matricidal mythos seeps in here, too.

First, despite the real differences,[100] the Genesis and Babylonian stories both concern the vanquishing of oceanic depths, "the deep." Again, in Genesis[101] this occurs without the dramatic warfare evident in the Babylonian epic, and the account does not speak of any other deity present. Still that *tehom*, "the deep," does share a common Semitic form with *Tiamat*,[102] the name of the Babylonian Goddess of the deep, and this term signals what is going on in the powerful subtext of the Genesis account. Note, too, that the transcendent God of Genesis commands and divides the deep waters. There is no bloody conquest, but conquest nevertheless. A predominantly masculine God stands over and against a subdued land and waters. The deep waters, maternal source of all life not only for Mesopotamian cultures but for many widely separate peoples as well,[103] is something divisible and conquerable.

Somewhere in the back of the minds of the writers of Genesis is the Tiamat world of dark and storm, and the story of the masculine warrior-God who creates the cosmos from out of chaos, splitting the dragon-mother's corpse as the initial act of creation. The transparent image of Marduk is thus superimposed upon Yahweh.[104]

Second, elements in later passages of the Book of Genesis reinforce the general primordial subordination of the maternal and the female. The very creation of woman, here Eve, is portrayed as an emergence from the body of the male. In this salient feature of the myth, not only are women's reproductive powers completely absent from the account of humankind's emergence, the woman's distinctive presence and her reproductive powers are actually derived from a male being. Feminist theorists sense that the male in this myth "usurps the female prerogative of childbearing."[105]

Another element in Genesis reinforcing the message of women's primal subordination concerns the link made between Eve and the serpent. The serpent has always been a troublesome feature of the creation account for theologians,[106] for here is a part of creation depicted as opposing the Creator's purposes. Here I am not so much concerned with the theodicy question of how there can be this opposition in or along with a "good creation" as with the nature of the opposition *as serpentine*. It is evident from a wide range of sources that the snake was a symbol of deity and fertility powers in the ancient Near East.[107] One theme, in fact, throughout world mythology is the link of serpents with female death and fertility, with the moon, and with other lunar animals.[108] The Genesis account, if viewed against this background, thus portrays women and their reproductive powers as the distinctive counter-principle to divine purpose. The message conveyed by Eve and the serpent's conspiracy is not just that this is how evil started, but it started with women and any serpentine valorizing of women's reproductive powers. Not only is the Creator's curse of the serpent punitive for the serpent (most cursed of all the animals) and for the woman ("I will greatly multiply your pain in childbearing; ... your husband ... shall rule over you"); the serpent and the woman are also put at enmity from each other. The message: Women's reproductive powers should not be seen as laden with divine good power but are an evil force requiring a subordination of women that entails even the multiplying of female pain. Keller's words also sum it up well: "The curse that alienates her from the serpent utters a suppressed truth: that of the brokenness of the All-Mother, leaving women frightened of our own power and divided against ourselves."[109]

A third indicator of the matricidal mythos evident in the Jewish and Christian scriptures emerges from passages in the poetic and prophetic scripture texts. Keller has collected the major texts. I will here juxtapose a passage from Isaiah with the words of Mot in the Ugaritic text in order to show the similarity between the Mesopotamian ethos and that of the Hebrew scriptures.

> If thou smite Lotan, the serpent slant,
> Destroy the serpent tortuous
> Shalyat of the seven heads.

Then compare:

> Awake, awake, put on your strength, O arm of YHWH
> Awake, as you did long ago, in days gone by.
> Was it not you
> Who hacked the Rahab in pieces and ran the dragon
>   through?
> Was it not you
> Who dried up the sea, the waters of the great abyss Tehom
> and made the ocean depths a path for the ransomed?[110]

The defeat of mother-identified powers is a pervasive feature of both Hebrew and Christian scriptural traditions. It remained for the Christian author of Revelation to characterize "that ancient serpent" as the Devil or Satan (Rev. 12:9-15, 20:2). "Thus the serpents of the primeval cosmic struggle, of the Garden of Eden and of the Ancient fertility cult are united with all that the . . . Satan had come to stand for, though this composite creature's ultimate end is to be cast forever into the lake of fire and brimstone (Rev. 20:10, cf. Matt. 25:41)."[111]

Historically, this matricidal and matriphobic mythos was enshrined in patriarchal cultures and proceeded hand-in-hand with a general diminution of women's cultural and economic powers. This is not to say that historically women's life was always better in cultural conditions that enshrined the goddesses or that women's lives were never improved in some respects under patriarchal cultural practice. In general, however, the married Jewish woman held a less favorable position, legally and culturally, than did her Babylonian counterparts. Unlike Babylonian women, women under the conditions of the patriarchal mythos and culture could not own property, sign contracts, or take legal action, nor were they entitled to a share in the husband's inheritance.[112] Furthermore, the Babylonian women had something else that the Jewish mythos denied to its women: female-specific as well as male-specific imagery of the divine.

The Great Goddess may have been demoted in the pantheon of the gods, but she continued to be worshipped in her manifold manifestations.

No matter how degraded and commodified the reproductive and

sexual power of women was in real life, their essential equality could not be banished from thought and feeling as long as the goddesses lived and were believed to rule human life. Women must have found their likeness in the goddess, as men found theirs in the male gods.[113]

The monster making and muting, or the monster making/monster slaying of women viewed as "wild" because of their reproductive powers, has been described as one of the founding metaphors of Western civilization. This mythic and symbolic devaluing of women in relation to the divine is accompanied by another founding metaphorical vision: the images of women pervading Aristotelian philosophy and Greek mythos.

The mix of misogyny, matriphobia, and matricide are evident here also. Only a few examples may be cited here. Hesiod in his *Works and Days* recasts the myth of Pandora so as to blame the world's evil on women and their sexual nature. Hesiod's *Theogeny* also expresses the subordinate position of women in Greek society in myths that tell of the storm-God Zeus' ascendancy to the highest position in the Greek pantheon. Zeus' battles on the way to the throne involve not only the overthrowing of his father but also the swallowing of his wife, Metis. This both prevents her from bringing forth a son to rival him and enables Zeus to take to himself her reproductive powers.[114] Zeus, in fact, by himself gives birth to Athena, who springs full-grown from his head. Athena is the "exceptional woman": successful, strong, and strikingly beautiful — born of man, not in need of a mother.

What Gerda Lerner refers to as "the symbolic downgrading of the mother" is continued in Aeschylus' *The Furies*, which is the last play of his *Oresteia* trilogy. The relevant climax comes when Orestes is confronted by the furies, who point out the atrocity of his killing his own mother: "Vile wretch, she nourished you in her own womb. Do you disown your mother's blood?" To absolve himself Orestes turns to Apollo to articulate a mode of denying his mother's parentage. Apollo utters the verdict of patriarchy: "The mother is not the parent of the child which is called hers. She is the nurse who tends to the growth of young seed planted by its true parent, the male. . . ."[115]

Athena, "the perfect patriarchal maiden, dutiful daughter and mouthpiece of the father,"[116] ratifies the point, lending an aura of female support to patriarchy: "No mother gave me birth. Therefore the father's claim and male supremacy in all things . . . wins my whole heart's loyalty."[117] With this turn of affairs, critics appropriately have seen in this play a last, though futile, defense of Mother-Goddess power against patriarchy. Not only does Zeus ascend to power by swallowing his wife and coopting her procreative powers, but now, too, the mother's slaying is consonant with male supremacy.

We cannot summarize all the myths here, but there follows a whole set of other myths regarding the sojourns of male heroes, whose egos and identities are fashioned out of the slaying of mothers.[118] Jung has described the "paternal principle" empowering these male journeys to identity: "its first creative act of liberation is matricide."[119] Kathryn Ann Rabuzzi's explorations also clearly document the source of male journeying in matricide.[120] By developing James Hillman's psychological analyses of woman hating, Keller suggests that the bedrock for Western self-consciousness is thoroughly misogynist.[121] Keller also provides examples of how matricidal mythologies are also paralleled by matricidal psychologies in the works of Freud, Jung, and others.[122]

We will turn to the role of the Christian mythos in the subsequent chapters on christology. There I will seek to present a christology that is emancipatory from the matricidal mythic culture that pervades our thought and practice. But it must surely be recognizable by now that the Christian salvation history and its doctrine can play quite ably into this matricidal and patriarchal schema. The figures of son and savior hero coalesce in a male Christ Jesus, easily conveying a message that denigrates the natural birthing capacity of women. Such a tradition can readily reinforce, in the already patriarchal minds of Western civilization, both misogyny and matricide.

Gerda Lerner surely is right when she identifies the two foundational metaphors of Western misogynist civilization as, first, the Hebrew devaluation of the feminine in relation to the divine, and second, the Aristotelian devaluation of women such that they are at best a natural deformity.[123] Nevertheless, we cannot forget the complicity of the Christian tradition in all this, whether we recall Augustine's misogynous discomfort with sexuality and women's bodies[124] or Aquinas's continuation of much of the Aristotelian devaluation of women,[125] or any of the currently reigning theological misogynies subtly or nonsubtly propounded by some Protestant evangelical and Roman Catholic theologies and often tolerated by so-called mainline Christian traditions. How we might formulate an alternative emancipatory christology for women, men, and all others of the earth is the task of later chapters.

4

SEEKING CONNECTIONS

Toward a Theory of an Infrastructure of Oppressions

And consider the profound etymological correspondence between matter, matrix, and mother, all transformed by history: matter from milk and sperm into shit; the matrix of symbols from vivid life into convulsed dead abstraction; and mother earth into the province of domination by men who repeat endlessly the fall of Adam from Eden to establish the kingdoms of power, machines.

Joel Kovell
White Racism

Attending only to sexism or the ways sexism relates to a female aesthetic is problematic in two major senses. First, it fails to acknowledge the different sets of problems named by racism, heterosexism, and classism, none of which can be reduced to those of sexism. Second, a singular focus on sexism would not even explore adequately the complexity of sexism itself — a complexity that includes a multifarious intersecting with other modes of oppression. To think of sexism fully is to think also of heterosexism, racism, and classism.

It is the purpose of this chapter to seek connections through which sexism links up with these other systemic distortions. In attempting this I claim neither that I will have achieved complete thoroughness nor that sexism is the prime causal distortion giving rise to the others. Instead of thoroughness I seek rather to articulate a few of the salient connections, sufficient to show the need for theorization of an infrastructure of oppressions. Instead of a conviction that sexism is the cause of other distortions, I proceed from sexism mainly because, given my social location, this is the procedure congruent with my present vision of the infrastructure.[1]

This chapter, therefore, continues the presentation of theories of explanation. Moreover, these theories also pertain to *political* forms of oppres-

111

sion, thereby developing analysis of the lives of oppressed peoples for which I acknowledged a privilege in the "understanding" of a cultural-political hermeneutics. In this chapter I will, where especially needed, draw also from *cultural* theories in anthropology to clarify the political analysis. In so doing, I seek to retain a sense of the plurality of political oppression, regarding both its many types and the many forms it can take in different cultural contexts. "Remembering Esperanza" thus again fosters reflection on both political subjugation and the cultural plurality that makes this subjugation so diverse.

ON THE ARITHMETIC OF OPPRESSION

Some approaches to the study of multiple forms of oppression have been characterized as an arithmetic of oppression. Such approaches cultivate awareness of the quantity of systemic distortions a given individual or group may be subject to, usually with the implication that a counting of these can illumine different degrees of oppression. According to this arithmetic approach, for example, an individual or group may be presented as uniquely oppressed if subject to the limitations of both racism and sexism, in contrast to those subject only to, say, those of sexism. Before setting forth my own way of interrelating the four systemic distortions I have selected, I want both to endorse and to qualify this arithmetic approach to the oppressions.

A sense of the value of the arithmetic approach, hence an endorsement of it, can emerge from noting the situations of pain out of which this approach comes. Especially among women of color, the approach has been expressed in the language of "double jeopardy" and "triple jeopardy." Frances Beale emphasizes that black women in the United States suffer a double jeopardy fostered by discriminations against them wrought by both racism and sexism.[2] They reel from the sexist oppression by white males from outside black communities and black males within them. In addition, they bear the burdens of a racist oppression emanating from both white men and white women, a racism that often sets them against black men and against their white sisters. Not only is the oppressive burden more intense, but the problematic of oppression with which they struggle is also more complex.

"Triple jeopardy," as discussed by Theressa Hoover or Jacqueline Grant, adds yet another systemic distortion to the two of sexism and racism already suffered.[3] Hoover refers to a kind of ecclesiasticism that attaches to black women who work in an official capacity in religious institutions. Grant identifies classism as a third systemic distortion, showing the triple burden shouldered by those who are women, black, and also economically poor.

Insofar as sexism, racism, and classism (and other systemic distortions, too), each having their distinctive problematics, cannot be reduced to one another, and in that they create different kinds and realms of suffering, this arithmetic approach warrants endorsement. In this way, one also gains a sense of how those who are privileged with respect to one or more of the oppressive systems actually possess different degrees of privilege. Sheila Briggs puts the matter clearly.

> If one's existence adheres fully to the cultural norm, if one is white, middle-class, male, straight, and in good health, neither too young or too old, then one does not experience a conflict in the lived experience of one's identities and their interpretations given to them in the way that a fully stigmatized person does, for instance someone who is hispanic, female, poor, and lesbian. Our different identities impose different loyalties upon us.[4]

If there is value in approaches that work in accord with an arithmetic of oppression, it lies in their awareness that those subordinate to oppression are not all of the same identity, that they have different kinds of "political identities," and that an oppressed group's or person's suffering can be compounded if they bear more than one socially constructed political identity.

When the arithmetic of oppression, however, becomes a way simply to compute a hierarchy of oppressions, or a way to discount the significance of another's oppression, then the arithmetic of oppression becomes oppressive itself. It becomes yet one more quantifying principle in a technological and quantifying Euro-American ethos that separates things and persons from one another. I have refrained in this book, therefore, from arguing that sexism is the most important oppression or the cause of all the others, even while trying to make clear my own tendencies to begin with sexism when theorizing about oppression. When an arithmetic of oppression creates a hierarchy of oppressions, then forces struggling for freedom are pitted against one another, unable to focus resistance against their sources of alienation.[5] For example, as Rosemary Radford Ruether has shown, sexism and racism are integrally related distortions in the United States context, and it becomes difficult to focus critique of those distortions if white women and black women spend time measuring their relative oppressions instead of resisting the ways sexism and racism contribute, in tandem, to both forms of suffering.[6]

While acknowledging the differences, then, between different political identities and different systemic distortions, our thinking needs to be focused on theoretical perspectives that connect them. This connecting is what I attempt to provide in this chapter. The primary aim in moving toward a theory of these connections is not simply to propose such a theory — something that social, political and historical analysts do best — but to bring to light a sufficiently complex picture of contemporary dominations so that I can subsequently address them in a cultural-political theology. In particular, these connections will be crucial to the christology that I unfold in chapters 5 and 6.

SEXISM: RECALLING THE PERVASIVE DYNAMIC

From the material presented in the previous chapter we need to retain a sense of the pervasive dynamic of sexism. According to our working definition of sexism, we are concerned with the systematic limiting of women's life-practices, life practices that are not limited for men as such. But what is the dynamic of the domination that perpetuates this unfair limitation with all its resultant pain?

As I developed it in the previous chapter, with the aid of both political and cultural theories of sexism, the operating dynamic is one of matriphobia and matricide. Men tend to envision women, by reason of their reproductive powers, as closer to nature, closer to that which is untameable. Women's connectedness to birthing and lactating calls forth the setting of women in relation to the mysteries of life's origins. In women's birthing and lactating, the mysteries of human origins are integrally bound up with processes of bodily conjoining and expelling, of blood, flesh, and fluid.

The male perception of women's connectedness to all this is not in itself the dynamic of sexism. This perception need not be viewed as a sexist one, even when women are described as "of the wild." Conceivably, that claim could be a positive valuation of the mysterious and untameable dimension of life origins insofar as these involve women's reproductive powers. But historically—and here is where the male perception grows into a sexist dynamic—women's "wildness" has been almost inseparable from a process of making them monsters, and further, monsters to be slain. The mythologies empowering Western civilization's worldviews, as I sketched them in the previous chapter, and those often still reigning in prevalent religious systems and theologies, either explicitly or implicitly reinforce the need to either kill or tame the wild mother. Sometimes this mythic message simply but powerfully lives on in cultural messages that generally devalue the maternal.

This dynamic of sexism that seizes on women's reproductive powers to make them monstrous and then mutes them also involves culturally disseminated beliefs about human development and maturity. These beliefs are characterized by notions that human development is fundamentally a separation from the mother, an acting out of one's autonomy from the mother/woman. Note: I write *mother/woman*, not because all women are mothers, or because women's roles should always and everywhere be reduced to maternal ones. Not at all. I do so because, given the prevalence of the matriphobic and matricidal mythologies, women tend to be responded to as "the mother" from whom one has come, and thereby as a potentially threatening source that one must control and tame. Men especially, but to a certain extent women, too, in a different way, are set on courses of "maturity" that call for a process of separating from the mother/woman. Part of the problem for a liberative analysis is to articulate how there can be, in the course of maturation, a legitimate *differentiation* from the mother without participating in the sexist dynamic that fuels matriphobic *separation* of egos from the mother. I will return to this problem below. It is this matriphobic dynamic of separation from the woman and from the maternal, represented in our mythology and systematically acted out in cultural practices, which powers and reinforces structures that reinforce recurring pain.

The tendency for this process of separation from the mother to be both similar and different for men and women provides occasion for making a crucial link to the distortion of heterosexism, or to what Janice Raymond terms "hetero-realism."

BETWEEN SEXISM AND HETERO-REALISM

Stay with the notion that the sexist and matriphobic dynamic is one that reinforces a vision of mature development as a process of separation from woman. Recall that this is a vision that will seem especially plausible in a North American child care arrangement in which (despite changing gender roles) women are still generally the primary caregivers for young children. As Dorothy Dinnerstein and Nancy Chodorow argue, in this kind of context maturation will often be characterized as a growth, beginning within infancy, away from the mother.

Identifying Hetero-Realism

One of the major accompaniments to this sexist child care arrangement is a prevalent hetero-realism, characterized, first, by alienation from passionate and intimate friendships with persons of one's own gender, and second, by alienation from one's own gendered body and sexuality.

Janice Raymond has most carefully developed the notion of hetero-realism as referring to "the worldview that woman exists always in relation to man," perceiving even "women together" as "women alone."[7] Raymond is writing about female friendship, but hetero-reality also has a negative impact on male friendship. Recasting Raymond's definition just a bit, we can remind ourselves that hetero-reality is also a worldview that man exists always in relation to woman (with the man dominant) and that often also perceives of men together as men alone. In both the female and male realms of hetero-realism, there is a devaluing of friendship with those of one's own gender and a devaluing of the body and sensuality shared with those of one's own gender. The advantage of Raymond's term, hetero-realism, is that it links heterosexism to a more fundamental general outlook—one that sees all human "reality" as characterized by persons' orientation only to others ("hetero-"). To say that hetero-realism is an oppression or distortion is not to reject authentic openness to others; it is to reject only that kind of otherness that overlooks the needs of the self and the possibilities for communality. Hetero-realism tends to take otherness as the only reality (in sexual relationships and elsewhere) and thereby devalues many experiences of sharing. How are these hetero-realist devaluations related to sexist structural arrangements?

Obstacles to Gyn-Affection among Women

Dinnerstein and Chodorow, who draw from object-relations theory, are helpful for responding to the question just posed. In a female-dominated child care arrangement that leads us to understand maturity as separation from the mother, there results for both genders an alienation from one's own gender, an alienation that occurs in different ways for men and women.

The process of differentiation for women, as Chodorow traces it, reinforces a boundary confusion in women's ego. This "boundary confusion" is viewed by Chodorow and a number of other feminist scholars as positive. Because girls share the same gender as the mother, their ego boundaries formed by separation from her cannot be so strictly drawn. The differentiation from the mother by which boundaries of one's ego are to be established (according to many reigning visions of development), is limited by the fact that the girl and her mother share the same gender. Among feminist theorists, this is often viewed as positive because it leads to a more relationally aware ego. This both slows and limits girls' differentiation process. "Chodorow concludes that girls' gradual emergence from the oedipal period takes place in such a way that empathy is built into their primary definition of self, and they have a variety of capacities for experiencing another's needs or feelings as their own."[8]

This relationality, especially in the tie to the mother, is fraught with ambiguity. Although they may be relationally oriented, sensing especially the power in relatedness to women, women are subject to an acculturation process that assimilates them into roles and self-understandings that stress their "being-for-a-man." This fact has long been explored by feminist writers as diverse as Simone de Beauvoir, writing in 1952, and Janice G. Raymond in 1986:

> Women are assimilated by the hetero-relational ideology that men are women's greatest adventure. Women learn not to expect a lively adventure with women. Men become the future—the eschatological saviors that women need only await. "Her youth is consumed in waiting, more or less disguised. She is awaiting Man."[9]

No wonder that the so-called "ego boundaries" of women are described as "confused."[10] Sensing the powers of cultivated affection with her own gender, she is nevertheless encultured into beliefs and practices that teach that power, adventure, and fulfillment are to be found primarily in cross-gender relationships.

This is hetero-realism in both its senses: as an alienation from one's gender and from one's female body. Why from one's body? Because a major feature of the hetero-realist ideology is that women's relation to their bodies is one in which it is seen as a gift to be given to or enjoyed with a man. It is rarely good in itself, especially given the matricidal and misogynous messages prevalent in Western societies influenced by the kinds of sexist mythologies outlined in the previous chapter. In hetero-reality, a construction of reality ordaining women's bodies to the other, it is hard for a woman to know her body as both good and her own. Working against hetero-realism, cultivating gyn/affection (by women, for women) thus includes a reclaiming of one's own body. Is this why even some heterosexual women who value heterosexual relations for themselves nevertheless say that friendship with their lesbian sisters has renewed their own sense of intrinsic worth and sensuality?[11] If so, the lesson may be that women's coming into friendship with their own gender and with their own bodies means a breaking out of the hetero-realist ideology that teaches (misteaches) them the primacy of "being-for-a-man."

Obstacles to Male Friendship and Life in the Body

Hetero-realism means an alienation from one's gender and body for men as well. Once again, this can be articulated in relation to the basic sexist dynamic of differentiation from the woman, that matriphobic impulse that powers reigning paradigms of "maturation."

The process of differentiation from the mother is different for boys and more marked and often more conflict filled, if for no other reason than that "both mother and son experience the other as a definite 'other.' "[12] This marked gender difference of boys from mothers drives the process of differentiation from the mother much more powerfully than in girls, who share a common gender with their mother. In contrast to what Catherine Keller has termed girls' more relational or "soluble" self that results from this similarity, the masculine self is not only differentiated but increasingly "separate."[13] Men's ego boundaries are more sharply drawn and are continuously strengthened.

This vigorous differentiation from the mother does not mean that we men have no memories of the mother-infant symbiosis. Quite to the contrary, it is simply more deeply repressed, and the continuing strengthening of our masculine ego comes through a continual repressing of this first relation, this repudiating of the mother tie.[14] This continual repressing has been interpreted as a "symbiosis anxiety," i.e., men's fear that they will not succeed in maintaining their separateness from the mother, their dis-ease about "sliding back" into the primordial oneness or symbiosis and being engulfed by it. Because women/mothers remind men of that oneness, they become objects upon which men rehearse their rituals of separation.

Nancy Hartsock has noted how studies of men's differentiation from the mother are supported by other studies focusing on male sexual excitement and perversion.[15] The continually repressed symbiosis and the anxieties entailed in that repression find expression in a variety of ways that include the fantasies by which masculine arousal toward women is triggered. Robert Stoller's studies of male fantasies of "harming the mother" reveal the role of these fantasies in shoring up the male self's repression of maternal symbiosis. These fantasies in which women, as displayed in pornography, are made objects or fetishes, enable the man "to isolate his mother and depict her as no longer being in contact with him, and therefore no longer threatening to merge with him to thus destroy his identity as a separate person."[16]

Stoller was studying the fantasies of "perversion," but other studies of "normal" patterns of male sexual excitement reveal how integral to the very event of "natural" arousal is the male sense of fear and of hostility toward them.[17] More than we men would probably like to admit, "natural" sexual *powers of* arousal are functions of our political and cultural *power over* women.[18] The rituals by which men repress their own symbiotic relation to mothers include not only the practice of hostility and domination in sexual excitement but also other phenomena: the fear of gender change prevalent among some male psychotics, the greater fear of homosexuality among men in contrast to women, and *machismo*, or hypersensitivity about one's masculinity expressed in the guarding of male privileges.[19] These phenomena, while by no means an exhaustive list, provide some sense of the pervasive practice of misogynist sensibilities along the way of the male's differentiation from women. The maternal monster is still being slain.

In what senses does the male's practice of this differentiation entail the hetero-realist alienation from gender (other men) and from one's body? One might think that this reinforcement of the male ego would lead to male bonding and union of men with one another and with their own bodies. Probing beneath the surface of so-called male camaraderie and below the rhetoric of male bodily pleasure, one can see signs of hetero-realist alienation from one's gender and body.

The alienation of men from men is evident in the wealth of literature documenting the difficulty men tend to have establishing intimate friendships with one another. James Nelson, in *The Intimate Connection: Male Sexuality, Masculine Spirituality*, devotes a chapter to the absence of genuine friendships among men. The studies are so extensive that they are hard to summarize here. The tenor of their conclusions is evident from one telling portion of Nelson's chapter.

> Daniel Levinson claims that adult friendships with either men or women is something rarely experienced by American men. Herb Goldberg writes, "Many men I interviewed admitted to not having one intimate male friend whom they totally trusted and confided in." Earl Shorris notes that in all the literature of business and management nowhere is there a single chapter on friendship. In the hierarchies of corporate life, relationships are always means to ends of the

organization and relationships get in the way if valued simply for themselves.[20]

A persistent theme through all these observations is that men have a deep-running fear of self-disclosure, and, as *The McGill Report on Male Intimacy* presents it, this is largely the cause of the dearth of friendships among men.[21] Even if one does not have a "fear of disclosure," it is difficult to find between men the spaces of trust, sufficiently free from competitive patterns, to allow for deep friendship.[22]

The problem of male friendship could be the topic of an entire book, but for our purpose of studying an infrastructure of oppressions it is important to see the structural connection between this hetero-realist gender alienation and the sexist dynamic outlined earlier. Men who form their ego boundaries, their selves, through continuing rituals of differentiation from their mother, who thus live by the matriphobic impulse, will tend not to be vulnerable and self-disclosive with men either. This is because such real dependence would allow a return of the repressed and, given the way we men have founded our egos, this would also mean a felt dissolution of our ego identities. The bounded male ego, differentiating from woman, becomes capable of competitive relationships with other men, but rarely of intimate friendship.[23] Self-disclosure and vulnerability is the stuff of mother-infant symbiosis and is to be avoided. One result of this is that men tend to make women their best and sometimes only friends. This in turn can put enormous strains on men's marriages and on the women who bear the burden of being the only friend.[24]

The other kind of hetero-realist alienation—from one's body—is also suffered by men. Again, with our culture's high valuation of the male athlete's physical prowess and our participation in various levels of athletics, one might think there exists among men a widespread positive valuation of their bodies. Celebrated athletic bodies, however, count for only a small proportion of the male bodies in our culture, and most athletic performances entail male displacement of their own body-love onto another (usually a televised image). No, men are often not-at-home in their bodies. Systematic paradigms of cultural expectations lead us to "know" our bodies, most intimately, in relation to actual or dreamed sexual/genital connecting with women. As I have already indicated this is an area of connecting that is heavily laden with male dominance and hostility toward women. Men's love for their own bodies often gets lost in the power plays operative in male sexuality toward women. What Nelson terms the "male genitalization" of their own bodies, as well as of women's bodies—a genitalization that often privileges qualities of "hardness, upness, and linearity"—easily blocks the comfort and at-homeness with one's body and emergence of a full-body sensuality.[25] There is all too much truth to what Dorothee Soelle has written about many of us in the white male culture: "The male's only relationship to bodies is to own them, his own included. He does not live in and with his body."[26]

Again, this hetero-realist alienation of men from their bodies can be articulated in relation to the matriphobic impulse of the sexist dialectic, without claiming that sexism is the primal cause. The differentiation from the mother and the repression of the male's own primal symbiotic relationships with the mother are also a denial of his own bodily existence, of his own dependency on flesh, blood, fluid, and bone, their growth and their decay. Matriphobia is then expressed here in yet another way, in the man's denial of his own body as good in itself, as good outside of dominative, largely genitalized relationships with women. For males to live in and with their bodies is difficult because it requires more than simply some ethic of body care or sensuality. It requires a thoroughgoing acknowledgment of human embodiment, an acceptance of that which an androcentric culture so often leads us to repress: our emergence from and dependence upon the maternal-infant symbiosis.

The Gay/Lesbian Struggles: In Suffering and Hope

These traits of hetero-realism provide one way to understand the suffering imposed on gay and lesbian persons in our times. That suffering includes outright physical abuse, violation of civil rights in housing and employment, scapegoating for the AIDS crisis, and consigning them to invisibility, silence, and virtual outlaw status. There are significant differences between the dynamics operating in gay and lesbian communities, hence they should not simply be lumped together as homosexuals, as our culture is often wont to do. In particular, gay men may not always manifest a resistance to sexism, to the problem of male dominance, though they may be conscious of heterosexist domination practiced against them.

Despite the real differences between the two groups, both gay men and lesbian women may be understood as the key resisters to the hetero-realism that is bound up with the sexist structures of male misogyny and matriphobia. In contrast to hetero-realism's gender alienation, gay/lesbian persons struggle to affirm affection and friendship with those of their own gender. Of course, central to this affection for one's gender are decisions and acknowledgments concerning one's own sexual orientation. But this sexual orientation, however we sort out its complexities (and I have not even tried to do that here),[27] should be seen as part of a larger struggle within a hetero-realist and sexist society and culture that alienates genders from meaningful intimacy with their own. Hence, the struggle for "gyn/affection," for example, understood as a personal and political movement empowering women amid woman-to-woman attractions and influences,[28] pertains to all of us, regardless of our practiced sexual orientation.

We can also understand gay and lesbian communities as sources for renewed affirmations of the body and sensuality. The writings of Audre

Lorde, especially her essay, "Uses of the Erotic: The Erotic as Power," suggest to a predominantly anti-body culture how sexuality and sensuality can serve as resources for replenishing creativity in all spheres of activity. The resisters of hetero-realism's anti-body messages renew women especially, perhaps, in gaining affirmation and control of their own bodies when these are wrested from them by forces of patriarchy.[29] It is perhaps no accident that women writing on themes in Christian theology and ethics have acknowledged that lesbian women exemplify and convey "the importance and intrinsic goodness, of sexuality in all human beings."[30] There are also signs that gay men's writings on male sensuality and sexuality have been helpful for both gay and nongay recovery of men's positive valuation of their own bodies and sexuality.[31]

The struggle against hetero-realism, against both its gender alienation and its body denial, is a painful one, especially for the lesbian and gay communities. This is because what they seek is ultimately a challenge to the pervasive misogyny and matriphobia structuring our culture and mythos, which operate on both personal and political levels. What they see and seek to practice turns everything upside down for members of the dominant culture, and that is so threatening that the dominant culture often responds with great hostility. In the long history of the West,[32] there have been periods when subcultural currents more open to gay/lesbian practice have gained momentum sufficient to inspire a gay or lesbian "aesthetic" in poetry and prose, similar to the "female aesthetic" articulated in the previous chapter.[33] There are signs that such subcultural trends are operative again, giving some support to gays/lesbians' struggle to voice their own aesthetic in speech and writing, i.e., their own forms of beauty, truth, and goodness celebrated in literature.[34] The recent AIDS crisis is a threat to this needed aesthetic, and the crisis is being seized upon by some groups as a warrant for reviving systemic repression of gay/lesbian culture and practice.

Present trends in North American culture may lead us to expect Christian church people and theologians to render negative judgments concerning the gay/lesbian struggle. Biblical and theological passages have been used, and are still used by many Christians, to proclaim same-sex orientation as unnatural and perverse. In addition, patriarchal theologies' worship of the Father-God, together with the matriphobic messages discussed in the previous chapter, also reinforce a hetero-realist vision of ultimate reality. This is especially evident in teachings that the church and all Christians constitute a composite bride to be in union with Christ the Son as bridegroom. Hetero-realist marriage of woman to man is thereby writ large in such a Christian soteriological vision.

Other elements of the Christian tradition, however — elements derivable from a historical view of the church — show that Christian theologies are not essentially negative.[35] Especially the church's emphases on concrete life and relationships of lived praxis, and its incarnational valuation of flesh (the word became flesh) — all this has occasionally provided, and still can provide, resources for a more affirming response to gays/lesbians involved in today's struggles against hetero-realism. I reserve to the presentation of christology below my own suggestion of what kind of theological response is possible today. Before this is done, it is necessary to examine other connections operative in an infrastructure of oppressions.

BETWEEN SEXISM AND CLASSISM

Relationships between sexism and classism have been, and are being, explored along many fronts. If sexism addresses both "the political and the personal," we should expect the problems of sexism to intertwine with those of classism. Again, this fact by no means suggests that the respective problematics are identical. Nor should we expect the problematics of one to be phrased completely in terms of another.

The relationships between feminist theories of sexism and Marxist theories of capitalist class society display this complex relationship. Feminist critiques are both indebted to Marxist critiques (as in feminists' uses of a notion like "consciousness-raising," as well as in their critiques of exchange economies) and openly critical of them. Because of the complex ways the two critiques intertwine, it may be better to speak, as Josephine Donovan suggests, of a "socialist feminism" or "feminist socialism" rather than Marxist feminism. Feminists have found elements of Marx and Engels illuminating for uncovering the plight of women in Western cultures, but they have also made their own contributions to the study of classism by subjecting Marxist studies to feminist critiques.[36]

This section of the chapter situates our reflection between sexism and classism by showing how feminist and socialist critiques join in a critique of the basic assumptions pervading capitalist exchange theory and practice. I then try to show how feminists intensify the socialist critiques of the tendency in capitalism to abstract from materiality, so that the sexist dynamic of abstracting from the woman/mother is here relevant once more, though in a new way. The complex evil discerned here does not lead to despair; to the contrary, I will try to show how the landless mothers of our period, who suffer the dismembering forces of both classist and sexist repression, still labor in hope.

Identifying "Classism"

As used here, the term *classism* names the systemic tendency of ruling classes to reinforce the distance between themselves and ruled classes by preventing the dispersal of power through a restructuring of wealth, privilege, and access to resources and technology. Classes, depending on the context, may be relatively open or closed to changes in membership, but a completely open system of class stratification is not known.[37] In fact, throughout most of the world today, class identity continues, and class differences, and the distances between them, are growing.

The deleterious consequences of classism often have been discussed as exploitation. Though there seems to be no agreed-upon meaning of this frequently used term, reinforcement of the class distance between ruled and ruler results in the following complex of alienation and suffering. This complex is what I will here take as the signs of suffering bound up with classism:

(1) The subordinate class experiences deprivations with respect to basic necessities such as food, water, air, sunlight, leisure, medical care, housing, and transport; (2) the ruling class enjoys an abundance of luxuries; (3) the luxuries enjoyed by the ruling class depend upon the labor of the subordinate class; and (4) the deprivations experienced by the subordinate class are caused by the failure of the ruling class to apply its power to the production of necessities instead of luxuries and to redistribute these necessities to the subordinate class.[38]

The exploitative suffering of classism and the phenomenon of class division itself are pervaded and sustained by certain fundamental visions of human nature and the organization of power. It is to these orienting visions and assumptions, especially concerning "rational economic man" and exchange theories of power, that we must first turn.

"Rational Economic Man" and Exchange Theories of Power

At the heart of the reasoning that flourishes in capitalist contexts spawning classism is the orienting notion of "rational economic man," which is also developed into an "exchange theory" of economic, social, and political power. Martin Hollis and Edward Nell have provided the most systematic presentation of these notions, and Nancy Hartsock's 1983 work, *Money, Sex and Power: Toward a Feminist Historical Materialism*, has been crucial for linking their presentation to issues of gender.[39] I will be relying heavily on Hartsock's book, not only because of its excellence in political theory and feminist thought, but especially because it enables us to articulate the connections between classism and sexism.[40]

Rational economic man — and below it will become clearer why *man*, although generically intended, works best as a gender-specific designation — envisions human nature as bent on the maximizing of interests. According to this vision, we do not know the particular interests of a given individual, but we do know that the individual will indeed seek to promote them and avoid their diminishment. In light of their interests, rational economic men seek to maximize larger shares of whatever benefits their interests and avoid what depletes the cultivation of their interests. Following Hollis and Nell, Hartsock summarizes: "He [rational economic man] is always at what he believes to be optimum, and is forever striking the best subjective balance between disincentive and reward. His behavior embodies the values 'which would be exemplified by a perfectly rational agent' under specific conditions."[41]

In Western capitalist contexts, it has been the market in which commodities are exchanged that has served as the arena for rational economic man to maximize interests. It is in this arena that people, pursuing their interests, become rational *economic* men.

> The market itself provides the means for bringing these independent, frequently isolated and presumably hostile beings together. The actors in the market, rational economic men, are individuals whose very humanity is based on their independence from the wills of others, and who may dispose of their own persons and capacities freely. . . . They enter relations only voluntarily in order to serve their own interests, and *construct a community by means of developing a circulating medium they can exchange. . . . The circulating medium [in the form of money] is the translator and bearer of the relation between the individuals involved in the exchange.*[42]

Adam Smith is perhaps the best-known codifier of this vision of rational economic man that emerged over the course of the eighteenth century,[43] but this basic vision is still operative for large numbers of present-day exchange theory economists, as for sociologists and political scientists who take this vision as a guide for understanding social life generally. The following passage reveals this. It is culled by political scientist Hartsock from the writings of George Homans, professor of sociology at Harvard University and past vice-president and president of the American Sociological Association:

> Social behavior is an *exchange* of goods, material goods but also non-material ones, such as the symbols of approval or prestige. . . . This process of influence tends to work out at *equilibrium* to a balance in the exchanges. For a person engaged in exchange, what he gives may be a cost to him, just as what he gets may be a reward, and his behavior changes less as *profit*, that is, reward less costs, tends to a *maximum*. Not only does he seek a maximum for himself, but he tries to see to it that no one in his group makes more profit than he does. . . . *It is surprising how familiar these propositions are: . . . Human nature will break in upon even our most elaborate theories.* Of all our many "approaches" to social behavior, the one that sees it as an economy is the most neglected, and yet it is the one we use every moment of our lives — except when we write sociology.[44]

There is, moreover, an extensive literature in many fields showing the prevalence of this perspective for understanding marriage, domestic violence, and diverse political processes.[45] It is because of this prevalence that Hartsock devotes extensive analysis and critique of the exchange theories of power and its central theoretical construct of rational economic man.

We cannot here follow out her critique in detail. Suffice it to say that her criticisms are threefold, all variations on the theme that exchange theories of power, whether referring to the market or social organization more generally, are complex "Panglossian efforts to persuade us that we live in the best of all possible worlds."[46] With this kind of critique she follows in the wake of Marx's critiques, which often were directed, with a special sarcasm, at the classical economists' trust in "the pre-established harmony of things—the auspices of an all-shrewd providence," conspiring by some invisible hand for everyone's "mutual advantage, for the common wealth, and in the interest of all."[47]

Hartsock's own threefold critique supports the aptness of this sarcastic critique. Her critique argues, first, that the exchange theorists' commitment to the notion that the desire to maximize one's satisfaction motivates economic behavior is not only circular but is viciously so. It is viciously circular because this notion is not only an assumption or construct that cannot be proven *a priori* but also one that rules out nonmaximizing behavior as a subject matter of economics.[48] Second, and more importantly, exchange theory and the rational economic man notion are fundamentally inaccurate in their assumption that individuals' market behavior is free from compulsion. This is especially evident in the exchange theorists' neglect of the coercive power that institutions and cultural norms exercise upon human behavior.[49] Finally, the exchange theories relating to "rational economic man" constitute an ethnocentric vision. Whereas exchange theorists tend to view the life-ways of rational economic man as universal among human cultural practices, almost no anthropological evidence supports that claim. Hartsock herself cites research by Martin Hollis, Edward Nell, Karl Polanyi and Marshall Sahlins. Other anthropological materials, not cited by Hartsock, could have been used to strengthen this aspect of her critique. Anthropological research of even twentieth-century capitalist societies suggests that the construct of rational economic man has few analogies in actual practice. Rational economic man is a vision that few human societies can in fact live by for any significant period.[50] Such anthropological studies only confirm Hartsock's critical conclusion that "even a cursory glance at the anthropological evidence does not suggest the universality of rational economic man."[51]

The claim that rational economic man the maximizer is a universal is really a reinforcement of the exchange theorists' own class and cultural location. If we now probe this location more fully, we will see that it is also a gender-specific claim, and this insight enables us to begin to see the connection between classism and the other distortions we have been examining.

The Exchange Abstraction and Separating Mind from Action

The emergence and codification of the vision of rational economic man, which lies at the heart of capitalist exchange theories, has had a particular social location in Western civilization. The developments are of course more complex than I am able to present, but both Albert Hirschman's study, *The Passions and the Interests*,[52] and Hartsock's studies are helpful guides.

At the time of capitalism's early development, especially in seventeenth- and eighteenth-century Western Europe, the emphasis on rational "interests" presented itself as the resolution of problems posed by unchecked passions, in particular, the passions of ferocity, avarice, and ambition.[53] According to both Hirschman and Hartsock, at the beginning of the eighteenth century, the calculated pursuit of interests seemed a healthy corrective to the unbridled plagues on society emanating from unrestrained practices of ambition, greed, lust for power, and sexual lust. The result was that greed was channeled underground. It took a less obvious form. In Hartsock's terms, "Greed itself was reincarnated as interest."[54] As interest, the abuses of passion wore the guise of calculation, deliberation, rationality. Through developments of the eighteenth century, the rational interests became more and more linked to economics and accumulation of money, especially as interests were calculated among the new commercial classes.[55]

From one perspective, this may seem like a desirable solution. What better remedy than one that tames the ferocity of socially destructive passions? The problem, however, is that it did not really tame them; it cloaked them with rationality and gave the powerful passion for accumulation a new systemic structure and respectability. Most problematic of all, perhaps, was the development of a perceived split between rational interests and passion. Thus there occurred not only the cloaking of the passion of greed in particular, but also the reinforcement of a general separation from the passions. A veritable culture of capitalist exchange came to feature this split of calculating mind from passionate nature and action. Hartsock's words ably summarize the problem with respect to even contemporary exchange theorists:

> For exchange theorists, human beings have ceased to be creatures with diverse responses to the world involving seeing, tasting, feeling, thinking, wanting, experiencing. They have become mere creatures of utility, whose every social and interpersonal action is an effort to maximize that utility. They are rational economic men.[56]

In relation to the historical and social location of this positing of interest over and against passion, we can understand the notion of "the exchange abstraction." This phrase names a posture in capitalist thought and practice of separating the mindful calculation of interest from the passionate realms of body, material, and sensing. This is especially evident in the way we view the commodity in a capitalist economy. In Marxist terms, we make a fetish of commodities. We make them objects of reverence, believing that these are not simply things but are that through which social relations take place. In the thoroughly developed capitalist experience, social relations become increasingly commodified, more and more understood in terms of exchange. Relationships between persons become expressed in exchange of commodities through the medium of money. Money itself passes through stages of abstraction.

> The concept of money began as a gift of something valued in itself, and passed through a stage in which valued objects were bartered for each other. Soon it was focused onto objects useless in themselves, though still concrete; then it became more abstract, until shells, stones, gold, coin and paper have led to cheques and credit cards. Soon, as the rationalization reaches its end state, it will become pure number. Money, which has been sought as the representation of all that is materially worthwhile, has become progressively more worthless in itself. And the economic system based upon this mental process, as it has perfected itself, has also become the representation of pure production as an end in itself, disgorging an endless supply of material things which, though more valued, are progressively less enjoyed.[57]

The exchange abstraction, especially as studied by Alfred Sohn-Rethel, includes much more than the increasing abstraction of forms of money. The abstraction of the medium of money is but one feature of the abstraction throughout capitalist systems.

The abstraction is evident in the pervasive dualities characteristic of exchange theory and of the theoretical construct of rational economic man. The abstraction of capitalist experience involves first setting up a duality and then pursuing practices of exchange in only one part of the duality. The following are some of the relevant dualities:

1. the opposition of quantity to quality
2. the separation of nature and interchange with nature from society and social interaction
3. the opposition of persons who are participants in the transaction
4. the division of mind from body, ideal from material (most particularly in the counterfactual assumption that the commodity does not deteriorate on the market).[58]

The result of these dualities is that the act of exchange that lies at the heart of capitalist experience is revealed as more and more abstract. Sohn-Rethel's conclusion is telling: "abstract movement through abstract (homogeneous, continuous, and empty) space and time of abstract substances (materially real but bare of sense qualities) which therefore suffer no material change and which allow for none but quantitative differentiation (differentiation in abstract, non-dimensional quantity)."[59]

As psychohistory studies of the exchange experience indicate — for example, in the studies of Joel Kovell — this abstraction is not wrong simply because it is quantitative or scientific. What is basically wrong is that the process of exchange, in that it is abstracted from materiality, makes materiality (land, senses, bodies, and so forth) primarily inert masses to be acted upon by the exchange system. Land, for example, is treated as inert mass to be acted upon and is treated like a commodity. Hence, abstraction *from* materiality becomes an abuse *of* materiality, because care and attention are spent in the abstracted world of exchange, while relations to the material world become a matter of taking from it to replenish the world of exchange. The disadvantages of this are summarized by Kovell:

> Land is not really a commodity, since it was not made by [humans] but made them instead. Yet in making the land into a commodity from which endless wealth can be extracted, [humans] have vented such aggressive energy upon it as to bring nature into abject submission. The submission is deceptive since, as we are beginning to learn, nature so traduced by technology has its ways of recoiling.[60]

Studies done by Sohn-Rethel, Kovell, and Hartsock are each in different ways indebted to Marx, though each also develops its own criticisms of his thought. Even though they have their own agendas, all agree in acknowledging Marx's role in identifying and challenging the conditions within which this abstraction thrives. In the next section I emphasize some of the terms in which Marx saw the abstraction, through his studies of production and modes of production. This enables us to connect the dynamics of capitalist class society with the other systemic distortions.

From Production to Reproduction: Re-Encountering the Exploitation of the Mother

The dualities set up and maintained in the exchange abstraction, discussed in expositions like Hartsock's, Kovell's and Sohn-Rethel's, are developments of Marx's critiques of capitalism. According to Marx, the exchange of commodities in capitalist systems rests on the duality or separation of a commodity's "exchange value" from its "use value." Exchange value is the quantitative value of a good that is being exchanged, basically qualityless and abstract, "stored in the *minds* of the people."[61] This exchange value is strictly separated from what Marx calls the commodity's use value. Use value is the worth of the commodity set in terms of its mode of production.

Exchange economies are abstracted from this realm of production. It is of the essence of capitalist economies to abstract from a commodity's use value. Marx's critique exposes precisely this abstraction, then explores the intricacies of the modes of production and the technical complexities of "relations of production" and "forces of production."

We need not in this project rehearse the whole complex of Marx's critique or even sketch its main lines. The major concern is to highlight again a duality that is relevant for suggesting an infrastructure of oppressions. What is crucial to see is that the exchange abstraction from the use value, which lies in the realm of production below the surface of exchange, implicates capitalist economic practice in a differentiation from the material not unlike what I have already indicated as integral to the matriphobic impulses discussed in sexism and hetero-realism. In fact, when commenting on Marx's understanding of use and use value, Sohn-Rethel uses maternal imagery and so suggests the confluence of classist and sexist supremacist logics. "Use" includes "all the material processes by which we live as bodily beings on the bosom of mother earth, so to speak, comprising the entirety of what Marx terms 'man's interchange with nature' in his labour of production and his enjoyment of consumption."[62]

The abstraction is away from "use value" as understood in the above terms, away from interchange with nature, with "mother earth" as matrix. Because Marxist critique identifies this abstraction, and because it presents capitalist economic systems as alienating from the material—from the maternal matrix from which we all spring and with which we remain in some kind of symbiosis (no matter how compulsive our abstracting behavior)—because of this, feminist critiques of sexism can view critiques of capitalism favorably. Marxist critiques of capitalism and feminist critiques of sexism can take up common cause because, in Hartsock's words:

> Women and workers inhabit a world in which the emphasis is on change rather than stasis, a world characterized by interaction with natural substances rather than separation from nature, a world in which quality is more important than quantity, a world within which the unification of mind and body is inherent in the activities performed.[63]

Although the concerns of both women and workers may coalesce in this critique of a mind/action or a mind/body separation, the feminist critiques go further.

Feminists attempt a move to a deeper level, a "level of reproduction." Or, we might say that the realm of production explored by Marx and Marxists is deepened to include the reproductive activity of women—an activity that not only involves the bodily producing of the producers, of the working laborers, but also (in societies where sexual divisions of labor mean women still do most of the housework and home nurture) includes the maintenance of the home that sustains laborers. Hartsock's words are again most telling:

> If, to paraphrase Marx, we follow the worker home from the factory, we can once again perceive a change in the *dramatis personae*. He who before [in the factory] followed behind as the worker, timid and holding back, with nothing to expect but a hiding, now [at home] strides in front, while a third person, not specifically present in Marx's account of the transactions between capitalist and worker [both of whom are male] follows timidly behind, carrying groceries, baby, and diapers.[64]

The feminist critique of capitalist society involves another layer, therefore, not just that of the surface level of exchange and then the level of production, but now also reproduction. That is, the context supporting classism and its exploration must be viewed as "three-tiered."[65]

The result of the feminist Marxisms or "socialist feminisms"[66] that formulate their critiques in this three-tiered manner is twofold. In the first place, it allows critical analysis of the distinctive economic situation of women and the household. Women's experience can be identified as alienated labor, and if one is both in the underclass and female this is alienated labor *par excellence*. A central concern has been the function of the household, in particular of women's domestic labor as part of the household, in capitalist society.[67] The second result of socialist feminism working with a three-tiered analysis is a still more striking disclosure of the anti-material, anti-body, and matriphobic impulses in capitalist settings, such that the phrase capitalist patriarchy is by no means inaccurate.[68] Although the first result leads to essential analyses, it is the second result to which I pay special attention here, since it more clearly discloses connections between oppressions that I am seeking to relate.

With this search for connections in mind, a crucial insight into capitalist society is that the exchange abstraction is not only a general movement away from nature and the material realms of labor and earthly substances. It is that, but it is also a movement away from the realms of women's reproductive powers. As such, the exchange abstraction joins and reinforces the masculinist abstraction from woman, from the mother, which can be discerned through political and cultural theories of sexism.[69]

It is important to state again that I am not arguing that the masculinist abstraction *causes* the exchange abstraction operative in classist supremacist logics, nor am I arguing for a causal relation moving in the reverse direction. I am saying, however, that the two abstracting processes strengthen each other in the Euro-American settings in which both work. This coalescence of masculine and exchange abstractions magnifies the suffering and exploitation endured by those from whom the abstractions occur. In our societies, moreover, those usually left behind and abstracted from are those who are the most vulnerable, the women laborers and the children of their households. This generalization is borne out by a wealth of data. Raymond starkly reminds us of them:

> Two-thirds of the world's illiterates are women.[70]
> Women earn 59.4 percent of what men earn.[71]
> Women are vastly more underemployed than men. While women represent over 50 percent of the world adult population and one-third of the official labor force, women perform for nearly two-thirds of all working hours and receive only one-tenth of the world income. Women also own less than 1 percent of world property.[72]
> Every seven minutes, a woman in the United States is raped.[73]
> Every eighteen seconds, a woman is battered.[74]

This exploitation is a function not only of exchange exploitation but also of masculinist abstraction. Masculinist and classist abstractions are both matriphobic in their pioneering drives to cut their ties to the concrete realms of daily life, "escaping from contact with the female world of the household into the masculine world of politics or public life."[75] The household is a place of material life, of bodies in dependence and interdependence, of secretions and substances. In it, as Hartsock and others such as Adrienne Rich have suggested, women's construction of self is nurtured in a way alternative to that of the masculinist abstraction: toward connectedness and toward valuing the concrete and the everyday. Rich has argued that in this place (and this is not just another romanticization of motherhood) there occurs that human experience where children are carried for nine months in the womb. In that experience, says Rich, the child is known "neither as me nor as not-me," there, "inner and outer are not polar opposites but a continuum."[76] This sense of the continuum emerges from what she discusses as "the fact that women's bodies, unlike men's, can be themselves instruments of production: in pregnancy, giving birth, or lactation, arguments about a division of mental from manual labor are fundamentally foreign."[77]

To abstract oneself and an entire social system from the household is not just to abstract from the concrete and from nature, it is also to differentiate from the woman/mother. Given the connections we have already traced between this abstracting differentiation in sexism and hetero-realism, we can discern how the exchange abstraction also joins and reinforces the hetero-realist alienations suffered and resisted by gays and lesbians.

One might object that it would surely be too much to call the exchange abstraction matricidal, as we did following out the implications of the matricidal mythos about monster slaying. Unfortunately we do indeed need to say precisely this. The exchange abstraction, seen as a move away from the household, is a move fraught with hostility. The household, always pitched close to women's reproductive powers, if not in fact, then at least in men's and women's memories, is always threatening, especially to the man seeking entry into the abstract world of commodity exchange. To be sure, the nuclear family and the mother in it are both usually objects of praise. However, the praise is often a smoke screen for male hostility; better said, it is a strategy for securing male freedom from the concrete, messy demands of bodily connectedness so as to better compete with other abstracting agents in the market. The household is a threat to that competition. The sense of ties to it and to the woman/mother must be severed, its influence conquered. A veritable master/slave struggle is at work between the male participant in the public world of exchange and the woman participant in a private world of reproductive and domestic labor. Moreover, as Hegel discerned regarding the master/slave struggle, the struggle is one of life and death, of a hostility that includes attempts to kill the other, as I consider in the next section. The brokenness of women in poverty, dis-membered in households that are isolated from the flow of an exchange system's wealth — is this really very different from the slaying of the mother *Tiamat*, from that dismemberment of the mythic woman/mother? Matricide is a classist crime as well as a sexist one.

The Suffering and Hope of Landless Mothers

Perhaps nowhere is the coalescence of misogyny and classism more manifest than in the diverse plights of third-world women (women of the two-thirds world). As the exchange systems of North Atlantic economies become ever more abstract, as quantities of money are managed and invested through multinational business practices and strategies, the flow of life-sustaining goods is abstracted from, drawn away from, the mothers who labor to support themselves and their families.[78] There is a real dis-memberment of women's lives ongoing in the wake of multinationals' "development," in spite of these organizations' claims to be "improving" living conditions.[79] What is more, when women organize and attempt even the most basic structural remedies of their plight, local elites with financial interests and supports in multinational business communities not only resist their efforts but often respond with ruthless physical attack on women's bodies. Multinational systems of exchange are not only anti-maternal in their general abstraction from the poor households of the world's mothers, often they are also quite literally matricidal for those women who struggle against the systemic effects of the abstraction.

Women are taking up this struggle in different locations: in South Africa, El Salvador, Guatemala, the Philippines, and in the urban settings of North American cities.[80] Most striking perhaps are the organizations of mothers formed to find information about their "disappeared" children and husbands, usually the victims of military or security forces or of death squads variously related to controlling militarized governments that protect classist privileges. The CO-MADRES group in El Salvador and GAM (Mutual

Support Group for the Appearance Alive of Our Loved Ones) in Guatemala are primary examples that have analogues in other nations throughout Central and South America.

In Guatemala, GAM was organized in 1984 by five mothers whose sons and husbands had disappeared. They have galvanized other women to join in the search for some 38,000 disappeared relatives. It should be noted that men are not the only ones being sought; women are looking for their disappeared sisters, too.[81] The vast majority of these will never be found, because they have been killed. One entire wing of GAM is needed just for the task of identifying bodies in Guatemala.[82] Although there are 1,200 members of GAM, this is a small percentage of those who have lost loved ones. Blanca Rosal, a member of GAM makes clear why: "Most people are afraid to join or participate in GAM, because they fear for their lives or their safety. You need to be very brave to participate in such a group in Guatemala."[83] The threat that deters participation is not just random violence; rather, it is the systematic repression of organizations that threaten to restructure elements of Guatemalan life to benefit the now largely impoverished Amerindian and poor Ladino populations.[84]

Most dangerous of all, perhaps, is for mothers of the disappeared to work with labor union groups or with any organization that challenges the privileges maintained by the landed elites and business classes, all of whom are dependent on extensions of multinational exchange economies in Guatemala. To challenge those economies and the livelihood of the local Guatemalan representatives of those economies is to invite threats of death and torture. Mothers of the disappeared often feel constrained to participate in labor union activity because they know that many of their personal losses are traceable to aberrant economic and political structures, to local structures as well as to the multinational ones that perpetuate the extraordinary force wielded by local elites.

Rigoberta Menchu, a politically active exiled Guatemalan, Quiche woman, has decided that it is not worth being a mother, because to be that in Guatemala is to know that half of your children will die of malnutrition. Motherhood also means living in struggle against insuperable odds. Rigoberta Menchu lost an older brother to illness when her highland family was forced to work the coastal plantations. She watched her brother being tortured to death by the Guatemalan military for alleged participation in labor union activity. Her father participated in a 1979 march on Guatemala City to demonstrate at the Spanish embassy for Guatemalan peasant rights, only to die there when Guatemalan security forces attacked the embassy.[85]

Rigoberta Menchu's mother is perhaps the most striking example of the contemporary matricidal dimensions of complex exchange systems. Her mother organized women in many provinces other than her own, lecturing and strategizing with women at specially called meetings as well as during the women's daily duties of making tortillas. She was particularly committed to harnessing women's anger and bitterness over their severe losses and channeling them into organized resistance. Often this organizing was supportive of the labor union activity in which her sons and husband had been involved, activity that regularly calls forth accusations of being "communist" as a prelude to torture and death.[86] In our own North American towns, other Guatemalans now in exile live with their own physical and psychological scars of torture for labor union activity in Guatemala.

The story of Menchu's mother is a painful one, told in wrenching detail in Menchu's autobiography. Menchu knows every step of the fate that befell her mother. It included not just kidnapping on April 19, 1980, as she was returning from organizing work, but multiple rape, starvation, beatings, close confinement in a pit, facial and other bodily dismembering, revival by serum injections, more rape and torture, then being left still alive under a tree, guarded by a permanent sentry, to a slow death from wounds that festered with insects and larvae over days. "After that my mother was eaten by animals; by dogs, by all the *zopilotes* [vultures] there are around there, and other animals helped. They [the army] stayed for four months until they saw that not a bit of my mother was left, not even her bones, and then they went away."[87] A woman and mother dismembered. Matricide in the mountains of one of our exchange system's "blue-chip investments," Guatemala.

I know there are not always direct, one-to-one connections between specific practices of North Atlantic business cultures and matricides in a troubled nation's countryside. But the links are no less real for all that. The matricidal rituals are of a piece with a mode of organizing production, life, and consciousness that maintains survival by increasingly and everywhere abstracting from nature, dis-membering the maternal, reducing it to inert mass.

Five months after Rigoberta Menchu's mother died, in September of 1980, Fred Sherwood was interviewed. He is an ex-president of the American Chamber of Commerce in Guatemala and a "leading spokesman for the North American business community."[88] In 1954 he flew with the CIA orchestrated air force that supported the overthrow of a Guatemalan government that had challenged United States business interests in their nation.[89] Since that time his investments in Guatemala have grown with the nationwide encouragement of practices that allow foreign corporations to establish businesses in the country.[90]

> Question: The State Department says the government hasn't been doing enough to deal with the death squads. Do you think that's reasonable?
> Sherwood: Hell no. Why should we do anything about the death squads? They're bumping off the commies, our enemies. I'd give them more power. . . .
> Question: Do all the U.S. businessmen feel the same way?
> Sherwood: Of course they do. After all they're trying to do busi-

ness. The commies are trying to stop them from doing business . . . to stop the economic growth. . . . It's a hell of violence going around. No one approves of violence, I don't. But if it's a question of them or me, I'd rather it be them. . . . We grew up on the basis of private enterprise. Private ownership of capital. . . . But these peasants, they don't know how to run something. Really, I'm not downbeating them, but they don't. They're dumb, damn savages.[91]

Sherwood's words, against the backdrop of Rigoberta Menchu's and other *campesinos'* struggles in Central America, seem so utterly and incredibly blind and heartless that my recording them here risks making my argument an exercise in overkill. I retain the words of his interview, here, however, because heartless overkill has in fact been a feature of North American relations to Central American life. Such words have to find their place in analyses of the matricidal dimensions of classism.

BETWEEN SEXISM AND RACISM

In his studies of the supremacist logics of racism, Cornel West again cautions that we should accept no monocausal expositions. Racism is a multileveled distortion involving a "complex interaction of economic, political, cultural and ideological regions in social formations."[92] Similarly Kovell wrote, at the outset of his 1970 study, *White Racism: A Psychohistory*, that "white racism in America is no aberration, but an ingredient of our culture which cannot be fully understood apart from the rest of our total situation."[93] Given these admonitions, it is important that we identify the complexity that white racism is, not collapsing it into other forms of oppression, while being just as cautious not to isolate it from the others.

Identifying Racism

"Racism" as a general term, can refer to the systematic exclusion and exploitation of almost any group. Racism thus includes anti-Semitism, the heinous obliteration and sequestering of Native Americans in the United States, and practices of discrimination against Hispanic, Asian, and Asian-American peoples. I am here focusing on white racism, however: white North Americans' systemic use and abuse of Africans' bodies and lives. In our North American racism, the skin color of the enslaved both ignited and was seized upon by Caucasian groups as a mark of their enslavability. Many ethnocentrisms and exclusions have occurred on our soil, but it is hard to dispute Kovell's sense that "none approaches in strength that of the black people by white people, the distinction of a self and an other according to the mysterious quality of skin color."[94] This is the multileveled distortion of white racism, which demands acknowledgment not only as a unique systemic distortion but also as one that must be seen as suffusing our total situation and therefore as closely connected with the other oppressions.

It is crucial to note that there are different types of this racism. White racism in the United States has varied with different historical and social conditions. Kovell has identified three types of racism in the United States: dominative, aversive, metaracist.[95] The first two types involve a direct relationship between human agents, while the third is usually not mediated through individual encounters.

Dominative racism is marked by direct physical oppression and sexual obsession. Intrinsic to this type is an explicit acting out of bigoted viewpoints. When blacks threaten the power of whites, the dominative racist responds with outright violence. This form belongs historically to the Old South, but it is still manifest in the present wherever threats to white supremacy meet with white violence.

Aversive racism is just as strong a type of racism, but it does not feature a direct acting out of the dominance. It is marked by white responses of aversion and coldness. When threatened by blacks, the bigoted person turns away, relies on cultural patterns that enable whites to wall themselves off from blacks' lives. The aversive racist believes in white supremacy but regularly suppresses expression of it and rarely acts it out directly. According to Kovell, this is the racism of the North, experienced as debilitating by many African Americans when they moved from southern regions into the larger urban areas of the North.

Metaracism is the most abstract but is no less real. In fact, because it is more elusive, involving technological and impersonal cultural patterning, it is more difficult to identify and resist. It is the racism diffused throughout late-capitalist society. It is a more impersonal violence. In metaracism, even nonbigoted individuals are metaracists, i.e., those who acquiesce to a larger cultural order that is debilitating to African American lives.

It is important to identify these different types of racism because they provide different kinds of resources for theorizing the connections of racism to the other distortions that have been discussed here, in particular the connections of racism to classism and sexism. The connection to classism is best seen by the probing of metaracism, while the connection to sexism is perhaps most dramatically (but not only) evident in dominative racism.

I am here assuming that we know racism to be an enduring plague in North American society, signaled, if by nothing else, by the host of indicators showing the systemic disadvantage at which African Americans are placed. It is intrinsic to metaracism to obscure this knowledge, to perpetuate (especially among whites) the sense that things are "getting better" in race relations. Although certain "advances" need to be acknowledged, such as perhaps the growth in the numbers of black mayors in this country,[96] in current metaracist systems of the United States economic inequality (in median family income, unemployment) between the races has persisted and grown over recent decades,[97] and blacks have remained exposed to substantially higher rates of general and infant mortality, deaths from homicides, imprisonment, first admissions to mental hospitals, alcoholism, and childhoods spent in families below the poverty line.[98]

Racism's Capitalist Context: But Why Africa?

An understanding of racism is facilitated by viewing it in the context of the capitalist exchange systems discussed earlier. Insofar as there are links between sexism and classism, we may expect that viewing racism in the context of issues of class and capitalism should also enable us also to find connections between racism and sexism. As I hope will become apparent, however, the capitalist context is only partially helpful. In order both to understand the racism and to view it in relation to sexism, one must acknowledge and examine the distinctive psychohistorical dynamics of racism. These dynamics do not automatically present themselves when looking at white racism solely through the lens of analyses of capitalism. Nevertheless, they provide an important starting point.

The phenomena of white racism have their economic-historical conditions set by the rise of the slave trade that forced millions of Africans into the Americas. The height of the slave trade occurred in the late eighteenth and early nineteenth centuries, with 6 million being exported from Africa between 1710 and 1810 and at least another 2 million between 1810 and 1870.[99] This trade in people was not a totally new phenomenon. Europe had a long history of providing slaves to Byzantium and also to the Islamic world. Other contexts of slavery could also be cited.[100]

As Eric Wolf argues in his magisterial 1982 book, *Europe and the People Without History*,[101] between the fifteenth and seventeenth centuries patterns of economic supply and demand between European colonizing interests and developments in African lineage groups and kingdoms helped shape the emergence of the slave trade. Europeans took the initiative for organizing and financing a delivery system that linked European demand and African supply.[102] This system set in motion a complex set of influences: the slave trade was influenced by changes in the modes of production in Europe and, conversely, the slave trade had significant impact on the European economic structures. Eric Williams has even proposed the controversial thesis, in his book *Capitalism and Slavery* (1944), that the slave trade impact was such that it supplied the capital that made England's propulsion into the industrial revolution possible. This thesis has been questioned on the ground that it is monocausal. The takeoff of England into the industrial revolution was surely due also to dynamics in its own domestic markets. Once this kind of qualification is made it still remains true, however, that the slave trade contributed to England, and to much of Europe, a "principal dynamic element."[103] One British mercantilist referring to the slave trade defended it as "the first principle and foundation of all the rest, the mainspring of the machine which sets every wheel in motion."[104]

The initiating action of European systems dovetailed with African political ones. Wolf suggests that African systems functioned primarily in relation to the capture, control, delivery, and maintenance of captured Africans awaiting transfer. He also identifies and discusses three mechanisms in African cultural-political life that shaped the African conditions of participation in the slave trade: the institution in Africa of pawnship, certain judicial processes, and the practice of capture in war.[105]

While such economic, cultural, and political conditions — in Africa as well as Europe — are essential and are ably discussed, Wolf's analysis of the slave trade is not sufficient for an understanding of racism, perhaps even for an understanding of the slave trade. The problem emerges in the form of a question that Wolf himself raises: Why Africa?

Wolf considers three possibilities. He offers a first response when considering the possibility that Europeans could have pressed some of their own into slavery. In the past, Europe had indeed been a supplier of slaves to the Moslems and the Byzantines. During the rise of the Atlantic slave trade, however, the presence of mercantilists in Europe would have stressed the importance of "conserving domestic manpower."[106] Africa presented a fresh supply of manpower that could be gained without depleting the labor pool used for Europeans' domestic economies.

Wolf also recalls an important historical point that constitutes a second kind of response to the question. Western Mediterranean areas were cut off from slave trade with the Eastern Mediterranean, which earlier had been an area supplying slaves. In 1453, the Ottoman takeover of Constantinople and the subsequent blockading of trade routes to the East made this area inaccessible.[107] This restriction reinforced other inclinations to turn to Africa as major supplier.

Why Africans, though, instead of Native Americans? Wolf's third response to the query seems to be his major consideration. The Spanish and indeed some English settlers are known to have enslaved the native inhabitants of the Americas.[108] But Native American slaves posed a problem for the development of slavery not unlike problems posed by enslaving white bondsmen: both would be able, to varying extents, to call on the support of their own groups. The capture, enslavement, and transport of Africans, by contrast, yielded a slave group in the New World that could be isolated from kin and neighbors. Further, "upon arrival in American ports, slaves of different ethnic and linguistic origin were then deliberately mixed to inhibit solidarity."[109] If these slaves escaped, the skin color of Africans provided a ready mark to patrollers who, seeking financial reward, would recapture and return them.

All three of these responses by Wolf constitute generally economic or economic-historical responses to the question, Why Africa? Only in relation to the last response, when discussing skin color as an identifying mark of runaway slaves, does he also name the factor of racist sentiment. This is an important naming, for, according to even Wolf, this sentiment fostered Africans' special segregation from white bondsmen and Native Americans.

In order to answer the question, Why Africa?, this racist sentiment needs to be further explored.

The consideration of racism within the context of capitalism is therefore a necessary move. The white racist sentiments toward Africans need to be considered in relation to historical changes in economic modes of production and political life that were occurring, especially in Europe, but also in Africa. It nevertheless remains the case that a fuller understanding of the connections between capitalism and racism emerges with study of the psychohistorical dynamics of racist sentiment. Moreover, it is in probing these dynamics that we are able to identify links not only to classism but also to sexism and hetero-realism.

A Sinister Psychohistory

We can glimpse the relevant dynamics of this racist sentiment by focusing on the white racist fixation on skin color in relation to the symbolic meaning for whites of blackness, especially as these were played out in the discovery of Africa and the enslavement of African bodies.

Many Europeans, especially the English who dominated the African slave trade throughout the eighteenth century,[110] drew upon fantasies of blackness that were already present in European culture.[111] Kovell notes that even before Africans came in view to Europeans, blackness and evil were already being coordinated with each other. The *Oxford English Dictionary* shows the predominantly negative meanings blackness held even prior to the sixteenth century. These meanings included:

> Deeply stained with dirt; soiled, dirty, foul. . . . Having dark or deadly purposes, malignant; pertaining to or involving death, deadly; baneful, disastrous, sinister. . . . Foul, iniquitous, atrocious, horrible, wicked . . . indicating disgrace, censure, liability to punishment, etc.[112]

A wealth of material in anthropological culture theory reminds us that a culture's use of colors is not just an exercise in natural perception. Rather, colors are often organized to encode culture's significant distinctions.

> Colors are in practice semiotic codes. Everywhere both as terms and concrete properties, colors are engaged as signs in vast schemes of social relations: meaningful structures by which persons and groups, objects and occasions, are differentiated and combined in cultural orders.[113]

Perhaps there are no more dramatic instances of colors being pressed into the service of a vast scheme of social relations than in that of white racism, which fostered and justified the pressing into slavery of black Africans for a white Euro-American cultural project.

When darker-skinned peoples were discovered in Africa, the color symbolism of blackness went into effect and was intensified. Kovell traces its basic moves: "these people were black; they were naked; they were unchristian: ergo, they were damned." They were, to recall other meanings of blackness for the European, the atrocious, the filthy, the horrible. Winthrop Jordan reports the basic response: blacks "in colour so in condition are little other than Devils incarnate."[114]

But more was going on than simply the use of European color symbolism to degrade the being of African lives. In this fusion of blackness and evil a denial and repression of whatever Europeans find threatening in themselves was also in motion. Recognition of this fact enables us to see the defaming of Africans by means of color symbolism as a projection of white Europeans' self-abhorrence. This fact will be essential for seeing links between racism and the other distortions. Drawing on the eloquent rage of Frantz Fanon in *Black Skin, White Masks*, Kovell puts in place the key elements of this complex use of color symbolism:

> Whatever a white man experiences as bad in himself, as springing from what Fanon described as "an inordinately black hollow" in "the remotest depth of the European consciousness," whatever is forbidden and horrifying in human nature, may be designated as black and projected onto a man whose dark skin and oppressed past fit him to receive the symbol.[115]

A psychological approach like Kovell's can then go on from the meaning of blackness to everything in the European id, in that European well of repressed forces, that unconscious body of repudiated infantile strivings.

Do we really need to employ psychological categories (the id, unconscious, and others) in order to understand racism? I suggest that not only are we helped in doing so, it is necessary to do it. Only in such a way can we begin to make sense of the ways that hostility against blacks include their sexual oppression and their being identified with filth and excrement. In fact, as Kovell's work shows, other psychological categories may need to be used, particularly those seeking to clarify dynamics at work in the phallic-oedipal and anal phases of human development.

I again make no claims of having made an exhaustive analysis of these complexities. My primary purpose in this chapter must be kept before us: to seek connections between this racist oppression and the others that I have selected. With this purpose in view, I further select certain salient features of a psychohistory of racism that connect its supremacist logic to that of the sexist logic that valued a process of differentiating from women and maternal worlds. In what ways, then, does the supremacist logic of racism connect with that supremacist logic so oppressive for women?

I suggest that psychohistorical studies of racism display a racist dynamic which, like that of sexism, involves both monster making and monster slaying. In this there is not only a parallelism between the racist and sexist logics; the racist logic is often strengthened by hostility from the sexist one, and this hostility is played out in oppression of the black body. These connections, by way of parallel dynamics that reinforce each other, are evident in both the phallic-oedipal and anal registers of racism's psychohistory.

1. *Phallic-Oedipal Connections.* Some students of racism have explored the connections between oppression of black peoples and fantasies about genital sexual activity with tabooed people and usually in settings of struggle and envy. There is a large literature on the highly sexualized character of racist psychology which is hardly known among even more educated people. Few have any idea of "the extent, organization, or intensity of such fantasies" that charge the racist mentality with sexual hostility.[116]

The phallic-oedipal connections between racism and sexism are especially evident in white racists' fantasies about black peoples' sexuality. Here sex and race are conjoined as subject matter to be worked over by the white mind and unconscious. If nowhere else, this is reflected in whites' general preoccupation with the category of Negro sexuality.[117]

This preoccupation signals a kind of obsession played out in the monster making/monster slaying dynamic. Black men as well as black women have first of all been characterized as sexually wild. As women generally were often envisioned as "wild" by reason of their reproductive powers, so blacks generally have been consigned to wild (nonwhite, uncivilized, savage) worlds in part because of their fantasized sexuality. Allegations concerning Negro males' sexual prowess were often linked to legends about the extraordinary and heroic proportions of their genitalia.[118] Indeed this fantasy was elaborated into a whole syndrome stereotyping black males' sexuality, referring not only to heroically sized genitalia but also to black males' enormous prowess in sexual performance and their "beastly" threat to white women's purity.

Black women, too, were subject to white racist obsession with black sexuality. Accompanying the white male's fear of black male sexuality was his preoccupation with the bodies of black females. "Black women were supposed to be more passionate than white women, and they doubtless were, since the whole of southern culture converged to force the white woman into being the most worshipped, the purest, the least vital, and certainly the least sexual of females."[119] Along with making black women's sexuality more passionate went the supposition that they were less human, more animal. On them, therefore, could be projected "the white man's own fear of his dark animality."[120]

The stereotyping and monster making of this people's sexuality was a prelude to systematic reinforcement of white domination and oppression of black men's and women's lives. Black men, whose sexuality was swollen by white fantasy into extreme proportions, were goaded into violating the "purity" of white women, at least by being placed in "compromising situations" from which a supposed rape of a white woman by a "black oversexed buck" could be "inferred."[121] The sinister outcome of this racist fantasy was manifest historically in the thousands of ritual castrations which, in the type called "dominative racism," so frequently accompanied the lynching of black men. One way of keeping the black male submissive—this one on whom white man's own dark animality was projected—was to castrate him whenever he could be charged with an offense, thus to inspire in him an abiding fear of castration. This fear and related threats connected to the lynching and burning rituals suffered by black men in the South is viewed by Trudier Harris as the key cultural-historical factor pervading black literary aesthetic, especially for the black male tradition of writers.[122] There are clearly both literary and historical referents for this fear. Infractions by black males, even before lynching-mob practice developed, were often punished with castration.[123] The monster making of the black male was prelude to his increasing oppression and often to his quite literal dis-memberment.

Black women, made to bear the stigma of "passionate animal," also became outlets for white male sexual passion. White racism therefore includes the institutionalized practice of rape of black women. The monstrous animalizing of black women's passions was, ultimately, a working out of white male dominance. While black women's rape was not a prelude to physical death as the black man's castration was for him in context of the lynching ritual,[124] systematic and recurring rape was still a brutalizing oppression full of physical and psychological trauma.

Can this monster making and monster slaying of black people's sexual lives be connected to that mix of hostile love/hate that pervades the process of differentiating from the woman/mother? The oppression of blacks by whites, in the past and present, is in itself sufficiently troubling to provoke anger, to mobilize resistance, and to demand theological and other critiques, without making any connections to sexist dynamics. But my sense is that unless we understand how racism is connected to sexism, we will not be able to sustain resistance very effectively.

The psychohistorical connections between racism and sexism are exceedingly complex and demand skills of analysis that go beyond my abilities. I can discern, however, some fairly significant signals suggesting that this monster making and monster slaying of a subordinated people's sexual lives is integrally bound up with sexist, gynophobic, and matriphobic impulses.

In the first place, research on racial hostility and sexuality suggests the connection. One frequently found way of working out the gynophobic process of differentiating from the mother is to defile the mother, to isolate her then harm her. A means of intensifying this process is to focus the mother/woman in a subordinated position. To find women among subordinated blacks, or generally to relate sexuality to exaggerated practices among blacks, is in the white racist/sexist mind to excite dynamics of attraction that are laden with hostility. The subordination and extended torture of black people's sexual lives are integrally bound up with the defiling of woman.[125]

In the second place, these complex psychological dynamics that are both sexist and racist are also evident in novels treating the psychic and sexual experiences of black people in white America. Is there a more powerful dramatization of these connections than in James Baldwin's story, "Going to Meet the Man?"[126] That story opens with Jesse, the white deputy sheriff of a small town, unable to mobilize sexual passion for his white wife. What psychosexual dynamics come into play to effect arousal? First, he recollects a beating he enjoyed giving that day, applying a cattle prod to various parts of a black demonstrator's body, including the testicles. Then, he recalls the particular pleasure he knew as a child while watching a lynching and burning at a festive picnic. Baldwin has Jesse call to mind the event in all its detail. The black victim's genitalia, displayed for Jesse and the rest of the crowd, are described as abnormally large ("much bigger than his father's"); all the more abnormally vicious, then, is the white man's knife that finishes the execution with bloody castration. "Then the crowd rushed forward, tearing at the body with their hands, with knives, with rocks, with stones, howling and cursing."

The sexist dimensions of this ritual of racist oppression become more evident in Baldwin's text when, after reminiscing on these scenes, Jesse wakes his wife and says, "Come on, sugar, I'm going to do you like a nigger, just like a nigger, come on, sugar, and love me just like you'd love a nigger."[127] The webs of oppression are exceedingly complex, but here a particularly striking link in the interaction of oppressions comes to the fore. Sexual activity between white man and white woman is facilitated by moods and motivations sustained by ritual acts of domination over black men (lynched, burned, castrated) and over black women (raped, sometimes lynched and burned).

Hostile domination of women generally is acted out in exploitation of black people's sexual lives and then refuels the sexual hostility coursing through relations between white men and white women.

2. *Anal Connections.* Some studies of racism are focused on how the oppression of black people is connected to fantasies of dirt and defilement. In his study of white racism in the United States, Joel Kovell refers to these fantasies as belonging to "a deeper level of our experience than that ordinarily thought of as sexual, and to a deeper aspect of historical power."[128] The anal phase is therefore presented as having "the greatest significance" for his psychohistorical study of racism.[129]

In order to understand the significance of this phase, we need to see how Kovell displays the basic dynamics of anality. For Kovell, there occurs an identification of excrement with dirt (excrement as hated) that then threatens to return to the body. To understand this identification and the negative charge in it, it is crucial to recall that anality is "a form of drive behavior"[130] that predominates during that time when children are painfully detaching themselves from their mothers and establishing themselves as separate persons.[131] In this context, excrement, material expelled from the body, "becomes symbolically associated with the ambivalent feelings a child has about his separation from his mother and the establishment of himself as an autonomous person."[132] Hated excrement is generalized in a far-reaching abhorrence of dirt and dirtiness that is evident in language about "soiling" the body and other objects, not only by excrement, but also by earth and mud.

The connections between excrement and dirt are signalled by a close look at etymology. Our English word *dirt* is an adoption from Middle English, Old Norse, and Dutch forms that specifically mean excrement. The *Oxford English Dictionary* still lists as the first entry under "dirt": dung, manure, excrement. That etymological connection may help to prepare us to find more of our anal anxieties about excrement to be operative in our language about dirt and dirtiness than we might otherwise expect.

We should be prepared, then, to discover anal drives operative in situations of oppression and exploitation such as racism. This is especially evident if we recall that almost every group that has been the object of prejudice has also been portrayed and spoken of as smelly, dirty, or both.[133] When that language of dirt merges with the fantasies constructed about black peoples' skin color, then anal anxieties readily get played out upon a specific people in a highly charged way. The hatred and anxiety that the white person has about excrement is projected upon blacks. They not only become associated with dirt and dirtiness, but also with "shit," a term that captures both the reference to excrement and the disgust toward it that characterizes Western consciousness. Kovell even argues that the dark color of the feces, especially in contrast with the light color of the Caucasian body, has been seized upon by anxious whites as a characteristic mark of negativity, "thus reinforcing from the infancy of the individual in the culture of the West the connotation of blackness as badness."

Really? The anal dynamics are so repressed and pervasive they are hard to focus. One may find it hard to believe. From time to time, however, anal behavior is especially evident in racist contexts, powerfully suggesting that white racists' avoidance and hostility toward black peoples is bound up with an avoidance and hostility toward feces.

Newsweek magazine surveyed white attitudes as manifest in their informal discussion.

In cafeterias here you go around and collect your food, then niggers paw over it and then you have to give them a tip to carry your tray. Big, old, dirty black paws pawing over your food and then you've got to eat it.

It's the idea of rubbing up against them. It won't rub off but it doesn't feel right either.

I don't like to touch them. It just makes me squeamish. I know I shouldn't be that way but it still bothers me.[134]

The sense of contamination from touching is pervasive. The anal threat that dirt expelled might return to befoul one's own body is clearly suggested here.

Sometimes anal behavior is more explicit. James Hamilton, in his article on the dynamics of prejudice, reminds his readers of what befell several white students who befriended James Meredith in his efforts to attend classes at the University of Mississippi. They went back to their rooms to find their walls smeared with excrement.[135] Kovell provides other examples of how a language of disgust explicitly invoking the terminology of filth and shit pervades hostility to black freedom drives.[136] To white racist minds, to let freedom ring for black people, to let them be alongside all their brothers and sisters, is to let filth and shit loose on the world.

Kovell's claim, then, is that "the root symbol between the idea of dirt and the blackness of certain people" is "this highly colored, strongly odored, dispensable and despised substance which the human body produces so regularly."[137] Kovell himself wonders, maybe even laments, the possibility of his having committed an analysis both overdrawn and reductionist. "How strange," he writes, "that this substance — which, after all, knows the body on the most intimate terms, and which is, aside from the pathogenic bacteria occasionally associated with it, certainly innocuous enough — should have received the brunt of such contempt and rage!"[138]

The suspicion of reductionism enters in response to Kovell's linking anal anxiety toward excrement with racial hostility. Writing thirteen years after his book's first publication, in its second edition, he himself considers this link his most outlandish psychological proposition.[139] Surely, one might think, the complexity of racism is here confined to too narrow a rationale. Surely, the dignity and intrinsic worth of black humanity has somehow in the past broken through into white minds to show forth a humanness sufficient to deny even the racist's capacity to cast black bodies into a category of filth to be worked over by the white mind.

Kovell admits the complexity of racism. His is not a monocausal theory at all. The linking of racism to anal dynamics is but one aspect of a theory of racism, albeit a most significant one. The anal fantasies about dirt need to be examined alongside the phallic-oedipal ones and within the context of classist and capitalist distortions. Kovell himself has suggested, in fact, that the exchange abstraction so central to capitalist theory and practice "is prior to and generates the specific psychology of racism."[140] Here, therefore, he notes the importance of macrostructural developments that condition and then are reinforced by racist psychology.[141]

Once we acknowledge that Kovell's approach is neither monocausal nor reductionist, we can give attention to the horrific reduction worked not by his scholarship but by the white mind, a reduction of a whole group of people to things, to "pieces of shit." To be sure, the white mind did not count on the many successful strategies created by black men and women to guard their dignity and build resources for struggle. Kovell does not adequately recognize the cumulative power of many heroic resistances of black peoples and groups, as these are recounted in many novels by black writers and especially by black women writers.[142] But Kovell's main goal was to trace the mechanisms of white racism, and among these mechanisms persists evidence for this degrading reduction. Hence, Kovell's "outlandish" psychological proposition is also of the greatest value. "The fantasy of dirt . . . is a quintessential fantasy of otherness—for the black body from which the white ego flees is his own body, lost in the Cartesian split of the cognito, and projected into the dark Otherness of the black."[143]

In this summary quotation it becomes clear that the projection which is a reduction of darker-skinned peoples to filth is also an abstraction. In the act of reducing some to the category of excrement, whites differentiate themselves from that category. In doing so, they abstract from that which is of their own dark, material being (". . . for the black body from which the white ego flees is his own body").

I suggest that this connection returns us to earlier examined issues, particularly to the issues of abstraction—both the exchange abstraction integral to capitalist exchange cultures and the masculinist abstraction central to sexist standards of development and cultural value. The linking of the racist abstraction to the exchange abstraction is one that Kovell treats at great length. Following out his discussion here enables us to see that the infrastructure of oppressions includes the dynamics playing between racism and classism. The love of property and the drives to accumulate are (and here Kovell expands his analysis of the anal phrase) efforts to gain back the loved part of one's excrement, only in a whitened and gilded (gold) form. Kovell not only expands his own studies of the dynamics of the anal phase; he also builds upon others', especially those of Sandor Ferenczi, who argued in his seminal 1914 paper, "The Ontogenesis of the Interest in Money," that humans' most valued possessions, gold and money, stem from the interest in their feces.[144] The abstraction process of exchange systems, from the material world to one where primarily quantities are dealt with, is thus connected to an abstraction from the body, from its regular interaction with external nature and its return of its excreta to that nature. Further studies of the connections between racism and classism in the infrastructure of oppressions would have to explore the interaction between these abstracting processes.[145] Here, however, we can only point in the direction of such studies on our way to reconnecting with the masculinist abstraction from the woman/mother which we discerned as so central to sexism.

The key for connecting racism to the sexist abstraction is suggested by the insight that the white racist is in one's abstraction, abstracting from one's own body, and indeed from close interaction with matter. Kovell himself, without really exploring the connection, suggests also that this abstraction entails a movement away from the maternal. For the mind of the white racist,

> this whole panoply of nature and society is but inert matter to be worked over destructively, foulness to be refined: shit. And this shit that we so abhor is but the concretized part of our body-ego, bearing in its harmless, dark, odorous, undifferentiated substance *the accumulated rage at separation from our maternal matrix. Maternal, matrix, matter — the same etymological root, the same symbolic root: a dimly receding, ambivalently held ground of being, pushed away by historical progress.*[146]

If Kovell is right, the rage and hostility of whites toward blacks, expressed systemically in both dominative and aversive racist structures is also rage and hostility toward our own matrix. It is another way to systemically mobilize our rage at the mother, the material web from which we have been generated and which ultimately will reclaim us. Note, I am not suggesting that racism can be reduced to this dynamic. It does, indeed, have its own integral problematic and its own structural constellations. Nonetheless, racism can be fruitfully related to the other systemic distortions by attending to this shared abstraction process. The abstracting from the mother, from the infant-mother symbiosis that is a matrix from which we never really become totally free, not only involves the continual subordinating of women to men celebrated in various mythologies of the dismembering of Tiamut (sexism); it also involves the alienation of women and men from intimate friendship with their own gender and from being at home with their own bodies (hetero-realism), the alienation of women and men from just distribution of the earth's goods (classism), and, further, the systemic dismemberment of black men and women's bodies and lives (racism).

Remembering Hope

I said earlier that perhaps Kovell gives too little attention to black men's and women's capacity to resist the horrific reduction worked by white racist minds and practices. Indeed, the varied attempts to fashion a black aesthetic in the writings of many African Americans displays that resisting capacity. These effects include the early black aesthetics movement associated with the black arts movement of the 1960s and 1970s, as this has been summarized and criticized by Houston Baker.[147] This movement sought to celebrate, to draw together the beauty and value of black peoples amid the dismembering pressures of racism.

The resisting capacity is also operative in the aesthetic visions antedating the black aesthetics movement, as Trudier Harris has explored it in the male traditions of Baldwin and Wright. Therein, the lynching and burning rituals are presented in grisly detail not for the purpose of praising their victimization but to commit tragedy to memory for the sake of remembering and reconstructing a people's resistance. As Harris tells it, the aesthetic literary practice of these black male writers was a ritual for exorcising black fears, to show the monstrosity of white historical practice and so facilitate an overcoming of racism. "Each literary depiction of a lynching or a burning, then, became a loud whistle to sustain a people past the graveyard of white suppression and brutality."[148]

Perhaps it is in the literature of African American women writers that hope and resistance are being most strikingly remembered. The study of African American women's literature is growing at a phenomenal rate in the late 1980s and 1990s. "Clearly we are in the midst," writes Henry Louis Gates, Jr., for the *New York Times*, "of a major international literary movement."[149] For our purposes what is striking about this movement is the display of black women's and men's "agency" under oppression. Literary critic Deborah E. McDowell argues, concerning the novel *Dessa Rose*, that African American writers place "a heavy accent on particular acts of agency within an oppressive and degrading system." She even argues that authority is placed "back into the hand of the slave." Black women and men, "victimized by southern patriarchy and its racial and sexual politics, find a power within that system by turning it back on itself."[150] In Delores Williams's words, African American "womanist" theologians are therefore allowed to explore God's relation to African American women, who long have been "making a way out of no way . . . making do/due when don't prevails."[151] It is fitting that African American women who suffer the triple jeopardy of oppression by racist, classist, and sexist systems should be the ones remembering the agency, resistance and dignity of black people and so reconstituting hope amid ongoing white racist systems of dismemberment. In many different ways, these writers are saying, we have been victimized, but we are not victims.

Here then is another fuller instance of remembering Esperanza. In the reconstituting of agency, in the indomitable strength and joy persisting among oppressed peoples, there endure movements of resistance that remember hope, no matter how seemingly unbreakable the chains with which oppressors bind them. Theorizations of an infrastructure of oppressions do not merely magnify a sense of radical systemic evil, they yield an awareness of subordinated peoples' resistance — still fighting, still being, still hoping.

We have seen along the way, whether looking at sexism, hetero-realism, classism, or racism, that Christians and Christian symbols have consistently reinforced these exploitative systems. Now we must consider what resources there are, within appropriations of Christian tradition, for supporting resistance instead of reinforcing dominance — for remembering hope for those whose lives are systemically dismembered. Further, in the complexity that is our North American context, we must ask whether Christian theology can support these movements of remembering and resistance without simply grafting its symbols on to one or more movements toward freedom from the dominations that are being discerned. The time has come for the discernment of a theological appropriation of Christian traditions, one that might address situations not only of plurality but also of these multifaceted and interrelated oppressions. In what ways can theology participate in remembering Esperanza?

5

CHRIST AS ROUGH BEAST

Revisioning Christ for
Reconciliatory Emancipation

It may be that some rough beast will slouch again toward Bethlehem, its haunches bloody, its name echoing in our ears with the din of history.
                                                                    Ihab Hassan

Christ, as central, crowning event of history, is an unfinished event.
                                                                    Severino Croatto

When Christian theologians risk exposure to their own pasts and to the tensions and brokenness of their times, especially when this brokenness has been reinforced by Christian language and traditions, the reconstructed theologies they offer may bear only a slight resemblance to generally accepted Christian traditions. This may be all the more true of our period, when plurality (political, cultural, religious) and an ever more complex web of dominations — not only of sexism, hetero-realism, classism, and racism, but also of militarism and the destruction of ecological structures — conspire to call forth theological response.

A piecemeal response to one or only a few of these demanding oppressions often founders with respect to others that are neglected. Indeed, it is true that there is a need to specialize, developing theological responses primarily toward, say, sexism or racism. As I have tried to show in previous chapters, however, many of these problematics are so interlaced that they cannot be analyzed separately, nor should they be theologically addressed separately. My way of relating several forms of systemic oppression while trying to preserve their distinctive problematics prepares the way for the christological response that I now begin to offer.

This chapter begins a christology that I hope is broad enough to address the interconnecting of oppressions I have identified while also featuring internal distinctions necessary to preserve christology from becoming yet another monolithic theology making imperialist, universal claims. This chapter begins the task by revisioning the lines of christological discussion so that the term "Jesus Christ" may be viewed as naming a socio-historical dynamic of "reconciliatory emancipation," a dynamic in which Jesus of Nazareth has a necessary role but not the only necessary role. The final chapter refigures reconciliatory emancipation more specifically as addressing the specific distortions of sexism, hetero-realism, classism, and racism that bind us all, oppressor and oppressed alike, but perpetuate a special enduring pain for the oppressed.

The Christ glimpsed by the end of this book may indeed seem a "rough beast" of unusual shape and unfamiliar lines, especially if one's only criteria for theological response are those that insist on consonance with received traditions. However, I believe that this christology, in Hassan's words, slouches toward Bethlehem and is significant because of that, even though the light showing the way for this christology shines not only from Bethlehem but from other sources as well, including many of the wondrous dark places of the present, where people are still struggling in hope.

CHRISTOLOGY AMID CHRISTOPRAXIS: A RETROSPECTIVE INTRODUCTION

While this chapter signals a new turn in the book's development, the christology does not leave the domain in which all this writing has been situated: in christopraxis. As I announced in the Prologue, the reflections of theologians who work within Christian religious practice are distinctive because of their emphasis on christopraxis: (a) focusing their action-related thoughts around the demands of action while not being simply reducible to this action, and (b) centering their action-related thoughts around the Christ symbol. Since my introduction of this theme, we have come to know more about the particular contours of this christopraxis, and these need highlighting as I formulate a christological mode of address. As an introduction to this chapter, we may cast a retrospective glance over the previous four chapters.

Contours of a Christopraxis

Three major moves have already been made in this book. These are important to note since they each influence the christology I propose. Each move works out a distinctive feature of a christopraxis, the christopraxis pertaining to thinking along my own actional routes and the systems of action in which I view North American discourse to be embedded.

The first move was a theoretical practice of "portraiture" by which, in chapter 1, I displayed contemporary situations in terms of a pervasive postmodern trilemma. This trilemma involves the distinctive impasses in which we often find ourselves when developing any one, or only two, of the following three commitments: to a sense of tradition, to plurality, to resisting oppression. While it can be shown that this postmodern trilemma pervades the action and thought of many in North American contexts, I have not argued this solely on the basis of a description of others' external conditions. The postmodern trilemma is clearly related to quandaries emanating from my own actional route, constructed from my own remembering of Esperanza, in which a received Christian tradition, a confrontation with cultural and religious plurality, and encounters of unjust and systemic oppression each left distinct, pervasive impressions.

I fully recognize that others who read these pages may also have had these experiences—one, two or all of them—with greater intensity, duration, or sophistication than I. Others may have had little that is analogous to them or to the way they are combined here. How a reader's own experience intersects with my descriptions of the postmodern trilemma will bear directly on evaluations of this entire project. For the present, it is crucial simply to note that my portrait of a postmodern trilemma for North American theology is a major move presenting a complex situation that will both shape and be addressed by the christology of these final two chapters.

A second move is the one embodied in chapter 2. In recognizing the features of a postmodern trilemma, I worked out an orienting vision for thought, a pervasive posture for thinking. This vision or posture, in order to respond to complexities characterizing the postmodern trilemma, had to be sufficiently constructed to orient those of us who would think in such a trilemmic context. I offered in that chapter, therefore, a hermeneutical understanding, envisioning (through critical engagement of Gadamer, Habermas, liberation thought, and others) how tradition might be appropriated within a conversation that both cultivates plurality and acknowledges certain privileges for oppressed voices needing emancipation. The christology begun in this chapter seeks to complete that vision: appropriating elements of Christian *mythos* (tradition) that privilege the needs of the oppressed for emancipation (resisting domination) while celebrating radical difference (affirming plurality).

It has not been possible, however, to move simply from a hermeneutical understanding to christology. Theories developing the understanding were necessary. Chapter 3 and chapter 4, therefore, provided a theoretical development of the hermeneutical understanding's orienting vision. I drew from *political* theories of explanation, primarily to develop that part of a hermeneutical vision that would grant privilege to the oppressed, organizing these theories, in fact, in terms of four politically analyzable systemic distortions: sexism, hetero-realism, classism, and racism. In order to preserve an accompanying sense of difference, also intrinsic to the hermeneutical vision, I drew from pertinent *cultural* theories of explanation to help articulate the diverse workings and interconnections of these oppressions. I drew, for example, from the cultural anthropologists' theories of Edwin Ardener and Peggy Reeves Sanday in order to qualify the political theories about sexism and male dominance. Both the political and cultural theories will provide categories for christological address, since the Christian mythos is not just a general response to political oppression and cultural difference but also to the diverse exploitations of women, gays and lesbians, the materially poor, and African Americans. To address these particular needs, christology requires something beyond general discourse about freedom; it must draw from discourses shaped to address specific forms of oppression.

These basic moves of the first four chapters I acknowledge as elements of a christopraxis. Of course, they are *not* "christology" as such, nor are they unrelated to the christology that will be proposed here. These moves in relation to christopraxis are "praxis" because they constitute reflection within and about scenes of action in which I am involved and of which I am aware. They are "christic" in that these reflections are inseparable from my various connections to religious communities that invoke the Christ symbol. It will be the job of these final two chapters to make explicit, in christology, the nature of the Christ symbol as connected (occasionally in albeit hidden and implicit ways) to the moves of reflection I have already made. From each of the three moves of reflection I have just summarized, we can hear a question for christology. What is the connection between christic living and the postmodern trilemma of North American discursive and extradiscursive affairs? How would christology articulate the Christ symbol in relation to a hermeneutical vision that not only celebrates plurality but also affirms a critical privilege for the voices of those needing emancipation? What particularly must christology become if it is to address the specific oppressions of sexism, hetero-realism, classism, and racism that political and cultural theorists have explored? This chapter engages most directly the first two questions, while the third question is taken up in the final chapter.

Toward "Address" for Proclamation and Action

It should be apparent that our concern with christology, while not removing us from christopraxis, does entail our taking up a distinctive "theoretical practice." In the first chapter, I identified three theoretical practices belonging to a cultural-political theology's engagement with situations: reflexive analysis, portraiture, address. All three are necessary if theology is to be preserved from varieties of fundamentalism, neo-orthodox transcendentalism, postliberal conservatism or the often nonreflexive correlational approaches of theological liberalism.

With christology we take up the theoretical practice of "address" that is just as essential to a cultural-political theology as reflexive analysis and portraiture. In the theoretical practice of address there is a more explicit speaking to and acting toward the situations thematized through reflexive analysis and portraiture. In address, we begin to identify and mine the richness of the Christian *mythos* (its narratives and communal practices) for their distinctive meanings. The theoretical practice of address especially aims to present the particularity of the Christ symbol, articulating the meanings of Christ in and for the situations approached reflexively and portrayed in cultural description and theory.

The theoretical practice of address is essential if a cultural-political theology is to have, as Clodovis Boff suggests, its own pertinency, its own distinctive resources for empowering speech and action in cultures and politics.[1] Cultural-political theology and its christology are not simply reflections of their cultural-political situations, even though they are always immersed in them and structured by them. Through its address cultural-political theology brings to speech and action something new; hence it is for the sake of, and makes possible, Christian proclamation and action.

Let me again stress that this bringing of something new does not entail stepping outside cultural-political situations. It does not mean having criteria untainted by experience, categories of thought and sociopolitical ideologies. It does not mean having a transcendent principle received from somewhere above the fray of cultural, historical, and political process. Nor does it mean having some deep foundation below a cultural, historical and political surface, which is somehow untouched by surface dynamics.

No, the distinctiveness of a cultural-political theology's address has its special character within the fray. The distinctive Christian mythos has its distinctiveness within cultural and political realms. The Christian mythos is distinctive by reason of the particular power of its mythic and symbolic language *as mythic and symbolic language* and by reason of the particular meanings of Christian mythic and symbolic language *as Christian*. Within distinctive cultural-political matrices, mythic and symbolic languages implicate their users in forms of awareness that are more than, or not yet fully disclosed in, any given cultural-political situation. As Christian, this mythic and symbolic language is given a particular shape in thought and practice — one that below I will present as reconciliatory emancipation.

SOTERIOLOGY AND CHRISTOLOGY

In insisting that any christology formulated by cultural-political theology is done within christopraxis, I am casting my lot with theological approaches that keep christology (discourse about Christ) inseparably connected with soteriology (discourse about salvation). Keeping christology within (though not merely reflective of) christopraxis is another way of underscoring the claim that christology is salvifically interested discourse. It begins in relation to human needs for healing, for release, for transformation.

Actually, much of the entire Christian tradition has recognized this in stressing that certain interests in salvation lead us to inquire about the figure of Jesus and to proclaim him "Christ." Melanchthon put the matter memorably: "Who Jesus Christ is becomes known in the saving action."[2] Perhaps Paul Tillich articulated the connection most emphatically in saying:

"Christology is a function of soteriology." I can affirm this language—elements of which were also evident in the theologies of Friedrich Schleiermacher, A. E. Biedermann, and Rudolf Bultmann—provided, first, that we not interpret this as meaning that christology is a mere reflection of soteriology and, second, that we go on to ask specifically of *whose* salvific interests is christology a function?

The group of theologians acknowledging the connection of christology to soteriology have not always formulated these two qualifications. Failing to formulate sufficiently the first qualification, they tend to lack ways of articulating the distinctiveness of christology as a contribution to soteriology. In not developing the question contained in the second qualification, they have risked formulating various "universal" visions of "human existence" that christology allegedly addresses. Tillich's tendency, for example, to take *Angst* (that particular post-World War I and II experience of North Atlantic cultures) as the basic predicament from which humanity needs deliverance, is an example of such problematic universalizing of salvific interests.[3]

Nevertheless, I affirm the statement made by Tillich, especially in opposition to alternative stances that would claim to start from "Jesus himself" or "Jesus' past history" itself as the grounding for talk of salvation. Wolfhart Pannenberg has perhaps most rigorously insisted on this alternative to my approach in his maxim: "Soteriology must follow from Christology, not vice versa."[4] However, Pannenberg cannot think christologically in a way consistent with this maxim. His own historical analyses of "Jesus himself" are laden with his own contemporary "apocalyptic" interests in salvific release from the existential traumas of death. Pannenberg acknowledges the interested character of his historical research when in conversation with positivist historians, but he does not develop the fact, which also must be acknowledged, that even for him soteriology cannot simply follow from christology. His historical explorations of Jesus emerge from, are accompanied by, and seek to inform a soteriological interest in hope given the threat he sees posed by death.[5] His failure to acknowledge this also appears to inhibit him from reflexively analyzing the particular kind of salvific interest out of which he is working. In shifting attention to christology and Jesus himself, Pannenberg allows himself to avoid the difficult question of *whose* soteriological interests he is developing and how his own soteriological interests are culturally and politically mediated.

The christology I present here, is unabashedly soteriological. I do not claim it is free from my own or others' projections of salvific interest, but I do hope to show that the christology is not reducible to my own or to any set of such interests. Again, the christology will have its own distinctiveness, its integrity.

Christology as a Mythos of Deliverance

Within the context of christopraxis and as inseparably related to soteriology, this christology can be portrayed as a mythos of deliverance. I will later clarify the meaning of the term *mythos* as it is being used in this work. At this point, suffice it to say that I mean it to be an expansive term, encompassing not only the kerygma or distinctive features of the Christian proclamation but also the scriptural narratives, the ritual, and the liturgy of Christian communities. The Christian mythos is constituted by all these, occurring in diverse manners.

Here my primary concern is to give greater specificity to the notion of what deliverance is from, leaving to later in this chapter my provision of a rationale for preferring *emancipation* as the term designating the specific kind of deliverance given and practiced in Christ.

First of all, and this is to be expected from the foregoing chapters, it is a deliverance from specific oppressions. We theologians have often resisted such specificity, leaving the task of addressing specific distortions to the laity and clergy laboring in particular fields of ministry. Classic traditions in theology have written more of salvation and deliverance as "from sin," "from death," and the like, all as general features of the human condition. I am not so much interested in replacing these concerns as I am with developing them more concretely. We here in North America do not struggle simply with sin—whether we identify this as pride or as sloth, as self-exaltation or as self-abnegation—we struggle with sin in the form of operative patterns and systems of distortion that warrant recognizing and naming. The sin from which I here take christology to proclaim deliverance is, as Schleiermacher identified original sin, a corporate or systemic phenomenon.[6] This should not be misunderstood as a denial of distortions and sin as operative in particular persons. Sin always has its individual form with its own personal enslavements. This cannot be denied. However, the sin and evil that beset us today are not simply failings caused by individual vices; they rise to meet us in the pervasive, deep-running, cultural-political structures that are with us from our birth and saturate our daily exchanges. Schleiermacher wrote that it is in its corporate character that human sin and guilt must be properly and fully understood and that Christ must be presented in relation to "a new corporate life."[7] So it seems especially today, however much we may need to move beyond Schleiermacher in other respects.

Theology, however, cannot rest content with a gospel that claims resistance to a pervasive corporate or social evil. That can become simply another generalist approach, though in a mode of sociality. We must name and resist particular major modes of sociality that are threatening North American life and culture. Even the carefully formulated notion of sin as "distorted relationality" used by Ruether in her *Sexism and God-Talk* as corrective to traditions that fix on sin as pride—even that, by itself, is insufficient. Ruether herself recognizes this, for her references to sin as distorted relationality appear within her specific address and naming of sexism and other distortions: militarism, ecological pollution, racism, and others.[8] The deliverances that I address christologically concern freedoms from the specific distortions that I have identified and selected as theorizable oppressions: sexism, hetero-realism, classism, and racism. Christology means a healing release from the systemic resistance imposed on women, gays and lesbians, the "underclass," and African Americans in our midst.

Throughout my discussion of these oppressions, however, I have been concerned not only with *political* theories that clarify the primary problem of domination but also with anthropological *cultural* theories that approach these dominations with a sensitivity to difference, an affirmation of the plurality of ways these oppressions can occur, can relate together, and can relate with other oppressions not selected for discussion in this book. If this affirmation of difference and plurality is to take place, deliverance from the specifically named oppressions also entails a deliverance *from ethnocentrism*, i.e., from the repression and devaluation of difference. This would be a deliverance *into* a life and study which, while privileging the problematic of dominance/oppression, never ceases to watch for difference. Thus, christology also addresses the need for deliverance from ethnocentrism, the failure and inability to celebrate difference, which pervades so many of the sexisms, hetero-realisms, classisms, and racisms of our times.[9]

Delivering Christology from Christian Traditions

There is a secondary sense in which christology is interested in deliverance. The primary sense focused on the needs for deliverance from sexism, hetero-realism, classism, racism, and their pervasive ethnocentrism. In order to articulate a christology that is really a mythos working deliverance amid these distortions, however, christology also needs deliverance from itself, from major elements and pervasive orientations in its traditions that have reinforced and even intensified the corporate and personal pain worked by these systemic oppressions.

1. We have already noted several instances of the tradition's complicity in oppressive systems, especially when theorizing sexism. The Hebrew and Christian scriptures and other elements of the Christian mythos are not only "androcentric," in Elisabeth Schüssler Fiorenza's term for general male-centeredness, they also reinforce patterns of male supremacy through messages that link the worship and spirituality of the church, explicitly or implicitly, to generally sexist or specifically misogynist and matricidal presumptions and practices. Even if "the brother" Jesus is interpreted as, say, a feminist, a hero crusading against the patriarchy, as indeed he has been — even then, he is still a male. This may not seem problematic until we recall that Jesus, as the tradition often has had it, is viewed as the unique incarnation in history of God's presence. Jesus, laden with ultimacy in this way, is an occasion in which women must identify themselves as "other" in relation to divine ultimacy's male coding. In fact, the incarnation's link to the man Jesus may give much reinforcement to women's stigmatizing as "the other." Gender identities play in incarnational thinking in this way,

no matter how fervently we theologians say that the incarnation, life, and work of Jesus is for all.

I am not suggesting that Christians' location of divine presence in a male Christ is necessarily without any transformative value for women and men. The sacrality of the male Jesus as the Christ can function in a positive way for men, especially those who see their Christian practice as a resistance against sexism.[10] Perhaps we can also agree, in part, with Cornel West's negative response to the question: "Is it contradictory and disempowering that Jesus Christ (male in human form) normatively grounds women's fight for freedom?" West suggests that it is no more contradictory or disempowering than "that Jesus Christ (Jewish in ethnic origins) normatively grounds Arabs' struggle for human dignity in Israel." West's query and response perhaps remind us that the coding of the Christ figure (male, Jewish, et al.) is not always without transformative function for women, non-Jews, and others.

The danger in West's response, however, is a major one. It underestimates the power of gender identities in the linguistic and ritual process of experiencing sacral power. We men receive an extraordinary empowerment by the predominance in language and ritual of male-coded references to Christ and God. The message is pervasive and deep: We can expect our gendered experiences of physicality, family, and social roles to be experiences of power. Women are far from powerless, but male-coded language about Christ and God has less to do with their experience of power, since the language transmits to them the message that they are *un*like the emergence in history of sacral power and ultimacy. Male-dominated Christ and God language—if no other options are available to them (e.g. sisterhood or woman-form images of sacral power)—leave women steeped in endless rituals of disempowerment.

Do our gender identities really have this powerful a role in our experiencing power? The answer, at least from ongoing anthropological and other social scientific study, is yes. Although the construction of gender varies from culture to culture, gender is everywhere—not just as a designation of sex, but as a whole system. Increasingly, it is necessary to speak of a *gender system*. This system is indeed culture's way of acknowledging physiological differences of sex and biology that involve two distinct developmental processes, male and female, occurring in at least five physiological areas: genes or chromosomes, hormones, gonads, internal reproductive organs, and external genitals.[11] Interwoven with these physiological areas of differentiation is a whole gender system associated with each category—a "wide range of activities, attitudes, values, objects, symbols, and expectations."[12] In the West, anthropologists themselves were so powerfully shaped by their own gender identities that it is only in relatively recent times that they have discerned the powerful function of gender systems in societies, particularly in those Western societies where male dominance is a pervasive feature.[13]

Our gender identities, therefore, must be viewed as part of a powerful gender system affecting almost every aspect of individual life and cultural practice. Given the power of gender systems, it is not surprising that gender becomes an issue in almost every experience, especially experiences of the sacred.[14] Predominantly male-coded religious language makes it more probable that women will experience themselves as "other" in relation to the sacred and also makes it probable that men will perceive women as not only other in relation to them (which may be fine) but also as other in relation to the sacred. This latter probability plays right into male-supremacist logics that are especially operative in the West, wherein women are taken to be other to God, and then also as symbols of evil.[15]

Insofar as our Christian traditions are dominated by male-coded Christ and God language, they contribute to the reinforcement and perpetuation of sexism. Here, too, christology will need deliverance from the Christian tradition.

2. Christology will also need deliverance from its heterosexism—from the hetero-realism that involves alienation from intimate companionship with one's own gender and from fully sensual experience of one's own and others' bodies.

I do not think the evidence shows that hetero-realist oppression is simply a result of a hetero-realist theology. It is not caused simply by Christian theologizing that rejects and punishes gay and lesbian practice. The causes of heterosexism are lodged, as are all oppressions, in cultural and political practices that structure our economic, political, and familial lives. However, theology often has reinforced repressive and punitive practices. To the extent that it has done so—through hetero-realist and heterosexist biblical interpretation, preaching, and ritualized exclusion of gay and lesbian persons from full participation in Christian communities as both leaders and the led—the Christian tradition is complicitous in fostering hetero-realist oppression.

Christology itself, as reflection on Jesus or on God's incarnation in history, has rarely been used to justify rejecting or punitive approaches to gays and lesbians.[16] Still, it needs to be delivered from a Christian tradition that from the beginning has marshaled specious arguments against gay and lesbian cultural and sexual practices by linking them to animal behavior, to "unsavory associations" with child prostitution or promiscuity, to unnatural ways of being, and to the undermining of social gender expectations.[17] Christology needs deliverance from these arguments of Christian tradition, as well as from those contemporary theological interpretations that continue rejecting-punitive motifs or are nonpunitive but still rejecting (as in the theology of Karl Barth).[18] Christology also needs deliverance from the Christian tradition's tepid qualified acceptance evident in Helmut Thielicke's barely more open stance.[19] Christology needs deliverance from this also, into a full acceptance of gays and lesbians within the visions of Christian community.[20] Only in such a manner can we begin to forge a Christian tradition, the mythos of which, in its proclamation, texts, and ritualized practice, is no longer used in North America or elsewhere to reinforce and justify cruel repressions and silencing of gays and lesbians.

I am aware that the issues of homosexuality, heterosexism and homophobia are complex issues for almost every current Christian tradition. They are difficult ones for the sexuality and spirituality of almost every Christian and for the ethics of almost every Christian church. Many of the very areas of the world where I discern Christian practice flourishing with an astonishing vitality and faithfulness — say, in Esperanza's Central America — are regions where homosexuality is still heavily repressed by individual, social and ecclesial sanctions.[21] Further, these issues will remain difficult. We have at hand now, however, a considerable expansion of literature on heterosexism, represented in my study by the research of Janice G. Raymond, John Boswell, and David F. Greenberg. In light of this literature and Christian valuation of freedom, the time is more than long due for a proclamation of deliverance from the role of our tradition in reinforcing the oppression of gay and lesbian persons.

3. Concerning classism, we might think that the liberation theologies of today — for example, in the theological texts of Jon Sobrino's *Christology at the Crossroads* or of Leonardo Boff's *Christ the Liberator*, and countless others — display clearly a deliverance of christology from classism. Indeed these christologies, as well as the dreams and practices of the world's poor, dramatize a christological resistance to classism by stressing God's opting with the poor, being present with the underclass, empowering resistance against the class divisions that perpetuate economic hardship and slow death.

It is an ongoing struggle, however, in North America and other parts of "Christendom" as well, to deliver christology from the classism that pervades Christian tradition. Among so-called evangelical traditions in North America, arguably one of the most active and influential ones in our midst, the notion prevails that we Christians can live in or enjoy "the benefits" of knowing Christ, having a "personal relationship with Jesus," "going to church," in short "be a Christian," without an active solidarity with the underclass on our continent and elsewhere. This apolitical spirituality, which in fact is a spirituality of compliance with political powers, is then often projected through North American televised media into third-world regions. Local elites often use this kind of Protestant "spirituality" to turn the disenfranchised away from labor union organizing and from other forms of social struggle.[22]

At best, if such solidarity with underclasses is practiced at all in this spirituality, it is as outreach, mission, or a witness that is secondary to a largely individual knowing of Jesus or to an associating with ecclesial communities in one's neighborhood. Christology continually needs deliverance from these distortions *into* a revisioned Christian praxis that understands life in or knowing of Christ as occurring, inseparably, *in the midst of* a practiced solidarity with the underclass. There may be many modes in which such solidarity can occur for North Americans.[23] Whatever the ways, they are not epiphenomenal, or secondary to, faith in Christ. To the contrary, these modes of solidarity resisting our own and others' classisms are the modes in which Christ's presence is known. The christology below seeks to reinforce this point.

4. Christian tradition's white racism is also something from which its christology needs deliverance. It should be clear from the previous theorization regarding white racism that christology cannot find its deliverance here simply by standing for the freedom of all peoples. That is necessary and will involve in this chapter a christological language of freedom and emancipation. This is not sufficient, however. I believe that more is necessary. Christian mythos needs deliverance particularly from the tradition's fantasies of blackness. We require a restructuring of our Christian mythos so we grasp the realities of "the evil of whiteness" and the fullness and goodness of blackness. Christology will thus need deliverance from the white/black color symbolism that is found in the pages of our scriptural texts and occurs much more frequently in the preaching, admonitions, and routine conversations of the Christian community. In this process a christological mythos must struggle toward deliverance from that entire ethos that mobilizes hostility toward black, darker-skinned peoples by stereotyping them as sexually monstrous or dirty, hence subject to muting and perpetual exploitation.

5. Finally, pervading all these needs for deliverance is another: the need for deliverance from ethnocentrism in Christian traditions. Christian traditions have not only been complicitous in the outright dominance of specific groups; they have also participated in a generalized defamation of aliens, of others from different cultures and life ways. The literature of anthropologists, from which the notion of ethnocentrism comes, suggests that this is not just a theologians' tendency; it is a tendency of their societies, indeed of many, if not all, human groups. There is a kind of repugnance or tremor in real encounters with others that many anthropologists take to be universal, however fervently they counsel against it. The repugnance is integrally bound up with the culture shock that is part of what needs enduring when one really lives with and affirms the other.[24]

However we evaluate claims that such ethnocentric impulses are universal, the tendency of such impulses to be widespread does not exonerate the Christian theological tradition's own ethnocentrism. That tradition has not simply borne impulsive tremors of repugnance; it has carried systematized thought and practice that speaks, in Enrique Dussel's apt words, a clear "No-to-the-Other."[25] Dussel is particularly concerned with Christian traditions of North Atlantic cultures and their predilections for viewing the poor as the other. He situates this within a distinctive tendency wherein that which is North Atlantic is "center" and that which is not (Asian, African, Indian, peasant, et al.) is "other." There is a dynamic practice of a generalized No-to-the-Other which, though all pervasive, is distinguishable from the more specific acts of domination (sexism, racism, classism, hetero-realism) that make some groups "other" for systemic exploitation. Christology needs deliverance from the whole generalized pattern of saying No-to-the-other, from the pervasive ethnocentrism that prefers and so gives ultimate value to our own ethnos. Christology needs deliverance *into* affirmation and celebration of the other, i.e., *into* thought and practice that says Yes-to-the-other. This does not mean rejecting one's own ethnos, but it should be valued in ways that are not ethnocentric.

This deliverance from ethnocentrism in Christian traditions is a deliverance not only from ethnocentrism as such but also from any absolutisms that ignore the plurality of forms characterizing the forms of domination. This is again congruent with the "understanding" that I developed in chapter 2. The deliverance from ethnocentrism enables a valuation of difference that sustains openness to the multifarious forms that sexism, heterosexism, classism, and racism themselves can take, openness also to the many intricate ways that these forms of domination interact with one another. The deliverance of christology from ethnocentrism in Christian traditions is necessary, then, to preserve a liberationist christology from becoming fixated on only one of the dominations or on only one form of a given domination.

THE NEED FOR AN EMPOWERING MYTHOS

Because the Christian tradition has participated in and reinforced systems of domination and their pervasive ethnocentrism, it is tempting to have done with the entire Christian mythos. In fact, I do not understand how any Christian theologian who has carefully analyzed the ways his or her mythos has nurtured atrocities of the most vicious forms and multigenerational slaveries of the most cruel intensity can fail to find within himself or herself a profound distaste and mistrust of the Christian religious tradition within which we find ourselves working.

We may frequently comfort ourselves with the protest: "Oh, but these were distortions of the tradition, not the tradition itself." More than we are often willing to admit, however, a symbolic or mythic tradition is indeed in accord with its use and performance. Moreover, as we have seen concerning the ties between sexism and the matricidal mythos of the tradition, the mythos itself can be viewed as flawed. There is no denying, however much we may wish to qualify the affirmation, that the scriptures are androcentric, patriarchal, at other points racist and anti-Semitic, too. I not only understand but also consider it an authentic and appropriate move, therefore, if post-Christian feminists such as Mary Daly and others come to hold that solidarity with the needs of others and their own means leaving behind the traditional Christian mythos. Similarly, gay and lesbian persons, some African Americans, many labor movement leaders and community organizers may also find little choice other than to find their most helpful communities outside Christian churches.

The lament of North American theologian David Tracy about Christian religious practice articulates a travail that often cannot be avoided:

Is it possible for a Catholic to read an account of the Saint Bartholomew's Day massacre and not be tempted to reject a tradition whose leader could sing a *Te Deum* in Saint Peter's to celebrate that betrayal of the central vision of Catholicism? Is it possible for a Protestant to read the story of Cromwell's savage destruction of Irish Catholics and not want to part company with the religiously empowered self-righteousness endorsing that disgrace? Is it possible for any Christian, after the Holocaust, to read the anti-Jewish statements in the entire tradition from the New Testament forward and not be tempted to have nothing further to do with so seemingly resentful a tradition? The demonic possibilities of all religions seem so ingrained in them that no one with the slightest historical knowledge need look far—even in our time—to find sufficient evidence to reject religion.[26]

The particular instances of destructive practice noted by Tracy are different from those explored in this book, but the systemic and pervasive presence of the distortions worked by sexism, hetero-realism, classism, and racism may also prompt Christians to reject not only the destructive patterns but their own religious tradition for its complicity in them. Tracy is, of course, not the only Christian theologian to have developed critiques of Christian religion. Just among Protestants we can recall Karl Barth and Dietrich Bonhoeffer. Both minced no words in subjecting distortions in Christian religious practice to vigorous critique.[27]

Although I also at times feel the pull to have done with the Christian mythos, I do not reject it. Nor do I take retreat, as I interpret Barth and Bonhoeffer generally to do, in a faith or revelation that occurs somehow outside of religion and myth. I remain with the Christian mythos, in the first place, because I am familiar with many religious communities whose struggles against the systemic distortions selected for this work are sustained by key elements of the Christian mythos—ranging from black churches in North America, whose worship and practice of Christian faith is a vital resource for survival and critique of white racism, to the Amerindian base communities of the Guatemalan highlands, whose Christian practice undergirds their struggle within conditions of genocide and military repression, to those few North American congregations whose Christian faith has led them into a practice of resistance to their own government's militarist policies.

In the second place, I still affirm the Christian mythos because the power of mythos—with its associated narratives, symbols, images, and ritualized gestures—is itself too vital a resource to give up. A tradition's mythos, as an imagistic resource, is not easily replaced by concepts and actions. In fact, it is difficult if not impossible to give ourselves to conceptual tasks, or to taking action, without mythos. Cornel West put it well when commenting on the need to resist the multileveled character of oppression: "Since energizing emancipatory visions are, to put it bluntly, religious visions, I see little alternative other than appropriating the subversive potential of Christianity and other religions."[28] Hence, I am committed to a remythologizing that serves an emancipatory christopraxis.

The Value of Myths

In theology as well as in other fields, the term myth has been used in an exasperatingly diverse manner. This diversity poses both an opportunity and a limitation for employing it here. The opportunity lies in the term's flexibility, its ability to refer to several kinds of functions. Its limitation, so evident in its diverse uses, prompts an entry here into the hoary problems of interpreting the nature of myth.

I have already suggested that the notion of myth or mythos as functioning in the phrase *Christian mythos* refers to the distinctive complex of traits constituting the Christian religion's "address" to and amid contemporary situations. This complex of traits includes not only the kerygma, or distinctive features of the Christian proclamation, but also the scriptural narratives and the ritual practice of ecclesial communities.

This linking of proclamation, narrative, and ritual practice within the notion of mythos or myth is supported by understandings of myth provided by the cross-cultural studies of the anthropology of religion, and it is from this field that we also begin to sense the ways in which we can speak of the value of myths.

Although multiple definitions that cannot be explored here abound in anthropology, anthropologist William A. Lessa provides a helpful orientation when he identifies myth as "a unifying concept which enables anthropologists to talk about etiological narratives and other forms which, for the society involved, make up a body of 'assumed knowledge' about the universe, the natural and supernatural worlds, and people's place in the totality."[29]

Several features of this quotation warrant comment. First, myth includes *narratives and other forms*. It includes not only narrative modes of expression, which employ strategies of emplotment and the building of characters and identities of agents who act and are acted upon in stories; it also includes other symbols, images, even these as acted and ritualized in touch and gesture. Although debates have raged in anthropology about whether myth or ritual is prior to the other,[30] more recent evidence suggests that divisions of myth and ritual are difficult if the aim is to claim one as prior to the other.[31] Mythic narratives are often completed in their ritual performance, and often ritual performance is the condition for the emergence and elaboration of narrative forms. It is best, then, to work with a view of mythos not as narrative over against ritual, but as narrative and ritual occurring together, in distinctive ways relative to particular societies.

Second, myth has a marked *etiological* character. Myths enable members of a given society to elaborate understandings of the causes and origins of the salient features of their living. This is done not simply to satisfy curiosity or only to provide accounts of origins but also, and often more importantly, to orient life in the present and toward the future. The etiological character of myths is not just pursuit of knowledge about the past, it is that as occasion for exploring and reinforcing senses of what is ultimately meaningful in the social group's present and future. This expanded understanding of the etiological character of myths leads to the next comment.

Third, myths are, as Lessa phrases it, *about the universe, and the natural and supernatural worlds*. It is not essential to myths that they be about supernatural agents and gods, though they often are.[32] More particularly, myths have a holistic orientation. They tend to elaborate awareness of the whole of life and of the unity of different dimensions of life. In Lévi-Strauss's terminology, myth has a totalizing function, tending to weave together in meaningful wholes the salient features of kinship practice, social organization, natural habitat, key historical events, actions of supernatural agents, political structures.[33] As totalizing and holistic, mythic expressions involve humanity at its limits. It is a "limit-language" in and through which people communally explore pervasive restrictions and limitations on human life (systemic political oppression, sickness, death, and the rest) and also imaginatively explore the whole within which they are limited parts.[34] Within a holistic vision, there is both the sense of restriction and the imagining of the larger, more pervasive realities within which we experience restriction. Mythic agents such as tricksters, heroes, heroines, spirits, ancestors, elements of nature, gods, God — all figures exploring the limits of life may be viewed as different ways of articulating and elaborating the holistic orientation of myths.

Fourth, it is characteristic of those who live, think, and work through myths that their knowledge has the status of *assumed knowledge*. Myth does not provide the knowledge of philosophical understanding, critical explanation or scientific data, though myth may be a dimension of each of these.[35] Myths, for their adherents, especially in patterns of religious myth, feature assumed knowledge that has a certain givenness, an "aura of facticity."[36] Even if believers in certain myths (such as the Genesis creation accounts) come to question and so develop a critical relationship that doubts the myths are literal descriptions of historical events, there often persists, along with the critical knowledge gained, what Paul Ricoeur has called a "second naivete," i.e., a willingness to assume, to be oriented by, such a traditional mythology and its powerful mythic expressions. Myth, despite all the tensions, can and often does dwell within the orienting assumptions of persons who have exercised explanatory critique, often in secular as well as religious communities.

Fifth and finally, we should note Lessa's acknowledgment, a significant one, that myth is a kind of heuristic device for scholars studying a given society's pattern of believing. It is a *unifying concept which enables the scholar* approaching these patterns. Myth—and the wide disagreement about myth's definition signals this—is a scholar's construct. As Ivan Strenski has argued in the excellent book, *Four Theories of Myth in Twentieth Century History: Cassirer, Eliade, Lévi-Strauss and Malinowski,* myth is an artifact of twentieth-century North Atlantic scholarship, created both to illumine the subject matter of anthropologists and historians of religion and also to serve certain interests—academic, social, political—within scholars' own contexts.[37] I am not claiming that myth is *only* a construct, strategically or heuristically employed by mythologists, for there are imagistic accounts among societies' belief patterns that invite the scholars' heuristic construction. We must not suppose, however, that *myth* is a term free from the interests and constructive concerns of the scholars of myth. Lessa's characterization of myth as an enabling, unifying concept is therefore a helpful reminder of myth's constructive character. While we can speak of a distinctive and disciplined science of mythology, there is no pure science of mythology in the sense of a study of myth separable from the mythologists' set of heuristic and strategic interests.[38]

This fifth feature of Lessa's orienting statement on myth, as well as the first four features, helps to clarify what is involved in the phrase *Christian mythos*. This way of characterizing Christianity's address in the light of contemporary practice is a heuristic and strategic move. It is not a description of the Christian tradition, as such, but tries to be a creative reinterpretation of elements of Christian tradition, in order to respond to the particular challenges posed by contemporary systemic distortions. I am also aware that, for many, to characterize beliefs as myth is to signify that they are untrue or unhistorical.[39] Strategically, I do mean to trouble any who think the central concerns of Christian faith and practice grow simply from truth and history, especially if they are thought to be free from creative and imaginative activity. Nonetheless, myth in my sense—or *mythos*, as I prefer to say in order to avoid some of the colloquial abuse suffered by the term *myth*— is opposed neither to truth nor to history.[40] Mythos, especially the Christian mythos demanded by our troubled times, weaves creativity into truth and history, moves us beyond the old dichotomies that pit imagination against truth and history.

All of this is part of the strategic and heuristic concern of my use of myth here. But the other four features of myth also contribute to an understanding of what the Christian mythos is; we must consider these too, though in reverse order.

In keeping with the fourth feature of myth, the Christian mythos concerns Christians' assumed knowledge. My discussions of the Christian mythos are ways to focus intentionally and explicitly on what for many Christians is often only assumed or implicit. Through intentional, explicit focusing and reinterpreting, I hope to reshape Christians' assumed knowledge for purposes of a transformative engagement with the systemic distortions of our period.

In accordance with the third feature of myth, the Christian mythos concerns a holistic orientation for Christian faith and practice. Presentation and elaboration of the Christian mythos is a way to say not only what the Christian project is all about but also what a Christian vision is of humanity in the totality of all creation. The Christian mythos, then, provides a holistic orientation for Christians amid human living, an orientation which is a response to the limitations encountered in that living and which often includes a language about the sacred as a way to thematize the whole that pervades and encompasses restricted human life and creation. The Christian mythos provides such a holistic orientation.

We must also recall the second feature of myth. The Christian mythos has an etiological dimension: That is to say, it concerns origins. The origins of what? As a specifically Christian mythos, it is an interpretation of the origins of the Christian movement, a movement variously bound up with the figure of Jesus of Nazareth and giving birth to the Christian church, though this movement should not be limited to any one official institutionalization as "church." Just what the relationship is of this Jesus to the Christian movement is the central concern of the Christian mythos as treated in this book. In that relation, I will argue, we can discern the central meanings of the Christian project that address the late twentieth-century challenges I have selected for this study. In relation to such movements, there is a retrievable tradition for current emancipatory practice. Through study of these central meanings, Christians may be led further to study beliefs about creation and divine power as origin of all life. For what I am here calling "Christian mythos," however, this etiological interest in the creation of all life, though necessary, is secondary to the etiological focus on the relation between Jesus and the rise of Christian movements. Even though this is only a part of the Christian mythos—understood as kerygma, narrative and ritual practice—it is the major portion of the Christian mythos attended to in this book.

We come now to the first feature of myth noted from Lessa's formulation: The Christian mythos is an interpretation of narratives and other forms. As interpretation of narratives, Christian mythos interprets the salient features of the New Testament scriptures. However, as interpretation of that nebulous phrase, "and other forms," Christian mythos cannot isolate that narrative from the historical contexts of the narrative, from the communal rituals associated with those narratives, or from the present-day readings and interests in those narratives. The Christian mythos thus gives a necessary place to New Testament narratives, but it is neither "narrativist" nor "intratextual," i.e., it is not simply produced by exploring meanings in the Bible's narrative world. In addressing its situations, Christian mythos draws from the salient features of that narrative world as situated in historical contexts, ritual contexts, and present-day social locations.

My clarification of Christian mythos by reference to categories drawn from an anthropology of myth may risk, in some readers' minds, a reduction of Christian particularity to categories of myth in social science or history of religions. Such reduction can be resisted by dealing directly with the Christian sources that I will examine in the rest of this chapter and the next chapter.

Here the main concern has been to locate Christian mythos in relation to myth generally, in order to suggest how, as mythos, it is valuable as a way to meet important human needs. In particular, as mythos it meets needs not met simply by concepts or actions, taken either alone or together. In particular, through uses of etiological narrative and other forms, myth provides a wholistic orientation for thought and action by dwelling in the assumed knowledge of a communal group. In dwelling there, myth has an empowering function for humans that should not be underestimated, even though we may cultivate very critical and learned views of our particular myths.[41]

Sallie McFague has seen this power of mythos quite clearly. In her book, *Models of God: Theology for an Ecological, Nuclear Age*, she is also critical of many traditional images, but she insists that any reconstruction "attempting to unseat the triumphalist, royal model, must be at least as attractive as it is."[42] The personal images as personal images have a power that even theologians who radically reconstruct the tradition must respect. The way to respect the power of these images is to take up the task of remythologization. Thus, there needs to be a retaining of "imagery reflecting the beginning and continuation of life, imagery of sex, breath, food, blood and water, as in the second birth, the breath of the Holy Spirit, bread and wine, blood of the cross, the resurrection of the body, and the water of baptism," among others.[43] McFague is concerned largely with the remythologizing of God, imaging God as Mother, Lover, and Friend, and with commenting on these new images as ways to revision a theology of relationships between God and the world. It remains to be asked, however: How are we to proceed with remythologizing when it is christology with which we deal, where the figure so prominent in the tradition is Jesus?

Toward a Mythos of Jesus' Life-Praxis

The Christian mythos, which is the heart of christology and provides the central meanings for a Christian address and that engages contemporary situations, needs to be derived not from the individual man Jesus, but from Jesus' life-praxis. Of course, Jesus' individuality is part of this life-praxis, but a life-praxis is bigger than any set of actions by its participating individual agents, Jesus included. What I mean by *life-praxis* is perhaps better articulated as a "sociohistorical dynamic." This is advisable because what is new, out of which christology emerges, is not just a heroic, individual life in history, a life of Jesus or anyone else. What is new is a whole complex of thought and action (praxis) occurring within a field of personal, political, economic, social, and religious contexts.

Christology's efforts to remythologize in a way that preserves the empowering features of myth while resisting the repressive functioning of many images need to be focused on the sociohistorical dynamic in which Jesus was a necessary participant and contributor but not the only necessary one. The Christian mythos is a mythos of this sociohistorical matrix, the whole life-praxis within which Jesus was a historical part. The empowering mythos we need is not only a mythos displaying, telling, and retelling the story of an individual hero, Jesus. It needs to become, more than the tradition has allowed it to become, a mythos of Jesus *and* other lives touching and contributing to his as he touches and contributes to theirs. Moreover, if sensitive to the dynamics of a sociohistorical praxis (in all its political, economic, social, and religious complexities), the Christian mythos will be primarily a mythos of a movement, constituted by images and symbols that nurture awareness, practice, and thought of the new transformative life constitutive of that movement. Christian mythos need not be a myth of the man Jesus or only a collection of individual stories, but of all these and more, the whole interpersonal movement catching all these up together.

A Christian mythos that takes seriously and works out of Jesus' *life-praxis*, not just from Jesus, enables us to revision christology in some new ways that are needed in our time. This will be the agenda, especially in the final chapter. Here, I am particularly interested in getting us accustomed to the notion that the Christian mythos is about something more encompassing than Jesus. One helpful illustration of the way we need to refocus the Christian mythos is given by Rita Nakashima Brock in *Journeys by Heart: A Christology of Erotic Power*:

> Jesus is like a whitecap on a wave. The whitecap is momentarily set off from the swell that is pushing it up, making us notice it. But the visibility of the whitecap, which draws our attention, rests on the enormous pushing power of the sea—of its power to push with life-giving labor, to buoy up all lives, and to unite diverse shores with its restless energy. That sea becomes monstrous and chaotically destructive when we try to control it, and its life-giving power is denied. Jesus' power lies with the great swells of the ocean without which the white foam is not brought to visibility.[44]

The task of christology is to formulate and elaborate a Christian mythos of that life-giving power that dwells with the great swells of the ocean and energized and transformed those caught up in the movement associated with Jesus. While Brock's quotation ably directs us to the whole enveloping power with which Jesus was associated, I am not sure it does justice to the significant role that Jesus plays in her own book's discussion.[45] Therefore, below, I will propose another metaphor—Jesus as leaven.

If you sense in the quotation from Brock a striking, though not exclusive, invocation of maternal imagery, then you also sense the direction in which I plan to develop a distinctive though not exclusive christology. This imagery can be developed in the direction of a remembering of the oceanic depths of life-renewing and reconnecting power that patriarchal mythologies and structures directly and indirectly repress and dismember. The christology that I present will preserve some of the experience of mystical oneness that characterizes this oceanic, transformative power but structures it in terms of a sociohistorical matrix I name reconciliatory emancipation. Before commenting further on the substantive themes of this christology, however, it is necessary to accustom ourselves further to the relocating of Christian mythos that I have proposed.

THE PARTICULARITY OF CHRIST

In several senses, what I am proposing is not new. First, numerous theologians have stressed that the key concern of christology is the event of redemption, salvation, or transformation—an event more encompassing and complex than Jesus' own lifestory—really a whole "salvation history worked by God" that involves present interests and practices, as well.[46] Except for a few,[47] however, most of these theologians still allow the event to be dominated by a mythos of Jesus, rather than a mythos pertaining to the whole transformative matrix. It is this latter kind of mythos for which I am calling here, in order to enable a cultural-political theology that addresses the specific oppressions I have discussed in previous chapters.

In another sense as well, this proposal for relocating the Christian mythos away from the individual Jesus might be seen as not innovative. The very name "Jesus Christ," traditionally taken as christology's subject matter, signals, within its own semantic construction, something more than an exclusive focus on the man Jesus. As Schubert Ogden puts it in his book, *The Point of Christology*, there is in the very name a predication or ascription of the title "Christ" to Jesus.[48] Many Christians, and theologians among them, when thinking or writing about Christ, have written and spoken as if Christ were merely the last name of the man Jesus, making little if any distinction between the words *Jesus* and *Christ*. Even those theologians who do make the distinction often still unpack the meanings of the christological predication in terms of the mythos of the man Jesus. The christology I propose here will not only make the distinction; it will also reconnect Christ with Jesus only through attention to the communal, sociohistorical matrix within which transformative power was experienced in relation to Jesus. Once again, this is to keep the Christian mythos oriented primarily to the whole matrix of a movement, and not just to a single life history. This calls not only for a knowledge of the context of the early Christian movement but also for a knowledge of the contemporary contexts within and in relation to which christological predication may still occur.

In christology, then, we do well to shift our understanding of "the particularity of Jesus Christ" *away from* exclusive preoccupation with the man Jesus *toward* the center of the Christ event, in the full complexity of the ongoing process of experiencing and predicating Christ of Jesus. This full complexity is christology's proper subject matter, and one best referred to at this point as an intersubjective, communal dynamic.

The locus of incarnation in Christ as an intersubjective, communal dynamic is ably articulated by Peter C. Hodgson in his 1989 work, *God in History: Shapes of Freedom*. There he writes: "God was 'incarnate,' not in the physical nature of Jesus as such, but in the gestalt that coalesced both in and around his person—with which his person did become identical, and by which, after his death, he took on a new communal identity."[49]

Hodgson's notion of incarnational presence as a gestalt is especially close, I think, to my notion of Christ as a sociohistorical or cultural-political movement in history. Other phrasing by Hodgson is helpful for clarifying the nature of the Christ dynamic:

God is efficaciously present in the world, not as an individual agent performing observable acts. . . . Rather, God is present in specific shapes or patterns of praxis that have a configuring, transformative power within historical process, moving the process in a determinative direction, that of the creative unification of multiplicities of elements into new wholes, into creative syntheses that build human solidarity, enhance freedom, break systemic oppression, heal the injured and broken, and care for the natural.[50]

Precisely this kind of shaping, configuring, and transforming power is what occurs in the Christ dynamic, and I will develop it more specifically as reconciliatory emancipation, in light of the challenges posed by our postmodern trilemma and contemporary oppressions.

I am less certain about the way Hodgson characterizes the relationship of the person of Jesus of Nazareth to the gestalt, to the dynamic movement of God in history. It is clear that for Hodgson the person of Jesus does not exhaust the meaning and content of the divine gestalt, but, if I read him correctly, he tends to accept "some sense" of Jesus becoming identical with the divine gestalt or becoming its bearer.[51] It is of course true that Christian traditions have often taken Jesus' words, deeds, death, and resurrection as identical to and as the bearer of the divine gestalt, and perhaps this is all Hodgson means when referring to Jesus as "bearer" or as in some sense identical with the gestalt. However, especially given the symbolic and social problems entailed in identifying the incarnation so closely to the male figure Jesus,[52] it is important today to emphatically resist that identification.

In keeping with my language of Jesus as a necessary but not the only necessary element of the Christ dynamic, I would prefer to characterize Jesus' relationship to the divine gestalt as that of a leaven that permeates the whole dynamic movement with an altering or transforming influence. As such, the leaven is necessary to the configuration of the whole rising mixture, but the other ingredients of the mixture are also necessary. In fact, a leaven is itself dependent on previously developed configurations; it is a part of already fermenting dough that is reserved to produce fermentation in a new batch. Hence, previously leavened mixtures are also necessary. Jesus' function in relation to the cultural-political movement that is the Christ event is like the relationship of leaven to the mixture that is caused to ferment and rise. Jesus is a necessary fermenting ingredient in the divine gestalt in history. As such his individual agency works not as an efficient cause of the Christ dynamic, but as permeating and enlivening the whole by interacting with other necessary personal agents: other men and women, other social, cultural, and political forces. The metaphors of leaven and ferment for characterizing Jesus' necessary, but not exhaustive, relationship to the Christ dynamic are not appropriate simply because they signal his creative role in the general formation of the gestalt in history; they also valuably connote a way of playing that role, as including fermenting activities like "agitation," or "unrest." Jesus is necessary to the sociohistorical, Christ dynamic, then, as a leaven is to a set of other necessary ingredients in a whole rising, expanding mixture. To identify the whole configuring, transformative mixture with the leaven would be to make too little of the mixture and too much of the leaven. So also, to identify the Christ dynamic or movement with Jesus both makes too little of that dynamic and too much of Jesus.

Reorienting our christologies toward this complex dynamic raises many problems for traditional christological and theological understandings. In this book I am more interested in crafting a Christian mythos for cultural-political theology's address of contemporary challenges than I am in assuaging worries about what becomes of many traditional notions indebted to formulations at Nicaea, Chalcedon, and elsewhere. Nevertheless, let me conclude this section on the particularity of Christ with comments — albeit too brief to do complete justice to their traditional complexity — about notions of the person, work, and divinity of Christ. What basic transformations of these notions are entailed in a christological revisioning of the Christian mythos as pertaining to a sociohistorical dynamic?

Concerning the language of *person* in christology, we need to speak less of the person of Christ and more of Christ as interpersonal. "Christ" issues from historical and communal relatedness to Jesus, through a movement of which Jesus is a necessary part. The complexity and richness of the Christ dynamic is truncated if its personal character is focused only on Jesus' person. Those who were diversely connected to Jesus — i.e., *who* they were and *what* their interests were — are just as essential to the *personal* character of the Christ event as is the person Jesus. Tillich's crisp language remains accurate: "the Christ would not be the Christ without those who receive him as the Christ."[53] This does not mean we simply substitute another striking person's life history for Jesus' (that of Mary, Jairus' daughter, Paul, Phoebe, or the Ethiopian Eunuch) as the central locus of christology. It does mean that other people can provide rich resources for a Christian mythos emerging from the divine gestalt in the incarnation, in the whole movement within which Jesus participated and to which he contributed.

This shift of the person of Christ away from Jesus as individual agent may seem like a move toward a less concrete, less human Christ figure. That is not really the case at all. It only seems to be the case because we, especially in North Atlantic cultures, are accustomed to identifying the human and the concrete with an individual (unconsciously often male) person. This move away from Jesus in christology is not a move away from the human, the concrete, or the historical, but rather away from an individualistic, largely androcentric vision. It is to locate Christ in the fuller, more complex, interpersonal nexus of history in which humanity is nurtured most fully. Individuals are only one mode of the concrete or the particular, by no means the only mode.

Similar transformations follow for the notions of Christ's work and divinity. If Christ is a particular kind of intersubjective, communal dynamic, then the *work of Christ* cannot be only the activity or practice of Jesus (his ministry, crucifixion, resurrection) but is rather *these as narrated and practiced by* historical communities of disciples contemporary with and subsequent to Jesus' period. The work of Christ is not the activity of Jesus, but the working that issued and issues from the intersubjective, communal network coalescing around Jesus, a coalescing which is never only an *imitation* of Jesus but may also include selective appropriations (involving suspicion as well as trust)[54] of Jesus' activity. These appropriations of Jesus' own activities may include suspicion as well as trust because what is disclosed to Christians are meanings derived from the whole sociohistorical movement of which Jesus was a part. These meanings may be more than, other than, at times even contrary to, specific acts characterizing the life history of Jesus.[55] Jesus is part of a disclosure or transformation more encompassing than the specifics dramatized in his own individual agency, consciousness, or historical activity.

Similarly, the *divinity* of Christ, from the perspective of a revisioned christology, shifts away from sole preoccupation with the man Jesus to historical realms of communal interaction through which Jesus was associated with transformative, salvific power. This approach to the divinity of Christ understands divine presence — ultimate and healing power, value and meaning — to be operative in a distinctive interpersonal communal praxis and in persons as participants in that communal praxis.

My suggestion here may seem to entail a de-divinizing of Jesus that some have lamented, especially with regard to feminist theology. Actually, this is not so much a de-divinizing process as it is a shifting of divinity from exclusive association with the male figure Jesus to the realm where women as well as men participate in a movement involving that figure. The man

Jesus may be a necessary feature of the communal dynamic we name Jesus the Christ, but necessary as he is, he alone is not sufficient to be the locus of divinity. To repeat, that locus is the realm of connections and interactions occurring among humans who together are connected to Jesus.

Despite differences we may have on other points, we may helpfully recall D. F. Strauss's eloquent way of urging this shift upon us. That which we value and is sacred (for Strauss, the *Idee*) is not wont "to lavish all its fullness on one exemplar . . . ; it loves rather to distribute its riches among a multiplicity of instances which mutually complete each other."[56] This does not mean that we need to lavish an equal degree of fullness on every potential exemplar. In my formulations below, I give a primacy to the early movement or sociocultural matrix associated with Jesus.

The interpersonal person of Christ and the communal work(ing) of Christ together constitute the locus and meaning of Christ's divinity. Images and names for Christ, which mediate our awareness of divine presence in history, need not fix only on the man Jesus. Hence it is conceivable, for example, that images such as Sophia and Christa, as employed by feminists, or of a black Christ, might better convey the meaning of the Christ dynamic than simple references to Jesus.[57] What is crucial is the character of the intersubjective, sociohistorical dynamic.

Each of these attempts to resituate the divine gestalt of Christ in a matrix enveloping the man Jesus, rather than simply in Jesus, is in fact consonant with Pauline understandings of the Christ event as comprised by a communal "body of Christ" — a body not dissociated from Jesus, but one that is often seemingly portrayed without extended discussion of Jesus of Nazareth.[58] While this biblical strand may be brought into the discussion as supporting the relocating of Christ in an intersubjective matrix, such biblical claims cannot serve, in the hermeneutics of a cultural-political theology, as a biblical "foundation" for the christological moves being made here.[59] They show merely an important consonance between biblical materials and this christology.

My resituating of the particularity of Christ tends to stretch the understanding of christology. Some may suspect a christocentrism. Although I focus in this work almost exclusively on Christian mythos because I believe that christic language distinguishes Christianity's religious practice, symbolic heritage and theology from others,[60] it is still true for me that locating Jesus Christ in the communal interactive realm makes this cultural-political theology christocentric only in a very complex sense. That is, to live after and think on Christ in the senses I have suggested is at once to consider ecclesiological and pneumatological issues as well. Jesus Christ is not really thinkable, or experienced, without also thinking and experiencing communities (inside and outside established churches) that mediate Christ, and without also thinking and experiencing the spiritual praxis characterizing such communities. To think christologically, as the rest of this book tries to show, is therefore to think also about the kinds of ecclesial community that occasion the working of Christ's spirit in the world.

THE CHRIST OF RECONCILIATORY EMANCIPATION

Insisting that christology begin with Jesus Christ as intersubjective communal dynamic is to locate its particularity, what I propose as christology's proper subject matter; it is not yet to identify or name the special character or themes of that dynamic. In our attempt to formulate a cultural-political theology that addresses the postmodern trilemma from a narrative and ecclesial tradition that is itself implicated in that trilemma, I shall name the special character of this Christ dynamic *reconciliatory emancipation.* The sign of the christic interpersonal presence in communal praxis that is of Christ is the presence of this reconciliatory emancipation. Precisely what reconciliatory emancipation is emerges through the subsequent discussion. Here at the outset I would say that the dynamic so named is *a freedom-making force that also unifies.* That is, it is emancipation that is reconciliatory. Hodgson's term "love-in freedom" is another way to refer to the substance of the dynamic, divine gestalt in history.[61] Freedom making, to be sure, entails conflict, strife, at times even division, but ultimately the Christ dynamic is one that unifies in the wake that freedom has made. Note that I have not claimed the reverse, that freedom comes in the wake of making unity. There is a primacy of freedom and emancipation over unity and reconciliation that is maintained even while insisting on the need to hold freedom making and unifying together.

Need for Both The Reconciliatory and the Emancipative

The problem of relating the reconciling and unitive meanings of the Christian gospel with its emancipative and liberative ones has been an ongoing concern wherever traditional North Atlantic theologies have come into conversation, often conflict, with more recent liberation theologies. It was a theme of Schubert Odgen's controversial statement on liberation theology in his book, *Faith and Freedom,*[62] and in a number of North American theologians' efforts to relate their traditions' beliefs about a gospel of reconciliation to the need and hope for liberation.[63] The conversation becomes conflictual concerning the South African *Kairos Document*, which argues that primacy given to reconciliation meanings of the gospel is often, especially in South Africa, a way to mask injustice and oppression. The document argues that justice and liberation must occur as a condition for reconciliation.

I will ultimately be in agreement with the *Kairos Document's* position about the primacy of justice. At this point, however, I am more concerned with making the simpler point that both reconciliatory and emancipative elements belong together in any understanding of the meaning of Christian faith and practice.

Hence, the first trait to note about the name, *reconciliatory emancipation*, for the special character of the sociohistorical Christ dynamic, is that it fuses both reconciliatory and emancipative dimensions. Both reconciliation and liberation/emancipation are components of the discursive elements of the tradition (scriptures, creeds, doctrines) and also of Christian traditions' extradiscursive elements (rituals, ministries, communal dynamics, institutional structure). More importantly, however, referring to the special character of the Christ dynamic as both reconciliatory *and* emancipative enables us to structure the tradition's Christ dynamic as addressing the two important prongs of the postmodern trilemma: difference (affirming plurality) and domination (resisting oppression).

In the proposed renaming, then, the reconciliatory element is there, making possible the Christ dynamic's address of the contemporary realities of fragmentation, difference, lack of unity amid intense and recalcitrant pluralism. The emancipative element is there to enable an engagement with, and resistance to, the realities of oppression and systematic exploitation. The two elements in reconciliatory emancipation work together to structure the salvific communal dynamic of Christ toward an address of difference and of oppressive forms of domination. As I hope to make clear, the reconciliation in question must not simply repress difference but seek a valuation of it that leads to alliance. The emancipation in question must not just proclaim deliverance but do so through address of specific oppressions in our period, from which deliverance is needed.

The Primacy of Emancipation

Reconciliatory emancipation, though a phrase insisting on an inextricable relation between the two elements of the Christ dynamic, does *not* entail the claim that they are equal in importance. To the contrary, I give primacy to the emancipative or liberative element. This primacy is signaled in my casting this element as the substantive noun when naming the Christ dynamic's special character. Once again, this is consonant with the privilege a cultural-political hermeneutics gives to the voices of the politically oppressed and to the explanatory theories pertaining to their oppression that I developed in chapters 3 and 4.The adjectival status I have given to the reconciliatory element, which signals its secondary significance, in no way denies that it is essential to the special character of the Christ dynamic. The reconciliatory element, the drive for unity amid differences, Christianity's well-known valuation of a *koinonia* community of love, is a *necessary* posture of Christian practice that pervades, qualifies, but never takes precedence over, the dynamic's movement for emancipation.

By "primacy," I mean that emancipation (liberation, or generally "freedom") is the basic, most pervasive christological concern and effect. This is not to say that emancipation is the only quality proper to the salvific dynamics of communal praxis we name Jesus Christ, but I suggest that it is the basic and pervasive one. Though many different things have been and can still be said about God's presence and work in Christ, freedom is the thing sayable that pertains most directly to the proper subject of christology, i.e., Jesus Christ as communal praxis. Saying this of Christ is to identify the special character of that praxis as making freedom for those dominated by oppression.

Several kinds of arguments together lead me to acknowledge primacy for the emancipatory element. Each kind of argument contributes to my own, involves a set of complex factors and rides a wave of literature and scholarship. I can in no way here summarize all these factors or all the issues raised in the bibliography of relevant texts. I can identify the kinds of arguments that are available that lead a christology to give primary focus to emancipation, thus enabling us to move on to the question of what a christology of reconciliatory emancipation might be for us today.

1. The first kind of argument is one that, in diverse ways, refers to Jesus as the radically free one. The argument here moves from views of Jesus' person and work. Latin American and North American black theologians have from the beginning focused on Jesus of Nazareth in order to center their christologies and theologies of liberation.[64] These scholars, to varying degrees, are aware of the problems inherent in trying to discern a historical Jesus, but together they have opened up new understandings of Jesus' pervasive concern, in teaching and ministry, with freedom.

One of the most careful yet emphatic developments of the notion of Jesus the Liberator is provided by Peter C. Hodgson, in his earlier work, *New Birth of Freedom: A Theology of Bondage and Liberation*. Citing Leander Keck, Hodgson is well aware of the danger of proof-texting abuses of the New Testament, not only by "the upper and middle-class pietistic right," but also by "the radical left."[65] He also knows, as more recent scholars have noted about the New Testament,[66] that one cannot find in Jesus an explicit language of freedom. Jesus even lacked a specific word for it, in large part because the available term for it, *eleutheria*, was a distinctly Greek concept that referred to an elite group whose freedom was integrally bound up with power over others. "Thus freedom meant autonomy, self-determination, power over oneself, membership in a privileged community (the *polis*) that excluded slaves, women, foreigners, manual laborers."[67]

Despite the difficulties posed by the fact that there is a shortage of an explicit terminology of freedom used by Jesus, Hodgson can proceed to develop a christology of Jesus the Liberator from sin, death, and every power. "He was the radically free person, and brought freedom to speech and praxis in a quite unprecedented way."[68] Combining these emphatic claims with a critical exploration of New Testament materials, Hodgson then proceeds to discern a gospel of liberation carried by the tensive metaphor, "the kingdom of God." He also interprets the accusations that led to Jesus' death as blasphemer and agitator as suggesting the political dimension of Jesus' ministry and a concern with freedom from oppressive political powers. Moreover, Hodgson's interpretation of "Jesus the Liberator" involves a reading of "salvation as liberation" in the texts attributed to Paul and John.[69]

All of this critical attention to the life teaching and ministry of Jesus in the context of New Testament literature and history is exemplary of a first kind of argument for the primacy of freedom, liberation, or emancipation in a christology. It is a strategy that, in the shaping of christology, makes continual reference to Jesus the Liberator and to his gospel of freedom, and it is a strategy pursued, in both critical and less critical forms, by diverse liberation theologians and Christians who interpret Jesus of the New Testament amid their struggles for freedom. It is a strategy evident in the writings of Ernst Käsemann, whose book title emphasizes that *Jesus Means Freedom*[70] and in the singing of oppressed peoples whose lyrics can make a similar point:

> Walkin' and talkin' with my mind set on Jesus,
> Walkin' and talkin' with my mind set on freedom.

Hodgson is aware, however, that in arguments for the primacy of freedom or emancipation more is going on than simply referring to Jesus and Jesus' message. That Jesus means freedom is not just a brute fact awaiting the encounter of a researching scholar or Bible-reading Christian. That there is something more going on suggests that within or associated with this kind of argument for the primacy of liberation, there is operative yet other kinds of argument.

2. A second type of argument proceeds within an interpretive strategy of incorporating the interpreters' interest or need for freedom into the discernment of Jesus' concern with freedom. The emphasis here is not so much on Jesus' person and work, but on the effects of that person and work on those who encounter Jesus, those who interpret him as "the Christ." As Schubert M. Ogden has reminded readers in his book, *The Point of Christology*, hitching christological arguments onto claims about the character, actions, or consciousness of Jesus is ultimately undermined by the impossibility of establishing empirical-historical conclusions about Jesus' sayings and deeds *apart from* existential-historical concerns in those conclusions.[71] For Ogden, this has always been the case with christological assertions, ranging from the earliest apostolic witness, to conciliar formulations, to contemporary scholars' constructions. Any christology, therefore, is a labor of interpretation, making an existential point.

Hodgson's own awareness of the important role played by such an existential point is evident in his acknowledgment that the presentation of Jesus as the Liberator is a construction. It is a construction laden with interests born of our world's struggles for freedom, as among African Americans, as well as from the interests in freedom evident in first-century Palestine. These struggles for freedom are not just something addressable by a message of Jesus Christ; rather the struggles are themselves resources for unlocking the meaning of that message. Thus the theme of liberation, so desired by those involved in contemporary struggles for justice, becomes a hermeneutical key to the message's meaning.

We may note that this kind of argument does not entail claiming that a christology of liberation is *only* a projection of christologists' own emancipative interests, but it does acknowledge a key role played by our present emancipative interests in constructing christologies and theologies generally. It is not contradictory to argue, on the one hand, that emancipation should be christologically privileged because it is "a thing most needed today" and, on the other hand, that the tradition's apostolic witness and scripture narratives also "provide ample support for the christology and liberation that we are seeking."[72] What is characteristic of this second kind of argument is that it acknowledges the role played by our own present emancipative interests in privileging a christology of liberation from traditional materials.

3. A third kind of argument stresses liberation and emancipation as characteristic of the movement associated with Jesus. The notion of the cultural-political, intersubjective *movement* is crucial here. The "Jesus movement" or the early "Christian movement" (sometimes these two named movements are used interchangeably, sometimes not) becomes the matrix within which to locate the special christological concern with emancipation and liberation. Edward Schillebeeckx and Elisabeth Schüssler Fiorenza are just two examples of scholars who construct their christologies, to a significant extent, out of a study of these movements.

For both scholars the character of the individual Jesus plays a role, as the first kind of argument would stress. For both also, however, their own and their contemporaries' experiences play important roles for interpreting the meaning of these Christian movements: Schillebeeckx emphasizes the importance of contemporary negative experiences of unjust suffering in interpreting Christian tradition, while Schüssler Fiorenza acknowledges the role of her own "advocacy stance for the oppressed" in her tasks of historical reconstruction of these movements.[73] What these scholars add is a particularly close analysis of *the movement* associated with Jesus and the early church, which involves not only religious and existential factors, but social, political, and economic factors as well.

Schüssler Fiorenza is probably the clearest example of this kind of argument for the primacy of emancipation. Although the phrase "Jesus movement," which she employs so often, features the name Jesus, I think it fair to observe that the force of her text locates the proper subject of christology not in the individual figure of Jesus himself but in the intersubjective movement coalescing around Jesus that brings him to prominence, a movement involving women as well as men. The primacy of emancipation emerges in her texts through study of this movement as a complex amalgam of narrative text and historical action in ecclesial praxis.[74]

An important contribution of Schüssler Fiorenza's book, *In Memory of Her*, is that it provides a portrait of this movement in such rich detail, particularly as it attracted dispossessed groups, including significant numbers of women—in short, many whose lives featured a need for emancipation. For Schüssler Fiorenza, the emancipation called for by the Jesus movement taught a radically inclusive love of God embodied in an equally inclusive discipleship of equals, one focused especially on "(1) the destitute poor, (2) the sick and crippled, and (3) tax collectors, sinners and prostitutes."[75] The fruit and special character of such a communal praxis, for women, as well as for all other outcasts, is liberation from patriarchal structure and ethos. The centrality of liberation is clear when she summarizes the *basileia* of the Jesus movement and praxis as what "empowers us to walk upright, freed from the double oppression of societal and religious sexism and prejudice."[76]

Schüssler Fiorenza's christology of liberation emerges from reconstructions focusing on this intersubjective communal movement, a movement difficult to reconstruct and focus because, among other reasons, it was so quickly patriarchalized by later Christian movements that eventually also became canonized in the New Testament, especially in its deutero-Pauline literature.[77] The important point to underscore as distinctive of this mode of arguing for the primacy of emancipation is that one works from this movement as a dynamic sociohistorical praxis.

Cornel West may be correct in his claim that Schüssler Fiorenza herself fails consistently to think out of this sociohistorical movement and instead relies on an individual hero, Jesus, portrayed in her text as a " 'woman identified man' with a *basileia* vision of a discipleship of equals, as if a reincarnate Jesus would join the contemporary feminist struggle against patriarchy."[78] While West is right in noting that she does not engage in an expected "thorough interrogation" of Jesus' "patriarchal sensibilities," her attention to emancipation emerges from study of a whole host of figures, including not only Jesus but other women and men who individually and together constituted a force of critique, resistance, and emancipation in the early settings of Christianity.[79]

My own reasoning for giving primacy to emancipation in naming the sociohistorical dynamic proper to experience of Jesus Christ draws from each of these arguments. The primacy of emancipation can indeed be developed through direct discussion of the figure of Jesus, as of texts bearing witness to him, as marshalers of the first kind of argument have shown (black and Latin American liberation theologians, Hodgson, and others). However, as these formulators of the first kind of argument would also stress, the primacy of emancipation emerges not just because Jesus or the Bible "tells us so" but also because emancipation is needed by so many.

This need for emancipation has been impressed on me, as person and theologian, in a variety of ways. The need has been presented in this text not only in the Prologue, but also as integral to a hermeneutical "understanding" adequate for responding to our postmodern trilemma (chapters 1 and 2) and as a need that is theorizable in terms of at least the four forms of sexism, hetero-realism, classism and racism that I selected for treatment in chapters 3 and 4. In fact, this awareness of the need for emancipation is so important for constructing a christology of emancipation that I expect readers who do not have this awareness will find it difficult to privilege emancipation as the basic and pervasive christological effect.

I am most dependent, however, on the third kind of argument for privileging emancipation: the one that focuses on the nature of the complex early movements associated with Jesus or early Christianity. This is not because I think that the earliest is best. Indeed, my insistence that present emancipative interests and advocacies partially constitute our understanding of Jesus' person and of any Jesus movement contravenes that assumption. What is especially important about these movements is that they are aspects of Christian tradition that are intersubjective and sociohistorical. They show forth the identity of Christianity's founding and orienting shape as a dynamic praxis of sociohistorical, ecclesial life. Accordingly, the tradition, from which I take cues about the primacy of emancipation is not only a scholar's set of historical studies about Jesus himself, not the biblical narratives alone, or creeds and doctrines alone, but all of these as variously seen through the early sociohistorical movements. What I am arguing, furthermore, is that *a study of these early movements, within contexts of our awareness of contemporary systemic need, yields a primary emphasis on emancipation.* In order to have a resource in tradition, one that can provide an empowering mythos and a certain normative status, we who live and work with a set of urgent emancipative interests more readily find that resource of tradition, that orienting mythos, in the distinctive concerns of these movements.

The Bible's Emancipatory Message

As the previous section indicates, this christology and its emphasis on emancipation as its most important theme emerges from what is admittedly a very complex source — one that involves interpretations of (a) Jesus' person and work, (b) the interests of those claiming to be disciples of Jesus in past and present, and (c) the early movements coalescing around Jesus and his followers in culture and history.

With so complex a source for a christology of emancipation, one might ask what place there is for a biblical reading that supports such a christology. Actually, it is only now that I can fairly present such a reading. To do so earlier would have been to imply that the Bible's message is somehow available to us apart from our interests and interpretations, apart from our understanding and theoretical explanations of the human situation.

Now that I have presented these elements of my social location and interpretive and theoretical stance, I can sketch briefly the main lines of a reading of the Bible that is consonant with a privileging of the themes of emancipation or liberation. My intention here is not to provide a "biblical foundation" for a christology of emancipation or explore all the liberative elements that might be presented by biblical scholars. My aim is more modest: to provide readers of biblical texts with at least some sense that the privileged interest in freedom and emancipation is not simply a projection onto the texts, but also, in some meaningful sense, a trait of the texts themselves. All *exegesis*, is, in fact, *eisegesis*, but there remains a need to display the traits of the texts themselves that are consonant with one's interpretation.

It must be noted first that the Bible's diversity, as well as its sheer length, make it a source within which one can find almost whatever one likes.[80] True as this may be, I argue here that the biblical writings manifest a primary interest in the emancipation of the culturally and politically oppressed. In chapter 2 I have already made an argument for "the privilege of the oppressed" as necessary for the hermeneutics of a cultural-political theology. Here I attempt to show how such a privilege is a trait of the biblical writings themselves. To do this just in the area of biblical studies would require another book, indeed, a series of books. In this section, I will develop the main lines of an approach that is informed by Severino Croatto's important, if brief, 1987 work, *Biblical Hermeneutics: Toward a Theory of Reading as the Production of Meaning.*

The Bible's own privileging of the emancipation of oppressed groups emerges out of analyses of three dimensions of the biblical text: historical, structural, and thematic. I will begin with observations about the historical dimension and then move to the structural one. While treating the historical and structural dimensions, I will discuss how analyses of the Bible's thematic content suffuses them both.

In the historical dimension, we may note an important point made by Croatto. He examines what it is that makes the Bible so open to a liberative reading in spite of the fact that, as it has been handed down, it is "a book put together and structured, by and large, by a comfortable middle class generally alienated from the people."[81] His response is the general one that stresses the Bible's growth "in the origin of the Israelites as a people." It has its origin in the liberation process in which Israel's history is so emphatically embedded. Even if one acknowledges the complexity of the Exodus event as more than a cultural-political occurrence, as a religious event, the political overtones of Israel's deliverance cannot be ignored.[82]

Much of the thematic content of the Hebrew scriptures reflects this origin in the Exodus liberation. The Israelite notion of Yahweh, the God of the Hebrews, is inextricably bound up with their experience and remembrance of deliverance from slavery in Egypt. "In that context, the *savior* God is identified with the *liberator* God."[83] Moreover, this God is also the *creator* God. Better said, creation is the savior God's first salvific act.[84] The liberating/saving God is the One being borne witness to in the creation accounts. Among liberation theologians, Gustavo Gutiérrez has offered one of the clearest interpretations of the convergence of liberation and creation motifs in the Hebrew scriptures. He particularly notes how the Isaiah passages, when praising Yahweh, employ images that are at once images of creation *and* of liberation.[85]

In the very giving of the law, Yahweh is identified as One whose grace was manifested in political deliverance from Egypt. The decalogue's occurrence in Exodus 20 is introduced thus: "I am the Lord your God who brought you out of the land of Egypt, out of the house of bondage" (Exodus 20:2). Michael Welker has carefully shown just how powerful a mark the Exodus event leaves on the formation of Israel's legal, cultic, and mercy codes.[86] Welker in particular identifies the powerful impact on Israelite law worked by the well-known "motive clause": " 'You yourselves were strangers in the land of Egypt' — therefore you shall not take advantage of and oppress a stranger" (Exodus 22:21, 23:9).[87] Welker eloquently reformulates the message that resounds in Israel's laws of liberation:[88]

The legal gains that you might attain by exploiting the stranger are incommensurable with the loss of that liberation experience and the complex social identity that rests upon it. If you take the risk of this loss, your identity will become without history, socially isolated, undifferentiated, insensitive, disintegrated, hardened. You will become foreign to yourself and to others in a disastrous way.

Not only is the law thus related to a God whose key qualifying mark is the "bringing out" of a people from an oppressive land and house; also "the Jewish religious festivals, the prophetic critique of the breach of the covenant, the heralding of a new order of justice, the messianic hope, Jesus' proclamation — all these, too, recall and retrieve the 'memory' of the exodus as liberative content."[89] The many links between these various institutional practices and the Exodus event of liberation are too numerous to summarize here.[90] Suffice it to say, and it is no small point, that the liberative concern in the textual presentation of these diverse religious practices gives the thematic content of the Hebrew scriptures a profound and pervasive emancipatory interest. Not only are institutional practices and prophetic critique informed by this Exodus event, so also are the understandings of God as creator and savior. What is the bearing of this for Christian readers of the New Testament? In order to respond to this question, it is necessary to discuss the structural dimension of the biblical writings.

For analyzing the structural character of the biblical writings as a whole, Croatto draws from semiotics. Essential to this kind of analysis[91] is the identification of semantic axes, or axes of meaning that are recurring themes or motifs structuring a text as a whole.[92] The major semantic axis of the

Hebrew scriptures is developed within the "complexus" of religious practices, narrative themes, and ideas that are displayed in the texts of the Israelite people who act, speak, think, and pray along the way of their liberation process. In other words, the historical origin of the Hebrew people in an event of liberation unites the other notions of God as creator, savior, and lawgiver. With this uniting there occurs a formation in the text, across the biblical writings, of a complexus within which extensive meanings are crafted and within which there can be identified a semantic axis — a constellation of meaning characterized by the recurring motif of God's historic activity of liberating the oppressed.[93]

This semantic analysis discernible on the level of the text becomes, on the level of message, a kerygmatic axis, a recurring motif to be proclaimed and acted out. The identification of this kerygmatic axis is crucial because, according to Croatto's analysis, this kerygmatic axis of liberation is not only central to the Hebrew scriptures, but also "is then projected into the new [Testament] in the salvific message of Jesus addressed *preferentially* to the poor of every sort and manner — in his options for the poor, in his death as a prophet rejected for his words and deeds."[94]

Croatto admits that this "projection" of a kerygmatic axis of liberation from the Hebrew scriptures into the New Testament is not due simply to some vitality in the text. His semiotic analysis of the text is enveloped in a hermeneutics of texts that views them as part of the complex event of reading.[95] The projection of a kerygma of liberation from the Hebrew writings into the New Testament ones, therefore, is due also to the active interpretations of "flesh-and-blood readers"[96] who are in need of liberation and thus read with emancipatory interests. However the text, because it features the semantic and kerygmatic axes of liberation, gives itself to such contemporary readings, is consonant with it, and stimulates it. The text is not simply an epiphenomenon of readers' interests.

It is understandable, therefore, that Croatto can move on to identify the semantic axis of liberation in the New Testament texts, most programmatically in the striking scene of Luke 4:16–30, where "Jesus rereads as 'fulfilled' in himself, the great text of Isaiah 61:1–2 on the proclamation of the good news to the poor, the deliverance of captives, sight to the blind and freedom to the oppressed."[97] Croatto is aware that the many texts and symbols of the New Testament each possess a reservoir of meanings that makes any monolithic reading inadequate. He is not the only liberation theologian aware of this complexity. Juan Luis Segundo also notes that while the poor were central to Jesus' preaching and ministry in the synoptics, "that central theme seems to disappear completely in the christology ... of the first eight chapters of Paul's Letter to the Romans."[98] Croatto also emphasizes that there are biblical narrations that do not sit comfortably with the semantic axis of liberation.[99] If one looks closely at the semantic axis operating in the Bible as a totality, however, then the primacy of its message of liberation for the oppressed comes to the fore. The various biblical narratives then can be read as different variations on the theme of the power of the hope of liberation.[100] Even with the shift in context from Hebrew to New Testament scriptures, "the liberation message permeates the pages of the New Testament. And the theology of the exodus — sometimes, to be sure, at a distance — echoes once again."[101]

It is this kerygmatic axis of the text that is not only consonant with an emancipatory reading but invites it. In fact, following Croatto, we may say that those in need of liberation are those to whom the Bible "belongs" — not in the sense that the Bible is an object manipulatable by the poor, but because the poor are those most in need of what the Bible offers, those whose lives most readily awaken and are awakened by the textual message of liberation.

In other terms (again those of Croatto in conversation with Ricoeur), one might say that the poor live in "the forward of the text,"[102] the message it puts forth for those most in need and in search of it. This *forward* is much like that world *in front of* texts that I examined in chapter 2, though here the focus is on the biblical text's projected meanings of liberation. While this suggests that the Bible belongs particularly to those most in need of liberation, it is still a message addressed to all. No one is excluded, even the nonpoor, those with relative wealth and privilege. However, its message must be received by these latter in accord with the high profile that the Bible gives to God's preference for the oppressed.

The "forward" of the biblical text is a very complex notion. It does not refer simply to the intentions or beliefs of the poor as individual readers who live in front of their received texts; it also refers to their struggles to find voice and life, struggles that include cultural practices and political organizations. All of us, rich or poor, subjugated to the key oppressive practices of our day or not, come into contact with this struggle going on in the forward of that biblical text. This book, from its Prologue on, has reflected some awareness of that struggle. From the perspective of Croatto's biblical hermeneutics, I can acknowledge here that this book has been a labor not in the biblical text *per se*, but in its *forward*. As such, this study has its biblical dimension, even though I have not explicitly examined biblical texts in detail. But now, with this observation, all kinds of liberative readings of biblical texts are not only possible, but also necessary.

We need to return now to additional analyses of the emancipation that is traceable, and for which we search, in front of the text. More needs to be said about the nature of this emancipation, especially if it is to be understood as a liberation for women in situations where they are structurally oppressed.

Beyond the Pater Familias: Emancipation as "Structuring Freedom"

Since the emancipative action of the Christ comprises a sociohistorical dynamic, it has some additional distinctive structures that can be sketched through commentary on the term *emancipation*.

My use of the term may seem a linguistic sign of departure from contemporary movements and theologies that pivot around the term *liberation.* I do not intend any such departure. Although this christology of reconciliatory emancipation may depart from major methods and claims of certain liberation theologians, including their claims regarding the primary normative function of Jesus of Nazareth,[103] within the context of North American academy and society, I mean this to be a work consonant with the central claims and reorientations demanded by the liberation theologies.

There are no meanings of the word *emancipation* that prohibit it from including all the main concerns usually carried by the term *liberation.* Emancipation means a concrete struggle for freedom, one realized in struggle, hope, and sometimes in actual historical transformation. It is a *freedom from* those social and political sufferings that compounds for many groups the existential anguish and suffering that generally accrue to humankind. Moreover, it is a *freedom toward* new social and political structures in history, that occasion a new kind of community with other people and a new participation in the mystery we encounter pulsing in life and often sense to be more than or beyond the mix of personal, social, and political factors through which we experience that mystery. If this book were attending to what has traditionally been called a "doctrine of God," I would develop such doctrine in relation to the encounter of mystery as we participate in such sociohistorical matrices. For reasons that will become clearer in the final chapter, such doctrine would have to think quite rigorously, and against much of the tradition, in terms of the mystery of "God/ess." The main challenge of such a doctrine, formulated from female-specific images of the sacred, would be to preserve that mythic imagery's emancipative function in a way that is also reconciliatory, uniting the different genders and diverse peoples' needs for a variety of emancipations.[104] Here, the main concern is with a *christology* of emancipation. As I have presented it thus far, emancipation is a concrete "freedom from" and "freedom toward" that does not set aside any of the vital concerns of already presented liberation theologies.

There is a connotation of the term emancipation, however, that may be troubling, in particular a paternalistic connotation exemplified in such usages as "emancipation edict" or "emancipation declaration," official proclamations connoting that freedom is something bestowed or granted by a powerful leader or assembly of privileged leaders. In contrast, the liberation theologians have often stressed a view of freedom that accents the renewed agency of the oppressed.[105] One might be suspicious, therefore, that using the metaphor of emancipation for the Christ dynamic presumes a freedom for oppressed peoples only if and when it is bestowed by established powers.

This faulty connotation, while worth noting, need not prevent us from making use of the term, especially given its other valuable meanings, which I will lay out below. In the first place, it is possible to develop a matrix of significance for more desirable connotations, giving shape to emancipation in ways that avoid elitist, top-down interpretations of emancipatory practice. Christology's emancipatory discourse, therefore, must be developed as naming sociohistorical dynamics involving both established power structures and also the agency of grass-roots organizations among the oppressed themselves. In the second place, there are already signs suggesting that emancipation is being used in connection with oppressed people's own calls to agency. I think most readily of the calls to action issued to the poor by Jamaican reggae singer Bob Marley, in "Redemption Song": "Emancipate yourselves from mental slavery."[106]

We may now consider two important meanings of the term emancipation, which I will be expanding in the next chapter.

First, the term emancipation can be developed in a way that signifies people's release from the *patria potestas*, from the powers of the *pater familias*. The first entry among definitions of the term "emancipate" listed in the *Oxford English Dictionary* has this meaning. To emancipate is to draw freedom, usually for a child or a wife, from the powers of the *pater familias*. True, this is a meaning that presumes some of the specificities of Roman law. These specifics, however, were directly relevant to major issues that concerned participants in the Jesus movement, which writers as diverse in their views as Elisabeth Schüssler Fiorenza and Wayne Meeks have noted.[107] In addition, this meaning takes on added importance if we recall how both political and cultural theories of sexism reveal the extent of organized patriarchal power, even in our contemporary North Atlantic societies that are seemingly so distant from the cultures of Roman patriarchal household codes. Given the veritable explosion of literature offering diverse theories of the pervasiveness of sexism and of women's and children's subordination to patriarchal powers bigger than us all, a Christ dynamic that highlights a sociohistorical praxis of freedom as emancipation from the *patria potestas* and the *pater familias* remains a relevant and striking claim.

The Christ dynamic needs to be further developed, christologically, as a dynamic of emancipation for women and children from patriarchal power — not only from the blatant abuse of power exercised in rape, child abuse, and neglect, but also from the socially sanctioned assumptions that the lives of women and children (and all of us) depend primarily or exclusively on the exercise of male authority and male leadership. This is not to rule out completely the exercise of male authority and leadership in given situations, but it is to experience freedom from the now-pervasive set of practices that still privilege, value, and make more likely men's assumption of power. Since this assumption of power is usually gained by men through acts of differentiation and abstraction from women and from the household worlds to which women are still largely consigned, this Christ dynamic means an emancipation of women from the patriarchal consignment to domestic spheres and an entry into new kinds of power arrangements in which women's involvement in reproductive labor does not mean loss of the power or the wealth necessary to meet their needs.

The Christ dynamic thematized as emancipation from the *pater familias* is also emancipative for men. For them, it may be an emancipation *from* the isolation, separation, and abstraction from body-to-body caregiving and *into* new kinds of power disbursements and practices in which the formation of a male identity hinges less on competition and the establishment of a sharply differentiated ego and more on mutual cooperation and on an ego identity distinguished by its mode of entry into ever-new configurations of solidarity and alliance.

Utopian? To be sure, it is, especially so if we recall that the patriarchal oppressions of sexism are interlocked with other distinctive modes of oppression that include hetero-realism, classism, racism, and others. But christology, insofar as it hopes for a salvific transformation of any evil, be it existential anguish or political oppression, has always featured elements of the utopian in its project of hope.[108] The project of hope does not only mean waiting. It means that, but it also means envisioning and dreaming in a way that entails working. The real challenge to a christology is not whether it might be labeled utopian. That is a charge we Christians will always have with us. The real challenge is whether what we aim for is complex and large enough to resist dismissal by a humanity that suffers a complex and enormous need.

To link the Christ dynamic to emancipation from the *pater familias* is often viewed as subordinating christology to a one-issue framework, to a marginalized "camp" that somehow fails to include the full human predicament. That concern can only arise from someone whose horizon of understanding is shaped by a position of dominance that feels nonprivileged by this theology. Actually, what more encompassing standpoint can there be than one that stays attentive to the needs of women and children for emancipation? If one wants to think in numbers, we do well to recall that over two-thirds of the world's economically disenfranchised are women and children.[109]

More significantly, if we recall the theorizeable connections between sexism and other systemic distortions explored in chapter 4, we are reminded that highlighting emancipation from the *patria potestas* unleashes concern with a whole range of freedoms. Just to recall some of the interlockings explored in chapter 4, the male abstraction from women and children, and its deleterious consequences, is connected to the abstraction characteristic of exchange economies that perpetuate classism and relates also to the alienation from gender and body in hetero-realism and to the abstraction from one's body, color, and "dirt" that in part feeds white supremacist logics. To formulate christology as emancipation from the *patria potestas* does not automatically mean that nothing more needs to be formulated regarding other forms of oppression. It does mean that to begin with emancipation from patriarchal powers is not at all to stake theology to a narrow project. Rather it is to think Christian freedom concretely, within a tangle of vast, interlocking needs. A christology that remembers the lives of women and children, these so frequently dismembered ones, seeks to address human need at its most radical, far-reaching levels.

We can note a second important meaning of emancipation. As several entries in the *Oxford English Dictionary* again make clear, to emancipate has an official or juridical meaning. I commented on the danger of construing emancipation as an official elite's bestowal of freedom rather than including an oppressed people's own actions of agency toward freedom. The official or juridical dimensions of the term provide the conditions for this unfortunate interpretation. The juridical sense may convey a legal and elitist connotation. In addition to the criticisms I have already made of that interpretation, however, I now suggest that the official or juridical senses can be developed christologically in a much more productive direction.

The official and juridical senses of emancipation can give the term a concrete, sociopolitical character. As the several dictionary entries on the word *emancipate* state, the person set free is done so *sui juris*, as one capable of assuming legal responsibilities and having legal power and functions in the structures of the polis.[110] As with the word *liberate,* to emancipate concerns a release, but it is a release focused especially on the structural mechanisms by which freedom is seized or granted and by which freedom is sustained. Emancipation links the salvific praxis of Christ to action and thought that seeks liberation as not only a *release* from oppressive structures but also a *restoration of structures* of freedom that weave together revolution and duration for the creating and sustaining of liberation.

Emancipation is structured and structuring freedom. As such, a christology of emancipation is challenged to call not just for a general emancipation for all but also for particular emancipations of those sufferers of systemic oppression in the christologist's own period. This does not necessarily mean linking christology to particular institutional forms and practices. It does mean shaping christology so that it is clear *whose* freedom is intended and *what kind of freedoms* are needed. Responding to these questions christologically is to develop freedom structurally in ways that may then invite strategic discussions about institutional practices and arrangements.

My very selection of oppressions and distortions for this project—sexism, hetero-realism, classism, racism, and ethnocentrism—suggests how specific categories of a christology of emancipation might be developed toward a structured and structuring freedom. In the final chapter, I will press emancipation language further in order to name specific emancipative practices that respond to these particular oppressions. There I will attempt to refigure christology's mythos in ways that specifically address the distortions of our time.

THE RECONCILIATORY PROVISO

Giving structural specificity to emancipation involves Christian faith and practice in ideological movements and commitments. This I do not deny, nor do I wish to deny it. Among established North Atlantic Christians and theologians there has often been a concern to "de-ideologize," to remove Christian faith from the realm of ideology. Insofar as people are politicized creatures with political and ideological dimensions of the worldview and ethos inhering in their sociohistorical location, however, people never extricate themselves from ideology, no matter how emphatically they seek to separate their faith from it, no matter how many ideologies they "de-mystify" or subject to "ideology-critique."[111] The real question for a christology of emancipation that structures freedom in particular ways is not *whether* it is ideological, but *what kinds of ideologies* it chooses to develop for Christian praxis. When the latter question is asked, it becomes especially important to look at the way various ideological commitments to structures of emancipation function in relation to other needs for emancipation.

It is precisely this will to analyze diversity and variety amid one's commitments to emancipation that is a mark of what might be termed the "reconciliatory proviso." As I discussed earlier, the Christ dynamic is not just emancipation. It is *that*, even primarily, but emancipation is always qualified by a necessary and pervasive reconciliatory posture. While the force of the Christ, as sociohistorical dynamic, is indeed for the emancipation of those who are the distinctive sufferers of classism, hetero-realism, sexism, and racism, and while their emancipation may involve conflict (involving uses of power employed in nonviolent action, as well as, conceivably, even a choice for violence in already violence-ridden contexts), the Christ dynamic as I am constructing it is marked by a startling openness to others, to diversity, to difference, even to "the other" who is enemy. The emancipation of the oppressed can never be subordinated to this reconciliatory openness to others, but neither can it be championed in a way that completely ignores the tasks of making-one, of reconciling within a differentiated humanity. We may insist that freedom making is primary while insisting that union making should be intended along the way. The reconciliatory proviso can both qualify and contribute to emancipation in three ways.

First, its valuation of difference and variety in ever-new community fosters openness to a diversity of oppressions. The Christ dynamic's force for emancipation must address a manifold of oppressions. While Christian theologies of emancipation and liberation may specialize in particular oppressions, it is a mark of *reconciliatory* emancipation to acknowledge the diversity of oppressions and to seek discourses of Christian emancipation that are relevant to those different forms of oppression and help address the interconnectedness of these oppressions. Emancipation thematized and practiced with such a spirit of openness to the manifold types and relations of oppressions is working under a reconciliatory proviso.

Second, the reconciliatory posture that continually celebrates difference also keeps theologies of emancipation aware of the role of diverse social locations and cultural contexts. Classism, to give an obvious example, cannot be resisted with the same theological discourse of emancipation for the Kikuyu of Kenya as for the poor ladinos and Amerindians of Latin America. The reconciliatory posture can help keep a cultural-political theology of emancipation from forcing crude generalizations about needs for emancipation. With respect to sexism, for another example, the needs for emancipation have to be developed out of respect for differences between the cultural and historical heritages of Caucasian and African American women in North America. It is almost a commonplace now to recognize that in North American Christian feminism, critiques of sexism and envisioned liberations for black and white women involve very different dynamics.[112] A reconciliatory posture in the Christ dynamic, along with the primary drive toward emancipation, respects and even cultivates such differences. The reconciliatory posture keeps Christians' emancipatory discourse clothed with "thick description"; that is, close-textured analyses of particular needs and forms of emancipation.

Third, the reconciliatory posture includes an openness toward, and intending of community with, even "the other" who is enemy. The call to love the enemy, for which there is warrant not only in the New Testament narratives but also in some early Christian movements, can be affirmed even amid the great pain oppressed peoples carry, and which leads them to cause pain to their oppressors while seeking their own emancipation. If oppressor groups use the call to love the enemy to mitigate the force of the oppressed's resistance against them, the call to love the enemy is being misused.

Liberation theologians have provided a vision for the proper use of the command to love the enemy. In opting for the poorest of the earth, there is of course a vigorous resistance against oppressors (violent or nonviolent). However, liberation theologians stress that Christian thought and practice of emancipation should also include an openness and invitation to the enemy oppressor. The link between a primary preference for emancipation of the earth's poorest with a reconciliatory openness, even to the enemy, has been reformulated by Gustavo Gutiérrez in the most recent edition of his work, *A Theology of Liberation*:

The universality of Christian love is, I repeat, incompatible with the exclusion of any persons, but it is not incompatible with a preferential option for the poorest and most oppressed. When I speak of taking into account social conflict, including the existence of the class struggle, I am not denying that God's love embraces all without exception. Nor is anyone excluded from our love, for the gospel requires that we love even our enemies; a situation that causes us to regard others as our adversaries does not excuse us from loving them. There are oppositions and social conflicts between diverse factions, classes, cultures, and racial groupings, but they do not exclude respect for persons, for as human beings they are loved by God and are constantly being called to conversion.[113]

In the first English edition, Gutiérrez commented on a citation from Giulio Girardi:

"The liberation of the poor and the liberation of the rich are achieved simultaneously." One loves the oppressors by liberating them from their inhuman condition as oppressors, by liberating them from themselves. But this cannot be achieved except by resolutely opting for the oppressed, that is by combatting the oppressive class. It must be a real and effective combat, not hate.[114]

In these articulations the reconciliatory proviso in the Christ dynamic operates with a necessary and powerful impact, without compromising the primacy of emancipation. Here also, I suggest, is a hope for the freedom of oppressors. Oppressors' suffering is not like that of the oppressed, but there is a sense in which oppressors, too, are enslaved by the systems of enslavement through which they oppress others. A full freedom for the oppressed would also mean genuine freedom for their oppressors, despite the hardship for oppressors that such full emancipation would bring. The reconciliatory proviso helps keep Christians envisioning that full kind of hope — that time when oppressors will also be emancipated through their being given the grace to live for and with the oppressed.

In sum, *reconciliatory emancipation* is the name proposed for a revisioned christology. "Christ," as an intersubjective, sociohistorical force with this special character, may seem a "rough beast," especially in comparison with the tradition's allegedly clear and distinct lines fixing on the individual figure of Jesus. In this chapter I have tried to show why the christopraxis of this work and its soteriological interests drive toward an empowering Christian mythos that is still "slouching toward Bethlehem," one that is arising not just from the figure of Jesus himself but also from contemporary appropriations of the Jesus movement. The particularity of the Christ who meets us in that way is an ecclesial praxis named "reconciliatory emancipation." By means of that notion, I have sought to appropriate Christian tradition in a way intended to navigate our period's struggle with both political domination and difference.

This navigation involved giving primacy to emancipation from domination as a structuring freedom that begins with an emancipation of those oppressed by the *patria potestas* and extends ultimately to all who suffer the ill effects of other interlocking oppressions. The reconciliatory element, though secondary in significance to emancipation, is necessary to emancipation and constitutes a Christian response to difference and plurality.

The coalescence of a manifold emancipation with a necessary, though not primary, reconciliatory posture amid differences, is not a frequent occurrence. When it happens, given all the hard labor and time it requires, its presence, however fragmentary, is heavily laden with a sense of mystery and gift. This mystery and gift—occurring, I stress, within a sociohistorical dynamic but still mystery and gift—are constitutive of a transcending[115] element, an impulse toward realization of something new and healing in contemporary life. It is in hope of this that all our efforts at connecting and remembering are undertaken. It must be in hope that such efforts are undertaken, for the Christ dynamic I have presented here is like most presentations of the Christ event by Christian theologians: both already underway, here and there, fragmentarily, and also "not yet," awaiting realization, still shrouded in mystery, a gift to be hoped for.

It is somewhat premature, however, for theological praise of a transcending mystery and gift. An understanding of reconciliatory emancipation requires still further revisioning for our time, a refiguring of categories especially pertinent for today's christological discourse. That is, a full-orbed christology of reconciliatory emancipation entails some specific emancipatory tasks that I now move to develop in the final chapter.

6

CHRISTUS MATER

Refiguring Christ for Today's Christopraxis

*If the first woman God ever made was strong enough to turn the world
upside down, all alone—these together ought to be able to turn it back
and get it rightside up again: and they is asking to do it. The men better
let 'em.*

Sojourner Truth, 1851

Sojourner Truth's quotation could be misused for placing the burden of
all transformative work of reconciliatory emancipation on women. Here I
issue no such call. The refiguring of christology is men's work as well as
women's, and christopraxis is something in which both participate. The
quotation does signal my proposal that collaborating theologians might well
begin with and be prompted by women's labor for their own and others'
emancipation.

In the context of christology, this means acknowledging and developing
links between the Christ dynamic in history and the sociohistorical emancipation of women. This connection may be developed in many ways, especially in our own times. In this final chapter, I will discuss several of these
ways, especially as they work to resist and redress structural oppressions.

The work of this chapter, then, is a further development of the revisioning undertaken in the previous chapter. There the concern was to revision
Christ as pertaining to a dynamic, sociohistoric praxis larger and more
complex than the individual figure of Jesus. Now the concern is to refigure
Christ still further, with the distinctive concerns of our period in view.

By "refiguring," I mean, first, a restructuring of christology so that
its subject matter—the Christ dynamic of reconciliatory emancipation—
addresses specific structural emancipations. By refiguring I also mean certain efforts to remythologize: identifying and developing those mythic
expressions, images, "figures," that attach the empowering qualities of
mythos to the requisite emancipatory processes. In both of these ways, there
is a refiguring of Christ for today's christopraxis, and this can be done

wherever there is a need for reconciliatory emancipation. We can affirm, and indeed hope for, christologies and whole theologies refigured to address the bondages of the aged and of children in our societies, of those differently abled because of physical injury, of Chicano/a, Hispanic, Asian-American groups in North American societies, and of Native Americans whose bondage has gone hand-in-glove with the Caucasian seizure of North American territories. For all these and more who are within the horizons of our christopraxis, reconciliatory emancipation is needed, demanding a refiguring of the Christ dynamic.

The refiguring I attempt here is conditioned by the selection and theorizations of structural oppression that have come before. I will be limiting my refiguring to the needs for reconciliatory emancipation posed by sexism, hetero-realism, classism, racism, and ethnocentrism. As I have underscored repeatedly, this is a particular selection of emancipative interests, but they are so systemic in character that they not only interlock with one another but also open out onto other distortions I am not explicitly addressing in this work: ageism, militarism, pollution of the nature system. The aim of this chapter is to refigure Christ for today's christopraxis in view of my five selected distortions.

CHRISTUS MATER

Before I discuss what the Christ of reconciliatory emancipation may be for each of the selected structural oppressions, I want to present a theologian's root metaphor that will guide subsequent refiguring for addressing those interlocking oppressions: *Christus Mater*. It is a metaphor intentionally crossing wires that are usually not crossed in Western traditions and theologies. It is a metaphor that conjoins the maternal powers of women (whether these are actualized or not) with the Christ taken by the traditions as locus of divinity and of salvific efficacy. It is an image for theologians, keeping them alert to the reality of convergence between christic ultimacy and womanform.

I suggest *Christus Mater* as metaphor for the distinctive character of what reconciliatory emancipation must become if there are to be movements of release from the sexism, heterosexism, classism, and racism of so much North Atlantic culture. *Christus Mater* is proposed as a "root" metaphor because its conjoining of the sacred with women's maternal powers, although refracted in different ways, provides a basic orientation for most of this chapter's refiguring. By risking the thought that "Christ is Mother," I am suggesting that to take seriously the Christ in our time is to take seriously the mother. "To take seriously the mother" is itself a phrase heavily laden with meanings that require elaborating. To take the mother seriously includes, but means far more than, simply respecting one's female parent. The latter by itself easily becomes trivialized into the kind of sentimentalized and only occasional reverence voiced on many a North American Mother's Day. To take the mother seriously here will mean a pervasive refiguration that characterizes the whole sociohistorical dynamic of reconciliatory emancipation in our time. Its meaning is developed by an important emancipative process that I will comment on in more depth later as "maternalization." *Christus Mater* is a root metaphor, then, for a general maternalization of human community and nature that is emancipatory for women in struggle against sexism, but also for a maternalization that includes the materialization of all creation's hopes for emancipation from that which enchains it, pollutes it, destroys it.

Please hear me. I know I run the risk of troubling a great many readers. This will be true for those who believe that it is part of some "scandal of particularity," which Christians just need to accept, that christology should occur in a male code. Others may be troubled too, especially feminists who sense in this metaphor of *Christus Mater* yet one more glorification/deification of mothers that is in fact a *reduction* of women *to* their reproductive functions. Christian feminists instead often prefer female-specific images that are not primarily maternal ones—images like *Sophia*, God/ess, or Christa.[1] All of these are, indeed, necessary images for christological refiguration, not only for resisting sexism but for dealing with other distortions as well.

I am arguing, however, that a mythic revaluation of maternal powers is also essential to Christian feminism. By themselves, without a maternal referent, I am not sure that womanform images of the sacred can successfully challenge the misogynous mythos and ethos of our culture, especially insofar as it is also a matricidal mythos and ethos.[2] I know not all women are mothers and that we must resist every patriarchal attempt to reduce women to mothering functions. True as this is, in a culture in which the oppression of women, whether they are mothers or not, is bound up with repression and fear of connectedness with the mother, it becomes strategically necessary for a christology of reconciliatory emancipation to link salvific emancipation with a sacral revaluing of maternal experience.

Because mothers tend to be the primary care givers in our culture, because of the unsettling mysteries (especially for patriarchal culture) of women's capacity for childbirth, because as our source mothers have kept us reminded of our finitude, of our "existence as a mere speck, a weak, blind, clot of flesh growing inside her body"—because of all this, the mother in our North Atlantic patriarchal societies and religions has become the object of formidable resistance and hostility. We must keep insisting on women's choice as to whether, when, and how they take on mothering roles, without allowing this insistence to lessen our struggles for the revaluation of mothering in a matriphobic society.[3]

This calls for creating a mythos and reflection that attempt to reverse, or at least resist, matricidal impulses. Of course, no new mythos by itself reverses or resists structural oppression. Sexism and the other distortions are not just linguistic challenges calling for a redressing mythic language.

However, oppressive mythic language is a reinforcing part of the oppressive praxis, and new mythic languages, with their accompanying reflection, need to become a reinforcing part of an emancipative christopraxis. *Christus Mater* is a metaphor that already guides some Christian women's and men's experiences of worship,[4] and I am here proposing it as a metaphor to guide theologians in their conjoining of what centuries of patriarchal religion and contemporary patriarchal practice would prefer to separate: christic ultimacy in history and women's maternal power and sexuality.

Many dangers are implicit in the sacral revaluing of women's maternal power. Because of these dangers, I have been hesitant to urge such a revaluation. *Christus Mater* may unfortunately be seized upon, as I have already acknowledged, as a reduction of women to solely mothering roles and functions, or as a reduction of their sexuality to reproductive powers. This metaphor may also be misunderstood as having only to do with women and not other people's issues and concerns (as if women were not always already related to those others!). Further, especially in North America's individualistic milieu, maternal imagery can lead to a sacralizing of individual mothers as heroines to merely complement or counter patriarchal heroes. In this chapter, I may come perilously close to these dangers in my christological reconstruction. But because misogyny is so pervasively matricidal, we need to risk revaluing the maternal, seeking to do so in ways that ward off the foreseeable dangers. Revaluations of the maternal usually run the risk of reinforcing sexist idealizations of motherhood. However, as Audrey McKinney and Mary L. Shanley remind us, "feminists must risk arming the enemy if feminism is to fulfill its liberatory potential and to be more than a call for equal rights, equal opportunity, or even economic redistribution."[5]

The theologian's root metaphor, *Christus Mater,* especially if left untranslated from the Latin for the time being, is fruitfully ambiguous. Its etymological and semantic features prompt women-specific imagistic thinking (maternal or not) in ways that connect with processes and issues we often do not associate with woman-specific concerns. Relating Christ, as a sociohistorical dynamic of reconciliatory emancipation, to *Mater,* is, to give one example, to implicate the Christ's salvific praxis not only in "maternal" care-providing functions, but also in the "material" needs of humanity and nature. *Mater,* the verbal form common to "maternal" and "material," has a still more expansive set of meanings. *Mater* is an Aryan root word for both "mother" and "measurement," giving rise to such English derivatives as matrix, matter, metric, as well as material and maternal. I suggest that to join *Christus* with *mater* is to focus divine transforming process in relation to a fabric of need that, if left unaddressed, threatens the material/sexual/ social/ecological/political matrix of peoples' lives together. I mean for the root metaphor of *Christus Mater* to provoke a sense of the christic emancipation of women's reproductive powers from matricidal repression, which also can be developed as an emancipation of others from related repressions.

Rendering the root metaphor for our christological efforts as "Christ as mother" or "Christ mother" certainly has some historical precedent and ably signals the maternal dimension of the Christ dynamic. But by itself, "Christ as mother" does not readily, in most contemporary contexts of discourse, provoke thought about all the dimensions in the matrix of christic transformation that we need to address in our time. For orienting the christologist's reconstructive task, I prefer here the untranslated root metaphor, *Christus Mater*.

"Christ our mother" might indeed be a usable image, alongside other kinds of images, including other female-specific images.[6] Given the active political/social/sexual roles of mothers in Latin American contexts, I actually find a Spanish rendering *Christus Madre*, or better, *Christus Co-Madres*, as more ably signaling the inclusive yet woman-focused features of the Christ dynamic as a movement of reconciliatory emancipation.[7] In the movements of *los madres de los desaparecidos* (the mothers of the disappeared), for example, there is a structured grass-roots organization not only on behalf of women's lost children and spouses, but often also on behalf of the sexual and reproductive freedom of women and of widespread social and political reforms.[8] *Christus Madre* or *Christus Co-Madres*[9] are two of many possible refigurations of Christ as reconciliatory emancipation. Their special power and desirability resides in their possessing a surplus of meanings from the *Christus Mater* metaphor.

In order to develop the inclusive logic of the theologian's *Christus Mater* metaphor, and guide the many possible refigurations in the form of *Christus Co-Madres*, "Sophia," "midwife," and many others, I propose a restructuring of christological categories. The rest of this chapter will be shaped in terms of such categories.

If we are to move our christological reflection closer to the demands of our contemporary christopraxis, I propose that the salvific praxis I have already named reconciliatory emancipation be further named as involving five particularized salvific dynamics. Let me simply announce what these dynamics are and which kinds of distortion they are designed to address. I will present four tasks of emancipation and one all-pervasive reconciliatory task. In the chapter's subsequent discussion of them, we will see the development of an expansive logic generated by the theologians' root metaphor, *Christus Mater*.

First, when in this chapter I articulate emancipation as *maternalization*, I am attempting to focus a resistance against sexism. When emancipation is, second, conceived as *sensualization*, it is a task primarily resisting heterosexism. Third, emancipation focused as an *emancipating of blackness* in Christian practice and theological discourse is a way to resist North American racism. Fourth, as *materialization*, emancipation can be thematized as a resistance to the distortions of classism. Each of these four emancipatory tasks is then enriched by a resistance to all ethnocentrism through a reconciliatory posture that is one of *admiration and liminality*. Taking together these four tasks of emancipation, as qualified by the reconciliatory posture that strengthens each task of emancipation, yields the meanings of reconciliatory emancipation for our time.

The terms I use here for identifying specific processes of reconciliatory emancipation (maternalization, sensualization, emancipating blackness, materialization, admiration/liminality) may at first seem cumbersome. I suggest, however, that they are no more so than a number of other theological terms we theologians are accustomed to using: salvation, reconciliation, liberation, regeneration, et al. Some such words as those seem necessary if we are to push christological, and ultimately theological, reflection toward closer and sustained engagement with the demands of our time. Yes, they are long words and reify life-giving processes; but they are important for marshaling thought about current needs for reconciliatory emancipation.

This chapter's major sections are devoted to each of these specific dynamics of reconciliatory emancipation. I begin with a discussion of the reconciliatory dynamic, then take up the four dynamics of emancipation. The reconciliatory dynamic, which I have named "admiration and liminality" in order to elaborate its unique way of seeking alliance amid the differences (cultural, religious, social, sexual, individual/personal) that keep us steeped in the quandaries of pluralism, is one I treat first because it is a posture attending and pervading each of the tasks of the primary christological concern: emancipation. In my comments about reconciliatory emancipation in chapter 5, I have already generally called for the reconciliatory concern to serve this subordinate but necessary and pervasive function in relation to emancipation. I begin, then, with the reconciliatory postures of admiration and liminality in order to later invoke them as needed when treating the major dynamics of emancipation.

MEETING CHRIST AMID DIFFERENCE: THE WAYS OF ADMIRATION AND LIMINALITY

The general purpose of this section is to show how experiences of Christ address the experiences of difference. What does it mean to meet Christ within contemporary experiences of difference, whether considering the differences between men and women, between a member of a Yoruban society in Africa and a Tzututil peasant in Guatemala, or between North Americans and Central Americans? In this section, I propose two terms for clarifying the nature of the Christian reconciliatory postures toward difference: *admiration* and *liminality*. Together these will qualify the specific christic emancipations that I will present in subsequent sections of this chapter.

Admiration is the term reserved especially for an affirmation of the other in her, his or their particular differences. Admiration entails affirming not just the difference of "the other," but also the differential traits of the one(s) who claim to identify and encounter "the others." If I portray Esperanza and her Zapotec world as "other," for example, admiration also involves affirming and exploring my own otherness, my own differentiating traits, as well as exploring those of her world. In this way, admiration affirms and cultivates difference.

Liminality is the term I reserve for the kind of life known "betwixt and between" differentiated persons, groups or worlds. This is an experience of the wonder, the disorientation and discomfort that can arise when one is suspended between or among different groups or persons. For example, in admiring Esperanza's Zapotec world and in affirming the differences between our worlds, I am in part pulled out of my world, challenged to enter a "liminal self-conscious world between cultures."[10]

I will suggest that both admiration and liminality need to be thought of together for an adequate Christian response to contemporary experiences of difference. Without an identification and affirmation of concrete differences through admiration, liminality becomes a free-floating and disengaged mode of living and thinking. Liminality here becomes sheer dismembering play, without a capacity to ally differentiated parties in new concrete interactions. Conversely, without the sense of suspension, shock, and disorientation that characterizes liminality, admiration would be little more than a compilation of differences, of incommensurable worlds. Admiration here would be without a capacity to move beyond identifying differences and into the kind of beneficial play needed to foster alliances between different groups and persons.

Both the sources from which I draw these two terms (admiration from French thinker Luce Irigaray, liminality from anthropologist Paul Rabinow) keep united the dynamics of admiration and liminality, even though they may themselves use only one of the terms. Rabinow, for example, writes mainly of liminality, but implicit in this notion for him are the characteristics of admiration.

Below, I will further discuss these two postures generally and then show how they can be understood as Christian postures.

The Reconciliatory Postures of Admiration and Liminality

I draw the term *admiration* from Luce Irigaray's writings on sexual difference, but I suggest that it appropriately applies to a general posture toward difference implied by reconciliatory emancipation. Irigaray explains the term as "What has never existed between the sexes. Admiration, keeping the two sexes unsubstitutable in the fact of their difference. Maintaining a free and engaging space between them, a possibility of separation and alliance."[11]

In discussions of "male feminism," this admiration has been proposed as one adequate response by men against sexism, a response that is a way of men viewing and acting toward women. It is a difficult response to make, because it requires an acknowledgment of gender difference, even a celebration of the otherness of women, without a confinement of women to restrictive gender roles and without a romanticization of woman as "the noble other" who all too often becomes the "exploited other."[12]

My own remembering of Esperanza, especially as I deal with its sexual encoding, is one example of this quest for admiration of women's difference. I can never claim, either through my memories or my dwelling as a neighbor in her *adobe* town's dwelling, that I am in union with her and her world. Her difference remains, and always was. Yet there was also a sharing—better, in Irigaray's language, an *alliance*—that somehow rested on the fact of her difference. If this memory and its intersecting memories have a more general, sexual or gender coding, the search for such an alliance extends to the wider network of relating with women family members, friends, and colleagues. The aim is not so much union or oneness; that is usually the rhetoric of relationships in which difference and identities are extinguished. The aim is more an alliance—an authentic participation in and with the other in which life together involves a surprising kind of engaging that is occasioned by difference.

This alliance, I suggest, is not only the aim of the sexes seeking co-participation with each other. It is also the aim for understanding relations, typically called "solidarity,"[13] between classes, people of different sexual orientation, different "races" and ethnic traditions, different religions. Sometimes we members of affluent communities—who also possess the benefits of male privilege, heterosexual "respectability," and Caucasian ethnic identities—claim a union of solidarity with those different from us, those who are systematically exposed to sexism, racism, heterosexism, and classism. It is an inauthentic co-opting of these others, however, to claim such a union if we do so without attending to the real differences. For example, for an affluent person to claim "solidarity" with "the poor" is inauthentic without coming to terms with the particular differences between worlds of affluence and poverty. Sometimes "the other" needs to be freed from the way we take him or her to be different, because our conception of their differences is an ill-informed stereotype. At other times, their differences need to be valued, celebrated in all their unsubstitutability, affirmed as both an obstacle and contribution to authentic co-participation, alliance with others.

Irigaray's reading is a rereading of Descartes' *Les passions de l'ame* and portrays admiration as "the sudden surprise of the new and the different that precedes objectification of the others as this or that quality, this or that characteristic."[14] The task of admiration is to live in and think out of this wonder at one's own and others' difference, to open up those spaces of radical difference that are not the old differences and that accent difference in all its particularity so that alliance occurs.

Admiration, despite some of its unfortunate connotations (perhaps it is too passive in connotation, or otherwise problematic, as in "her admirers"), I propose as a contemporary expression of Christians' reconciliatory approach to contemporary differences. Especially as developed by Irigaray, it heightens one's sense of difference (including conflict and confrontation) while doing so in ways that facilitate co-participation.

The dynamics of liminality are implicit within Irigaray's definition of admiration, particularly when she writes of "maintaining a free and engaging space between them [here, the "two sexes"], a possibility of separation and alliance." This space between, which is free and engaging and holds the possibility for both separation and alliance, is the domain of liminality. In order to clarify the dynamics operative in this liminal space, I propose turning to an example from anthropologist Paul Rabinow's intercultural experience. As Richard Bernstein has suggested, anthropology is crucial to philosophy and many other disciplines, especially because its fieldworking practice provides an excellent context within which to analyze the dynamics of knowing and communicating in the face of seemingly incommensurable differences.[15]

In his book, *Reflections on Fieldwork in Morocco*, Rabinow comments on his relationship to his informant, Ali, and thereby discloses the shifting terrain of liminality in intercultural practice.

Under my systematic questioning, Ali was taking realms of his own world and interpreting them for an outsider. This meant that he, too, was spending more time in this liminal, self-conscious world between cultures. This is a difficult and trying experience—one could almost say it is "unnatural"—and not everyone will tolerate its ambiguities and strains.

This was the beginning of the dialectic process of fieldwork. I say dialectic because neither the subject nor the object remains static. . . . With Ali there began to emerge a mutually constructed ground of experience and understanding, a realm of tenuous common sense which was constantly breaking down, being patched up, and re-examined, first here, then there.

As time wears on, anthropologist and informant share a stock of experiences upon which they hope to rely with less self-reflection in the future. The common understanding they construct is fragile and thin, but it is upon this shaky ground that anthropological inquiry proceeds.[16]

Four elements of Rabinow's passage can be elaborated to clarify the notion of liminality, and these assist us in understanding better the experience of this Christian reconciliatory posture.

First, the "liminal self-conscious world between cultures" which Rabinow discusses is characterized by questioning. This questioning is not simply the raising of just any question (though the haphazard, groping, and awkward queries are often also essential to fieldwork). It is a dialectical process of systematic questioning. As dialectical, questioning in this liminal world is aimed to reveal the valuable biases of the questioner and the questioned. Dialectical questioning in fieldwork breaks the barriers of the questioner's world by highlighting the particularity of each party in the dialogue.[17] Through such questioning in fieldwork, as Gadamer writes about questioning in conversation generally, the real unity that makes intercultural understanding possible emerges from a play of question and answer that focuses differences.[18] To the final page of his book, Rabinow is aware of the crucial role of otherness, and yet this otherness is not completely opaque; it is the very means to alliance with those who are other.[19] Here, within Rabinow's notion of liminality, is admiration, an affirmation of otherness, the insistence on what Irigaray termed "unsubstitutable difference."[20] However, other elements of Rabinow's notion of liminality show what is operative in liminality.

He emphasizes, secondly, that the liminal world is a mutually constructed one. "Neither the subject nor the object remains static." In fact, it is no longer right to speak of subject comporting with an object. More accurately, we see a mutually constructive activity that is a play of subjects, ultimately a play of subjects who are each embedded in their own historical and cultural situations. Any knowledge of the other that the anthropologist is able to disclose is mutually constructed by them and the ones they describe.

Third, the liminal world is shared. As Rabinow puts it, through the questions and actions of both subjects seeking to accent differences, there is an alliance. There is for both a "stock of experiences upon which they hope to rely with less self-reflection in the future." Elsewhere, Rabinow writes that through the play of question and answer, a "doubling of consciousness" occurs. Both anthropologist and Ali become conscious not only of their own cultural and linguistic worlds, but also of the liminal world that is born between them and through encounter with each other's self-reflection.[21] In the active process of making crucial space between each other by highlighting their differences, they are caught up in shared webs of signification spun in their dialogical encounter.[22]

Lest we think this shared web is some common ground, we must note how Rabinow qualifies the sense of unity with the other in the liminal world. It is a realm of only "tenuous common sense." The liminal world's common understanding is fragile and thin. Rabinow stands, at best, on shaky ground that is always "breaking down, being patched up, and re-examined, first here, and then there." To make clear the qualification, Rabinow later explicitly denies as proper to this liminal consciousness any "privileged position" or "absolute perspective."[23]

As shifting, without privilege and absolute perspective, this shaky ground is understandably rough on those who enter upon it. It is "a difficult and trying experience — one could almost say it is 'unnatural' — and not everyone will tolerate its ambiguities and strains." Anthropologists' self-images are here thrown into doubt as they acknowledge themselves to be embedded in their own particular cultures and then give themselves to be reconstituted in the liminal encounter.[24]

Irigaray and Rabinow are both helpful for identifying the key traits of admiration and liminality as postures necessary for engaging the difference and otherness that characterize our experiences amid plurality. How is it, though, that we might speak of these postures as Christian reconciliatory postures? To respond to this question is the task of the next section.

Admiration and Liminality as "Christian" Postures

Both the narrative language of the New Testament that was produced by early Jewish and Christian movements and the communal praxis in these movements contain features that allow us to speak of admiration and liminality as *Christian* reconciliatory postures. As I have already indicated, Christian practices and postures have often manifested neither admiration nor liminality in response to others. In Dussel's words again, the basic posture has been one that utters a "No-to-the-Other."[25] However, there are some often untapped resources in Christian traditions that allow us to forge a closer alliance between these needed postures of admiration and liminality, and the Christian tradition. Turn first to the narrative language of the New Testament where, for the Christian community, the identity of Jesus as the Christ is formulated. Analysis of both the form and meaning of these narratives suggests that New Testament narratives themselves foster not only the affirmation of others that is intrinsic to admiration, but also the sense of suspension and disorientation that is essential to liminality.

Ricoeur and others have stressed that the *form* of the gospel narratives, particularly in the parables, is qualified by a structural trait intrinsic to the narrated action. This trait, or qualifier, is the narrative's tendency to highlight the extravagant, the paradoxical, the hyperbolic.[26] The gospel narratives intensify ordinary experience to the point of the extraordinary, not to distract from the ordinary but to illumine it from within. So, for example, the parable of the Good Samaritan is not only recommendation or illustration of a virtuous life-style. It is extravagant portrayal of compassion without limit.

The narrative form, structurally charged with extravagance of this sort, has the particular function for readers of dislocation. Even though the plot of the narrated story of Jesus may culminate in reorientation for readers, our experience of this in the narrative is not without a jarring, disorienting encounter with an intensified vision of the ordinary. The narrative form "dislocates our project of making a whole of our lives." Even with later reorientation, Ricoeur suggests that the dislocation is so radical that it occurs "without ever perhaps allowing us to remake a whole."[27]

This dislocating function is paralleled by the *subject matter* of the gospel narrative. The whole narrative story of Jesus moves from an announcement that leads to challenge, and then scandalous condemnation and execution, before any vindication of Jesus in the resurrection. Further, the one vindicated always remains the one who was dislocated and who experienced to the point of death the discomforts of that dislocation. The whole story is laden with extravagance and hyperbole as Jesus, the individual on whom the narrative focuses with ever greater intensity,[28] carries love to extremity, to the point of his own death. This death, viewed as consequence of his radical existence for others, especially for the oppressed others, is startlingly the occasion for confession of his being from God, of his being the Christ. "In these narratives, that reign of God is now recognized as not coercive power but as the sovereignty of agapic, other-regarding love from God to all."[29] The meaning of the narrative itself, as carried by the plot, is also dislocating, because readers are led to expect both full humanity and God in and through the kind of dislocation that is agapic transcendence for others. In these ways the narratives foster admiration and liminality.

Next note the communal form of life that is suggested by the narrative, that embodies that narrative and mediates it to us. Communal existence is implied by the very narratives themselves, suggesting as they do through form and meaning that dislocation is always toward life lived for and with others, and in that way, for and with God. The narrative impels to sociality not just as obligation subsequent to experience of God, but as the way humans are led to redemptive experience of the divine. Among contemporary theologians, Edward Farley's social phenomenology of Christian redemptive existence is particularly helpful in relating the gospel narrative to its congruent communal life in a way that shows the meaning of Christian existence for experiences of liminality and admiration.

Farley's major claim is that Christian faith occurs in a "faith world, a social matrix" that he terms ecclesia.[30] Ecclesia is the concrete cultural-linguistic form through which the reality of God is mediated. Most pertinent to my concerns here is Farley's thesis that the distinctive trait of ecclesia's intersubjective life "derives from the strange way in which the human being who is not a participant in ecclesia is present to those who are participants."[31] Repeatedly, Farley stresses that Christian intersubjective experience is one wherein members co-intend "the stranger." Ecclesia is a concrete, "determinate" community, but one that is always hard to define because its character is to have an unformulatable boundary.[32]

In this sense, then, Christian communal existence, while always concrete and specific to some culture, nation, ethnos, and language, may be viewed as a liminal form of existence in those communities. By co-intending strangers as its mode of bonding, it is also always de-centering. "Agape's radical character is disclosed only when it is coupled with the repudiation of all determinate social units as conditions of God's presence. . . . In agape the stranger is intentionally drawn into ecclesia."[33] At the heart of Christian ecclesial formation, there is both an affirmation of the other (admiration) and a de-centering, co-intending of strangers that takes Christians into spaces with unformulatable boundaries (liminality).

The notion of the word *intending* in Farley's phrase, "co-intending strangers," needs further clarification. The sense of intending does not mean, as common parlance has it, something that individuals aim at, attempt, but never quite practice: "What I really intended was. . . . " No, intending in *co-intending* refers to a form of intersubjective communal life. To say, therefore, that Christian community is marked by the co-intending of strangers is to say that its communal life, ranging from explicit corporate activities to its members' prereflective intentions of will, have this feature. Liminality, as this co-intending of strangers, is a Christian reconciliatory posture that does not refer simply to an individual's attitudinal intents but to a communal praxis.

The notion of "stranger" also requires careful attention. The Christian reconciliatory postures toward difference, through admiration and liminality, involve a turning to the stranger in at least two of the primary meanings of "strange." First, the stranger is one who is different by reason of some individual trait(s), physical appearance, custom, distant location, or cultural practice. The strangers who are co-intended, toward whom Christian reconciliatory communities are always turning, are first of all these strange ones who are different, in whatever way, from a given Christian community.

Second, the stranger is also one who is estranged, alienated from a given Christian community, one whose estrangement may in fact be due to oppression by structures in which Christians participate. Co-intending strangers in this sense, therefore, may often mean a praxis with and for them that is also a praxis of resistance against one's own oppressing structures. Whatever particular kind of praxis is called forth, the stranger in this sense is not just the different one but is one who is made different; the stranger is then not just an other but an exploited other.

In the actual practice of co-intending strangers, it is often not possible to separate the two senses of the word *stranger*. In North American church communities (especially patriarchal ones), women, for example, are not just other by reason of gender or distinctive cultural experiences; often they are also exploited others.[34] The exploitation itself frequently involves seizing on the mere fact of strangers' differences, then developing this in a way that entails their exploitation. As we have seen with respect to white racism, the difference of African culture and skin color were seized upon and developed so that they became not just different (strange), but also made different as exploited others (estranged).[35] Christian reconciliatory postures certainly attend to, focus and celebrate strangers in all their differences; more, they attend to, focus and resist their estrangement and alienation.

The Christian reconciliatory postures of admiration and liminality expressed in practice toward the stranger understood as alienated and estranged, connect reconciliation to the major concerns of emancipation that I will treat in the following sections. These alienated ones whom we co-intend demand a work of emancipation. Before examining emancipation as a christological task, however, we can summarize the christological import of this section's discussion.

Admiration and liminality together comprise a Christian reconciliatory strategy for dealing with human differences. To be "in Christ," i.e., to be a Christian participant in the sociohistorical dynamic of reconciliatory emancipation, is to be caught up in a particular way of navigating the realities of difference and plurality. This way is neither one that flattens out difference within a homogeneous vision of human life nor one that abides easy relativisms that see human life as but an endless play of incommensurable viewpoints and practices. As admiration, the Christian reconciliatory posture resists homogenizing tendencies, affirming the other as other, cultivating senses of others' unique traits, and also of one's own otherness.[36] As liminal, Christian reconciliatory practice involves a posture that risks taking admiration's affirmation of others to the point of the disorientation and suspension that attend living in new spaces of human interaction. In liminality, Christians dwell in those strange spaces where affirming the other (admiration) becomes an always unsettling but creative co-intending of strangers—unsettling because the Christian knows herself or himself to be in lands the boundaries of which are always being refashioned, and creative because forged from this unsettled dwelling "betwixt-and-between" are new shared experiences and ways of living.

To be in Christ, therefore, is *to admire*, thus affirming in theory and practice the unsubstitutable differences between women and men, Zapotec and North American, Asian and Latin American, African and European— better, between Pawnee, Pueblo, Norwegian immigrant to North America, Mam, Cakchiquel, Chorti, Kikuyu, and others. Such admiration is an experience of being given to the wondrous, often seemingly endless plurality of life differences. To be in Christ, however, is also *to be liminal*, to risk being given toward the others one affirms. It is thereby to undergo the disorientation, sense of homelessness, play, and suspension that attends one whose thought and practice, while for others, can never become those others. To be liminal in this way often involves alienation from one's own previous spaces without being able to settle in others' spaces. But precisely this liminal dwelling can be the source of reconstructing new alliances between one's own and others' worlds, a discovery and creation of "stocks of experience" that bring together different, often alienated, lives.

The Christian reconciliatory postures of admiration and liminality tend to embrace, therefore, both radical otherness and new alliances among others. This is indeed the stuff of hope. It is a reconstituting of hope, a remembering Esperanza. This hope may seem only the wishes of a sanguine spirit, especially from the customary perspectives of Western thought, wherein affirming radical otherness is often thought to be antithetical to forging new alliances and shareable experience. Nonetheless, *Christus Mater* instills unrest concerning such an antithesis and inspires a resistance to it.

Christus Mater challenges us to recall that life with, for and among radically differentiated others, in spite of the pain and disorientation that goes with that life, does not rule out sharing and alliance with others. The *Christus Mater* metaphor is particularly powerful for creating this hope because otherness and alliance are perhaps nowhere more strikingly conjoined than in the body of a mother—a body that is one, but also two or more. It is a body the mind of which speaks—especially in times of pregnancy, birthing, lactating, and at other times—of "me" and "not me." Radical otherness, the mystery of another's source and vitality, is other to the mother's body, but also interior to her.[37] To meet Christ or to be in Christ in the ways of admiration and liminality is to have a reconciliatory posture toward others like that of a mother's being toward the new life in her. *Christus Mater* inspires hope for this kind of reconciliatory posture.

The reconciliatory postures of the *Christus Mater* will suffuse my unfolding of the other christological tasks of emancipation still to be presented. The first of these to be discussed is that which works freedom as maternalization.

CHRIST AND EMANCIPATING THE MATERNAL

The first of four necessary tasks of emancipation is *maternalization*. I am suggesting that Christ as a dynamic of reconciliatory emancipation entails emancipating the maternal in North Atlantic practice and Christian religious language. Maternalization together with the other three tasks of political emancipation have primacy in relation to reconciliation. This is consonant with the privilege I have been acknowledging for the political throughout this work. Nonetheless, the reconciliatory postures of admiration and liminality play a *necessary* auxiliary role, and suffuse Christian discourse and practices of emancipation. Therefore, at the end of this section, I will return to the reconciliatory postures, to show how they shape and qualify the emancipatory task of maternalization.

The notion of maternalization could be misunderstood in any number of ways, some of which I have already anticipated. Because of possible misunderstandings, I urge that very specific meanings of maternalization be explored. By maternalization, therefore, I am referring to movements for the emancipation of women from sexism that involve two ongoing, mutually reinforcing efforts: a revaluing of women's reproductive powers and a relocating of society's maternal functions. Both of these efforts must work together.

Against the stream of matricidal devaluations of women's reproductive powers, christology must insist upon a thoroughgoing *revaluing* of those powers and of the connectedness with natural process they entail. To insist upon this, however, without also calling for a *relocating* of maternal functions, risks simply enshrining women's reproductive powers without supporting women in the exercise of those powers or freeing them from shouldering disproportionate shares of child care labor. Conversely, to relocate society's maternal functions without also insisting on the revaluing of women's reproductive powers would be to overlook what remains a major feature of women's difference and would entail yet one more co-optation of the reproductive powers that are theirs. How to both revalue those powers and relocate maternal functions within a wider communal practice is the major challenge for a christology that understands emancipation as maternalization.

Taking maternalization as a first task of emancipation is consonant with that originary meaning of emancipation as a release from the *patria potestas* and *pater familias*. This was a release partially characteristic of the movements coalescing around Jesus before more intense repatriarchalizations of the tradition became established. I have already discussed the works of Elisabeth Schüssler Fiorenza, Rita Nakashima Brock, and others who have discussed this dimension of early Christian movements. My leading off with christological discussion of emancipation from sexism (as maternalization) seeks to heed those insights.

It will not be an easy task to articulate a contemporary Christian notion of maternalization as emancipatory for women, not only because of the complexities of the subject matter, but also because there are some peculiar risks for a male theologian.

In relation to their mothers, men, in practice and in writing, have both idealized mother love and sought to separate themselves from it.[38] Both the idealization and separation often function, as Adrienne Rich shows in her essay, "Mother and Son, Woman and Man," as strategies for consolidating a sexual division of labor that consigns an idealized mothering, and often parenting generally, to a private sphere, the burdens of which fall primarily to women.[39] Although men often abstract themselves from the idealized mother of the private sphere in their relations with women, they often expect women to play mothering roles, roles that not only short-circuit mutuality in the relationship but also increase burdens upon women.[40] Because of the pervasiveness of sexist practice, we may suspect that men's theological efforts to develop emancipatory strategies from sexism can easily become not emancipatory for men or women but simply one more male exercise in patriarchalized, often sentimentalized, notions of woman as mother. This suspicion should motivate our careful attention as to how we revalue women's reproductive powers and relocate maternal care-giving functions so that they are supported by the whole human community.

Christic Revaluing of Women's Reproductive Powers

Has there been before a christic valuing of women's reproductive powers? Yes and no. Yes, in the sense that from ancient periods, especially in the times of the goddess, women's reproductive powers have been sacralized. Reverence for those powers, for the flow of blood, for the female sexuality joining with male's that produced life, for the regular changes in women that were a piece of cosmic, seasonal, and agricultural changes — reverence for all these has been a major feature of human history and religious language.[41]

In Christianity's own history, often differentiated by its established interpreters from the legacy of the goddess, there have also been numerous cases of Christ titles and language intertwined in ways that give a sacral value to women's reproductive powers. Perhaps this is most striking in the medieval Christian mysticism of Julian of Norwich, in which there are interwoven references to God and Christ as both mother and father, involving specific invocations of terms like "Our Mother Christ" and "Jesus Christ . . . our very Mother" in relation to the transformation of female life and sensuality through use of maternal images of birthing and suckling.[42] Rosemary Radford Ruether and other scholars have collected a number of other references in which early Christian martyr texts can refer to a woman slave as "another Christ" or Christ as "our sister." Further, mystical, utopian sects such as the Shakers could reverence Mother Ann Lee as a female Christ.[43]

Although the presence of these formulations in the legacy of Christianity is significant, these images of the Woman Christ or Mother Christ tend to suffer three weaknesses.

First, these images have often been forced to occupy a place subordinate to those marked out by male-specific images of a Father God and a male Christ, usually developed through primary development of the male hero and savior, Jesus. Even Julian, who frequently mixes gender-specific metaphors in a way that sometimes seems to make the Mother primary in power, usually refers to "our Father" as the one in whom we have "our higher part." So also for the Shakers, where Mother Ann Lee and the female Christ tend to occupy subordinate positions. Such subordinationism easily reinforces and legitimizes ecclesial and social subordination of women to men.[44]

Second, even when an approximate parity of female-specific and male-specific images was achieved, as in the androgynous christologies of some counter-establishment spiritualities, the cost was often a disembodied spirituality that valued a female Christ spiritually but did not value processes associated with woman's embodiment. This was part of the androgynous christologies' dualistic disparagement of the body, easily reinforcing women's (and men's) practice of splitting their female or male spiritualities from their physical, embodied experiences.

Third, the Mother Christ and Woman Christ images tend to be individual figures rather than figures denoting sociohistorical or political practices. Perhaps this is to be expected in the context of centuries of patriarchal oppression, in which there was little space to elaborate the expansive meanings of such woman-specific metaphors. To the extent that these metaphors were often subordinate to the male-specific ones or were spiritualized apart from embodied practice, it would be difficult to elaborate the sociohistoric and communal meanings of revering the sacred in womanform images.

At present, in order to critique and resist in hope the misogynist ethos and mythos of our period, the female-specific images need formulating in ways that avoid their being subordinate to male-specific ones, that affirm and even celebrate processes of women's embodiment, and that keep to the fore the sociopolitical implications of a Christian faith and practice centered on such imaging.

If any single image can be adequate in these respects, I suggest that one that comes closest to the surplus of meanings carried in the theologian's root-metaphor, *Christus Mater*, is the complex image used by Rita Nakashima Brock: Christa/Community.

In this term, the dynamic of Christ is given a distinctively female or womanform. "Christa" is a christic image, signaling the divine ultimacy and power in womanform. Christa was the name of a female figure depicted on the cross in the Cathedral of Saint John of the Divine in New York City.[45] But by using the Christa image alongside the term *community,* Brock signals that the locus of ultimacy and transformation is not just an individual figure, male or female, on the cross or anywhere else, but, more in my terms, a womanform, communal dynamic.

Brock, drawing primarily from the New Testament scholarship of Elisabeth Schüssler Fiorenza and Elizabeth Struthers Malbon, shows how Jesus was himself both a contributor to and was empowered by a transformative dynamic operative in women's actions. These actions include the initiative exercised by the hemorrhaging woman who violates social taboo to touch Jesus and so knows a healing power between them. They include also the acts of solidarity exercised by women present with one another and Jesus at his death, present also to affirm the emergence of new life, joy, and relation in the resurrection.[46] As Schüssler Fiorenza has shown, women and the movements of women can be understood as paradigms of true discipleship. What I am suggesting is something more: Their paradigmatic movements toward healing and emancipation, imaged as Christa/Community, in fact constitute the locus of divine ultimacy in history and society. For us to be in Christ, therefore, is to be a participant in such Christa/Community.

If Christa/Community is to be an emancipatory event revaluing of women's reproductive powers, then Christa/Community and any other womanform and communal images need to bring out three essential meanings that give further concreteness to what it means to be in Christ.

The being in Christ that is a revaluing of women's reproductive powers means, first, an affirmation and celebration of women's sexuality and reproductive powers. As emancipatory, such affirmation and celebration mean these powers are first and foremost women's, exercised in their freedom, agency, and control. In resistance to a North American society that projects an ideal body image for all women, that teaches that women's bodies are for men, for families, for children, being in Christ is women's coming into being for the goodness of their bodies as for their own created good selves. This affirming and celebrating of women's sexuality and reproductive powers also mean resisting the damaging effects coming from patriarchal fears and anxieties of the flow of women's blood. As Penelope Washburn writes, there *is* a pervasive fear and anxiety attaching to the sign of that blood's flow—especially its first flow at puberty—an anxiety that need not be shunned and needs expression to give acknowledgment to the state of crisis, transition, and change that are parts of life.[47] The church, however, has not given expression to this right fear. Instead, for centuries it has, through its superstitious horrors of women's menstrual blood, practiced an unjust quarantining of women. St. Jerome claimed, "Nothing is so unclean as a woman in her periods; what she touches she causes to become unclean." Between the eighth and eleventh centuries, church codes prevented menstruating women any access to church buildings. Even today, the Catholic church and other churches more subtly continue the notion that ordination of women is impossible because "a menstruating priestess would pollute the altar."[48]

Affirming and celebrating women's sexuality and reproductive powers mean being in Christ such that this Christian abhorrence is resisted. It means growing into new modes of life and practice, wherein menstruation and all processes of female embodiment are seen as graceful experiences, in which women and men accept those processes as symbols of the potential of women's bodies for the enrichment of self and others. Moreover, this is an enrichment entailing a trusting and liking of one's body.[49] The blood flowing in Christa/Community may never cease to create some anxiety and tension for the whole community, but rather than denying this, it can be accepted and celebrated as part of the life that accepts death, change, crisis, tension, and finds amid those newness and hope. How powerful and renewing it is when parents, especially mothers, succeed—amid all the patriarchal devaluations—to enable their daughters to celebrate the events attending their bodily growth.

Second, revaluing women's reproductive powers does not mean celebrating these in themselves. It means that, but it also means celebrating and affirming these as a caring connectedness to all of nature. As Washburn writes for women, "The potential procreativity is not a personal power but the linking of ourselves to the creative power of nature. . . ." For the entire Christa/Community, for lives that are in Christ, revaluing women's reproductive potential means focusing not just on female reproductive powers but also on their entire matrix and nature. Celebrating what happens physiologically in a woman's body each month is ultimately a celebration of the temporality of all creation. It is to note humanity's connectedness to moons and tides, to the planets of space's vastness, to the oceanic depths of the earth's waters. All of created nature is encompassed and, in its being, affirmed and celebrated as something to be cared for and accepted because it is what encompasses and empowers us.

Being in Christ in this way is to be in resistance to the exploitation of nature that has often accompanied misogyny. What needs resisting is the joint exploitation of women and nature. The exploitation of these two together is evident especially in our language about land. We have wanted land that is rich, "virgin," "productive," and "wild." As men coveted the virgin, so they sought virgin land. The likening of land or earth to women is not unique to North American Caucasian settlers, but in their actions there is a vicious analogue between misogyny and land abuse. Mark Gerzon develops the analogy:

Once the land had been won, it was treated like a fallen woman. Commerce replaced romance. The wilderness, once conquered, was no longer wild, the virgin land, once used, lost her innocence. The frontiersman and his followers could win the land, use her, and then abandon her, leaving behind a commodity that other men would exploit until they too moved on. Instead of wooing the earth, we began to waste her . . . we treat the land neither reverently, as our mother, nor chivalrously, as a virgin, but contemptuously, as if she were no better than a whore. We rape her. And when we are done, we leave her — and our wastes — behind.[50]

How unlike the care of the Native American peoples, whose posture to the land was in resistance to the settlers' rapacious ways.

"You ask me to plow the ground," Chief Smoholla said to the military authorities of the far Northwest. "Shall I take a knife and tear my mother's bosom? You ask me to dig for stone. Shall I dig under her skin and bones? . . . You ask me to cut grass and make hay and sell it, and be rich like the white men. But how dare I cut off my mother's hair?"[51]

To be in Christ is to live in this similar reverence for the earth, for all of nature, with which women's and ultimately all our bodies are in a delicate, living relationship. To be sure, there can be no naive repristination of Native American spirituality; nor is that spirituality irrelevant to our complex technological society's abuse of our resources, however. It prompts us to forge our own new Christian spiritualities to revalue women's bodies and earth's material resources.

Third, revaluing women's reproductive potential is to affirm and celebrate that potential as a caring connectedness to all of social and political life. Affirming women's reproductive powers is a celebration pertinent to the dynamics that play in society and history as well as in women's bodies and nature. Emancipation as maternalization in this full sense is most evident to me in the hopeful labor of contemporary Mayan women.

There is in the labor of the Mayan Zutuhil women, for example, a difficult struggle for freedom over their own reproductive power—a struggle that is, in a sense, with their own Zutuhil men. The reproductive potential and life of each Zutuhil woman are in large part outside her control, but she seeks to forge new respect for her own agency by emphasizing the mystical power of female sexuality and menstrual blood.[52] When, as a result of both choice and compulsion, Mayan women are entrusted with care of their offspring, their children are taught the importance of care of nature and land, which is generally a feature of Maya-Quiche cultures. About the land, Mayan peoples offer testimonies like the following:

> There appeared the trees, we appeared ourselves, there appeared our tortilla, there appeared our atole [maize gruel], there appeared our beans, there appeared our squash, there appeared our chayote [vegetable pear]. All those things appeared in the world. But only the holy earth gave them to us. For that reason, there is an obligation. For that reason we say prayers for our maize field. For that reason we give offering because the earth gives us food.[53]

Further, when land is not available for the Maya-Quiche women, their spouses, and children to work and to own, they are motivated toward sociopolitical movements for the restoration of social structures that will both preserve the life of the land and their access to it in the face of development by the small percentage of elite groups who own the land and guard it for their own use.[54] The Guatemalan mothers, as we saw in the case of Rigoberta Menchu's family, are giving their lives for the restoration of those structures.[55]

Being given to this struggle, to this revaluing of women's reproductive potential—as a struggle for women's control over their own reproductive and sexual power, as a caring connectedness to nature and to just social structures—is to find oneself in Christa/Community. Now being in Christ, seen as emancipatory maternalization, comes into its fullest sociohistorical and political complexity. This is true because being in Christ in this struggle demands a resistance that articulates the concerns touching women's and men's sexual lives together, their joint dependency upon nature, and also the intricacies playing between societies' labor and social movements, international trade policies, and multinational use and abuse of economic power.

With the emergence of these complexities at the heart of a revaluing of women's reproductive potential, we cannot think (as if we ever could, really) that this revaluing is only a woman's issue. Hence, whatever we thought a maternal function was, it can now no longer be understood as being something that an individual woman does with her reproductive power, or what women as a whole do in some domestic sphere. The whole maternal function is understood as being inclusive of more factors than usually attributed to it. This means that the maternal functions of a society need to be relocated, or resituated, in larger contexts. This relocation warrants explicit discussion.

Relocating Society's Maternal Functions

It is essential to stress this notion of relocation. Without it, the revaluing of women's reproductive powers would only serve to sacralize patriarchy's identification of women and women's practices with maternal functions and legitimize women as primary care givers for children, nature, and society. The christic maternalization that I am proposing also involves relocating society's maternal functions within a wider communal praxis, in which the efforts of caring for life—for its children, its supporting network of institutions, its groups of women and men, its ecological infrastructure, its political systems—are shared by both women and men, by individuals, groups, and institutions.

The christic emancipation here involves a release of maternal functions from present patriarchy's assignment of them to domestic spheres in which women have the primary role and a release into a wider communal praxis. The obstacles to such a relocation are many. Not only are North Atlantic cultures prone to social structures and ideologies reinforcing separate spheres, as explored by Jean Bethke Elshtain's *Public Man, Private Woman*.[56] Other cultures as well, such as some Latin American ones, shore up the practice of separate spheres with a feminine cult of *marianismo*, in which women experience power predominantly in a domestic sphere attended to with a spirit of self-sacrifice, humility, sadness, and patience.[57]

"In Christ," we are coming into emancipation from all this. This is true of women first, who already bear a disproportionate share of maternal care giving in our societies,[58] but of men, too, who need release into greater participation in child care providing and into all the other systemic care giving—for nature and for social structure—that is integrally connected with it.

There has been much talk among both men against sexism and women feminists about the importance of male participation in child care.[59] In addition, with changing gender roles in our culture, men are "helping more" in the domestic sphere when women achieve opportunities for employment in contexts beyond the home.

The christic and emancipatory relocation, however, is something more than this general, often sporadic, "helping" provided by "sensitive males." Christian emancipatory relocation, in fact, leads Christians to critique that helping, especially if it glosses or tends to replace the need for systemic changes in the social, political, and economic structures that are needed if women are to be free from the inhumane costs of maternal responsibilities and if men are to become fuller co-participants in child care. All this involves developing any openness to genuinely shared parenting and care providing that now exists between men and women into new configurations of business, professional, and labor practices, such that no "spheres" are isolated from the ever-present need to provide for our children and so that all of us, while at work or at home, are more available to the worlds of children.

To demand this makes the envisioned relocation a radically eschatological reality, because the structural changes required for such relocation are so many and so intricate that they are probably beyond realization in our time. That fact is, again, not new to Christian faith and practice. Nonetheless, this eschatological dimension does not prevent us from seeing now that there are being birthed new child-providing practices and organizations in church, neighborhood, school, and work—contexts that anticipate new emancipatory structures. It is the work of a Christian practice of emancipatory maternalization to be given to the nurture of these new configurations, critiquing them, reshaping them in order to ensure a relocated maternal function.

An important qualification to all this must be registered. This christic emancipation that includes male participation is not a male takeover of women's maternal functions. As Janice Raymond and others remind us, patriarchy has often bridged the gap between public and private spheres, but it has done this by way of a nonemancipatory co-optation of women's powers.

> For example, the takeover of the female world of birth and midwifery by men is a blatant example of this transformation, demonstrating among other things the hetero-relational imperative that men must have access to women in all circumstances. What was traditionally and primarily a woman-centered event between mothers, midwives, and female kin and friends has become a hetero-relational drama with, once again, the man (doctor) on top in the hospital-based obstetrical script. Even the new so-called natural childbirth scenarios give primary emphasis to male inclusion rather than to restoring the tradition of birth as an event that brings women together. . . . Unfortunately, many women succumb to the hetero-relational rhetoric of making men "equal" and "active" participants in the birthing process, and the traditional bonding of women at this event is obscured and forgotten.[60]

The lesson here is that any emancipatory relocating of maternal functions must be done in relation to the revaluing of women's reproductive powers as *women's* powers. Adrienne Rich, in her visions of an emancipatory future of child care, has insisted that "women . . . must and will take leadership in demanding, drafting, and implementing such a profound structural and human change."[61] Actually, it has seemed to me that women who are engaged in the demands of mothering, whether feminist or not, already show some remarkable survival skills—cooperating with other mothers (sometimes with their spouses) and other agencies to keep child-care duties spread out in a broad network of responsibility. This does not always happen, of course; patriarchal nuclear families often enculturate women to see themselves as omnicompetent care givers going it alone. But the communal impulses already operative in women's care-giving practices are discernible, and women should retain the initiative as we men increasingly step forth to provide our needed presence in systems of child care. This means that, in our responses, we men do well to allow women to lead, as they seek "to possess still more consciously" their own "realms of unconscious, proverbial knowledge as mothers, biological or not."[62] In the relocating effort, therefore, a fully emancipatory maternalization effort never leaves behind the need for revaluing women's distinctive connectedness to reproductive power.

This does not in the least deny the revolutionary priority that men must give to their own participation in the relocated provision of maternal care. While stressing the role of women's leadership and special connection, Adrienne Rich has also stressed the point that assimilating significant numbers of men into a comprehensive system of child care is crucial.

I believe that would be the most revolutionary priority that any male group could set itself. It would not only change the expectations children—and therefore men—have of women and men; nor would it simply break down gender-roles and diversify the work-patterns of both sexes; it would change the entire community's relationship to childhood. In learning to give care to children, men would have to cease being children; the privilege of fatherhood could not be toyed with, as they are now, without an equal share in the full experience of nurture.[63]

With this kind of relocation, always in league with the revaluation, both men and women will be in different relations not only within families, but also within the *polis*. Again, an authentically emancipative maternalization, as in the struggles of Guatemalan mothers, needs to extend to the personal, the familial, and the political. Working for and realizing this aspect of emancipation is to participate in Christa/Community. It is to be in Christ in the light of today's sexist structural oppression.

Maternalization and the Reconciliatory Postures

The reconciliatory postures attending christology's primary theme of emancipation lead us to ask what value admiration and liminality have for emancipation understood as maternalization. How do Christians, who delight in difference (admiration) and co-intend strangers in that often disorienting free and engaging space between others (liminality) influence the christic dynamic of maternalization? Three major implications should be noted.

First, the reconciliatory postures keep the Christian struggle for a revalued and relocated maternalization vigilantly attentive to personal and life-history differences. In my comments about emancipatory maternalization, I have formulated my christological constructions in response to general social structures and expectations to which many of us are exposed. But people's individual histories intertwine with others' and with these structures in wondrously diverse ways. Individual experiences of travel, child abuse, divorce, family illnesses, deaths, unique religious practices, special friendships — all these and more have the capacity to refract the drive for emancipatory maternalization in different ways. The reconciliatory postures attend to these differences as real differences, seeking to forge meaningful alliances among them in the drive for emancipation as maternalization.

Second, the reconciliatory postures of celebrating and risking exposure to difference leave us fundamentally unsatisfied with emancipation *only* as maternalization, as only a freedom from sexism. Awareness of difference makes us equally attentive to the constraints of hetero-realism, racism, and classism, each of which has its distinctive problematics yet calls forth its own discourse of christic emancipation. The struggle for maternalization will take a very different form for African American women than for white women, even though we might still be able to speak, concerning both groups, of needs for emancipation as both a revaluing of women's reproductive powers and a relocating of maternal functions. As Christians, our reconciliatory postures never allow us to assume this. We must ask about the difference and acknowledge particularities in the effort to reconcile, to forge new alliances. The reconciliatory postures of admiration and liminality allow the differences posed by classism and racism (not just sexism) to have their impacts on the understanding of emancipation.

Finally, the reconciliatory postures extend to include the enemy. And who is the enemy with respect to the emergence of emancipatory maternalization? Well, it is we men. I say this not out of guilt, despair, or misanthropy, but simply out of an observation of the configuration of power that has for so long and still keeps us men abstracted from maternal functions in the specific and broadest senses. Acknowledging, even accepting this status as enemy, can be a beginning of emancipatory work and hope in solidarity with those who suffer more than we from sexist structures. Acknowledging this status may mean accepting being told by women to just stay away. But more often it means accepting their invitation to work and hope in emancipatory struggle. That invitation can be heard even amid critiques of patriarchy as radical as Adrienne Rich's. We need expect, however, no special praise from women for our response to the invitation. To respond positively is *not* for any man to become, for a woman, a praiseworthy, fully understanding comrade in the struggle against sexism. That is only:

the phantom of the man-who-would-understand,
the lost brother, the twin—

This is the phantom, as Adrienne Rich develops it in her poem, "Natural Resources," for which women left their mothers and denied their sisters over and over,[64] not something we men can expect to become.

Nor should we expect special treatment from women in reward for some sensitive male participation in household chores, in daily care of children, or even for working for the comprehensive systemic changes needed to make all this participation really possible. All these things are simply that to which we men are called, to which we have long been called, as contributors to the human project. We are called back from our lives in abstraction from systemic care giving, back to the contexts where bodies grow, thrive, and need tending through the creation of supportive social and political networks. Responding to the call in this way is to enter into an alliance with women, based on their invitation when it is there, that is not only reconciliatory but emancipative. In Christ, in Christa/Community, there is this form of reconciliatory emancipation as maternalization.

CHRIST AND EMANCIPATING SENSUALITY AND FRIENDSHIP

An emancipatory maternalization in Christa/Community, through both the revaluing and relocating moves I have identified as significant for empowering women and the entire birthed and birthing community, introduces a partial resistance against hetero-realism. To revalue and relocate maternal powers in public communal praxis is also to begin restoring friendship with one's self and with one's own gender and body. As such, it is to begin to set conditions for emancipation and justice for currently oppressed gay and lesbian communities. Why is this so?

The dominant patriarchal code that restricts maternal functions to a private sphere not only oppresses women, whose duties are disproportionately heavy in that sphere. It also oppresses those who are oriented to fulfill their needs for intimacy outside of the reigning paradigms for male and female functioning. Those paradigms are usually allotted to spheres governed by a sexual division of labor. The gay male is often subject to oppressive constraints not simply because he violates pervasive heterosexual notions of sexual bonding but also because he threatens male identity, an identity that is based on a public persona of distance from privatized maternal spheres in which he yet holds the most power. The gay male's identity, public or private, is not constituted by holding a place of dominance over women in a private sphere, even though gay males may also practice their own forms of misogyny and should never be idealized as free from sexist practices. Similarly, the lesbian is a woman not only outside a privatized maternal sphere (though the experience of mothering may still be hers), but she is also thereby outside male control.

Emancipation as maternalization, provides a christic sacralizing that revalues women's reproductive powers and a christic sacralizing of those spaces of wider, supportive communal praxis in which maternal functions are relocated. In so doing, emancipation in Christ both sacralizes sexual difference and sacralizes resistance to the two-spheres vision of male and female roles, therefore also undermining the patriarchal and misogynist ideologies about male and female senses of identity and maturity, according to which gays and lesbians are so frequently judged aberrant. From the perspective of a christology of reconciliatory emancipation, gays and lesbians are judged neither by the fact of their sexual orientation nor by their departure from reigning gender roles and nuclear-family arrangements, but in accord with their participation or nonparticipation in christic revaluing of women's reproductive powers and the christic relocating of society's maternal care providing. Gays and lesbians are called, together with "straights," to the task and vision in Christ of emancipating women from the matricidal mythos and ethos worked upon all women and of emancipating the whole creation that needs tending by those of every sexual orientation. This, I believe, entails granting every civil and ecclesial right needed by gays and lesbians—not only for accepting them, but also for working fully with them at the tasks of reconciliatory emancipation.

Christic Sensualization

More is needed, however. Reconciliatory emancipation as maternalization, though necessary, is not sufficient for redressing heterosexist and homophobic domination. Nor is it sufficient, though it helps, to observe, against the backdrop of the central emancipation motif, that gay and lesbian communities are unfree and so in need of emancipation.

As a second major task of emancipation which needs to enter a restructured christology, I therefore propose sensualization. By this I mean a christic sacralizing of the human body such that its role as incarnating the divine presence is emphasized and developed. This is not to privilege the body above other modes of incarnating divine presence. After all, our experiences of the body are inscribed in communal, social, and political matrices. These matrices, too, must be acknowledged as incarnating divine presence. However, given Christian traditions' long and manifold history of looking away from the body as if it were both irrelevant and antithetical to the divine presence, an emancipatory task of sensualization must at last show forth the human body as graced in its very being with divine presence.

Given the well-known traditions of Christian thinkers who have demeaned the body, if in no other way than by looking away from it to find "God," perhaps it is more honest to give up on formulating a christological response, to cease talking of such a sacralization as christic. I continue to do so, however, for three reasons.

First, in part a christology is in its essence a response to contemporary need. Christology is always, in part, soteriology. In previous chapters I have already discussed the suffering and need created by alienation from the body and the way that suffering contributes to the matricidal and misogynist abstraction from, and alienation of, women and men. That complex soteriological need represented in alienation from the body itself calls forth the response of a christological mythos.

Second, it must be noted that as anti-body as much of the tradition has been, there are significant resources within the traditions—for example, the narrative texts, the early Jesus movements, and alternative Christian communities—to enable us to develop Christian critiques of anti-body postures and of body-soul dichotomizing. As John Fortunato writes when exploring Christian spirituality in the context of the AIDS crisis, disembodiment can be viewed as the church's "orthodox heresy."[65]

The very ability on our part to identify this as heresy suggests the availability of body-affirming resources in Christian tradition. Indeed there are many. These begin in the Hebrew scriptures, in which divine presence dwells within a people who are released from an oppression that is depicted both bodily and politically. These scriptures can be read as a testimony to divine incarnation not simply in history but in the interaction of bodies in history as well. Human offspring and reproduction, though biblically still cast in a patriarchal mode, are nevertheless means for continuation of the divine presence. *The Song of Songs*, for all of its disembodied allegorization by both rabbis and Christian patriarchs, still has a power, beauty, and candor sufficient to help call our spiritualities back home to the body and to a preservation of its sensuality.

Third, traditions representing the movement of reconciliatory emancipation in which Jesus was a participant depict no consistent ideals of ascetic body denial. John Fortunato has indicated that although Jesus exhibited periods of withdrawal to isolated places, this can in no way be taken as license for ascetic body denial. To the contrary, Jesus feasted often, accepted anointments of head and feet with oil. In the absence of specific denigrations by Jesus of sexuality, it is impossible to accept him as fully human and not think that he both knew sexual feeling and valued it. Moreover, his ministry suggested that he not only valued and respected life in the body, but it is also surely included in the configuration of beings and events in which divine presence was located and announced: "The Kingdom of God is at hand" (Matt. 4:17); "The Kingdom of God is in the midst of you" (Luke 17:21); "The Kingdom of God has come upon you" (Matt. 12:28).[66] This is not to say that bodies are the only incarnation of divine presence; but in light of this life and these messages, there are no grounds for excluding the body from the locus that we celebrate as divine presence.

There are these and other reasons, therefore, for an understanding of emancipation as sensualization. What I am calling sensualization, or a christic sacralizing of the human body, has already begun to be quite ably articulated by scholars such as James B. Nelson, Sallie McFague and others.

Nelson's contribution has been to call for a sexual theology that interprets experiences of growing sensuousness as a growing in grace and rereads the symbol "resurrection of the body" as, among other meanings, a radical renewal that begins now with a radical self-acceptance of our bodies as "grace-full."[67] Similarly, though with greater emphasis on metaphors for the divine, McFague also moves in the direction of sensualization. Human desire and passion, as including full love expressed between embodied agents, is an occasion for speaking of God as love; and in so doing we highlight regions of embodied loving as loci of God's relating to the world.[68] These and other efforts in theological construction contribute to sensualization as a task both for christology and a lived christopraxis. Instead of continuing discussion of this task in general terms, we must now return to its value for a resistance to hetero-realism.

Emancipating Sensuality and Friendship for All

For christic sensualization to be seen as one of emancipation from hetero-realist domination, a link needs to be drawn between heterosexist repression of gays/lesbians and a pervasive nervousness about and devaluation of the body. Beverly Harrison has helpfully traced a number of the unexplored connections between misogyny and homophobia. She argues also that the crucial connector is the pervasive, dualistic denial of the body in our North Atlantic cultures.[69]

Feminist theorists have documented the nervousness and even dislike by women of their own bodies within heterosexist paradigms.[70] One's body is harder to love when it is in the power of a patriarch who controls it, whether this power is wielded in subtle and paternalistic forms of control or in the more blatant forms of domestic violence. It is also increasingly probable that men are also not comfortable with their bodies, that the use and abuse of women's bodies (from objectification in advertising to rape) reflect not love of bodily pleasure but its absence.[71] Within the paradigm of domination between the sexes, love of the body in itself is easily lost. Sexism often puts us out of touch with our bodies and hence with ourselves. We relinquish a being in touch with our bodies to an experience of another's control over it or to our experience of being in control of another's body.[72]

For people who envision and practice their sexuality in modes outside heterosexist power arrangements — and this is often, though not always, true of gays and lesbians — a valuation of one's own body is often discovered, and this can become a self-empowerment with communal impact. Being in touch with and affirming one's body can occur in heterosexual relationships, but this often requires moving against the sexist dynamics that structure most heterosexual bondings and growing toward new practices and frameworks of heterosexual loving.

Sensualization as christic sacralizing of the body seeks to emphasize that bodies (along with all creation) are to be enjoyed as bodies, not as dominated and dominating physical forces.[73] The primary life in the body known in heterosexist relations is often one that is not a love of bodies as bodies but is rather a functioning of bodies in accord with patterns of domination.[74]

Gay and lesbian communities manifest their own forms of domination and hence should not be romanticized as fully emancipative communities. There, too, for example, can be found the distortion that degrades and alienates one from his or her body. Nonetheless, for many of the gay and lesbian writers who reflect on their sexualities, there exists in gay and lesbian communities a definite aim to affirm the giftedness of erotic power in a way not often found in heterosexual contexts.[75] They often awaken to this erotic power in ways that entail a broad understanding of sexuality as full sensuality, freer from the genitalization of sex often prevalent in the sexist paradigm.[76]

Sexism, as male domination in heterosexual relationships, moves against gays and lesbians as heterosexism and homophobia in part because affirming relatedness to the body affirms a very powerful part of human being in the world, to which heterosexists are often not open and of which they are often afraid. Dominating and being dominated by each other, and dominating others to protect our games of domination, can seem safer than unleashing our own bodily power. To really do so would call into question the entirety of the structuring of power that constitutes our world.

I propose, then, this christic sacralizing of the body as an essential component of a refigured christology and christopraxis. It is designed to work against every tendency (direct and indirect) to present the body as antidivine, and to set in place a christological counter-strategy directed toward the major distortion in heterosexism's supremacist logic: the dualism of body/spirit. Our emancipatory rhetoric on behalf of gay and lesbian communities, our concerned ministries, and our counter-explanations of problematic biblical passages are surely necessary. But unless the emancipation worked by the Christ is understood as sensualization, we will not have an effective strategy for countering the supremacist logic that reinforces cultural practices of oppression toward gays and lesbians. Christology must therefore address the dualism that devalues the body, and it must undertake this by employing its most powerful strategy: naming and thinking embodiment as locus of the Christ, of the sacred in human life and history.

The theological concern expressed in this strategy is not just a concern for gay and lesbian persons. It is that, but the cries of these oppressed ones alert the entire community to its need for emancipation, given the present alienation from our bodies, from those of our own gender, from ourselves.

To be in Christ is to be on the way to revaluing one's body, its sexuality, its known processes, its mysteries, even its decay and death; it is to live in and with the body in all its frailty and particular fullness. Perhaps an acceptance of our bodies' death is the hardest of all. Our fear of bodies and death is so intertwined. This is powerfully evident in current apathy and insensitivity to the AIDS crisis. In that crisis, our heterosexist-supremacist logics seize upon AIDS in its death-dealing capacity and often interpret this as just desert for the homosexual's affirmation and celebration of embodiment and sexuality outside heterosexist spheres. Resistance to this supremacist logic of heterosexism must also entail a life of solidarity, in writing and practice, with those of any sexual orientation whose bodies are being lost to AIDS.[77]

To be in Christ, understood as emancipatory sensualization, is also to be on the way to rediscovery of friendships with those of one's own gender. For women, this would seem to mean the good news that one's body and being are not ordained to man, but are given, within their agency and orientation, to themselves, to their sisters and brothers, within a whole range of mutually edifying relationships. For men, being in Christ means growing into friendships with other men, whether gay or not, free from the competition that characterizes so much male bonding and free from the camaraderie built around misogynist assumption and banter. Such friendships may be full and intimate without being projected as involving sexual imagery. Against the backdrop of men's alienation from their own gender, which I developed in chapter 4, this view of growth can breathe new, positive meaning into even the androcentric translations of Jesus' words about friends: "Greater love has no man than this, that a man lay down his life for his friends" (John 15:13). Jesus was part of a movement in which his associates were called not servants but friends. Understandably, emancipated into such friendship with their own, men are also freed for new alliances and friendships with women. This is because in this way of being in Christ, it is easier to shake free from having to depend on women as the "all-nurturing ones" or from viewing them fearfully as the "monstrous" ones.

Here is emancipation in Christ as sensualization, restoring both men and women to friendship with their bodies, with those of their own gender and across genders in new, healing ways.

Sensualization and the Reconciliatory Postures

More can be said about the reconciliatory postures of admiration and liminality, here as qualifying and enriching sensualization.

First, their celebration of alliance in difference keeps thought and practices of emancipation aware of both the connections and the distinctions between the different forms of emancipation in Christ. Concerning the two thus far presented (maternalization and sensualization), there is a general connection in that both emancipations involve structural releases from the abstraction from the woman made into monstrous mother (in sexism) and abstraction from the body (in hetero-realism). The structural emancipation of both maternalization and sensualization is connected in seeking to reverse that abstracting process and its oppressive consequences, especially for women and for gay and lesbian communities, but ultimately for the whole community.

The reconciliatory admiration and liminal co-intending of difference, however, does not allow the process of maternalization and sensualization to be taken as identical. They are both distinctive practices of Christian resistance, calling for the initiatives of different groups (women in the one case, gays and lesbians in the other) and demanding distinctive dynamics of solidarity from others who may support their struggles for emancipation.

Second, the reconciliatory postures of admiration and liminality keep all our practices of emancipation as sensualization aware of the different modes of body experience inside as well as outside North Atlantic societies. Without this awareness, the rhetoric of emancipation easily replays much of the sweeping generality and stereotypes featured in contemporary homophobia. In particular, the celebration of difference will lead us to recall that analogues to gay and lesbian practice in some other cultures and historical periods have not been forced to assume the outlaw status they have in our present sociohistorical period.[78] Our theological discourse, therefore, may be influenced by study of the mythological and religious language of other cultures and of other historical periods, language that may give greater worth to gay and lesbian practice than is true in our own religious traditions. Reconciliatory postures oriented to the wonder of difference will allow a freedom for heterosexual, gay, and lesbian groups from the stereotypical generalizations so regularly attached to them.

CHRIST AND EMANCIPATING BLACKNESS

If there is to be a thoroughgoing critique of and resistance to white racism, then I suggest that christology needs to articulate emancipation as a freeing of blackness as a set of images and symbols that relate to the real freedoms sought by black peoples in North America. Gayraud Wilmore has suggested that what the churches need is a "blackenization." Wilmore uses this term to refer to a process by which white people expose themselves to black culture "no less than they have always expected blacks to act white in order to be accepted."[79] This is a crucial part of the christology I will emphasize here, one that emancipates blackness within and for a new christopraxis. Emancipating blackness involves a process by which christological symbols and meanings become emancipating for blacks no less than they have in the past reinforced blacks' oppression.

Christology does not achieve such transformation by itself, but in its capacity of informing an emancipatory communal christopraxis, it can begin to do this. Above all, christology's logic of participation "in Christ" must be developed as a counterstrategy to white fantasies of blackness that reinforce — not only in whites but sometimes also in African Americans[80] — a general abstraction from the material, the bodily, the matrix of being, the dark.

The Blackness of Christ

In twentieth-century North American theology, the blackness of Christ has been a theme for reflection in Albert Cleague's *The Black Messiah*, James Cone's *God of the Oppressed*, Allan Boesak's *Black and Reformed*, and to a certain extent in the work by Dutch scholar Theo Witvliet, *The Way of the Black Messiah*. In these works and others, writers propose and consider such phraseology as "Jesus is black," "The black Christ," the "black messiah."[81] In my theology courses, and in the churches generally, I think, such phrases scandalize even more than another phrase, also frequently troubling to white Christian communities: "black theology."

Talk of the black Christ provokes a more notable disorientation because we are not referring simply to a specific theology done by black scholars (as in "black theology" or "black theology of liberation"). Rather, blackness is being attributed to that which names the locus of divine incarnation, the central salvific power in Christianity: "Christ." That move cannot help but scandalize and disorient what Kovell has termed our "metaracist" societies.[82]

I suggest that it is precisely this kind of disorientation that christological reflection and proclamation need, not to glory in disorientation itself but to inscribe in thought a reorientation for action against white racism. Sustained action against white racism, against its complex, deep-running fantasies of blackness, will require among other strategies a countering mythos that utilizes semiotic codes revaluing symbolism of the color black.

To speak or write about the blackness of Christ, the central symbol of sacral presence in culture and history for Christians, is markedly provocative in face of the supremacist logic that operates in both the conscious and unconscious registers of white racism. It weaves together what is often most devalued (blackness and all its meanings) with the central value of Christian faith and practice (Christ). Until we allow this to happen, until we allow the Christ to meet us as black, white theologians' calls for the liberation of African Americans easily becomes only one more form of paternalistic liberalism. Such calls do not quite let go of the culturally learned prejudice that white is preferable. Until blackness is allowed to be sacralized as christic, it will rarely be taken by Christians to be as full of truth, goodness, and beauty as whiteness.

To invoke the blackness of Christ is consonant with the logic of christology I have already presented. "Christ" names a sociohistorical dynamic of reconciliatory emancipation. Insofar as that Christ dynamic works emancipation for black peoples who suffer white racism, that Christ is black, met in the rising up to structured freedom of black bodies and cultural practice. Even Jesus is black, insofar as he is an agent or leaven participating in that christic emancipation of blackness. The actual skin color of Jesus of Nazareth is not the main point, although the probability that his pigmentation as a Jew in Palestine was substantially darker than that of most North

Atlantic white racists is not irrelevant. What is crucial is that Jesus can be viewed as an agent in a Christ dynamic working emancipation for black sufferers of racism.

A christology that presents emancipation as freeing blackness for Christian symbols and meanings, primarily through acknowledging the value in "the black Christ" lifted up by black theologians, offers for christopraxis new understandings of what it means to be and grow in Christ, and some of these may be discussed here.

The mythos of the black Christ will generate different meanings of being "in Christ" for African Americans than for most whites. What it means for blacks is best articulated by blacks themselves. A mythos of the black Christ would seem to me to mean for African Americans neither a rejection of their blackness (their past being and present cultural experience) nor a romanticization of blackness. Still less would it be a call to blacks to "assimilate" to predominantly white structures by engaging in the metaracist system's pursuit of status, wealth, and prestige.[83] Rather, faithfulness to the black Christ as an emancipating of blackness in African American practice means something more like what Cornel West called a "humanist" response in *Prophesy Deliverance!*. This response is a movement aiming to

> foster the fulfillment of the potentialities and capacities of all individuals, encourage motivation and originality in Afro-American culture, and expand people's control over those institutions which deeply affect their lives. . . . Afro-Americans are viewed as both meek and belligerent, kind and cruel, creative and full — in short, as human beings. This tradition does not romanticize or reject Afro-American culture; instead, it accepts this culture for what it is, the expression of an oppressed human community imposing its distinctive form of order on an existential chaos, explaining its political predicament, preserving its self-respect, and projecting its own special hopes for the future.[84]

For whites, emancipating blackness will mean learning about our participation in movements of solidarity with this African American struggle. Our being and growing in Christ as emancipating blackness is not our working *for* them, but a participating *with and for* them in that christic emancipation moving in our midst as well as in theirs. But there are some particular tasks for the white theologian that should not be relegated to anyone else. I refer to the task of suggesting a christic growth by whites into awareness of our own blackness. How to articulate this in a way that really resists the powers of supremacist logics is the challenge of the next section.

The Meanings of a Blackenized Christian Mythos

When examining the psychohistory of racism in chapter 4, I noted that the fantasy of blackness that renders darker-skinned peoples monstrous and exploitable and reinforces power arrangements oppressive to blacks is in large part a projection by whites of their hatred for their own "dark animality"—hatred for their own passions, drives, senses of embodied finiteness. There must begin, precisely in resistance to this hatred, a whole new way of seeing into our own darkness. This is not a kind of seeing that directs a glaring light at the dark regions of our being; it is one that looks into the darkness accepting its mystery, its obscurity. Maybe the darkness can be valued precisely as darkness, as spaces that are just as much a part of us (our power, our strength, our origin, and our telos) as those spaces we think we have brought to clarity "in the light."

Largely undeveloped components of Hebrew and Christian traditions suggest possibilities for revaluing blackness through and beyond its christic sacralization. Indeed, in a number of settings blackness has already been used as a means of positive valuation, and these uses prepare the way for discerning better the beauty and value of a blackenized mythos.

Traditions of African American women poets impressively point the way toward the richness, comprehensiveness, and promise of blackness. This revaluation of blackness is, as Gwendolyn Brooks wrote, first and foremost a "Primer for Blacks."

> Blackness
> is a title,
> is a preoccupation,
> is a commitment Blacks
> are to comprehend—
> and in which you are
> to perceive your glory.

More is going on here than glorying in a particular group. The glory resides in a ubiquity, fullness, and endurance of blackness through all creation.

> Blackness
> stretches over the land.
> Blackness—
> the Black of it,
> the rust-red of it,
> the milk and cream of it,
> the tan and yellow-tan of it,
> the deep-brown middle-brown high-brown of it,
> the "olive" and ochre of it—
> Blackness
> marches on.[85]

The pivoting between bold affirmation of black peoples' particularity and an equally bold comprehension of history and cosmos as dark, black matrix

is also strikingly present in Margaret Walker's "THIS IS MY CENTURY
. . . Black Synthesis of Time":

> O Man, behold your destiny.
> Look on this life
> and know our future living;
> our former lives from these our present days
> now melded into one.
> . . .
> The dying Western sky
> with yawning gates of death,
> from decadence and dissonance
> destroying false and fair;
> worlds of our galaxies,
> our waning moons and suns
> look on this living hell
> and see the rising sun.
> . . .
> This is my century
> I saw it grow
> from darkness into dawn
> . . .
> The fireworks overhead
> flame red and blue and gold
> against one darkened sky.
> . . .[86]

In the blackness wherein these poets see their own peoples revalued,
decked in an all-encompassing glory, is there not a shock of recognition for
us whites? We along with all humanity seem not only to be held in, tran-
scended by, maybe even engulfed in blackness. Have we whites feared
precisely this? Have we responded to the fact of our beginning in the
opaque, and to the fact of our returning *to* the opaque, with a dread concerning darkness, a dread projected outward in semiotic color codes
through which we desperately, viciously, try to tame the darkness by dealing
death, torture, and racist enslavement to the darker ones among us? It
would indeed appear that whites, ourselves suspended in a web of an
opaque, dark, all-encompassing realm, have defensively spun out our own
imaginary symbolic codes and institutional practices, catching up blacks and
"the colored races" as so many instances of stain, defilement, things to be
exchanged and systemically oppressed.

In truth, have not we been suppressing ourselves in the process of inflict-
ing racist horrors upon others? If so, emancipation as freeing of blackness
must not only mean release of blacks from white racism through the movement and agency of blacks (which it must surely be, first of all). It must

also mean a release of whites from those racist dynamics that abstract from our own darkness, from those powerful, threatening forces of the opaque, in our bodies, our unconscious, our passions. In Paul Tillich's language, we have reacted to the "shock of non-being" by seeking to secure our being at the expense of other beings, especially, as in racism, by making black peoples and their skin color the symbol of our own hated (repressedly loved?) nonbeing. An emancipation that frees and sacralizes blackness will mean release from this repression into new ways of being in relation to nonbeing. We are not released simply into a macabre dance, into a drifting in nothingness, wherein we celebrate only the abyss, though the release must mean these things in part. Being, our lives and light, are only in relation to nonbeing, death, and the darkness. Not to see this is to deny our own constitutive matrix, and all too often this denial has entailed denying quality life to others. Whiteness, then, becomes a terror let loose upon the world, and white skin becomes, in fact, a symbol of a pallid ash destroying all.

Where are the Christian theologians who might extend reflection on the disorienting "black Christ" into a reoriented theology that can inform a ritual and practice sensitizing us to the whiteness of evil and sin, reminding us that the Creator/Creatress spoke and acted to bring forth light from a dark home and that the earth's people were formed from the browning earth?[87] In this darkness we connect with our own matrix, meeting that which surely is mystery, more than us, but nonetheless part of our own being. Here again we may encounter *Christus Mater*. Thinkers who reorient theology in the way of a black Christ may come, if from nowhere else, from the ranks of Christians of all colors who know that their own darkness and coloring are being emancipated to fill in a new, beauteous, densely textured garden.

Freeing Blackness and the Reconciliatory Postures

The reconciliatory postures of admiration and liminality are already well at work in this task of emancipation. The affirmation of difference is powerfully implied in the symbolisms of blackness noted above. The blackness that is appropriated as the strength and glory of a particular people is also all encompassing: "It stretches over the land." You cannot think blackness without thinking also, in Brooks's words, of "the black of it," too, "the rust-red of it,"

> the milk and cream of it,
> the tan and yellow-tan of it,
> the deep-brown middle-brown high-brown of it,
> the "olive" and the ochre of it.[88]

A first task of the Christian postures of reconciliation concerning emancipation as freeing blackness, then, is to preserve this wondrous difference in blackness, its fullness, its variegation. What Wilmore terms "blackenization" has to do primarily with the emancipation of darker-skinned peoples from oppressive structures of white racism, whether these structures are in the United States, South Africa, Brazil, or anywhere else. At the same time, this christic emancipation, if qualified by reconciliatory postures, always seeks alliance among the different groups seeking this emancipation: African Americans of the United States with the African Americans of Brazil, "coloreds" with "the Blacks" in South Africa, and all of these with one another. Again, the purpose of these postures is not to merge these in a melting pot but to nurture that blackness which calls forth the fullness of difference in alliance.

A second task of these reconciliatory postures in relation to what I have termed the freeing of blackness is to focus attention on the diversity of racisms. Although we may speak of white racism as a fundamental racist distortion that North American Christians must resist, a Christian admiration and liminality will further insist that wherever racisms are found, critical thought and action meet them with resistance and hope for transformation. Christian admiration and liminality demand full critical response also, for example, to the United States government's past and present repression of Native American peoples, to the anti-Semitisms of our day, to ladino racism against Amerindian peoples in Guatemala and elsewhere in Latin America.

A third task of the reconciliatory postures respecting the freeing of blackness is one parallel to the tasks already specified in relation to maternalization and sensualization. The Christian postures of admiration and liminality also nurture an orchestration of differences among the various forms of oppression. The distinctive problematics of racism must be thought in relation to sexism, hetero-realism, and classism. Hence, the emancipation as freeing blackness is a struggle in hope that Christians, in thought and action, need to undertake with a conscious awareness also of the other emancipations: maternalization, sensualization, and also of the materialization that I will present in this chapter's last section.

The reconciliatory postures among emancipatory struggles that preserve the distinctiveness of each struggle are strikingly evident in the recent work of James H. Cone, especially in his book, *For My People*. The posture, tone, and critical agenda of that volume display his own increasing openness to critique of the plurality of oppressions and of the cultural diversity of those dominations—even to the point of identifying some inadequacies in his own earlier writing without retracting any of the force of his critique of white supremacy or his primary commitment to a black theology of liberation.[89] Here I identify the Christian reconciliatory postures at work, insisting on the primacy of the struggle for emancipation from white racism while seeking connections to the other struggles, to the struggles against other racisms and against the other distortions of sexism, hetero-realism,[90] and classism. From another direction, which emphasizes classism and the needs of the poor, Gustavo Gutiérrez has called for a new sensitivity among Latin American theologians to racism and sexism.[91] That too is a sign of the Christian reconciliatory posture in theology.

Finally, as a fourth task of Christian reconciliatory postures, I suggest that the bold sacralization of blackness, viewed as both color meaning and as cultural movement for emancipation, needs to develop away from notions of human difference based on skin color toward those based on more complex and manifold differences of ethnicity and culture. The white racist fixation on skin color and physiognomy has demanded a counter-strategy in North America of emancipatory symbolism that revalues blackness. Nonetheless, the admiration and liminal co-intending of difference, ever vigilant against stereotypes and ever pursuing the differences that make for authentic alliance, must move to celebrate also the differences occurring among peoples who share the same skin color and physiognomy. The cultural differences among black peoples can be considerable, of course. The cultural differences between the Ndembu of northwest Zambia and African Americans in North America constitute an obvious example. The central point is that once blackness is revalued in resistance to white racism, there abides the task of admiring cultural differences, beyond the often insufficient categories provided by a prism of colors. Human difference is more variegated and complex than any color schema can differentiate. Ultimately this means that what we might call color-coded theologies. if they really celebrate human difference, will have to become culturally coded ones as well. We cannot expect from the Ndembu or the Bantu, or even from every black group in North America, a single black theology. Christian admiration and liminality look toward a time in which celebration of cultural differences can occur in the wake of emancipation from white racism.

CHRIST AND THE MATERIALIZATION OF HUMAN LIFE AND HOPE

The task of emancipation that is pertinent to classism I name materialization. *Christus Mater* began the movement of reconciliatory emancipation, at least as I have traced it in this chapter, with a maternalizing impulse working freedom for women and, after challenging and enabling us to seek the freedoms of sensualization and blackenization, *Christus Mater* works an emancipation for distorted and threatened material infrastructures.[92]

The relation of Christian faith and practice to matter and to materialism is a complex one. Marxist notions of historical materialism have notoriously been viewed as antithetical to Christian faith and practice by people both inside and outside Christian circles. Yet many have recognized that we can also speak of a Christian materialism, in the sense of a thoroughgoing valuation of material creation and of that which preserves it.[93] To the extent that this valuation entails a critique of classisms that often destroy the material health of people and creation, conversation with the different Marxist critiques of classism will also be fruitful. Although Christian faith and practice have often reinforced classist oppression, it has also reinforced proletarian struggle. Given the witness of the *comunidades de base* throughout Latin America, it is almost banal to make such a point. Often this has meant, as well, that Marxism and Christianity can share many of the same values, despite real differences between them.[94]

In this section, my primary concern is with the christic valuation of material creation and some suggestions of what that valuation means for contemporary constructive christology and the church's christopraxis. How, I ask, does that valuation mandate a refiguring of christology and christopraxis?

The Christic Valuation of Material Practice

Materialization, as a dynamic of Christian emancipation, has a particular structure. The first element of the structure of materialization is a revaluing of the earth's resources, contributing to the restructuring of processes that channel those resources to those most in need of them. It is a dynamic that can also be referred to as a "material practice." This is a practice of revaluing the life-giving elements of material creation themselves; it is also a practice of building, maintaining, and rebuilding structures and policies that give life to those denied their material needs and sustenance rights.[95] This material practice is predominantly focused on such life-giving work, hence it is a positive work, though it necessarily bears a negative feature as well. That is, the practice is also a movement of resistance against all structural arrangements that devalue material creation and fail to disburse those elements justly. Recalling my definition of classism, we may understand the negative dimension of Christian material practice as a resistance against classism, the systemic tendency of ruling classes (well-meaning or not) to reinforce the distance between themselves and subordinate classes by preventing a dispersal of power through a restructuring of wealth, privilege, and access to resources and technology. Resistance against classist structures that complements the revaluation of the earth's resources can take many forms. Here I am primarily concerned with how a constructive christic vision can be developed that both contributes to this resistance and might help nurture ongoing programs that structure our material being in life-nourishing ways.

Members and groups in Christian traditions have often marshaled their reflection and action in order to serve those who suffer material deprivation.[96] Concerning North American churches of many sorts, we only need to observe the rhetoric and actions bound up with mission budgets, social witness, "church and society" committees, stewardship, and more, to note that at least a general "social concern" or sensitivity to "the poor" is often considered integral to Christian discipleship (even in ecclesial settings where the "spirituality" actually practiced seems to fail to manifest social concern).

Emancipatory materialization, as I am developing it here, however, is something more demanding, more grace-full. I am interpreting the revaluing of the earth's elements and the restructuring of their distribution in materialization as a participation "in Christ." Materialization is a being caught up in the sociohistoric dynamic of reconciliatory emancipation that I have been presenting as distinctive to the Christ's interpersonal working in society and history. In revaluing material elements, working for their life-nourishing functions, and resisting classism, there resides nothing less than a participating in Christ, a being in Christ. *Mater* and material practice are loci of the incarnational mystery. We must note here, then, a christic sacralizing of *mater* and material practice that makes the material practice of Christians not just faithfulness to Christ, much less a matter of just "doing good" or "serving the poor." Rather, being given to this material practice is also a veritable being in Christ. Although there are surely many ways of engaging in this material practice, to fail to manifest this material practice at all means not yet being graced with the presence of Christ.

Note how the convergence here of Christ with material practice does not simply mean a resistance to the distortion that is generally termed classism. If we recall my earlier exploration of critiques of classism, we will, more specifically, observe the need to resist the abstracting from matter that was so powerful a force in capitalism's "exchange abstraction."[97] A Christian material practice cannot simply be a matter of making money in capitalist systems and then sending some to the poor. It may include that in some fashion. More fundamentally, this material practice means challenging the abstracting propensities that lie at the very heart of capitalist perspectives as we know them, propensities that not only drive the capitalist frame but also reinforce distance between the makers and controllers of monetary systems, on the one hand, and those who lack needed access to the earth's goods, on the other.

The Christ met in emancipatory materialization is, therefore, not easily adapted to a life of practice in a capitalist mode. In fact, Christ involves Christians in a life of resistance to familiar capitalist practice, even when there are intentions to "do good for," or to "develop," the worlds of the poor. Participating in this Christ, therefore, will often mean that Christian discipleship is, as Metz observes, a "discipleship as class treason."[98] Metz's words are worth recording in full:

Did not Jesus himself incur the reproach of treason? Did not his love bring him to that state? Was he not crucified as a traitor to all the apparently worthwhile values? Must not Christians therefore expect, if they want to be faithful to Christ, to be regarded as traitors to bourgeois religion?[99]

Christians, Metz continues, will often be dismissed, and their efforts will be "branded as treason by those who are infatuated with our system of exchange and barter and whose rejection of the inhuman consequences of capitalism is at most only verbal."[100]

This is not to say that such a "treasonous" material practice mandates a total withdrawal from involvement in every structure or monetary resource related to capitalist systems. That is hardly possible in the late twentieth century as it is presently structured, nor do I think it would be an effective Christian material practice. Emancipation in Christ does insist on nothing short of the sacralizing of *mater* and of its material practice; in so doing, *Christus Mater* sets Christians against the central dynamic of capitalist practice and against the abstracting mechanisms beating at its heart. Consequently, though there can be no naive casting off of every capitalist entailment, Christians seem called by the Christ of emancipatory materialization to work against capitalism's exchange abstraction and to dream powerfully of a world in which the elements of the earth are shared in systems free from capitalism. The kingdom of Christ we await is not simply a perfected exchange economy.

The christic valuation of material practice can be articulated in relation to a crucial New Testament passage, the eschatological parables of Matthew 25:31ff., in which members of the Christian community have their connectedness to the Christ[101] through action that meets human need for food, drink, clothing, welcome to strangers, visitation in sickness, being present to the imprisoned, and the like. The passage is particularly important because here the classical distinction between the Christ's person and work is inseparably connected to a communal praxis for "the least of these," and this praxis is, as the final lines of the parable suggest, the mark of a community which enters eternal life.

Matthew 25:31ff. has a long, varied history of interpretation. A central emphasis cannot be missed, however. Here, human agents are presented as "in Christ" — as in One whose coming means transformation into fulfilling and enduring life — when they are given to a life of meeting the material needs of the hungry, the thirsty, the stranger, the naked, the imprisoned. This is not simply a divine imperative from Christ to go into faithful service; no, more accurately, the message is that to serve in this way is to serve the Christ. The full radicality of the passage is underscored by the use of the emphatic formula, "Truly I say to you. . ." Then we find the startling juxtaposition that takes both the faithful and the unfaithful by surprise: ". . . as you did it to one of the least of these who are mine, you did it to me" (Mt. 25:40).

Here there is a valuation of Christians' material practice and a sacralization of it. Christians come to life in Christ by being at work with and for the material needs of the least of these. Doing unto these is not a second act, occurring after or in addition to knowing and being in Christ. The latter is the kind of spirituality that permits so many of us North Americans to call ourselves Christians without resisting the systems that wreak material suffering upon so many of the world's poor. No, doing unto the least of these is the act in which the Christ of life is met. Abiding in material practice for the least of these is an abiding in Christ.

In North American communities, perhaps especially in Protestant ones, two objections are frequently registered against this christic sacralization of material practice. First, the emphasis on material practice can be feared as compromising the primacy of grace as the condition for participation in Christ. If we need to be doers of such a material practice in order to be in Christ, so wonder those who raise this objection, does this not make our life in Christ dependent on our own labor? Some Protestants especially may be inclined to see here yet another "works righteousness."

In response, it should be observed that the sacralizing of material practice, i.e., the insistence on material practice as a necessary mark of being in Christ, does not entail claiming that we are the sole agents who effect the material practice, or that our labor achieves a major salvific transformation of ourselves or others. The language of gift and grace can still be affirmed. Affirming the sacrality of our material practice does not supplant the Christian experiences of gift and grace; rather it emphatically clarifies the nature of the gift. We are given to enter this material practice. To be sure the volition of the agent is involved; no specious piety of grace and gift should force us to overlook that. Nonetheless, agents of material practice themselves usually bear witness to the fact that the material practice that is of the essence of knowing or being in Christ, without which they would not be in Christ, is caused by that which is more encompassing than their volition, something to which they have come or have been given. Doing is a gift. Material practice is a gift. To avoid material practice because it is somehow thought to issue in "works righteousness" is really a disguised effort to avoid the demands of the greater gift.

A second objection made against the sacralization of material practice is that it reduces Christ or the Incarnate One to a material level, particularly to our material practice. Two responses need to be made here. It should be noted first of all that this objection usually assumes precisely that dualism of Christian spirit and matter that has been a central concern of this project. The fear in the objection is that the material, often presumed to be a locus of evil or as somehow anti-divine, will detract from the spiritual. To the extent that this objection rests on that problematic dualism it must be criticized, as I have suggested in previous chapters.

We can also provide a second kind of response to the objection that sacralizing material practice "reduces" Christ to our material practice. It simply needs to be observed that affirming the sacrality of our material practice does not, in logic or practice, necessitate the view that now the sacred is exhaustively "contained in" or "reduced to" material practice. One might say that material practice is the only way we encounter Christ without claiming that not *all* of the sacred mystery of Christ's being in the world or with us, is known in that way. What does remain true, however, and what I have been suggesting throughout, is that the mystery is known and we participate in it not by looking away from material practice but by being given to it. We know the mystery especially from within material practice. That claim insists on a particular *kind* of encounter with the sacred; at the heart of materiality it does not reduce the sacred to the dimensions of our encounter. A christic sacralization of material practice, essential to emancipatory materialization, therefore, entails a supplanting of neither Christians' experience of grace nor of their experiences of the unfathomable wonders of divine mystery.

Christic Material Practice and Sacramental Practice

With the christic revaluing of the earth's resources and of the material practice that distributes them to those in need, a Christian motion of resistance to the exchange abstraction is initiated. For Christians to be in Christ is to be moving in the path of valuing the earth's resources, resisting any classist structure that prohibits their just distribution, working also to build and rebuild more adequate structures. Many kinds of actions are needed and are intrinsic to such a material practice. They may include citizen lobbying groups to end world hunger, community organizing projects in North American cities, land reform movements in Central America, or any number of strategies designed to rectify the "economic apartheid" emerging in many areas of development in the United States. None of these efforts of material practice, as part of the christic valuation I have proposed, is reducible to efforts in social concern and social witness, generally defined. They are a participation in Christ.

In order to sustain this conviction within Christian material practice, however, it is not sufficient to revalue material practice in the form of many world-engaging acts. We must also restructure the Christian community's own worship and other ritual practice so that these actually nurture Christian movements that engage world structures with a faithful, effective material practice.

There are many ways to work for this transformation in Christian communities. Here I want to turn especially to churches' celebrating of the sacraments. Notably, for the sake of a Christian material practice it is necessary to bring the christology I have been developing into relation with a sacramental practice of the Eucharist or Lord's Supper.

There is perhaps no area of traditional Christian community that more displays our traditions' alienation from *mater*. Here is a communal practice in which the elements of the earth — food and drink, bread and wine — are prepared, celebrated, and distributed, while the meanings of these are often systematically abstracted from the earthiness of those elements. Further, the celebration is often abstracted from women in that it is still difficult for women, in Protestant as well as in Roman Catholic churches, to be regular celebrants of these rites. In reverent tones a celebrant usually recites, "This is my body which is broken for you. This is my blood shed for you." And yet, during times of intense concentration, with bowed heads and bended knees, we are often led to search for spiritualized meanings away from the stuff of earth, of food, drink, body, and blood. We are often ritualized away from looking to our material practice. Perhaps the abstracting look is directed inward to an individual's guilt consciousness, perhaps upward in search of an ascendant spirituality that lifts one above the fray of material struggle and practice.

The very history of the Eucharist shows the abstraction, the spiritualization of this Christian sacramental practice. The celebration of the Eucharist in the earliest periods of the Christian movement was conjoined with an "Agape meal" or "love feast," an informal supper of the church for purposes of community (*koinonia*) and sharing with the poor. It is not clear precisely what the distinctions were between the Eucharist and the Agape, between the sacramental memory or presence of Christ in the Eucharist and the social practice of *koinonia* and sharing with the poor. Whatever the distinctions were and however clearly they were drawn, it is certain that by the time of Justin Martyr (100–163?) the two types of observances were still conjoined.[102] Indeed, if the early Christian movement was as marked by a reconciliatory emancipation, as I have suggested in chapter 5, we would expect some elements of social practice and community to be integrally related to the sacrament.

While there is no record of the actual time and place that the Agape was detached from the sacramental Eucharist, it is clear that the separation eventually occurred. There seems no unanimity among scholars as to the reasons for the detachment, though various theories have been put forth: linking the two meals allowed too many possibilities for abusing one or the other, or, perhaps, practical considerations stemming from the growth of larger congregations made it difficult to maintain the connection.[103] Whatever the reasons, with its detachment from the Agape meal, the Eucharist itself underwent important modifications. Among the several changes was a tendency to give primary stress to interpretations of the sacrament as "supernatural food." Christian spirituality could easily abstract its sacramental practice and religious meanings from the events of meal preparation, eating, drinking, and sharing of the elements.

Although clearly making an end run around a whole number of complications in Christian sacramental theology, the anthropologist Marvin Harris has noted the abstraction I am attending to, and he also issues challenges to Christian practice:

Protestant and Catholic thinkers have spilled much blood and ink over the question of whether the wine and wafer are actually transubstantiated into the corporeal substance of Christ's blood and body. The real significance is that by spiritualizing the eating of the paschal lamb and by reducing it to a nutritiously worthless wafer, Christianity long ago unburdened itself of the responsibility of seeing to it that those who came to the feast did not go home on an empty stomach. The point . . . is that the nutritive value of the common feast is virtually zero, whether there is transubstantiation or not.[104]

A similar challenge emanates from the provocative words of Mary Daly. She comments on

the significance of the fact that the bread and wine of the "Eucharist" are called "elements." In traditional catholicism people must will to believe that they are not eating and drinking bread and wine, and thus acquire the habit of self-deception about the elemental acts of taking food and drink.[105]

Any number of responses could be made to both Harris and Daly, contesting the precise accuracy of their assumptions or the fairness of certain aspects of critiques. What cannot be missed, and what I suggest should not be dodged, is their challenge to sacramental practice and to leaders of Christian communities generally that it is necessary to consider whether or not our sacramental practice of the Eucharist meets elemental human need or whether it distracts people from seeing that need.

Actually, some Christian leaders, often in situations where human material need and classist distortion cannot be ignored, have themselves seen the deception and hypocrisy operative in a sacramental practice shorn of a faithful material practice. Priests of Ecuador, for example, had to break from automatic practice of the sacrament and cry:

The hour has now come for us as servants of the People of God in Ecuador, to unite our voices to the cry of the people and the voice of the apostle Paul: we cannot continue calmly to celebrate the event of liberation in the Eucharist, while oppressors and oppressed eat the same bread and drink the same wine—without any true reconciliation.[106]

A "true reconciliation" is effected when we are given to an emancipatory materialization that begins to release oppressed groups from the classist oppression that so often denies them sustained food and drink. How can our sacramental practice be joined to such an emancipatory material practice?

The understanding of Christ already developed through the last two chapters yields a notion of Christ's "real presence" that we need to allow to reshape our understanding of the sacramental practice of the Eucharist or Lord's Supper. The Christian tradition, in one way or another, has emphasized that celebration of the Eucharist involves a participation in the "real presence" of Christ. Perhaps this language is more explicit in Roman Catholic than in most Protestant traditions, but even in the latter the memorializations and celebrations are filled with Christians' awareness of the special presence of Christ in their sacramental practice of the Eucharist.

Christology can join with a sacramental theology of the Eucharist precisely at this point of reflection on the "real presence" or special presence of Christ in the sacramental act. Recall that the name Christ, as used throughout this work, names a sociohistorical dynamic of reconciliatory emancipation. As further developed in this chapter, this emancipation is a materialization involving a christic revaluing of the earth's material elements, a material practice that distributes them to those in need and which resists classism's exchange abstraction.

This sacralization of Christians' material practice is precisely what the earthy rite of the Eucharist needs to sustain and celebrate by means of regular sacramental practice. Christians experience a "real presence," the distinctive presence of Christ in the sacrament, through that rite's powers to restore them to a revaluing of the earthy elements of creation, to a material practice of distributing the elements to those in need and to resisting classism.

The Eucharist as sacramental practice, then, needs to become interpreted and structured as a practice for the overall material practice that is so central to an emancipatory resistance and recreation of human life in the face of classist distortions. From this perspective it is possible to affirm one observation made by John Paul II in a Lenten address. There he spoke of the Eucharist as "the active school of love for the neighbor."[107] Sacramental practice will only become such an active school when it is situated within a matrix of theological and homiletical interpretation that allows the sacraments' materiality to come forth as christic and emancipatory power.

Such interpretations need to be allowed to shape the form of the sacramental practice so that the Eucharist's or the Lord's Supper's character as a material practice is accentuated. The elements of bread and wine are not signs directing Christian faith, reflection, and practice away from these earthy elements so we can think of something else. Rather, they invite participation in the divine mystery through their materiality and through their inaugurating a sharing of these material, life-sustaining goods with others in need. This sacramental celebration of the earth's material elements, therefore, properly becomes a performance enabling a materialization of the earth's elements for those in need of them. From this perspective, all those bodies moving from church seats to fronts of gathered congregations partaking of the Eucharist can be viewed as Christians on the move to receive, give, and distribute the earth's food and drink, the earth's hungry and thirsty above all. The Eucharist's sacramental practice is a recurring, centering activity in the church that begins and highlights the essential character of Christians' material practice in the world.

This view of sacramental practice is not merely the stuff of futurist hopes. In some of today's most vital Christian communities these links between sacramental and material practice are evident. They are evident in those *comunidades de base* in Latin America where Christian worship and Bible study groups celebrate the Lord's Supper in close conjunction with the sharing of a meal. Especially when practiced in contexts of extreme material need, the materiality of sacramental practice is difficult to overlook.[108] Links between sacramental and material practice are manifest in those ritualized actions of some North American congregations that involve placing food-stuffs around the communion table or altar as part of the celebration of the Eucharist. These links are also evident when the words of institution are interwoven with communion prayers focused on the specific material needs of the church's local and global communities. When that happens the words of institution become "performative utterances" in ecclesial praxis, in which hearing those words and partaking of the elements set Christians in motion working for just distribution and redistribution of the earth's good elements.

Sacramental practice is not supplanted by material practice. Nor am I arguing for a replacement of the Eucharist by the Agape love feast. A sacramental practice of the Eucharist does need to be constructed in relation to Christians' material practice. Sacramental practice, in turn, needs to be seen as Christian participation in the structuring of the Christ's emancipatory materialization of life, especially for those whose lives are a slow death because of structures that deny them the earth's sustenance and nurture.[109] The emancipatory materialization of Christ in which we participate must have this impulse to structure in it, for the unequal distribution of wealth, and hence of the earth's resources, is obviously a structural problem. The Christian community's rituals, especially its sacramental practice of the Eucharistic supper, sustain a structuring of practice within the church that also sustains the structuring of community organizing, grass-roots citizen movements, and larger scale political actions designed to meet communities' material needs. Being a part of the hands-on, usually lifelong movements that are entailed in such struggles for emancipatory structures is nothing short of a participation in Christ. It is, again, to move and be moved in the way of the *Christus Mater*.

Materialization and the Reconciliatory Postures

The reconciliatory postures of admiration and liminality are no less important in emancipatory materialization than they were in relation to the other tasks of emancipation. Three meanings of the reconciliatory postures are especially important for christic materialization.

First, admiration as an approach to difference implies an important understanding of solidarity between members of different classes. Keeping in view the approach to difference articulated by Irigaray through commentary on sexual difference, we must insist, concerning class differences, that reconciliation between classes means acknowledging the realities of difference. This is essential for opening a space of solidarity between classes that is both free and engaging. Nothing is more tinged with *bathos* and *hubris* than the efforts of well-meaning members, usually of privileged classes, proclaiming their solidarity with subordinate classes.[110] Real solidarity is rooted in neither easy assumptions of unity, nor in "common humanity," nor in paternalistically designed strategies for "development" and "modernization" of the underclasses. Instead, through first attending to the depth and extent of alienation and difference, which involve not only differences of material wealth but also of worldview and social practice, we come into the kind of alliance that is characteristic of an authentic reconciliatory emancipation. Given the recognition of the extent of alienation, there then can be the Christian struggle to remove, wherever possible, the dehumanizing barriers of class.

Second, the reconciliatory posture's respect for difference and its vigilant resistance to every ethnocentrism preserve an essential respect for the cultural plurality of class formation and conflict. The dynamics of class are culturally variant. This does not make cross-cultural generalizations about class and classism impossible, but a reconciliatory admiration of difference here opens out into a particular kind of collaboration with post-Marxist, culturally specific class analyses that do greater justice to the cultural diversity of class formation.[111] These reconciliatory postures in class analysis are especially important as we North American theologians work with liberation theologians from a wide variety of continental locations. A materialized theology of emancipation from class domination risks a great disservice to the worldwide ecclesia if it develops a universal theological vision of class conflict that is unmindful of the significantly different cultural forms that class realities and struggles can assume.

Finally, the impulses of the reconciliatory postures to value difference will also resist viewing all domination from which emancipation is needed in strictly classist terms. Human exploitation and oppression cannot and should not be reduced to class dynamics. A Christian reconciliatory proviso, in relation to a materialization that resists classism, will lead both christology and christopraxis to not leave unattended the dominations I have discussed earlier: sexism, heterosexism, racism. This means not just naming them oppressions but allowing Christian discourse and practice to be shaped by their distinctive problematics.

As can be seen from a number of claims that I have already advanced, because the reconciliatory postures attend to these different problematics, we are thereby allowed to theorize connections between oppressions. These connections can provide conditions for orchestrating the different tasks of emancipation: maternalization, sensualization, blackenization, materialization.

Epilogue

RE-MEMBERING ESPERANZA

Throughout this work a key theme pertaining to connections between oppressions has been that of *abstraction*: abstracting from the woman/ mother in sexism; from the body and same-gender friendships in hetero-realism; from one's self and finitude in racism; from the earth and a sharing of its resources in classism. A fully reconciliatory emancipation from the oppressions that are built up around this abstracting practice must seek to ally the different emancipatory tasks that focus on different forms of oppressing abstractions. With the emergence of an alliance of such eman-cipatory strategies, there begins to occur a "remembering Esperanza"—a reconstituting of hope for all victims who are dismembered by the abstract-ing practices of oppression.

This interlocking resistance for emancipation, though having an eschat-ological component, is not mere futurist dreaming. To be sure, the eman-cipations for which we work will never fully be realized in any cultural-political situation of our time. Nor can any movement claim to manifest fully the reconciliatory emancipation needed. Nonetheless, that reconcili-atory emancipation is at work in our times, borne in some particularly striking places, though not the places around which powerful established churches often center their institutional practices and understandings of the Christian life.

One of the places to which we can look for examples of reconciliatory emancipation occurring as a sociohistorical dynamic involving different interlocking oppressions is in the Christian practice of landless mothers and their relatives organizing politically to find their "disappeared" children and fight for their children's future. Whether we are considering organi-zations like MADRE, Women for Guatemala, Somos Hermanas in the United States, or GAM and CO-MADRES in Central America, we can discern, in all its many meanings, the *Christus Mater*. There is at work in those efforts the power toward emancipation that is both a maternal and a material practice. There is, in other words, a christic revaluation of wom-en's reproductive powers, a caring connectedness to all of life, and a christic sacralization of the material practice working to make the earth's life-giving resources available to those denied them.

Writing and speaking of the Christ as operative in these places, in the labor of this kind of engagement, enables us to write, to pray, and to act with a whole new sensibility—really to reconstitute and to remember hope. Julia Esquivel, in one of the powerful poems she has written as a Guatemalan exile, does not let us forget the power that is at work at the heart of such movements. In the struggle of those in these movements, all of us are "Threatened with Resurrection."[1] In them the Christ rises to meet us, a dynamic, hope-making, emancipatory force.

It is the silent warm weeping
Of Indian women without their husbands,
it is the sad gaze of the children
fixed there beyond memory,
They have threatened us with resurrection.

Because they live
today, tomorrow, and always
on the streets—baptized with their blood
and in the air which gathered up their cry.

It is to the deaths, suffering, hope and joy of the world's movements of women and children, and all their families, that we should look to find the Christ and our life in Christ. This is not because Christians worship weakness and these movements show forth suffering in its acutest forms. Quite to the contrary. Here, and in places like them, we can see the Christ powerfully at work, refusing to abstract from the material worlds tended by these women in the hope of a new *familias* and a new *polis*. Here is the Christ effecting a structuring freedom from what is entailed in the *patria potestas*. Will the blood and struggle of these women's movements be acknowledged as transformative power, as the region of Christ's working, inviting authentic solidarity among all peoples? Women, it seems to me, keep daring to think so, dreaming against a stream of matriphobic practice, that somehow their bodies and blood should not be just the objects of abhorrent abstraction, but instead affirmed as a cleansing, transformative power that gives life. Such dreaming can be found powerfully at work among those who know their transformative power in spite of their being denied power and access to leadership roles in celebrating the sacraments.

Did the woman say,
When she held him for the first time in the
dim dark of a stable,
After the pain and the bleeding and the crying,
"This is my body; this is my blood"?

Did the woman say,
When she held him for the last time in the dim
rain on the hilltop,
After the pain and the bleeding and the dying,
"This is my body; this is my blood"?

Well that she said it to him then.
For dry old men,
Brocaded robes belying barrenness,
    Ordained that she not say it for him now.[2]

Women, on the basis of their calling by Christ, have an equal right with men to the ordination that enables them to say officially for Christ and the church, "This is my body, this is my blood." More, they may have a special effectiveness in saying precisely those words, because by their labor and their blood they ever bring the very materialization of life into new being, thus inviting all of us to do the same. Until all our churches can recognize, confess and meet the Christ in the life-praxis of women whose bodies and lives are so central to the emergence and sustenance of life—whether they become biological mothers or not—until then the church will be prone to reinforcing the abstractions that are so oppressive and death-dealing, the abstractions from women and their bodies, from friendship and sensuality, from the good darkness holding all life, from the earth that is our home.

Re-membering Esperanza, therefore, is far more than resistance to the abstractions that oppress women; it is also to practice with equal seriousness a resistance to those related abstractions of a white supremacism that oppresses African Americans, of a hetero-realism that subjugates gay and lesbian persons, and of the classism that impoverishes the underclasses. Until this *full* emancipatory practice becomes our churches' christopraxis, North American churches will more be the tools of oppression than the agents of reconciliatory emancipation. Until then, our calling is to struggle, celebrate and pray in the way of *Christus Mater*.

NOTES

PROLOGUE: AUTOBIOGRAPHY, RE-MEMBERING, THEOLOGY

1. See Claude Lévi-Strauss, "Race and History," in his *Structural Anthropology*, vol. 2 (New York: Basic Books, 1976), pp. 328-30. Lévi-Strauss demonstrates both traits in his *Tristes Tropiques* (New York: Atheneum, 1955), pp. 388-93.

2. See Dell Hymes, ed., *Reinventing Anthropology* (New York: Pantheon, 1969).

3. Johann Baptist Metz, *Faith in History and Society: Toward a Practical Fundamental Theology* (New York: Seabury, 1980), p. 219.

4. The Mudflower Collective, Carter Heyward, ed., *God's Fierce Whimsy* (New York: Pilgrim Press, 1985), pp. 87-142.

5. Robert Bellah, *Habits of the Heart: Individualism and Commitment in American Life* (Berkeley: University of California, 1985), pp. 142-63.

6. Calvin O. Schrag, *Communicative Praxis and the Space of Subjectivity* (Bloomington, Ind.: University of Indiana Press, 1986). Schrag's voice is an important one that needs a wider hearing. The great value of this book is that Schrag provides a deft review of North Atlantic philosophies over the past fifty years and then crafts a valuable proposal that moves us beyond the positions and counter- positions of modernism/postmodernism debates, to new tasks of reflection and action.

7. Ibid., p. 134.

8. On memory's capacities to effect this kind of awareness, see Metz, *Faith in History*, p. 194, and his discussions of memory in the writings of Herbert Marcuse, Walter Benjamin, and Theodor Adorno.

9. Ibid., pp. 220-21.

10. Edward S. Casey, *Remembering: A Phenomenological Study* (Bloomington and Indianapolis, Ind.: Indiana University Press, 1987), pp. 11-12.

11. Ibid. Casey actually discusses many more traits. My own are sometimes additions and sometimes combinations of the traits he identifies.

12. Ibid., p. 24.

13. Ibid., p. 27.

14. Lévi-Strauss, *Structural Anthropology*, pp. 328-32.

15. E. E. Evans-Pritchard, "Religion Among the Anthropologists," *Blackfriars* 41 (1960):110.

16. See anthropologist Kenelm Burridge, *Encountering Aborigines: Anthropology and the Australian Aboriginal, A Case Study* (New York: Pergamon, 1973), p. 17, for commentary on how in fact the very rise of modern, cultural anthropology is intertwined with missionary enterprises.

17. For the controversial study of the Wycliffe translators, see David Stoll, *Fishers of Men or Founders of Empire?: The Wycliffe Bible Translators in Latin America* (London: Zed Press, 1982). For a critique of Stoll's work and an anthropologist's

assessment of missionary experience and ethnographic work, see Robert B. Taylor, "The Summer Institute of Linguistics/Wycliffe Bible Translators," in Frank A. Salome, ed., *Missionaries and Anthropologists*, Part III, *Studies in Third World Societies* 26 (1985): 93-116.

18. Mark Kline Taylor, "In Praise of Shaky Ground: Christ and Cultural Plurality," *Theology Today* 43 (April 1986): 36-51.

19. Casey, *Remembering*, p. 23.

20. Beatriz Manz, *Refugees of a Hidden War: The Aftermath of Counterinsurgency in Guatemala* (Albany, N.Y.: SUNY, 1988), pp. 30, 239-40.

21. On the links between U.S. business interests in Guatemala, disdain for Amerindians, peasants and workers, and the death of these Guatemalans, see the words of Fred Sherwood, U.S. businessman and former president of the American Chamber of Commerce in Guatemala, "To Defend Our Way of Life: An Interview with a U.S. Businessman," by Allan Nairn, in *Guatemala in Rebellion: Unfinished History*, ed. by Jonathan L. Fried, Marvin E. Gettleman, Deborah T. Levenson, and Nancy Peckenham (New York: Grove Press, 1983), pp. 90, 91. For a detailed study of the way U.S. political and economic interests have long been imposed on Guatemala, see Richard H. Immerman, *The CIA in Guatemala: The Foreign Policy of Intervention* (Austin, Texas: The University of Texas Press, 1982).

22. This is carefully documented in Roy Gutman, *Banana Diplomacy: The Making of American Policy in Nicaragua 1981-1987* (New York: Simon and Schuster, 1988).

23. The phrase is the subtitle of a recent study of Guatemalan cultural and political life. See Jean-Marie Simon, *Guatemala: Eternal Spring, Eternal Tyranny* (New York: W.W. Norton, 1988). For anthropological documentation, see Manz, *Refugees of a Hidden War*. For the indispensable views of Latin Americans themselves, see the historical studies by Eduardo Galeano, *Las venas abiertas de América Latina*, 53rd ed. (Mexico City: Siglo Veintiuno Editores, 1988) and Severo Martínez Peláez, *La Patria del criollo: Ensayo de interpretactión de la realidad colonial Guatemalteca*, 8th ed. (Puebla, Mexico: Universidad Autónoma de Puebla, 1987).

24. See Gerda Lerner, *The Creation of Patriarchy* (New York: Oxford University Press, 1986), pp. 10, 238. Here I am invoking a distinction between sex and gender that is frequently employed. As one example, see Gerda Lerner's formula of "sex" as the biological given for men and women and "gender" as "the cultural definition of behavior defined as appropriate to the sexes in a given society at a given time."

25. On this valuation of difference, see Luce Irigaray, "The Fecundity of the Caress: A Reading of Levinas' Totality and Infinity, section IV, B, 'The Phenomenology of Eros,'" in *Face to Face with Levinas*, ed. by Richard A. Cohen (New York: SUNY Press, 1986), pp. 231-56. In the North American context, see Marilyn Chapin Massey, *Feminine Soul: The Fate of an Ideal* (Boston: Beacon, 1985), pp. 1-29, 163-88.

26. On this commitment by men to feminism as both "necessary and impossible" see Stephen Heath, "Male Feminism," in *Men in Feminism*, ed. Alice Jardine and Paul Smith (New York: Methuen, 1987), pp. 1-2; and Jon Snodgrass, "Men in the Feminist Movement," in his *A Book of Readings for Men Against Sexism* (Albion, Calif.: Times Change Press, 1977), pp. 6-11.

27. On these two types of theory and others on the North American scene, see Josephine Donovan, *Feminist Theory: The Intellectual Traditions of American Feminism* (New York: Ungar, 1983), pp. 1-63.

28. The necessity of self-implicature or of a radical self-locating consciousness

is based on the various critiques of objectivism in recent studies. My stress here on the intersubjectivity of the self arises from the critique and reformulations of the notion of the self and "subjectivity" also evident in recent studies. For summaries of the critique of objectivism, see Richard J. Bernstein, *Beyond Objectivism and Relativism: Science, Hermeneutics and Praxis* (Philadelphia: University of Pennsylvania Press, 1983). For summaries of the "end" and "retrieval" of notions of self and subjectivity see Schrag, *Communicative Praxis* (note 6), pp. 115-57.

29. Alice Jardine, "Men in Feminism: *Odor di Uomo* or *Compagnons de Route,*" in *Men in Feminism*, ed. by Alice Jardine and Paul Smith (New York: Methuen, 1987), p. 60.

30. See Hans-Georg Gadamer, "What is Practice? The Conditions of Social Reason," in his *Reason in the Age of Science*, trans. Frederick G. Lawrence (Cambridge, Mass.: M.I.T. Press, 1981), pp. 81-82, and Karl Marx, "Theses on Feuerbach (1845)," especially nos. III and IV, in Robert C. Tucker, ed., *The Marx-Engels Reader*, 2nd ed. (Princeton: Princeton University Press, 1978), p. 144. For this understanding of praxis which, because of its inclusion of reflection and theory, is fuller than the notion of "practice," see Hans-Georg Gadamer's critique and retrieval of Aristotle's notion of praxis, as well as Karl Marx's notion of "revolutionizing praxis." Neither notion opposes praxis to theory, as practice is often opposed to theory; instead they dialectically relate action and reflection *within praxis*.

31. See Matthew L. Lamb, *Solidarity with Victims: Toward a Theology of Social Transformation* (New York: Crossroads, 1982), pp. 82-83. For Lamb, theory is productive in its critical role of explicating "its own foundations in transformative praxis" (p. 82). But the primacy of praxis is maintained: "No theory *qua* theory can sublate praxis, although praxis can sublate theory" (p. 83).

32. Ibid., pp. 21-25, on the need and nature of theology's collaboration with other disciplines.

1. A POSTMODERN TRILEMMA

1. Todd Gitlin, "Hip-Deep in Post-modernism," *The New York Times Book Review*, November 6, 1988, pp. 1, 35-36.

2. See the essays in Hal Foster, ed., *The Anti-Aesthetic: Essays on Postmodern Culture* (Port Townsend, Wash.: Bay Press, 1983).

3. See George Lindbeck, *The Nature of Doctrine: Religion and Theology in a Postliberal Age* (Philadelphia: Westminster Press, 1984), p. 118. I am thinking especially of Lindbeck's insistence that "the direction of interpretation" in theology should be *from* a scriptural framework to extrascriptural realities.

4. Francis Schüssler Fiorenza, *Foundational Theology: Jesus and the Church* (New York: Crossroad, 1984), pp. 303-304.

5. Rosemary Radford Ruether, "Is a New Christian Consensus Possible?" in *Consensus in Theology? A Dialogue with Hans Küng and Edward Schillebeeckx*, ed. Leonard Swidler (Philadelphia: Westminster Press, 1980), p. 67.

6. Rosemary Radford Ruether, "Feminist Interpretation: A Method of Correlation," in *Feminist Interpretation of the Bible*, ed. Letty M. Russell (Philadelphia: Westminster Press, 1985), p. 117.

7. Elisabeth Schüssler Fiorenza, *Bread Not Stone: The Challenge of Feminist Biblical Interpretation* (Boston: Beacon Press, 1984), p. 13.

8. Lindbeck, *Nature of Doctrine*, p. 118.

9. Ibid., p. 118. Despite his explicit preference for "the direction of interpretation" from text to world or from Bible to believer, Lindbeck's discussions of this directionality often suggest the difficulty in really enforcing the primacy of that direction. Lindbeck rejects the notion that "believers find their stories in the Bible" and approves the notion that "they make the story of the Bible their story." Lindbeck fails to give attention to the meaning and complexity of the phrase *they make*. The fact that *they make* the Bible their own story, suggests more of a dialectical relation between text and believers' experience than Lindbeck treats theoretically.

10. See Rebecca S. Chopp, "Practical Theology and Liberation," in *Formation and Reflection: The Promise of Practical Theology* (Philadelphia: Fortress Press, 1987), pp. 120-138. This critique of the method of correlation is the centerpiece of an essay that focuses more broadly on practical theology's relation to the method of practical theology. For fuller treatment of these ideas, see Rebecca S. Chopp, *The Praxis of Suffering: An Interpretation of Liberation and Political Theologies* (Maryknoll, N.Y.: Orbis Books, 1986). Especially on pp. 138-148 of *The Praxis of Suffering*, the contrast between liberation theology and the method of correlation is not so strong, but her commentary here is helpful in identifying specific points at which liberation theology departs from the method of correlation.

11. See Clodovis Boff, *Theology and Praxis: Epistemological Foundations* (Maryknoll, N.Y.: Orbis Books, 1987), pp. 70-71. My definition of "theoretical practices" is consonant with the term as used in Clodovis Boff and Louis Althusser, but the theological project here need not endorse the other strategies of those thinkers.

12. Edward Farley, *Ecclesial Reflection: An Anatomy of Theological Method* (Philadelphia: Fortress Press, 1982), p. 197.

13. Ibid., p. 200.

14. Robert S. Lynd, "The Pattern of American Culture" in his *Knowledge for What?* (Princeton, N.J.: Princeton University Press, 1945), pp. 56-101.

15. Marvin Harris, "The Anthropology of the USA," in his *Cultural Anthropology* (New York: Harper and Row, 1983), pp. 288-318.

16. David Schneider, *American Kinship: A Cultural Account* (Englewood Cliffs, N.J.: Prentice-Hall, 1968).

17. Mary Douglas and Aaron Wildavsky, *Risk and Danger: An Essay on the Selection of Technological and Environmental Dangers* (Berkeley, Calif.: University of California Press, 1982), pp. 152-173.

18. Ihab Hassan, *The Postmodern Turn: Essays in Postmodern Theory and Culture* (Columbus, Ohio: Ohio State University Press, 1987), p. 85. For an alternative history of the term *postmodern*, see Hans Küng, *Theology for the Third Millennium: An Ecumenical View* (New York: Doubleday, 1988), pp. 2ff.

19. Two important offerings of Richard Rorty's thought are to be found in his *Philosophy and the Mirror of Nature* (Princeton, N.J.: Princeton University Press, 1979) and *Consequences of Pragmatism* (Minneapolis, Minn.: The University of Minnesota Press, 1982).

20. See the essays by Kenneth Frampton, "Towards a Critical Regionalism: Six Points for an Architecture of Resistance" and Rosalind Krauss, "Sculpture in the Expanded Field" in Hal Foster, *The Anti-Aesthetic*, pp. 16-30, 31-42.

21. E. Ann Kaplan, *Rocking Around the Clock: Music Television, Postmodernism and Consumer Culture* (New York and London: Methuen, 1987).

22. Friedrich Nietzsche, *On the Genealogy of Morals* (New York: Vintage Books, 1967), p. 80.

23. Hassan, *Postmodern Turn*, p. 173.

24. Ibid., pp. 168-173.

25. Mark C. Taylor, *Erring: A Post-modern A-theology* (Chicago: University of Chicago Press, 1984).

26. Peter C. Hodgson, *Revisioning the Church: Ecclesial Freedom in the New Paradigm* (Philadelphia: Fortress, 1988), pp. 11-19.

27. Stanley Rosen, *Hermeneutics as Politics* (New York: Oxford University Press, 1987), p. 17 and *passim*.

28. See Jürgen Habermas, "Modernity—An Incomplete Project," in Foster, *The Anti-Aesthetic*, pp. 3-15.

29. Hassan, *Postmodern Turn*, p. 169.

30. See the analyses of Jeffrey Stout, *Ethics After Babel: The Languages of Morals and Their Discontents* (Boston: Beacon Press, 1988), pp. 191-219.

31. Alasdair MacIntyre, *After Virtue: A Study in Moral Theory* (Notre Dame: University of Notre Dame Press, 1981), pp. 9-10.

32. Ibid., p. 245.

33. Foster, *The Anti-Aesthetic*, pp. xi-xii.

34. MacIntyre, *After Virtue*, p. 245.

35. Ibid., p. 241.

36. I take "postliberalism" in theology to be but one form of a more widespread postmodern ethos. Here, even more specifically, it is one form of a postmodernism of reaction.

37. See the review symposium on George Lindbeck's work in *The Thomist* 49 (July 1985). Cf. Stanley Hauerwas and L. Gregory Jones, "Seeking a Clear Alternative to Liberalism," *Books and Religion* 1, 2 (1985); 7; William H. Willimon, "Answering Pilate: Truth and the Postliberal Church," *The Christian Century* (January 28, 1987): 82-85; Paul Giurlanda, "The Challenge of 'Post-Liberal Theology': Testimony, Community & Nonviolence," *Commonweal* (January 30, 1987): 40-42.

38. Lindbeck, *Nature of Doctrine*, p. 23.

39. Ibid., pp. 30-45.

40. Hans W. Frei, *The Eclipse of Biblical Narrative: A Study in Eighteenth Century Hermeneutics* (New Haven, Conn.: Yale University Press, 1974). See also his "The Literal Reading of Biblical Narrative in the Christian Tradition: Does It Stretch or Will It Break?" in *The Bible and the Narrative Tradition*, ed. Frank McConnell (London: Oxford University Press, 1986), pp. 36-77.

41. See Garrett Green, ed., *Scriptural Authority and Narrative Interpretation* (Philadelphia: Fortress Press, 1987).

42. Lindbeck, *Nature of Doctrine*, pp. 134-35.

43. Ibid., p. 136, n. 5.

44. On reader-response criticism, see Hans Robert Jauss, *Toward an Aesthetic of Reception*, trans. Timothy Bahti (Minneapolis, Minn.: University of Minnesota Press, 1982); on social symbolic approaches to narrative, see Fredric Jameson, *The Political Unconscious: Narrative as Socially Symbolic Act* (Ithaca, N.Y.: Cornell University Press, 1981); on feminist and Afro-American literary criticism, see, respectively, Elaine Showalter, ed., *The New Feminist Criticism: Essays on Women, Literature Theory* (New York: Pantheon, 1985), and Henry Louis Gates, Jr., *The*

Signifying Monkey: A Theory of Afro-American Literary Criticism (London: Oxford University Press, 1988).

45. I say "almost all" because, as I suggest below in chapter 2, a vigorous celebration of plurality need not rule out every experience of guiding normativity, and may in fact entail a certain normative vision, critique and practice.

46. Hassan, *Postmodern Turn*, pp. 167-169.

47. See, for example, Thomas Kuhn, *The Structure of Scientific Revolutions*, 2d ed. enl. (Chicago: University of Chicago Press, 1970). For a discussion of the "incommensurability" debates in natural science, see Richard J. Bernstein, *Beyond Objectivism and Relativism: Science, Hermeneutics, Praxis* (Philadelphia: University of Pennsylvania Press, 1983), pp. 79-93.

48. On these so-called "rationality debates" between MacIntyre and Winch, see Bryan R. Wilson, ed. *Rationality* (Oxford: Basil Blackwell, 1970), especially pp. 1-17, 62-77.

49. On this influence, see Joel C. Weinsheimer, *Gadamer's Hermeneutics: A Reading of Truth and Method* (New Haven: Yale University Press, 1985), pp. ix-xii, and 1-59.

50. In theology, for example, see Sallie McFague's *Metaphorical Theology: Models of God in Religious Language* (Philadelphia: Fortress, 1982), pp. 62-66.

51. Hans-Georg Gadamer, *Truth and Method* (New York: Seabury, 1975), p. 275.

52. John D. Caputo, *Radical Hermeneutics: Repetition, Deconstruction, and the Hermeneutical Project* (Bloomington, Ind.: Indiana University Press, 1987), p. 115.

53. See Susan R. Suleiman and Inge Crosman, eds., *The Reader in the Text: Essays on Audience and Interpretation* (Princeton, N.J.: Princeton University Press, 1980), and more recently the developments in Ricoeur's theories of narrative in Paul Ricoeur, *Time and Narrative*, vol. 3 (Chicago: University of Chicago Press, 1988 [1985]), pp. 157-79.

54. For one of the most helpful summaries of types of feminist theory, see Josephine Donovan, *Feminist Theory: The Intellectual Traditions of American Feminism* (New York: Ungar, 1985).

55. Francis Schüssler Fiorenza, *Foundational Theology*, p. 289.

56. Bernstein, *Beyond Objectivism*, p. 92.

57. David Tracy, *The Analogical Imagination: Christian Theology and the Culture of Pluralism* (New York: Crossroad, 1981). See esp. pp. 318-19 for his discussion of criteria in relation to a pluralism that he views as "fundamentally enriching."

58. See Cornel West, "Marxist Theory and the Specificity of Afro-American Oppression," in Cary Nelson and Lawrence Grossberg, eds., *Marxism and the Interpretation of Culture* (Urbana and Chicago: University of Illinois Press, 1988), p. 27, n. 15. These distinctions are set out in one of his footnotes and are prompted by Michel Foucault's work.

59. For Foucault's notion of "discursive practice" see Michel Foucault, *The Archaeology of Knowledge and the Discourse on Language*, trans. A. M. Sheridan Smith (New York: Harper & Row, 1972), pp. 48-49.

60. West, *Marxist Theory*, p. 27, n.15.

61. Antonio Gramsci, *Selections from the Prison Notebooks*, ed. and trans. Quentin Hoare and Geoffrey Nowell Smith (New York: International Publishers, 1971), p. 12.

62. Mark C. Taylor, *Erring*, pp. 25-29.

63. Ibid., p. 134. Taylor is citing Hegel's *Phenomenology of Spirit*, A.V. Miller

and J.N. Findlay (Oxford: Clarendon, 1977), pp. 113, 112.

64. Caputo, *Radical Hermeneutics*, p. 259.

65. Ibid., p. 260.

66. Ibid., p. 261.

67. Ibid., p. 262.

68. Ibid., p. 264.

69. Hassan, *Postmodern Turn*, p. 182.

70. Langdon Gilkey, "Events, Meanings and the Current Tasks of Theology," *Journal of the American Academy of Religion* 53 (December 1985): 728.

71. For further commentary on these examples see, concerning the trinity, both Robert Magliola's discussion of "Christian differentialism" in his *Derrida on the Mend* (West Lafayette, Ind.: Purdue University Press, 1984), pp. 133-64, and Jürgen Moltmann's discussion of the trinity and human freedom in *The Trinity and the Kingdom: The Doctrine of God* (New York: Harper & Row, 1981), pp. 212-22. Concerning the mystics of Angelus Silesius (1624-77), see Magliola, *Derrida*, pp. 153-59. Another work probing Christian tradition for resources that in fact celebrate difference and plurality is Joseph Stephen O'Leary, *Questioning Back: The Overcoming of Metaphysics in Christian Tradition* (Minneapolis, Minn.: Seabury, 1985).

72. Mark C. Taylor's critique is throughout Part I of *Erring*, pp. 3-93.

73. Carter Heyward, "Heterosexist Theology: Being Above It All," *Journal of Feminist Studies in Religion* 3 (Spring 1987):29-38. Heyward's critique of liberal Christianity may be affirmed without uncritically affirming her explication of Paul Tillich as "a paradigmatic modern liberal." On the ambiguities of Tillich's contribution to contemporary problems noted by Heyward, see my Introduction, in Mark Kline Taylor, *Paul Tillich: Theologian of the Boundaries* (New York: Harper & Row, 1987), pp. 11-34. As an example of one thinker's view of how taking a stand can occur even in the liberal's "final vocabulary," see Richard Rorty, *Contingency, Irony, and Solidarity* (Cambridge: Cambridge University Press, 1989), pp. 189-98.

74. On the need in Guatemala to examine ethnic plurality within the political struggle, see Norman B. Schwartz, "Ethnicity, Politics, and Cultural Survival," *Cultural Survival Quarterly* 7 (Spring 1983): 20-23. See the awareness of Guatemala's "Guerilla Army of the Poor" concerning both "class contradiction" and "ethnic-national contradiction" in *Compañero*, no. 5 (Guatemala City, 1982): 11-20.

75. Van A. Harvey, "The Pathos of Liberal Theology" (review of David Tracy, *Blessed Rage for Order: The New Pluralism in Theology* [New York: Seabury Press, 1975]) in *Journal of Religion* 56 (1976):382-91.

76. James Cone, *God of the Oppressed* (New York: Seabury, 1975), pp. 7-8, 247, n.2.

77. Cf. Cornel West's "disenchantment" with this development and with others in his *The American Evasion of Philosophy: A Genealogy of Pragmatism* (Madison, Wisc.: The University of Wisconsin Press, 1989), pp. 7-8.

2. A CULTURAL-POLITICAL HERMENEUTICS OF TRADITION

1. See Mark 5:1-20.

2. Ernesto Cardenal, *The Gospel in Solentiname*, vol. II, trans. Donald D. Walsh (Maryknoll, N.Y.: Orbis Books, 1978), pp. 194-95.

3. Paul Ricoeur, *Time and Narrative*, trans. Kathleen McLaughlin and David Pellauer, vol. 1 (Chicago: The University of Chicago Press, 1984), p. 81. This world

"in front of the text" is, for Ricoeur, part of the function of any "poetic" work (a myth, metaphor, narrative). The function is one that "aims less at restoring the author's intention behind the text than at making explicit the movement by which the text unfolds, as it were, a world in front of itself." The notion of world "in front of" texts was earlier discussed in Paul Ricoeur, "The Task of Hermeneutics," *Philosophy Today* 17 (1973):112-28. In this book, I attempt to develop the notion of a world "in front of" texts so that it refers to the complex social locations within which different interpreters receive and construct the meanings of texts.

4. See Willard M. Swartley, *Slavery, Sabbath, War and Women: Case Studies in Biblical Interpretation* (Scottdale, Pa.: Herald Press, 1983), pp. 224-28 for a text that helpfully explores relationships between meanings found "behind," "in," and "in front of" texts.

5. On hermeneutics as a discourse occurring in situations of cultural crisis, see David Tracy, *Plurality and Ambiguity: Hermeneutics, Religion, Hope* (San Francisco: Harper & Row, 1987), pp. 7-10.

6. Hans-Georg Gadamer, *Philosophical Apprenticeships*, trans. Robert Sullivan (Cambridge, Mass.: M.I.T. Press, 1985), p. 177.

7. Kurt Mueller-Vollmer, ed., *The Hermeneutics Reader: Texts of the German Tradition From the Enlightenment to the Present* (New York: Continuum, 1985), p. 10.

8. John D. Caputo, *Radical Hermeneutics: Repetition, Deconstruction and the Hermeneutical Project* (Bloomington, Ind.: Indiana University Press, 1987), pp. 95-206.

9. Joel C. Weinsheimer, *Gadamer's Hermeneutics: A Reading of Truth and Method* (New Haven: Yale University Press, 1985), p. 9.

10. Richard Rorty, *Philosophy and the Mirror of Nature* (Princeton: Princeton University Press, 1979), pp. 315-56.

11. Ibid., p. 360.

12. Hans Frei, *The Identity of Jesus Christ* (Philadelphia: Fortress Press, 1975), p. xvi.

13. Hans-Georg Gadamer, *Truth and Method* (New York: Seabury, 1975), p. xxiv.

14. Tracy does this by developing not only Gadamer's hermeneutics, but that of other hermeneutical theorists, as well as literary critics, historians, and social scientists. See David Tracy, *The Analogical Imagination: Christian Theology and the Culture of Pluralism* (New York: Crossroad, 1981).

15. For discussion of this move, see Paul Rabinow and William M. Sullivan, *Interpretive Social Science: A Reader* (Berkeley, Calif.: The University of California Press, 1979).

16. Paul Ricoeur, *Hermeneutics and the Human Sciences* (Cambridge: Cambridge University Press, 1981), pp. 192-221.

17. In religious ethics, see Gibson Winter, *Liberating Creation: Foundations of Religious Social Ethics* (New York: Crossroad, 1981); in pastoral care, Donald Capps, *Pastoral Care and Hermeneutics* (Philadelphia: Fortress, 1984).

18. See, for example, the important place given to language in the hermeneutical phenomenology of *Truth and Method*, pp. 345-448. Cf. Gadamer's specific comments on Wittgenstein's concern with language in his "The Phenomenological Movement (1963)" in *Philosophical Hermeneutics*, trans. and ed. David E. Inge (Berkeley, Calif.: University of California Press, 1976), pp. 173-77.

19. Paul Ricoeur, *Interpretation Theory: Discourse and the Surplus of Meaning* (Ft. Worth: Texas Christian University, 1976), pp. 1-23.

20. Gadamer, *Truth and Method*, p. 446.

21. Roy J. Howard, *Three Faces of Hermeneutics* (Berkeley, Calif.: University of California, 1982), p. 32. See the more comprehensive account by Terrence N. Tice, *Research Guide to Philosophy* (Chicago: American Library Association, 1983), pp. 150-56, 161-72.

22. *Vorurteilen* in Gadamer's work. See Gadamer, *Truth and Method* pp. 235-45.

23. Paul Ricoeur, "Explanation and Understanding," in Charles E. Reagan and David Stewart, eds., *The Philosophy of Paul Ricoeur: An Anthology of His Work* (Boston: Beacon Press, 1978), pp. 149-66.

24. Howard, *Three Faces*, p. 33. See also Tice, *Research Guide*, pp. 285-301.

25. This is especially to be found in Habermas' earlier work. See Jürgen Habermas, *Knowledge and Human Interests*, trans. Jeremy J. Shapiro (Boston: Beacon Press, 1968), pp. 25-42, 214-45.

26. Conference Advisory Board for Conversations: A Theological Project in Hermeneutics and Cultural Contexts, January 1986, Princeton Theological Seminary, Princeton, N.J. Board members attending: Charles Amjad-Ali, David Tracy, Craig R. Dykstra, Michael Fishbane, Elisabeth Schüssler Fiorenza, Hans W. Frei, Susan Handelman, Matthew Lamb, Margaret R. Miles, Dan O. Via, Cornel West, Charles M. Wood.

27. Elaine Showalter, ed., *The New Feminist Criticism: Essays on Women, Literature, Theory* (New York: Pantheon, 1985), p. 140.

28. Hans-Georg Gadamer, *Reason in the Age of Science* (Cambridge, Mass.: M.I.T. Press, 1981), p. 150 (emphasis added).

29. Rorty, *Philosophy*, p. 318.

30. Ibid., p. 377.

31. Jaci C. Maraschin, "Messengers of the Gods: Hermeneutics and Communication in Latin America," *Media Development* XXX (1/1983). See also Clodovis Boff, *Theology and Praxis: Epistemological Foundations* (Maryknoll, N.Y.: Orbis Books, 1987), pp. 132-58.

32. See, for example, Severino Croatto's commentary on Gadamer and others, and his extensive use of Ricoeur, in *Biblical Hermeneutics: Toward a Theory of the Production of Meaning* (Maryknoll, N.Y.: Orbis Books, 1987).

33. For a helpful delineation of forms of plurality and relativity, see Jeffrey Stout, *Ethics After Babel: The Languages of Morals and Their Discontents* (Boston: Beacon Press, 1988), pp. 82-105.

34. See, for example, Gadamer's discussions of "effective historical consciousness" (*wirkungsgeschichtliches Bewusstsein*) in his *Truth and Method*, pp. 267-74.

35. The Christian theologian who perhaps most reflects on the salient concern of plurality, both historical and sociocultural, is David Tracy. All of his works wrestle with the issue. See his *Blessed Rage for Order: The New Pluralism in Theology* (New York: Seabury, 1975), *The Analogical Imagination*, and most recently *Plurality and Ambiguity*.

36. Again, see Gadamer for the application of this kind of language to the event of interpreting written literature: "In its [writing's] deciphering and interpretation a miracle takes place: the transformation of something strange and dead into a total simultaneity and familiarity." Gadamer, *Truth and Method*, p. 145.

37. Ibid., p. 446.

38. Rorty, *Philosophy*, pp. 389-90.

39. Ibid., pp. 318, 377-78.

40. In Afro-American scholarship, for example, see Houston A. Baker, Jr., *The Journey Back: Issues in Black Literature and Criticism* (Chicago: University of Chicago Press, 1980); Renita Weems, "The State of Biblical Interpretation: An African-American Womanist Critique," presented at the Conference on "Gender, Race, Class: Implications for Interpreting Religious Texts," Princeton Theological Seminary, May 17, 1988, unpublished; and Mary Ann Tolbert, ed., *The Bible and Feminist Hermeneutics, Semeia* 28 (Chico, Calif.: Scholars Press, 1983).

41. Caputo, *Radical Hermeneutics*, p. 3 (emphasis mine).

42. Robert Sullivan, "Translator's Introduction" to Hans-George Gadamer, *Philosophical Apprenticeships* (Cambridge, Mass.: M.I.T. Press, 1985), p. ix.

43. Weinsheimer, *Gadamer's Hermeneutics*, p. ix.

44. For Gadamer's rehabilitation of tradition and authority, in light of Enlightenment suspicions of both, see *Truth and Method*, pp. 241-53. While Gadamer's rehabilitation is clearly a search for a nondogmatic authority and for a tradition of openness, he gives little attention—and this is his major fault, I think—to the possibility that interpreters will have to resist tradition. Herein persists the basic "conservative" cast of his thought.

45. Ibid., p. 261.

46. Ibid., p. 274.

47. Ibid., p. 304.

48. Ibid., p. 281.

49. Ibid., p. 275 (emphasis mine).

50. Ibid., pp. 345ff.

51. For Gadamer's unfolding of this analogy, see his *Truth and Method*, pp. 321-24.

52. Caputo, *Radical Hermeneutics*, p. xxx.

53. For examples of the photographic and journalistic idealization and romanticization of these groups, see Nelle Dorr, *The Bare Feet* (New York: The New York Graphic Society, 1962). The photographs in Dorr's volume are freer of the romanticizing impulse that is so apparent in her textual commentary.

54. Gadamer, *Truth and Method*, p. 324.

55. Ibid., p. 319.

56. For historical and contemporary studies of this subordination, see not only Beatriz Manz but also Kay B. Warren, *Symbols of Subordination: Indian Identity in a Guatemalan Town* (Princeton, N.J.: Princeton University Press, 1978) and Jonathan L. Fried, Marvin E. Gettleman, Deborah T. Levenson, and Nancy Peckenham, *Guatemala in Rebellion: Unfinished History* (New York: Grove Press, 1983).

57. In theology, the most thorough discussion and citation of literature supporting this approach to truth and reasoning is in Francis Schüssler Fiorenza, *Foundational Theology: Jesus and the Church* (New York: Crossroad/Continuum, 1984), pp. 301-21.

58. On the early usage of "reflective equilibrium," see John Rawls, *A Theory of Justice* (Cambridge, Mass.: Harvard University Press, 1971), pp. 49, 51. According to Francis Schüssler Fiorenza, "the advocacy of wide, in distinction to a narrow, equilibrium comes to the fore in Rawls' later works." See Fiorenza, *Foundational Theology*, especially p. 320, nn. 153 and 154.

59. Cited from Bernstein in Rorty, *Philosophy*, p. 224.

60. See Donna Kate Rushin, "The Bridge Poem," in Cherrie Moraga and Gloria Anzaldua, *This Bridge Called My Back: Writings of Radical Women of Color* (Kitchen Table: Women of Color Press, 1981/83), pp. xxi-xxii.

61. See Gustavo Gutiérrez's "Introduction to the Revised Edition: Expanding the View," in *A Theology of Liberation*, 15th Anniversary Edition (Maryknoll, N.Y.: Orbis Books, 1988), pp. xxv-xxviii.

62. Acknowledging this "privilege" can be done without either romanticizing the oppressed for having some supposedly noble "intuition" or legitimating their sufferings as some necessary means toward knowledge. The dangers of both this romanticization and legitimation require vigilance in each case, but their possibility should not prohibit the acknowledgment of unique insight from systemically oppressed groups.

63. Janice E. Perlman, *The Myth of Marginality: Urban Poverty and Politics in Rio de Janeiro* (Berkeley: University of California Press, 1976).

64. On this being true of the muted status of women in relation to dominant patriarchal cultures, see anthropologist Edwin Ardener's study, "Belief and the Problem of Women" in Shirley Ardener, ed., *Perceiving Women* (London: J.M. Dent & Sons, 1975), pp. 1-17, and that by literary critic Elaine Showalter, *New Feminist Criticism*, pp. 262-64.

65. Bell Hooks, *Feminist Theory: From Margin to Center* (Boston: South End Press, 1984), p. v.

66. On the need to hear the readings of the oppressed first, see David Tracy, *Plurality and Ambiguity*, pp. 103-04.

67. Gadamer, *Truth and Method*, pp. xiii, xxiv.

68. For two of the most helpful summaries of these debates, see Jack Mendelson, "The Habermas-Gadamer Debate," *New German Critique* 18 (Fall 1979):44-73, and Susan J. Hekman, *Hermeneutics and the Sociology of Knowledge* (Notre Dame, Ind.: University of Notre Dame Press, 1986), pp. 129-39.

69. See David Tracy, *The Analogical Imagination*, p. 152. Tracy has suggested that Gadamer's writing in *Truth and Method* suggests interpretation that is more "truth *or* method."

70. Without this strengthening, three of Habermas's critiques of Gadamer's hermeneutics of understanding would pertain also to this cultural-political hermeneutics: (a) that its far too radical disjunction of understanding and method grants control over the definition of scientific methods to positivists; (b) that it only asserts the power of a certain historical preunderstanding or only announces the presence of interpreters' prejudgments, without showing precisely how these preunderstandings and prejudgments operate in particular persons and social locations; and (c) that Gadamerian hermeneutics of understanding lacks resources for identifying and breaking the powers of authority and tradition when they rule with compulsion and fear. Concerning this latter problem, Habermas writes: "We have good reason to suspect that the background consensus of established traditions and language games can be a consciousness forged of compulsion, a result of pseudocommunication, not only in the pathologically isolated case of disturbed family systems, but in entire social systems." Jürgen Habermas, "On Hermeneutics' Claim to Universality," in Mueller-Vollmer, *The Hermeneutics Reader*, p. 317. Cf. Habermas, "A Review of *Truth and Method*," in *Understanding and Social Inquiry*, ed. F. Dallmayr and Thomas McCarthy (Notre Dame, Ind.: The University of Notre Dame Press, 1977), pp. 358ff.

71. For Gadamer's arguments for this claim, see Hans-Georg Gadamer, "Rhetorik, Hermeneutik und Ideologiekritik," in Karl-Otto Apel, ed., *Hermeneutik und Ideologiekritik* (Frankfurt: Suhrkamp, 1971), pp. 293ff.

72. Compare Houston A. Baker, Jr., *Blues, Ideology and Afro-American Literature: A Vernacular Theory* (Chicago: University of Chicago Press, 1984) and "New Directions of Black Feminist Criticism," in Elaine Showalter, *The New Feminist Criticism*, pp. 186-199.

73. See the entirety of Showalter, *The New Feminist Criticism*.

74. Terry Eagleton, *Criticism and Ideology: A Study in Marxist Literary Theory* (London: Verso, 1975).

75. Jean E. Kennard, "Ourself Behind Ourself: A Theory for Lesbian Readers" in Elizabeth A. Flynn and Patrocinio Schweickart, *Gender and Reading: Essays on Readers, Texts and Contexts* (Baltimore: Johns Hopkins University Press, 1986), pp. 63-80.

76. Jürgen Habermas, *The Theory of Communicative Action: Reason and Rationalization*, vols. 1 & 2, trans. Thomas McCarthy (Boston: Beacon Press, 1984, 1988).

77. Michel Foucault, *Power/Knowledge: Selected Interviews and Other Writings, 1972-1977*, ed. Colin Gordon (New York: Pantheon, 1972-1977).

78. Fredric Jameson, *The Political Unconscious: Narrative as a Socially Symbolic Act* (Ithaca, N.Y.: Cornell University Press, 1981).

79. Antonio Gramsci, *Selections from the Prison Notebooks*, ed. and trans. Quentin Hoare and Geoffrey Nowell Smith (New York: International Publishers, 1971), p. 12.

80. Joel Kovell, *White Racism: A Psychohistory* (New York: Pantheon, 1970), and Cornel West, "A Genealogy of Modern Racism," in his *Prophesy Deliverance!: An Afro-American Revolutionary Christianity* (Philadelphia: Westminster, 1982), pp. 47-65.

81. Two of many important texts are Nancy Chodorow, *The Reproduction of Mothering: Psychoanalysis and the Sociology of Gender* (Berkeley, Calif.: University of California Press, 1978), and Gerda Lerner, *The Creation of Patriarchy* (London and New York: Oxford University Press, 1986).

82. See, for example, Morton Fried, "On the Evolution of Social Stratification and the State," in Stanley Diamond, ed., *Culture in History: Essays in Honor of Paul Radin* (New York: Octagon Books, 1981), pp. 713-31.

83. Janice G. Raymond, *A Passion for Friends: Toward a Philosophy of Female Affection* (Boston: Beacon Press, 1986).

84. Richard Bernstein notes that many issues "come into sharp focus," such as the issue of "incommensurability," when entering the "wide-ranging discipline" of anthropology. See Bernstein, in Rorty, *Philosophy*, p. 93.

85. Two different texts are helpful for providing an overview of these culture theories: Marvin Harris, *The Rise of Anthropological Theory: A History of Theories of Culture* (New York: Thomas Y. Crowell, 1968), and Robert J. Schreiter, C.PP.S., "The Study of Culture," in *Constructing Local Theologies* (Maryknoll, N.Y.: Orbis Books, 1985), pp. 39-74.

86. Current anthropologists are taking up the difficult challenge of "how to represent the embedding of richly described local cultural worlds in larger impersonal systems of political economy." See George E. Marcus and Michael M. J. Fischer, *Anthropology as Cultural Critique: An Experimental Moment in the Human Sciences* (Chicago: University of Chicago Press, 1986), p. 77.

87. Reagan and Stewart, *The Philosophy of Paul Ricoeur*, p. 44; and Ricoeur, *Interpretation Theory*, pp. 75-80, 87-88.

88. I have attempted this more fully in Mark Kline Taylor, "Symbolic Dimensions in Cultural Anthropology," *Current Anthropology* 26 (April 1985): 167-69, and in Mark Kline Taylor, *Beyond Explanation: Religious Dimensions in Cultural Anthropology* (Macon, Ga.: Mercer University Press, 1986), pp. 70-75.

89. Ricoeur, in Reagan and Stewart, *The Philosophy of Paul Ricoeur*, p. 165.

90. Ibid.

91. Tracy, *The Analogical Imagination*, p. 244, n.18.

92. I myself have had this kind of theoretical challenge put to my own hermeneutical understanding. See anthropologist Steven Webster's critique of my work, appended to Mark Kline Taylor, "Symbolic Dimensions in Cultural Anthropology," *Current Anthropology* 26 (April 1985):167-85, esp. p. 179.

93. See Paul Ricoeur, *Time and Narrative*, vol. 3, trans. Kathleen Blamey and David Pellauer (Chicago: University of Chicago Press, 1988), p. 171. Ricoeur's own more recent work calls for analyses of readers' matrices, but he himself does not practice cultural-political treatment of those matrices. "To give full scope to the theme of interaction, the phenomenology of the act of reading *requires a flesh-and-blood reader*, who in actualizing the role of the reader prestructured in and through the text, transforms it" (emphasis mine).

3. THEORIES OF SEXISM

1. See Prologue, pp. 1,7, 12-15.

2. Sara Shute, "Sexist Language and Sexism," *Sexist Language: A Modern Philosophical Analysis*, ed. Mary Vetterling-Braggin (Boston: Littlefield, Adams, and Co., 1981), p. 27.

3. Bob Reiser and Pete Seeger, *Carry It On! A History in Song and Picture of the Working Men and Women of America* (New York: Simon and Schuster, 1985).

4. Jack Newfield, "Reasons to Believe," *Backstreets*, vol. 4, no. 4 (Winter/Spring 1986), pp. 21-24.

5. For discussion of this problem and some proposals, see Mark Kline Taylor, "Celebrating Difference, Resisting Domination: The Need for Synchronic Strategies in Theological Education," in Edward Farley and Barbara Wheeler, eds., *The Structure of Theological Study* (forthcoming).

6. See ch. 2, nn. 72–75.

7. Joel Kovell, *White Racism: A Psychohistory* (New York: Columbia University Press, 1984).

8. J. Deotis Roberts, *Black Theology in Dialogue* (Philadelphia: Westminster, 1987), p. 44.

9. See the argument developed throughout Barbara Ehrenreich's book, *Hearts of Men: American Dreams and the Flight from Commitment* (Garden City, N.Y.: Anchor Press, 1983).

10. Elaine Showalter, "Critical Cross-Dressing: Male Feminists and the Woman of the Year," *Raritan*, vol. 3, no. 2 (Fall 1983), p. 133.

11. Stephen Heath, "Male Feminism," in Alice Jardine and Paul Smith, *Men in Feminism* (New York: Methuen, 1987), p. 1.

12. Gayatri Chakravorty Spivak, "The Politics of Interpretation," in *The Politics of Interpretation*, ed. W. J. T. Mitchell (Chicago: University of Chicago Press, 1982), p. 366.

13. Daniel C. Maguire, "The Feminization of God and Ethics," Presidential Address to the Society of Christian Ethics, in *The Annals of the Society of Christian Ethics*, ed. Larry L. Rasmussen (Dallas: The Society of Christian Ethics, 1981), p. 2.

14. Gunnar Myrdal, *The American Dilemma* (New York: Harper & Row, 1944, 1962), p. 1073.

15. Sheila Briggs, "Images of Women and Jews in the 19th and 20th Century Germany," in Margaret R. Miles, et al., *Immaculate and Powerful: The Female in Sacred Image and Social Reality* (Boston: Beacon, 1985), pp. 250–51.

16. Gerda Lerner, *The Creation of Patriarchy* (New York and London: Oxford, 1986), pp. 212–14.

17. The term is that of Annette Kolodny in "Dancing Through the Minefield: Some Observations on the Theory, Practice, and Politics of a Feminist Literary Criticism," in Elaine Showalter, *The New Feminist Criticism: Women, Literature, Theory* (New York: Pantheon, 1985), pp. 144–67.

18. Houston A. Baker, Jr., *Blues, Ideology and Afro-American Literature: A Vernacular Theory* (Chicago: The University of Chicago Press, 1984), pp. 2, 115–16, 183–84.

19. Ibid., see esp. pp. 84–112.

20. Heath, "Male Feminism," p. 1.

21. On this as both "disarming and yet provocative of suspicion for women feminists", see Alice Jardine, "Men in Feminism: *Odor di Uomo* or *Companons de Route?*," in Jardine and Smith, *Men in Feminism*, pp. 59–60.

22. Kovell, *White Racism*, pp. 51–92.

23. Elaine Showalter, "Introduction: The New Feminist Criticism," in Showalter, *New Feminist Criticism*, pp. 3–17.

24. Ibid., p. 5.

25. Phyllis Trible, *Texts of Terror: Literary-Feminist Readings of Biblical Narratives* (Philadelphia: Fortress, 1984).

26. These texts include Patricia Meyer Spack's *The Female Imagination* (New York: Alfred A. Knopf, 1975); Ellen Moer's *Literary Women: The Great Writers* (Garden City, N.Y.: Doubleday, 1976); Elaine Showalter's *A Literature of Their Own: British Women Novelists from Bronte to Lessing* (Princeton, N.J.: Princeton University Press, 1977); Sandra Gilbert and Susan Gubar's *The Madwoman in the Attic: The Woman Writer and the 19th Century Literary Imagination* (New Haven, Conn.: Yale University Press, 1979). To these we need also to add Gilbert and Gubar's *Norton's Anthology of Women's Literature* (New York: W.W. Norton, 1985).

27. Elisabeth Schüssler Fiorenza, *Bread Not Stone: The Challenge of Feminist Biblical Interpretation* (Boston: Beacon Press, 1984), p. 20.

28. Showalter, *New Feminist Criticism*, p. 6 (emphasis mine).

29. Patrocinio P. Schweickart, "Reading Ourselves: Toward a Feminist Theory of Reading," in Elizabeth A. Flynn and Patrocinio P. Schweickart, *Gender and Reading: Essays on Readers, Texts and Contexts* (Baltimore: Johns Hopkins University Press, 1986), p. 38.

30. Shute, "Sexist Language," p. 27.

31. Ibid., p. 28.

32. See especially Michelle Zimbalist Rosaldo and Louise Lamphere, eds., *Woman, Culture, and Society* (Stanford, Calif.: Stanford University Press, 1974), pp. 1–15.

33. Mark Gerzon, *A Choice of Heroes: The Changing Face of American Manhood*

(Boston: Houghton Mifflin Co., 1982), pp. 126–27; and Gerda Lerner, "The Lady and the Mill Girl: Changes in the Status of Women in the Age of Jackson," in Jean E. Friedman, et al., eds., *Our American Sisters: Women in American Life and Thought,* 4th ed. (Lexington, Mass.: D.C. Heath, 1987).

34. Eric Wolf, *Europe and the Peoples Without History* (Berkeley, Calif.: University of California Press, 1981).

35. Amaury de Riencourt, *Sex and Power in History* (New York: D. McKay Co., 1974), cited in Gerzon, *A Choice of Heroes,* p. 128.

36. Gerzon, *A Choice of Heroes,* p. 128.

37. Ibid., pp. 128–129.

38. Lerner, *Creation of Patriarchy,* pp. 36–53.

39. Louise Kapp Howe, *The Future of the Family* (New York: Simon and Schuster, 1972), p. 21.

40. Heidi Hartmann, "The Unhappy Marriage of Marxism and Feminism: Towards a More Progressive Union," in Lydia Sargent, ed., *Women and Revolution* (Boston: South End Press, 1981), p. 1.

41. Ehrenreich, *Hearts of Men,* p. 7. This book is limited in that it insufficiently treats class factors in its discussion of sexism and the "family wage system." Yet her thesis of the elite and the popular cultural support for male flight from commitment is both well documented and important. For important reviews illuminating the strengths and weaknesses of Ehrenreich's contribution, see Laurel Richardson, *Journal of Marriage and the Family* 46 (May 1984):503; Jan Rosenberg and Fred Siegel, "Fighting over the Family," *Dissent* 31 (Spring 1984):240–42; and Arlene Kaplan Daniels, *Signs* 11 (Spring 1986):576–78.

42. Ibid., p. 11.

43. Gerzon, *A Choice of Heroes,* p. 132.

44. Barbara R. Bergmann, *The Economic Emergence of Women* (New York: Basic Books, 1986); Rosanna Hertz, *More Equal than Others: Women and Men in Dual Career Marriages* (Berkeley, Calif.: University of California Press, 1986).

45. *New York Times Book Review,* October 26, 1986, p. 43. Review of Bergmann and Hertz as cited in preceding footnote. For an important recent analysis of the power held by men in contemporary society, see Arthur Brittan, *Masculinity and Power* (Oxford: Basil Blackwell, 1989).

46. Ehrenreich, *Hearts of Men,* p. 9.

47. Ibid., p. 8.

48. Cf. Gerzon, *A Choice of Heroes,* pp. 169–216; May Sarton, *Journal of a Solitude* (New York: W.W. Norton, 1973), pp. 70–71; *New York Times Magazine,* October 26, 1986; and especially Dorothy Dinnerstein, *The Mermaid and the Minotaur: Sexual Arrangements and Human Malaise* (New York: Harper & Row, 1976).

49. See the chapter on "Mothers and Sons," in Adrienne Rich, *Of Woman Born: Motherhood as Experience and Institution* (New York: W.W. Norton, 1976), pp. 186–217, esp. p. 211.

50. Dinnerstein, *Mermaid,* pp. 40–58.

51. Ibid., pp. 59–71.

52. Ibid., pp. 163–79.

53. Ibid., pp. 258–76.

54. See Ehrenreich, *Hearts of Men,* pp. 29–143.

55. Catherine Keller, *From a Broken Web: Separation, Sexism, Self* (Boston: Beacon Press, 1986), p. 120. Keller also criticizes Dinnerstein's tendency to assume

that the ideal for children's development is that of ego separation. See pp. 120–121.

56. In addition to Dinnerstein's explorations, Dinnerstein, *Mermaid*, see Rich, *Of Woman Born*. Additional perspectives are offered in Kathryn Allen Rabuzzi, *Motherself: A Mythic Analysis of Motherhood* (Bloomington and Indianapolis, Ind.: Indiana University Press, 1988).

57. Dinnerstein, *Mermaid*, p. 93.

58. Hendrik M. Ruitenbeek, "Men Alone: The Male Homosexual and the Disintegrated Family," *The Problem of Homosexuality in Modern Society* (New York: E.P. Dutton, Inc., 1963), p. 80.

59. Therese Benedek, "Fatherhood and Providing," in E. James Anthony and Therese Benedek, eds., *Parenthood: Its Psychology and Psychotherapy* (Boston: Little, Brown, and Co., 1970), p. 167.

60. H. A. Overstreet, *The Mature Mind* (New York: W. W. Norton, 1950), cited in Ehrenreich, *Hearts of Men*, p. 18.

61. For summary and fuller discussion of these eight steps, see Ehrenreich, *Hearts of Men*, pp. 18-20.

62. Lionel Oversey, M.D., *Homosexuality and Pseudo-homosexuality* (New York: E. P. Dutton, 1969), pp. 24–25; and Ehrenreich, *Hearts of Men*, pp. 20–27.

63. Collette Dowling, *The Cinderella Complex: Women's Hidden Fear of Independence* (New York: Summit Books, 1981), p. 62.

64. Bruce Springsteen, "Factory," on *Darkness on the Edge of Town*, Columbia Broadcasting System, 1978. Cf. Suzanne Vega, "Luka," on *Solitude Standing*, A&M Records, 1987; Tracy Chapman, "Behind the Wall," on *Tracy Chapman*, Elektra Asylum Records, 1988.

65. Gerzon, *A Choice of Heroes*, p. 275, n. 92; Richard J. Gelles, *Family Violence*, 2d ed. (Newbury Park: Sage Publications, 1987).

66. Gerzon, *A Choice of Heroes*, pp. 192-193.

67. Jesse Bernard, *The Future of Marriage*, 2d. ed. (New Haven: Yale University Press, 1982). See also "Adult Sex Roles and Mental Happiness," *Changing Women in a Changing Society*, ed. Joan Huber (Chicago: University of Chicago Press, 1973).

68. Gerzon, *A Choice of Heroes*, p. 127.

69. Ibid., p. 212.

70. Ibid., p. 122.

71. Rosaldo and Lamphere, *Woman, Culture, and Society*, pp. 3, 71. As I note below, this still valuable study has been superceded by more recent research. For the important reviews of this book see Joan Vincent, *Journal of International Affairs* vol. 30, no. 2, 1976–77, pp. 268–70; Stella Silverstein, *African Studies Review*, vol. 18, no. 3, pp. 125–27; Beverly Chias, *American Anthropologist* 77 (1975):92–93.

72. Rosaldo and Lamphere, *Woman, Culture, and Society*, 71.

73. Sherry B. Ortner, "Is Female to Male as Nature Is to Culture?" ibid., pp. 67–87.

74. Peggy Reeves Sanday, *Female Power and Male Dominance: On the Origins of Sexual Inequality* (Cambridge: Cambridge University Press, 1981), pp. xv, 113–114, 172–179. For the definitions of "power and authority" she ascribes to women in certain cultural contexts, see esp. p. 114. On the importance and limitations of Sanday's work, see Mary Douglas, "Morality and Culture," *Ethics* 93 (July 1983):786–91; Lynne Brydon, *Man* 17 (December 1982):802–803; Faith Robertson Elliot, *British Journal of Sociology* 34 (December 1983):603–604; Susan Carol

Rogers, *American Anthropologist* 86 (June 1984):436–37; and Jean E. Jackson, *Signs* 9 (Winter 1983):304–307.

75. Sanday, *Female Power*, pp 5–6.

76. Sanday does discuss cultural myths and legends about dominating female giants and monsters that are used to justify maintaining female subordination. Ibid., pp. 180–81.

77. Ibid., p. 231.

78. Ibid., pp. 215–31.

79. Lerner, *Creation of Patriarchy*, p. 45. For ethnographic examples of the occurrence of these events, see the case studies in Sanday, ibid., pp. 184–211.

80. This is similar to Sanday's claim that male dominance arises as a response to a cultural group's situation of stress. Sanday, ibid., pp. 183, 184–87.

81. Ibid. pp. 49–50.

82. See Lerner, "A Working Hypothesis," *Creation of Patriarchy*, pp. 36–53. For two of the more helpful reviews of the strengths and weaknesses of Lerner's hypothesis, see Deborah Gewertz, *American Ethnologist* 15 (August 1988):595–96; Nancy Barnes, *Signs* 13 (Summer 1988):857–59.

83. Elaine Showalter, "Feminist Criticism in the Wilderness," in Showalter, *New Feminist Criticism*, pp. 243–70.

84. See Shirley Ardener, ed., *Perceiving Women* (London: J.M. Dent & Sons, 1975). For reviews of this early anthropological study of women, see Michelle Z. Rosaldo, *American Anthropologist* 80 (June 1978):407–409; Deborah Pellow, *African Studies Review* 20 (April 1977):117–26; Virginia Luling, *Man* 11 (June 1976):288.

85. E. Ardener, "The 'Problem' Revisited," in Ardener, *Perceiving Women*, p. 23.

86. Ibid., p. 7.

87. Ibid.

88. Elaine Showalter, "Feminist Criticism in the Wilderness," in Showalter, *New Feminist Criticism*, p. 263.

89. Showalter, "Toward a Feminist Poetics," ibid., p. 141.

90. Sallie McFague, *Metaphorical Theology: Models of God in Religious Language* (Philadelphia: Fortress, 1982), pp. 112–64.

91. Elisabeth Schüssler Fiorenza, *In Memory of Her: A Feminist Theological Reconstruction of Christian Origins* (New York: Crossroad, 1983), pp. 61–64.

92. Rosemary Radford Ruether, "Postscript: Woman/Body/Nature: The Icon of the Divine," in *Sexism and God-Talk: Toward a Feminist Theology* (Boston: Beacon Press, 1983), pp. 259–66.

93. Ardener, *Perceiving Women*, pp. 8–9.

94. Lerner, *Creation of Patriarchy*, p. 11.

95. Sanday, *Female Power*, p. 215.

96. Keller, *From a Broken Web*, pp. 73, 74, 75.

97. Paul Ricoeur, *The Symbolism of Evil*, trans. E. Buchanan (Boston: Beacon Press, 1969), p. 180. See Keller's discussion, *From a Broken Web*, pp. 76–77.

98. For the discussion of Michael Fishbane's position, see Keller, *From a Broken Web*, pp. 81–82. For a commentary similar to Fishbane's, on the relation of Genesis primeval history to the epics of neighboring religions, see Gerhard Von Rad, *Genesis: A Commentary*, rev. ed. (Philadelphia: Westminster, 1972), pp. 45–67.

99. Keller, *From a Broken Web*, p. 80.

100. Anthropologist Sanday has suggested that the differences are great enough

that one might even have in Genesis an implicit endorsement of equality between the sexes. Sanday, *Female Power*, p. 225.

101. Scholars wishing to make other points about the Genesis text may find it useful to distinguish the two creation accounts in Genesis (1:1–2:4a and 2:46–25). It may be possible, for example, to forge a more positive theological reading of the first account than of the second. The distinction between accounts, however, is basically a scholar's distinction. In the history of the tradition's effects in culture and history, that distinction has not been observed. In this sketch of sexism in the tradition's religious myth, therefore, I discuss Genesis without making the distinction between accounts.

102. A. Heidel, *The Babylonian Genesis: The Story of Creation*, 2d ed. (Chicago: University of Chicago Press, 1951), pp. 83–88, 98–101; Keller, *From a Broken Web*, p. 82; J.J. Jackson, "Tiamat," *The Interpreter's Dictionary of the Bible*, vol. 4 (Nashville: Abingdon, 1962), p. 639.

103. Mircea Eliade, *Patterns in Comparative Religion*, trans. Rosemary Sheed (New York: Meridian, 1958), pp. 188–215.

104. John A. Phillips, *Eve: The History of an Idea* (San Francisco: Harper & Row, 1984), p. 5, cited from Keller, *From a Broken Web*, p. 83. Phillips's imagery about the story being "somewhere in the back of the minds of the writers of Genesis" does not mean that his insight grows out of a confidence in Phillips's or any scholar's ability to discern the mind or intention of the writer. Rather, the observation grows out of a study of the structural and thematic similarities between the Genesis text and the story of Marduk.

105. Keller, *From a Broken Web*, p. 83.

106. Peter C. Hodgson and Robert King, *Christian Theology: An Introduction to Its Traditions and Tasks* (Philadelphia: Fortress, 1980), pp. 76–77.

107. G. Contenau, *Everyday Life in Babylon and Assyria*, (London: E. Arnold, 1954), and W. S. McCullough, "Serpent," *Interpreter's Dictionary of the Bible*, vol. 4 (Nashville: Abingdon, 1962), pp. 289–91.

108. Eliade, *Comparative Religion*, pp. 163–71.

109. Keller, *From a Broken Web*, p. 84.

110. J. B. Pritchard, ed., *Ancient Near Eastern Texts Relating to the Old Testament*, trans. and annot. W. F. Albright, et al. (Princeton, N.J.: Princeton University Press, 1971), Ugaritic Text (I, AB [i] lines 2–4). The second passage is from Is. 51:9–10; cited from Keller, p. 84.

111. McCullough, "Serpent," p. 290.

112. Lerner, *Creation of Patriarchy*, p. 171.

113. Ibid., pp. 158, 160.

114. Robert Graves, *The Greek Mythos*, vol. I (New York: G. Braziller, 1959), pp. 37–47. Also see Lerner's summaries, *Creation of Patriarchy*, pp. 204–205.

115. Lerner, *Creation of Patriarchy*, p. 205.

116. Keller, *From a Broken Web*, p. 56.

117. Lerner, *Creation of Patriarchy*, p. 205.

118. In 1988, as I write, news services report on the widespread popularity among North American males of video games that "every American boy wants." One of the most popular is one that involves plans "to destroy the dread Mother Brain." *New York Times*, December 4, 1988, Section D, pp. 5–6.

119. Keller, *From a Broken Web*, p. 62.

120. Rabuzzi, *Motherself*, pp. 32–34.

121. James Hillman, *The Myth of Analysis* (Evanston, Ill.: Northwestern University Press, 1972), p. 298. Keller, *From a Broken Web,* pp. 67.

122. Keller, ibid., pp. 93-154.

123. Aristotle, *Genesis of Animals,* 4:4, 735A 14–16. Cf. Lerner, *Creation of Patriarchy,* pp. 205–11.

124. Margaret R. Miles, *Augustine on the Body* (Missoula, Mont.: Scholars Press, 1979).

125. Thomas Aquinas, *Summa Theologica,* vol. 13 (London: Burns, Oates and Washburne, Ltd., 1914), question 92. Cited from Keller, *From a Broken Web,* p. 127.

4. SEEKING CONNECTIONS

1. See above, chapter 3, pp. 80ff.

2. Frances Beale, "Double Jeopardy: To Be Black and Female," in Gayraud S. Wilmore and James H. Cone, *Black Theology: Documentary History, 1966–1979* (Maryknoll, N.Y.: Orbis Books, 1979), pp. 368–76.

3. Theressa Hoover, "Black Women and the Churches: Triple Jeopardy," and Jacqueline Grant, "Black Theology and the Black Woman," in Wilmore and Cone, *Black Theology,* pp. 377–88, 418–33.

4. Sheila Briggs, "The Politics of Identity and the Politics of Interpretation," in Conference address, Conversations: A Theological Project in Hermeneutics and Cultural Contexts, Princeton Theological Seminary, May 18, 1988, p. 14, unpublished.

5. Hynes seems to have been the first to develop a critique like this on the arithmetic of oppression. See H. Patricia Hynes, "On 'Racism and Writing,' " *Sinister Wisdom* 15 (Fall 1980): 105. See also the discussion in Janice G. Raymond, *A Passion for Friends: Toward a Philosophy of Female Affection* (Boston: Beacon Press, 1986), pp. 191–93.

6. Rosemary Radford Ruether, *New Women, New Earth: Sexist Ideologies and Human Liberation* (New York: Seabury, 1975), pp. 115–33.

7. Raymond, *A Passion for Friends,* p. 3.

8. Nancy C. M. Hartsock, *Money, Sex and Power: Toward a Feminist Historical Materialism* (Baltimore: Johns Hopkins University Press, 1983), p. 238.

9. Raymond, *A Passion for Friends,* is here concluding her comments by quoting Simone de Beauoir, *The Second Sex,* trans. and ed. H. M. Parshley (New York: Bantam, 1952), p. 307.

10. Hartsock, *Money,* p. 238.

11. The Mudflower Collective, Carter Heyward, ed., *God's Fierce Whimsy: Christian Feminism and Theological Education* (New York: Pilgrim Press, 1985), pp. 191–92.

12. Nancy Chodorow, *The Reproduction of Mothering: Psychoanalysis and the Sociology of Gender* (Berkeley, Calif.: University of California Press, 1978), pp. 105–109; Hartstock, *Money,* p. 238.

13. The terms *soluble* and *separate* for men and women's selves is developed in Catherine Keller, *From a Broken Web: Separation, Sexism, Self* (Boston: Beacon Press, 1986), pp. 7–46.

14. For the development of this argument, see Jane Flax, "The Conflict Between Nurturance and Autonomy in Mother-Daughter Relations and in Feminism," *Feminist Studies* 6 (June 1978).

15. Hartsock, *Money*, p. 239.

16. Stoller's argument as summarized, ibid., p. 240.

17. In addition to his study of *Perversion* (New York: Pantheon, 1979), see Robert Stoller, *Sexual Excitement: The Dynamics of Erotic Life* (New York: Pantheon, 1979).

18. For some careful and honest explorations of the relationships between male dominance and sexual arousal, see Jack Litewka, "The Socialized Penis," in Jon Snodgrass, ed., *A Book of Readings for Men Against Sexism* (Albion, Calif.: Times Change Press, 1977), pp. 22–23.

19. Hartsock, *Money*, p. 239; Stoller, *Perversion*, pp. 149–51.

20. James B. Nelson, *The Intimate Connection: Male Sexuality, Masculine Spirituality* (Philadelphia: Westminster, 1988), p. 48. For Levinson's comments, see Daniel J. Levinson, *The Seasons of a Man's Life* (New York: Ballantine, 1978), pp. 12, 335. Goldberg's comments are in *The Hazards of Being Male* (New York: New American Library, 1977), p. 136. Earl Shorris's perspective is summarized from Sam Keen, "Male Friendship: A Gilt-Edged Bond," *Gentleman's Quarterly*, May 1984, p. 238.

21. Michael E. McGill, *The McGill Report on Male Intimacy* (New York: Harper & Row, 1985), pp. 172–80.

22. On competition as obstacle to intimacy, see David F. Greenberg, *The Construction of Homosexuality* (Chicago: University of Chicago Press, 1988), p. 356–60.

23. On the deeply ingrained character of this competitiveness, see James E. Dittes, *The Male Predicament: On Being a Man Today* (New York: Harper & Row, 1985), pp. 172–80.

24. James B. Nelson, *Intimate Connection*, pp. 50–51.

25. Ibid., p. 37.

26. Dorothee Soelle, *The Strength of the Weak: Toward a Christian Feminist Identity*, trans. Robert and Rita Kimber (Philadelphia: Westminster, 1984), p. 51.

27. For a detailed treatment focusing especially on the cause of social rules that construct homosexuality as deviant, see David F. Greenberg, *Construction of Homosexuality*.

28. Raymond, *A Passion for Friends*, pp. 7, 8.

29. Audre Lorde, *Sister Outsider: Essays and Speeches* (Trumansburg, N.Y.: Crossing Press, 1984), p. 58.

30. See The Mudflower Collective, Carter Heyward, ed., *God's Fierce Whimsy*, pp. 191–92.

31. See, for example, John Stollenberg, "Refusing to Be a Man," and "Love-Making with Myself," in Snodgrass, *Men Against Sexism*, pp. 36–41, 4–44.

32. For a historical view, see John Boswell, *Christianity, Social Tolerance and Homosexuality: Gay People in Western Europe from the Beginning of the Christian Era to the Fourteenth Century* (Chicago: University of Chicago Press, 1980), pp. 44–45.

33. On the notion of a lesbian aesthetic, see Bonnie Zimmerman, "What Has Never Been: An Overview of Lesbian Feminist Literary Criticism," and Showalter's bibliography, "Lesbian Feminist Criticism," both in Elaine Showalter, *The New Feminist Criticism* (New York: Pantheon, 1988), pp. 200–24, 385–86; Carolyn Burke, "Gertrude Stein, the Cone Sisters, and the Puzzle of Female Friendship," and Catharine R. Stimpson, "Zero Degree Deviancy: The Lesbian Novel in English," in *Writing and Sexual Difference*, ed. Elizabeth Abel (Chicago: University of Chicago Press, 1982), pp. 221–42, 243–59. Concerning homo-relationality or "homosociality"

in men's writing, see *Between Men: English Literature and Male Homosocial Desire*, ed. Eve Kosofsky Sedgwick (New York: Columbia University Press, 1985), esp. pp. 1–20.

34. On the recent North American developments, see David Altman, *The Homosexualization of America* (New York: St. Martins Press, 1982), p. 6; Barbara Ehrenreich, *Hearts of Men: American Dreams and the Flight from Commitment* (Garden City, N.Y.: Anchor Press, 1983), pp. 126–30; Greenberg, *Construction of Homosexuality*, pp. 455–81.

35. See Boswell, *Christianity*, pp. 137–66, 243–66. Cf. Greenberg's critique of theorists who fault religious traditions for the oppression of gay and lesbian communities. Religious traditions cannot be blamed so easily. Greenberg, *Construction of Homosexuality*, pp. 12–13.

36. For a summary of this interaction, see Josephine Donovan, *Feminist Theory: The Intellectual Traditions of American Feminism* (New York: Frederick Ungar Publishing, 1985), pp. 65–90.

37. Marvin Harris, *Cultural Anthropology* (New York: Harper & Row Publishers, 1983), p. 160.

38. Ibid., p. 172.

39. Martin Hollis and Edward Nell, *Rational Economic Man* (New York: Cambridge University Press, 1975); Hartsock, *Money*, esp. pp. 38–54.

40. For the important reviews of Hartsock, see Gwendolen M. Carter, *Political Science Quarterly* 99 (February 1984):549–50; Joy Huntley, *The American Political Science Review* 78 (December 1984:1187–88; Audrey McKinney and Mary L. Shanley, *The Journal of Politics* 47 (November 1985):1298–1301; and Judith Van Allen, *Signs* 10 (Spring 1985):577–79.

41. Hartsock, *Money*, p. 38; Hollis and Nell, *Rational Economic Man*, pp. 55.

42. Hartsock, *Money*, pp. 38–39.

43. Ibid., p. 48.

44. Ibid., p. 20.

45. See Hartsock's extensive bibliographical note, ibid., p. 33, n.4. For her explicit discussions of "mainstream theorizations of power," indebted to exchange theory, see her discussions of Harold Lasswell and Abraham Kaplan, *Power and Society* (New Haven, Conn.: Yale University Press, 1950); Nelson Polsby, *Community Power and Political Theory* (New Haven, Conn.: Yale University Press, 1962, 1980); Talcott Parsons, "On the Concept of Power," and Roderick Bell, David Edwards, and Harrison Wagner, eds., *Political Power* (New York: Free Press, 1969); and Robert Dahl, "The Concept of Power," ibid. Hartsock's critique, *Money*, extends from pp. 55–75.

46. Hartsock, *Money*, p. 51.

47. Karl Marx, *Capital* (New York: International Publishers, 1967), I:176. Cited from ibid., p, 40.

48. Hartsock, *Money*, p. 51.

49. Ibid, pp. 40-43.

50. See Harris, *Cultural Anthropology*, pp. 288–95, 317–18. Harris writes that while from the viewpoint of U.S. natives the political economy is said to be capitalist it in fact is a mixture of socialism and capitalism. Harris' studies of U.S. political economy also confirm Hartsock's claim that exchange theories based on the freedoms of rational economic man actually screen the extent to which power and coercion structure the political economy. Harris writes: "the capitalist sector of the

economy is viewed as being based on free enterprise price competition; . . . however, the degree of concentration of economic resources in the largest conglomerate corporations creates a situation of oligopoly that precludes the setting of prices through competitive market supply and demand" (p. 317).

51. Hartsock, *Money*, p. 46.

52. Albert Hirschman, *The Passions and the Interests* (Princeton, N.J.: Princeton University Press, 1978).

53. Hartsock, *Money*, p. 47; Hirschman, *Passions*, pp. 28–31.

54. Hartsock, *Money*, p. 47.

55. Ibid.

56. Ibid., p. 48.

57. Joel Kovell, "Radix Malorum," in Kovell, *White Racism: A Psycho-History* (New York: Columbia University Press, 1970), pp. 86–149.

58. Hartsock, *Money*, p. 97.

59. Alfred Sohn-Rethel, *Intellectual and Manual Labor: A Critique of Epistemology* (London: Macmillian, 1978), p. 53. Cited from Hartsock, *Money*, p. 100. For Hartsock's differentiation of her analysis from Sohn-Rethel, see *Money*, p. 111.

60. Kovell, *White Racism*, p. 117.

61. Marx, *Capital*, 1:137, cited in Hartsock, *Money*, pp. 98, 111.

62. Sohn-Rethel, *Intellectual and Manual Labor*, p. 27; Hartsock, *Money*, p. 98.

63. Hartsock, *Money*, p. 234.

64. Ibid.

65. Ibid., p. 10.

66. Donovan, *Feminist Theory*, pp. 65–66. Donovan prefers this phrase instead of those retaining the terms *Marxist* or *Marxian* because many of the feminisms have gone well beyond Marxian formulations.

67. For literature on this and related themes, see Heidi Hartmann, "The Unhappy Marriage of Marxism and Feminism: Towards a More Progressive Union," in Lydia Sargent, ed., *Women and Revolution* (Boston: South End Press, 1981); Angela Davis, "Reflections on the Black Women's Role in the Community of Slaves," *The Black Scholar* 3 (December 1971): 7; Zillah Eisenstein, ed., *Capitalist Patriarchy and the Case for Socialist Feminism* (New York: Monthly Review, 1979), p 11.

68. See Eisenstein, *Capitalist Patriarchy*.

69. On the relations between capitalism and heterosexism, see Greenberg, *Construction of Homosexuality*, pp. 347–56.

70. United Nations, "Review and Evaluation of Progress Made and Obstacles Encountered at the National Level in Attaining the Objectives of the World Plan of Action," item 8a of the Provisional Agenda 80-14909, World Conference of the United Nations Decade for Women: Equality, Development, and Peace, Copenhagen, Denmark, 1980. See Raymond, *Passion for Friends*, p. 262.

71. United States Department of Commerce, Table 12, Comparisons of Median Earnings of Year Round Full Time Workers by Sex, 1955–1978, in *Money Income of Families and Persons in the U.S., Current Population Reports 1957–1977: Money Income and Poverty Status of Families and Persons in the U.S.*; 1980 census. See Raymond, *Passion for Friends*, p. 262.

72. United Nations, "Program of Action for the 2nd Half of the U.N. Decade for Women: Equality, Development, and Peace," item 9 of the Provisional Agenda 80-12383, World Conference of the United Nations Decade for Women: Equality,

Development, and Peace, Copenhagen, Denmark, 1980. See Raymond, *Passion for Friends*, p. 262.

73. United States Department of Justice, *F.B.I. Uniform Crime Report: Crime in the United States, 1980*. See Raymond, *Passion for Friends*, p. 262.

74. D. Moore, *Battered Women* (Beverly Hills, Calif.: Sage, 1979). See also Raymond's discussion of women's material conditions in *Passion for Friends*, pp. 206–07.

75. On the split between private and public worlds in the philosophies of the West, see Jean Bethke Elshtain, *Public Man, Private Woman* (Princeton, N.J.: Princeton University Press, 1981).

76. Adrienne Rich, *Of Woman Born: Motherhood as Experience and Institution* (New York: W.W. Norton, 1976), pp. 64, 167, cited in Hartsock, *Money*, p. 242. Rich can make this point while also insisting that the family context in which women have been forced to work is a "most dangerous place," from which they need their freedom.

77. Hartsock, *Money*, p. 243. For an extensive bibliography that documents this as an accurate portrayal of women's experience, see p. 251, n. 41.

78. See the figures in Raymond, as well as the statistics and descriptions of women's economic situation in Robin Morgan, ed., *Sisterhood is Global: The International Women's Movement Anthology* (Garden City, N.Y.: Anchor Books, 1984).

79. On the effects and nature of multinational organizations, see Richard J. Barnet and Ronald E. Miller, *Global Reach: The Power of Multinational Corporations* (New York: Simon and Schuster, 1974). For a defense of the effects of these extensions of the capitalist enterprise, see Peter L. Berger, *The Capitalist Revolution: Fifty Propositions about Prosperity and Equality of Liberty* (New York: Basic Books, 1986). My major critique of Berger is that his defenses of "the capitalist revolution" are developed on macrolevels, rarely including fine-grained, "thick description" of the social and political lives that are fashioned in the wake of "the capitalist revolution." On the need to study capitalism and multinationals' impact, see anthropologists George E. Marcus and Michael M. J. Fischer, *Anthropology as Cultural Critique: An Experimental Moment in the Human Sciences* (Chicago: University of Chicago Press, 1986), pp. 77–110.

80. For one review of specific organizations of mothers, see Joyce Hollyday, "Mothers of Sorrow and Hope," *Sojourners* (May 1988):14–20.

81. Marilyn Anderson and Jonathan Garlock, *Grand-daughters of Corn: Portraits of Guatemalan Women* (Willimantic, Conn.: Curbstone Press, 1988).

82. Hollyday, "Mothers of Sorrow and Hope," p. 16.

83. Ibid., p. 16.

84. About 61 percent of Guatemala's population is Amerindian, and they constitute the vast majority of those in poverty. There are, however, poor "Ladinos" (non-Indians) who also suffer from an unequal distribution of wealth and land control. Fifty percent of Guatemala's population earns $80 per year or less, and 80 percent of the arable land is owned by 2 percent of the population.

85. For one of the more judicious explorations of these embassy deaths, see Philip Berryman, *Christians in Guatemala's Struggle* (London: Catholic Institute for International Relations, 1984), pp. 44–48.

86. Elisabeth Burgos-Debray, ed., *I . . . Rigoberta Menchu: An Indian Woman in Guatemala*, trans. Ann Wright (London: Verso, 1984), pp. 174–77.

87. Ibid., p. 200.

88. Allan Nairn, "To Defend Our Way of Life: An Interview with a U.S. Businessman," *Guatemala in Rebellion: Unfinished History* (New York: Grove Press, 1983), p. 89.

89. For this story's documentation, see Richard H. Immerman, *The CIA in Guatemala: The Foreign Policy of Intervention* (Austin, Tex.: University of Texas Press, 1982).

90. Nairn, "To Defend Our Way of Life," pp. 89, 100–105.

91. Ibid., pp. 90–91. Concerning the inclusion in this text of the interview with Sherwood, I am grateful to conversation with Paul Knitter.

92. Cornel West, "Marxist Theory and the Specificity of Afro-American Oppression," in *Marxism and the Interpretation of Culture*, Cary Nelson and Lawrence Grossberg, eds. (Urbana and Chicago: University of Illinois, 1988), p. 25.

93. Kovell, *White Racism*, p. 3.

94. Ibid., p. 15.

95. Ibid., pp. ix–x, 54–55, 211–30.

96. Ibid., xxv–xxvi. As Kovell points out, this "advance" is at best ambiguous. It gives blacks the *problems* of power at the very intense local level, without the *resources* of power that must come from access to macrolevel resources.

97. See Kovell's summaries of the problem, not only as it increased during the Reagan presidency, but as it was also problematic prior to Reagan. Kovell, *White Racism*, pp. xii–xvi.

98. See the diverse essays collected in James D. Williams, ed., *The State of Black America 1986* (New York: The National Urban League, 1986). This should be supplemented by more recent studies, such as Richard P. Nathan, *New York Times*, January 26, 1987, A1, A27. Drawing from both 1970 and 1980 census figures, and also from later surveys, this reports the rise of extreme poverty in fifty urban centers, but also the substantial growth of blacks' exposure to extreme poverty, while the number of poor whites so exposed actually declined (p. A27).

99. Eric R. Wolf, *Europe and the People Without History* (Berkeley, Calif.: University of California Press, 1982), p. 196.

100. Ibid., p. 195.

101. See especially the critical but emphatically appreciative review of Wolf's book in Peter Worsley, "A Landmark in Anthropology," *American Ethnologist* 11 (February 1984):170–75. Cf. J. H. Galloway, *The Journal of Historical Geography* 10 (January 1984):119–24; and Katherine Verdery, *Ethnohistory* 31 (1984):225–27.

102. Wolf, *Europe*, p. 204.

103. For discussion, see Eric Williams, *Capitalism and Slavery* (Chapel Hill, N.C., University of North Carolina Press, 1944); Wolfe, *Europe*, pp. 199–200.

104. Cited in Wolfe, *Europe*, p. 198.

105. Ibid., pp. 204, 207.

106. Ibid., p. 202.

107. Ibid, p. 204.

108. Gary B. Nash, *Red, White and Black: The Peoples of Early America* (Englewood Cliffs, N.J.: Prentice-Hall, 1974); Theda Perdue, *Slavery and the Evolution of Cherokee Society 1540–1866* (Knoxville,Tenn.: University of Tennessee Press, 1979).

109. Wolf, *Europe*, p. 203.

110. Ibid, p. 196. "Between 1701 and 1810, England exported from West Africa . . . about two-thirds of the total number shipped by the three major powers in the slave trade [England, Portugal, France]" (p. 198).

111. For an excellent pictorial gallery of the ways blackness and black people functioned in the art of Western civilization, see Jean Vercouter, et al., *The Image of the Black in Western Art*, 3 vols. (Cambridge, Mass.: Harvard University Press, 1976).

112. Kovell, *White Racism*, p. 62.

113. Marshall Sahlins, "Colors and Cultures," in Janet L. Dolgin, David S. Kemnitzer, and David M. Schneider, eds., *Symbolic Anthropology: A Reader in the Study of Symbols and Meanings* (New York: Columbia University Press, 1977), p. 167. Sahlins's essay also includes references to most of the significant anthropological research on color symbolism.

114. Winthrop Jordan, *White Over Black* (Chapel Hill, N.C.: University of North Carolina Press, 1968), p. 24, cited from Kovell, *White Racism*, p. 63.

115. Kovell, *White Racism*, pp. 65–66. He is citing Frantz Fanon, *Black Skin, White Masks* (New York: Grove Press, 1967), p. 190.

116. Ibid., p. 97.

117. Ibid., p. 67.

118. See Trudier Harris, *Exorcising Blackness: Historical and Literary Lynching and Burning Rituals* (Bloomington, Ind.: Indiana University Press, 1984), pp. 91–92, in Kovell, *White Racism*, p. 67.

119. Kovell, *White Racism*, p. 69. Note here how the oppression of white women by white men is integrally bound up with the white male's oppressive stereotyping and monsterizing of black women's sexuality. Ruether also explores this in *New Women*, pp. 115–33.

120. Kovell, *White Racism*, p. 67.

121. See the summaries of the way fantasy could construct such situations and were dramatized in literary texts like Chester Hime's *If He Hollers Let Him Go* (Chatham, N.J.: Bookseller, 1945) and James Baldwin's *Another Country* (New York: Dell 1962), in Trudier Harris, *Exorcising Blackness*, pp. 53–61.

122. On this concern as a feature of a black aesthetic vision, see esp. Harris's discussions in *Exorcising Blackness*, pp. 95–128, of Richard Wright's novels. Her reflections on this being largely a male tradition occur on pages 188ff.

123. Kovell, *White Racism*, p. 67.

124. Harris develops this point in *Exorcising Blackness*, pp. 188–90.

125. On these connections see Stoller, *Perversion* and *Sexual Excitement*; and Calvin C. Hernton, *Sex and Racism in America* (New York: Grove Press, 1965). See also Hartsock, *Money*, pp. 157–61.

126. James Baldwin, "Going To Meet the Man," *Going To Meet the Man* (New York: Dell, (1965), pp. 198–218.

127. Ibid., p. 210.

128. Kovell, *White Racism*, p. 81.

129. Ibid., p. 48.

130. Ibid., p. 49.

131. Unfortunately, Kovell does not discuss how this claim needs to be qualified with respect to the gender of the child. The projection of this separation process as identical for female and male children, and hence as universal, is itself an element of sexism in psychoanalytic theory. On feminist critiques of psychoanalysis, see Donovan, *Feminist Theory*, pp. 91–116. Kovell does seem to limit his claims about the presence of this separation process to "Western civilization," but he does not take into consideration the way gender may qualify the "drive behavior" he asso-

ciates with anality. In this study I take Kovell's description to apply mainly to the drive behavior of white males, which, in fact, is what the entire context of Kovell's study implies without actually stating. For Kovell's own later self-critique of his confidence in psychoanalytic theory, see Kovell, "Preface," *White Racism*, 1983 Morningside ed., pp. xxxviii–xlvi.

132. Kovell, *White Racism*, p. 49. I retain Kovell's usage of masculine pronouns here, because I believe he is talking primarily about male drive behavior.

133. Ibid., pp. 81–82.

134. *Newsweek*, October 21, 1963, pp. 48–50, cited in Kovell, Ibid., p. 83.

135. James Hamilton, "Some Dynamics of Anti-Negro Prejudice," *Psychoanalytic Review* VIII (1966–1967), pp. 5–15.

136. Kovell, *White Racism*, pp. 86–90. Kovell draws his examples mainly from white language formed in response to a fair-housing drive in Ann Arbor, Michigan.

137. Ibid., p. 87.

138. Ibid.

139. Ibid., p. xlv.

140. Ibid., p. xlvi.

141. On the need for "macrostructural analysis" in the study of racism, see Cornel West, "Marxist Theory."

142. See summaries of this literature by Deborah E. McDowell, "New Directions for Black Feminist Criticism," in Elaine Showalter, *The New Feminist Criticism* (New York: Pantheon, 1985), pp. 186–199.

143. Kovell, *White Racism*, p. xlv.

144. Sandor Ferenczi, "The Ontogenesis of the Interest in Money," in his *First Contributions to Psychoanalysis* (London: The Hogarth Press, 1952), pp. 319–31. See also Kovell, *White Racism*, pp. 134–35.

145. For Kovell's fuller discussions of these links, see his chapter, "Radix Malorum," in his *White Racism*, pp. 107–37.

146. Ibid., p. 157 (my italics).

147. Houston A. Baker, Jr., *Blues, Ideology and Afro-American Literature: A Vernacular Theory* (Chicago: The University of Chicago Press, 1984), pp. 64–112. See also Baker, *The Journey Back: Issues in Black Literature and Criticism* (Chicago: The University of Chicago Press, 1980), p. 11ff.

148. Trudier Harris, *Exorcising Blackness*, p. 195.

149. Henry Louis Gates, Jr., "Reclaiming their Tradition," review of Mary Helen Washington, *Invented Lives: Narratives of Black Women 1860–1960* (New York: Doubleday, 1987), in *New York Times Book Review*, October 4, 1987, p. 3.

150. Deborah E. McDowell, "Negotiating Between Tenses: Witnessing Slavery After Freedom, Dessa Rose," unpublished paper, presented at Princeton Theological Seminary, May 16, 1987, pp. 34, 30–31.

151. Delores S. Williams, "Womanist Theological Perspectives on the Hagar-Sarah Story," unpublished paper, Princeton Theological Seminary, May 17, 1987, p. 21.

5. CHRIST AS ROUGH BEAST

1. Clodovis Boff, *Theology and Praxis: Epistemological Foundations* (Maryknoll, N.Y.: Orbis Books, 1987), pp. 67–90.

2. Philip Melanchthon, Preface to *Loci communes* (1521), cited in Wolfhart

Pannenberg, *Jesus — God and Man* (Philadelphia: Westminster Press, 1963), p. 38.

3. John Herman Randall, "The Ontology of Paul Tillich" in Charles W. Kegley, ed., *The Theology of Paul Tillich* (New York: The Pilgrim Press, 1982), p. 193. About the importance Tillich gave to this *Angst*, Randall remarked adroitly: " 'The ontological anxiety of finitude' may well express the way many Continental Europeans feel these days. But in this country I seriously doubt whether for many it can mean more than the latest fashion in theological apologetics."

4. Pannenberg, *Jesus*, p. 48.

5. Ibid., pp. 82–88.

6. Friedrich Schleiermacher, *The Christian Faith*, ed. H. R. Mackintosh and J. S. Stewart (Philadelphia: Fortress, 1976), pp. 282–304.

7. Ibid., p. 365.

8. Rosemary Radford Ruether, *Sexism and God-Talk: Toward a Feminist Theology* (Boston: Beacon Press, 1983), pp. 159–64.

9. On ethnocentrism as a widespread cultural phenomenon and as exacerbating oppression, see Claude Lévi-Strauss, "Race and History," in *Structural Anthropology*, vol. II, trans. Monique Layton (New York: Basic Books, 1976), pp. 323–62.

10. David L. Shields, "Christ: A Male Feminist View," *Encounter* 45 (Summer 1984): 221–32. On the complex issue of men's need for both male-specific *and* female-specific imagery, see Arthur Green, "Bride, Spouse, Daughter: Images of the Feminine in Classical Jewish Sources," in Susannah Heschel, ed., *On Being a Jewish Feminist: A Reader* (New York: Schocken, 1983), pp. 248–60.

11. John Money, "Psychosexual Differentiation," in *Sex Research: New Developments*, ed. John Money (New York: Holt, Rinehart and Winston, 1965), p. 11.

12. Salvatore Cucchiari, "The Gender Revolution and the Transition from Bisexual Horde to Patrilocal Band: The Origins of Gender Hierarchy," in *Sexual Meanings: The Cultural Construction of Gender and Sexuality*, ed. Sherry B. Ortner and Harriet Whitehead (Cambridge: Cambridge University Press, 1981), p. 32.

13. On the role of gender ideology in the study of gender systems, see Sherry B. Ortner and Harriet Whitehead, "Introduction: Accounting for Sexual Meanings," in Ortner and Whitehead, *Sexual Meanings*, pp. 6–9.

14. Note also the power of "maternal" and "paternal" images, and their different functions in formulating children's views of the sacred, in Anna-Maria Rizzuto, M.D., *The Birth of the Living God: A Psychoanalytic Study* (Chicago: University of Chicago Press, 1979), pp. 142–44, 149–52, and 185–90.

15. Peggy Reeves Sanday, *Female Power and Male Dominance* (Cambridge: Cambridge University Press, 1981), p. 215.

16. On the lack of connections in early Christian tradition between arguments against same-sex eroticism and homosexual practice, on the one hand, and the teachings of Jesus, on the other, see John Boswell, *Christianity, Social Tolerance and Homosexuality* (Chicago: University of Chicago Press, 1980), p. 63. See also David F. Greenberg's counsel against interpretations of homophobia as simply the product of a "Judaeo-Christian tradition" in David F. Greenberg, *The Construction of Homosexuality* (Chicago: University of Chicago Press, 1988), pp. 12–13.

17. The summary of these modes of arguments in early Christian tradition occur in Boswell, *Christianity, Social Tolerance and Homosexuality*, pp. 137–66.

18. See James B. Nelson, *Embodiment: An Approach to Sexuality and Christian Theology* (Minneapolis, Minn.: Augsburg, 1978), pp. 189–96.

19. Ibid., p. 196–97. Nelson summarizes the effect of Thielicke's position, since

it represents a third theological approach, that of "qualified acceptance" regarding gay/lesbian practice. The other two are "rejecting/punitive," and "rejecting/non-punitive" approaches. See ibid., pp. 180–205.

20. On "full acceptance," see ibid., pp. 197–99. My own christology of full acceptance occurs in the final chapter.

21. For discussion of this problem and possibilities for change in Latin America, in particular, in Nicaragua, see Carter Heyward, Anne Gilson, The Amanecida Collective, *Revolutionary Forgiveness: Feminist Reflections on Nicaragua* (Maryknoll, N.Y.: Orbis Books, 1987).

22. For studies that further articulate these connections, see Hugo Assmann, *La iglesia electronica y su impacto en America Latina* (San Jose, Costa Rica: Editorial DEI, 1987), pp. 127–28; Quentin J. Schultze, "The Mythos of the Electronic Church," *Critical Studies in Mass Communication* 4 (1987):248. I wish to thank D. A. Smith for calling my attention to these sources in his address, "Whose Gospel? A Reflection on the Pastoral and Ideological Impact of Evangelical Broadcasting on Central American Christians," presented at the Institute for the Study of American Evangelicals, Wheaton College, Wheaton, Ill., September 1988.

23. For one summary of options available, see Alice Frazer Evans, Robert A. Evans, and William Bean Kennedy, *Pedagogies for the Non-Poor* (Maryknoll, N.Y.: Orbis Books, 1987).

24. Lévi-Strauss, "Race and History," pp. 328–32.

25. Enrique Dussel, *A History of the Church in Latin America: Colonialism to Liberation* (Grand Rapids, Mich.: Eerdmans, 1981), pp. 8–13.

26. David Tracy, *The Analogical Imagination: Christian Theology and the Culture of Pluralism* (New York: Crossroad, 1981), p. 156.

27. See Karl Barth, *Theology and Church: Shorter Writings 1920–1928* (New York: Harper and Row, 1962); Karl Barth, "The Revelation of God as the Abolition [*Aufhebung*] of Religion," in *Church Dogmatics* I/2 (Edinburgh: T. & T. Clark, 1956), pp. 280–361. For Bonhoeffer's critiques see Dietrich Bonhoeffer, *Letters and Papers from Prison*, ed. Eberhard Bethge, 3d ed. (New York: Macmillan, 1967), 6/8/1944: pp. 178–82; and 4/30/1944, pp. 152–53. For critiques of Barth's position, see not only Bonhoeffer, but also Paul Tillich, "What is Wrong with the 'Dialectical' Theology?", *The Journal of Religion* 15 (1935):127–45. For critiques of all of these and other Protestant theologies as insufficiently critical of cultural-religious formations, see Gustavo Gutiérrez, *The Power of the Poor in History*, trans. Robert R. Barr (Maryknoll, N.Y.: Orbis Books, 1983), pp. 222–34.

28. Cornel West, "Marxist Theory and the Specificity of Afro-American Oppression," in *Marxism and the Interpretation of Culture*, ed. Cary Nelson and Lawrence Grossberg (Urbana and Chicago: University of Illinois, 1988), p. 29n.25.

29. William A. Lessa, "The Analysis of Myth: Introduction," in *Reader in Comparative Religions: An Anthropological Approach*, 4th ed., William A. Lessa and Evon Z. Vogt, (New York: Harper & Row, 1979), p. 168.

30. For an early example of the debate, see Clyde Kluckhohn, "Myths and Rituals: A General Theory," in Lessa and Vogt, *Reader in Comparative Religions*, pp. 66–78.

31. On this complex relationship, see William A. Lessa, "The Apotheosis of Marespa," ibid., pp. 169–73. Cf. G. S. Kirk, *Myth: Its Meaning and Functions in Ancient and Other Cultures* (Berkeley, Calif.: University of California Press, 1970), pp. 16–31.

32. Kirk, *Myth*, pp. 9–12.

33. This is a theme that runs throughout Lévi-Strauss's four-volume *Mythologiques*, but for more succinct discussion, see Claude Lévi-Strauss, *The Savage Mind* (Chicago: University of Chicago, 1966), pp. 250–262.

34. On "limit-language," see Tracy, *The Analogical Imagination*, pp. 160–67, and his earlier *Blessed Rage for Order: The New Pluralism in Theology* (New York: Seabury, 1975), pp. 91–119, 204–36. Tracy considers limit-language mainly in relation to fiction and the New Testament's christological language, instead of in relation to myth. I take Tracy's two notions of limit, as "limit-to" and "limit-of," as corresponding to my phraseology of myth's exploration of pervasive restrictions and limitations (Tracy's "limit-to") and its imaginative explorations of the whole (Tracy's "limit-of").

35. On the relationship between science and myth, see the early essay by Stephen Toulmin, "Contemporary Scientific Mythology," in *Metaphysical Beliefs: Three Essays*, ed. Alasdair MacIntyre (New York: Schocken, 1957), pp. 3–71.

36. Clifford C. Geertz, "Religion as a Cultural System," *Interpretation of Cultures* (New York: Basic Books, 1973), p. 90. Geertz is writing about religion understood as a cultural system.

37. See Ivan Strenski, *Four Theories of Myth in Twentieth Century History: Cassirer, Eliade, Lévi-Strauss and Malinowski* (Iowa City: University of Iowa Press, 1987), pp. 70–128. See especially Strenski's discussion of Eliade's project in the history of religions in relation to his Rumanian political context. Strenski comes close to discounting these scholars' contributions to mythic scholarship, almost "reducing" them to the diverse contexts of the scholars. Nevertheless, his work is a valuable reminder that the category of myth, and the use of it, is not just subject matter to describe and analyze, but also a heuristic and often strategic device.

38. My approach to myth here may be viewed as a "hermeneutical" one, provided that we not take the word as being antithetical to "explanatory" approaches. It is a hermeneutical approach because it integrates the social, political, and personal interests, or prejudgments, of mythologists into the mythologists' explanatory analyses. A hermeneutical approach to myth is similar to Eliade's hermeneutical approach to religion, though his "creative hermeneutics" has often been viewed as so speculative that the concerns of an explanation of myth are not preserved in his approach. See Mircea Eliade, "Methodological Remarks on the Study of Religious Symbolism," in *The History of Religions: Essays in Methodology*, ed. Mircea Eliade and Joseph M. Kitigawa (Chicago: University of Chicago Press, 1959), pp. 86–107; for a recent critique, see Strenski, *Four Theories*, pp. 104–11, 118–22.

39. As an example, see North America's perhaps most prolific evangelical theologian, Carl F. H. Henry. "Myth," he writes, "is fable." See his book, *God, Revelation and Authority, Volume I: God Who Speaks and Shows* (Waco, Tex.: Word Books, 1976), p. 48. For the entirety of his argument on myth, see pp. 44–69. "Truth or falsity must then pertain only to the nonmythical" (pp. 64–65).

40. On relations between myth and truth, see Schubert Ogden, "Myth and Truth," in his *The Reality of God and Other Essays* (New York: Harper & Row, 1963/1977), pp. 99–119. For discussion of ties between myth and history, as critique of any easy separations of these from one another, see anthropological studies, especially Marshall Sahlins, *Historical Metaphors and Mythical Realities: Structure in the Early History of the Sandwich Islands Kingdom* (Ann Arbor, Mich.: University of Michigan Press, 1981), pp. 3–32.

41. Gordon Kaufman's critiques of past metaphors and personal images in the traditional Christian mythos are therefore necessary and valuable. Kaufman's calls for reconstruction, however, do not readily seem to include remythologizing through new uses of personal images and anthropomorphisms. This book will propose such a remythologization as necessary to any theological reconstruction. For the relevant passages in Kaufman, see Gordon D. Kaufman, *Theology for a Nuclear Age* (Philadelphia: Westminster, 1985), pp. 32, 41–43, 58.

42. Sallie McFague, *Models of God: Theology for an Ecological, Nuclear Age* (Philadelphia: Fortress, 1987), p. 80.

43. Ibid.

44. Rita Nakashima Brock, *Journeys by Heart: A Christology of Erotic Power* (New York: Crossroad, 1988), pp. 105–106.

45. Ibid., pp. 71–104. In these chapters, though Brock gives needed attention and significance to figures often neglected in commentaries on Jesus' life, Jesus still seems to function for her in a way that is more essential than the simile presenting Jesus "like a whitecap on a wave."

46. See Claude Welch, *Protestant Theology in the Nineteenth Century*, vol. I, 1799–1870 (New Haven, Conn.: Yale University Press, 1972), pp. 139–169. Such christologies are featured in various nineteenth century Protestant theologies, ranging from Hegel and Schleiermacher to later theologians of the nineteenth and twentieth centuries who made distinctions between the "Jesus of history" and the "Christ of faith."

47. I am thinking especially of Rita Nakashima Brock, *Journeys by Heart*, and of Tom Driver, *Christ in a Changing World: Toward an Ethical Christology* (New York: Crossroad, 1981).

48. Schubert M. Ogden, *The Point of Christology* (New York: Harper and Row, 1982), pp. 20–40.

49. Peter C. Hodgson, *God in History: Shapes of Freedom* (Nashville, Tenn.: Abingdon Press, 1989), p. 209. For an example of another scholar's work, which moves in a direction similar to mine, though in a different way and in the context of interreligious discussion, see Paul Knitter, "Jesus-Buddha-Krishna: Still Present," *Journal of Ecumenical Studies* 16 (1979):651-71.

50. Ibid.

51. Ibid., pp. 209, 214.

52. See above discussion, pp. 157–60.

53. Paul Tillich, *Systematic Theology* (Chicago: University of Chicago Press, 1967), III:149. Tillich, of course, is not claiming that the Christ is *only* a function of "those who receive him as the Christ." For Tillich, (see II:97–99), the Christ event has its "factual" side also, i.e. the "concreteness" of Jesus' life. See also Knitter, "Jesus-Buddha-Krishna."

54. For the postures of suspicion in relation to scholars' reconstruction of the early Christian movements, see Elisabeth Schüssler Fiorenza, *In Memory of Her: A Feminist Theological Reconstruction of Christian Origins* (New York: Crossroad, 1983), pp. 26ff. and especially her *Bread Not Stone: The Challenge of Feminist Biblical Interpretation* (Boston: Beacon Press, 1984), pp. 15–22. The notion of a "hermeneutics of suspicion" is developed by Schüssler Fiorenza from Paul Ricoeur's early work. See Paul Ricoeur, *Freud and Philosophy: An Essay on Interpretation*, trans. Denis Savage (New Haven and London: Yale University Press, 1970), pp. 32–36.

55. If we take up the question, as some readers may want to at this point, of

what criteria are able to justify or discredit Christian actions that are "contrary to those of Jesus," I can only answer that while the actions of Jesus are an important part of Christian criteria they cannot be "the foundation" for judging Christian actions. Ultimately, we must have recourse to ethical reflection ongoing in the whole communal dialogue, wrestling with the meaning of the whole Christ dynamic disclosed in the Christian movement in light of dialogue about contemporary needs. For discussion of communal, nonfoundationalist understandings of criteria, see Richard Bernstein, *Beyond Objectivism and Relativism: Science, Hermeneutics and Praxis* (Philadelphia: University of Pennsylvania Press, 1983), pp. 223–31, and Francis Schüssler Fiorenza, *Foundational Theology: Jesus and the Church* (New York: Continuum, 1984), pp. 285–311.

56. David Friedrich Strauss, *The Life of Jesus*, trans. George Eliot (1835), Section 149. For fuller discussion of Strauss's christology, see Welch, *Protestant Theology*, pp. 147–54, esp. 150.

57. On "Sophia" images in Christian feminist theology, see Hal Taussig, Susan Cady, and Maria Ronan, *Sophia: The Future of Feminist Spirituality* (New York: Harper & Row, 1987). For images of "Christa," see Brock, *Journeys by Heart*, pp. 67–72. On discussions of the black Christ, see Albert Cleague, *The Black Messiah* (New York: Sheed and Ward, 1968); James Cone, *God of the Oppressed* (New York: Seabury, 1975), pp. 133–37; Theo Witvliet, *The Way of the Black Messiah: The Hermeneutical Challenge of Black Theology as a Theology of Liberation* (New York: Meyer & Stone, 1985), pp. 213–30.

58. See J. Christiaan Beker, *Paul the Apostle: The Triumph of God in Life and Thought* (Philadelphia: Fortress, 1980), pp. 135–212, and Oscar Cullman, *The Christology of the New Testament* (Philadelphia: Westminster, 1963), pp. 166–80.

59. I treat the issue of readings of the bible in the section below, "The Bible's Emancipatory Message," pp. 181–85.

60. See Prologue, pp. 18–20.

61. Hodgson, *God in History*, pp. 209, 214.

62. Schubert M. Ogden, *Faith and Freedom: Toward a Theology of Liberation* (Nashville, Tenn.: Abingdon, 1979). See the important critique of Ogden formulated by Dorothee Solle, *The Challenge of Liberation Theology: A First World Response* (Maryknoll, N.Y.: Orbis Books, 1981), pp. 4–20.

63. For example, see Daniel Migliore, "Jesus Christ, the Reconciling Liberator: The Confession of 1967 and Theologies of Liberation," *Journal of Presbyterian History* 61 (Spring 1983):33–42. The major concern in this issue is to examine the Presbyterian Church (U.S.A.)'s "Confession of 1967" in relation to liberation theology, and in the process show how both biblical themes of reconciliation and liberation need each other. In this particular essay, Migliore is not arguing, as I will here, for the primacy of emancipation in its mutually coinherent relation with reconciliation. However, see Daniel L. Migliore, *Called To Freedom: Liberation Theology and the Future of Christian Doctrine* (Philadelphia: Westminster, 1980).

64. See, for example, Jon Sobrino, *Christology at the Crossroads: A Latin American Approach* (Maryknoll, N.Y.: Orbis Books, 1978), pp. 1–6, and Cone, *God of the Oppressed*, p. 115–20.

65. Peter C. Hodgson, *New Birth of Freedom: A Theology of Bondage and Liberation* (Philadelphia: Fortress, 1976), p. 209. Hodgson is citing Leander E. Keck, "The Church, the New Testament and Violence," *Pastoral Psychology* 22 (October 1971):7–8.

66. Wayne A. Meeks, *The First Urban Christians: The Social World of the Apostle Paul* (New Haven, Conn.: Yale University Press, 1983), pp. 189–92.

67. See Hodgson, *New Birth*, p. 216. Cf. pp. 8, 20. For the etymological and historical details making *eleutheria* a problematic word for Jesus and Christians because of its integral relation to privileged peoples, see esp. Hodgson's footnote on page 50.

68. Ibid., p. 215.

69. Ibid., pp. 253–64.

70. Ernst Käsemann, *Jesus Means Freedom* (Philadelphia: Fortress Press, 1969).

71. Ogden, *The Point of Christology*, p. 111.

72. Ibid., p. 123.

73. Edward Schillebeeckx, *Christ: The Experience of Jesus as Lord* (New York: Seabury, 1980), p. 36, and Elisabeth Schüssler Fiorenza, *In Memory of Her*, pp. 26–36.

74. Schüssler Fiorenza, *In Memory of Her*, pp. 152, 100, 127.

75. Ibid., p. 122.

76. Ibid., p. 154.

77. Ibid., pp. 243–79, 285–334.

78. Cornel West, review of *In Memory of Her*, in *Religious Studies Review* 11 (Jan. 1985):4.

79. See her studies of the discipleship of diverse women and "of equals," and of the house church movement, in her book, *In Memory of Her*, pp. 130–51, 162–68, 175–84.

80. Severino Croatto, *Biblical Hermeneutics: Toward a Theory of Reading as the Production of Meaning*, trans. Robert R. Barr (Maryknoll, N.Y.: Orbis Books, 1987), p. 51. For case studies of this, see Willard M. Swartley, *Slavery, Sabbath, War and Women: Case Issues in Biblical Interpretation* (Scottdale, Pa.: Herald Press, 1983).

81. Croatto, *Biblical Hermeneutics*, p. 51.

82. See Childs' discussion of this point in Brevard S. Childs, *The Book of Exodus: A Critical, Theological Commentary* (Philadelphia: Westminster, 1974), pp. 213–14.

83. Croatto, *Biblical Hermeneutics*, p. 52.

84. Gerhard von Rad, *Old Testament Theology*, vol. 1, trans. D. M. G., Stalker (New York: Harper and Brothers, 1962), p. 139.

85. Gustavo Gutiérrez, *A Theology of Liberation: History, Politics, and Salvation*, trans. and ed. Sister Caridad Inda and John Eagleson, 15th Anniversary Ed. (Maryknoll, N.Y.: Orbis Books, 1988), pp. 87–88.

86. See Michael Welker, "Security of Expectations: Reformulating the Theology of Law and Gospel" *The Journal of Religion* 66 (July 1986):237-60.

87. Ibid., p. 252.

88. Ibid., p. 254.

89. Croatto, *Biblical Hermeneutics*, p. 52.

90. For one summary of many of these links, see Severino Croatto, *Exodus: A Hermeneutics of Freedom* (Maryknoll, N.Y.: Orbis Books, 1981).

91. Croatto's analysis here is not the kind of structuralism found in Lévi-Strauss or Greimas, although those figures stand very much in the line of intellectual ancestry informing Ricoeur's approach to structuralism, from whom Croatto takes so much. See Paul Ricoeur, "The Narrative Form," in *Semeia* 4 (1975):29-74.

92. Croatto, *Biblical Hermeneutics*, pp. 89–90.

93. Ibid., pp. 53, 58.

94. Ibid., p. 53.

95. Here I am following Croatto's distinction between "semiotics" as pertaining largely to texts, and "hermeneutics" as the whole complex life process wherein readers' worlds and textual worlds interplay.

96. See Paul Ricoeur, *Time and Narrative*, vol. 3, trans. Kathleen Blamey and David Pellauer (Chicago: University of Chicago Press, 1988), p. 171. The phrase is one I cite from Ricoeur, the major hermeneutical theorist from whom Croatto draws. This phrase emerges from writings by Ricoeur not cited by Croatto in his book *Biblical Hermeneutics*.

97. Croatto, *Biblical Hermeneutics*, p.53.

98. Juan Luis Segundo, *The Historical Jesus of the Synoptics*, vol. II, *Jesus of Nazareth Yesterday and Today* (Maryknoll, N.Y.: Orbis Books, 1985), p. 19.

99. For examples, see Croatto, *Biblical Hermeneutics*, p. 58.

100. In addition to Croatto's *Exodus*, see the hermeneutical work in biblical studies done by J. C. Maraschin, "Boas novas aos pobres e libertaçao aos presos e opremidos," *Simpôsio* 21 (1980):36–51; and J. Pixley, "El Reino de Dios, ¿Buenas nuevas para los pobres?," *Cuadernos de Teología* 4/2 (1976):77–103.

101. Croatto, *Biblical Hermeneutics*, p. 53.

102. Ibid., pp. 50–53.

103. As just one example, see again Jon Sobrino's comments on the historical Jesus in *Christology at the Crossroads*, pp. 1–16.

104. For just a few of the scholars who have begun to integrate female-specific imagery toward doctrines of God/ess, see Ruether, *Sexism and God-Talk*, pp. 47–71; Brock, *Journeys by Heart*, pp. 50–70; and Nelle Morton, *The Journey Is Home* (Boston: Beacon Press, 1985), pp. 147–75.

105. See especially Paulo Freire, *Pedagogy of the Oppressed*, trans. Myra Bergman Ramos (New York: Herder and Herder, 1970).

106. Bob Marley, "Redemption Song," on *Uprising*, an album by Bob Marley and the Wailers (New York: Island Records, 1980).

107. Schüssler Fiorenza, *In Memory of Her*, pp. 118–54, and Meeks, *The Moral World of the First Christians*, pp. 108–113.

108. On relationships between the place of utopias in Christian theologies of hope, see Gutiérrez, *A Theology of Liberation*, pp. 135–139.

109. For additional resources beyond those given in chapters 3 and 4, and for qualifications concerning this claim, see Ruth Leger Sivard, ed., *Women . . . A World Survey* (Washington: World Priorities, 1985), and Michael Harrington, Robert Greenstein, and Eleanor Holmes Norton, *Who Are the Poor? A Profile of the Changing Faces of Poverty in the United States in 1987* (Washington: Justice for All, 1988).

110. See, again, the *Oxford English Dictionary*, where both the first and second senses indicate that the legal status from which and to which the emancipated one comes is important. *The Compact Edition of the Oxford English Dictionary*, vol. I (London: Oxford University Press, 1971), pp. 847–48.

111. For explorations of ideology as an inevitable feature of human existence, and hence as not necessarily lamentable, see Geertz's call for "a genuinely none-valuative conception of ideology," (Clifford Geertz, "Ideology as Cultural System," in his *The Interpretation of Cultures*, (New York: Basic Books, 1973), p. 196; Geuss's identification of ideology in a "descriptive," "positive" as well as "pejorative" sense, Raymond Geuss, *The Idea of Critical Theory: Habermas and the Frankfurt School* (Cambridge: Cambridge University Press, 1981), pp. 4–26; and for Mannheim's

important view of ideology as "a general aspect of the human condition," see Susan J. Hekman, *Hermeneutics and the Sociology of Knowledge* (Notre Dame, Ind.: Notre Dame University Press, 1986), p. 64; Gunter Remmling, *The Sociology of Karl Mannheim* (London: Routledge & Kegan Paul, 1975), p. 57; and F. W. Rempel, *The Role of Value in Karl Mannheim's Sociology of Knowledge* (The Hague: Monton, 1965), p. 19. For one theologian's attempt boldly to relate faith to ideology—even to insist on faith *with* ideology—see Juan Luis Segundo, *Jesus of Nazareth Yesterday and Today, Vol. I: Faith and Ideologies* (Maryknoll, N.Y.: Orbis, 1984), pp. 119–44.

112. See Bell Hooks, *Feminist Theory* (Boston: South End Press, 1984), pp. 1–15.

113. Gutiérrez, *A Theology of Liberation*, p. 160.

114. Ibid., p. 276. Gutiérrez is citing Giulio Girardi. See also p. 285.

115. On the value of using "transcending" instead of "transcendence," as I do here, see Nelle Morton, *The Journey Is Home*, pp. 98–99.

6. CHRISTUS MATER

1. On *Sophia*, see Elisabeth Schüssler Fiorenza, *In Memory of Her* (New York: Crossroad, 1983), pp. 130–40; on God/ess, see Rosemary Radford Ruether, *Sexism and God-Talk* (Boston: Beacon Press, 1983), pp. 47–71; and "Christa/Community" in Rita Nakashima Brock, *Journeys by Heart* (New York: Crossroad, 1988), pp. 113–14 n.2 and 114–15 n.8.

2. In addition to the discussion on misogyny and matricide in chapter 3 of this work, see also Shulamith Firestone, *The Dialectics of Sex* (New York: Bantam Books, 1970), and Leonard Schein, "All Men Are Misogynists" in Jon Snodgrass, ed., *A Book of Readings for Men Against Sexism* (Albion, Calif.: Times Change Press, 1977), pp. 69–74.

3. See the summary above of the dialectic of sexism by which women are made monstrous and then muted, chapter 4, pp. 114–15.

4. Miriam Therese Winter, *Woman Prayer, Woman Song: Resources for Ritual* (Oak Park, Ill.: Meyer Stone Books, 1987), esp. pp. 25–29, but also *passim*.

5. Audrey McKinney and Mary L. Shanley, review of Nancy C. M. Hartsock, *Money, Sex and Power: Toward a Feminist Historical Materialism*, in *The Journal of Politics* 47 (November 1985):1301.

6. On the ascription of female-specific titles to the figure of Jesus, see J. M. Robinson, "Jesus as *Sophos* and *Sophia*: Wisdom Tradition and the Gospels," in R. Wilken, ed., *Aspects of Wisdom in Judaism and Early Christianity* (Notre Dame, Ind.: University of Notre Dame Press, 1975), pp. 1–16. On the "Jesus as Mother" tradition, see Caroline Walker Bynum, *Jesus as Mother: Studies in the Spirituality of the High Middle Ages*, (Berkeley, Calif.: 1982).

7. See above, pp. 132–34.

8. On the ways these play in relation one to another, see Elisabeth Burgos-Debray, ed., *I . . . Rigoberta Manchu*, trans. Ann Wright (London: Verso, 1984), pp. 59–78, 102–116, 163–71.

9. The phrase is taken from a particularly effective grass-roots organization in El Salvador to which there are analogues throughout Latin America (GAM in Guatemala, for example). *CO-MADRES* is a committee of relatives of political prisoners disappeared and assassinated in El Salvador. It is inspired by Christian faith and practice, and its members claim that "the sole objective that has led us

to organize has been to recoup what is ours and has been wrested from us: our children." Write *CO-MADRES*, P.O. Box 21299, Washington, D.C. 20009-0799. North Americans organizing in solidarity with these and other Latin American women's movements have organized *MADRE* at 121 West 27th St., Room 301, New York, N.Y. 10001.

10. Paul Rabinow, *Reflections on Fieldwork in Morocco* (Berkeley: University of California Press, 1977), p. 39.

11. Luce Irigaray, *Ethique de la difference sexuelle* (Paris: Minuit, 1984), p. 20.

12. On the dynamic of "woman as other" as a dynamic of women's oppression, see Simone de Beauvoir's now almost classic description of women "living in a world where men compel her to assume the status of the Other." Simone de Beauvoir, *The Second Sex*, trans. A. M. Parshley (New York: Alfred A. Knopf, 1952), p. xxviii.

13. See Jon Sobrino, S.J., and Juan Hernandez Pico, S.J., *Teologia de la Solidaridad Cristiana* (Managua: Coedicion, IHCA-CAU, 1983).

14. Stephen Heath, "Men in Feminism: Men and Feminist Theory," in Alice Jardine and Paul Smith, ed., *Men in Feminism* (New York: Methuen, 1987), p. 29.

15. Richard J. Bernstein, *Beyond Objectivism and Relativism* (Philadelphia: University of Pennsylvania Press, 1983), pp. 93ff.

16. Rabinow, *Reflections on Fieldwork*, p. 39.

17. Maria-Barbara Watson-Franke and Lawrence C. Watson, "Understanding in Anthropology: A Philosophical Reminder," *Current Anthropology* 16 (June 1975):251.

18. H. Gadamer, *Truth and Method* (New York: Seabury, 1975), pp. 325–33.

19. Rabinow, *Reflections on Fieldwork*, p. 162.

20. See above, pp. 200–201.

21. Rabinow, *Reflections on Fieldwork*, p. 119.

22. Ibid., p. 151.

23. Ibid.

24. Ibid., p. 119.

25. See above, chapter 5.

26. Paul Ricoeur, "Biblical Hermeneutics," *Semeia* 4 (1975):115–22.

27. Ibid., 125–26.

28. Hans Frei, *The Identity of Jesus Christ: The Hermeneutic Bases of Dogmatic Theology* (Philadelphia: Fortress, 1975), pp. 135–38. My arguments in chapter 5 for a mythos of Jesus' *life-praxis*, which is more encompassing than Jesus' individual identity, allows readings of the narrative that accent others' identities as well, besides the identity of Jesus that Frei highlights. The point can then still be made that the narratives' subject matter is laden with extravagance and hyperbole in order to prompt radical love for alienated humanity.

29. David Tracy, *The Analogical Imagination* (New York: Crossroad, 1981), p. 278.

30. Edward Farley, *Ecclesial Man: A Social Phenomenology of Faith and Reality* (Philadelphia: Fortress, 1975), p. 150.

31. Ibid., p. 158.

32. Ibid., pp. 171, 178.

33. Ibid., p. 178.

34. See above, chapter 4.

35. See above, chapter 4.

36. On the notion of Christian love as affirming the other *qua* other, see Outka's notion of "equal regard" in Gene Outka, *Agape: An Ethical Analysis* (New Haven, Conn.: Yale University Press, 1972), pp. 9–24.

37. For discussion of otherness in relation to experiences of mothering see Kathryn Allen Rabuzzi, *Motherself* (Bloomington and Indianapolis, Ind.: Indiana University Press, 1988), p. 77.

38. Nancy Chodorow, *The Reproduction of Mothering: Psycho-analysis and the Sociology of Gender* (Berkeley, Calif.: University of California Press, 1978), pp. 104–107.

39. Adrienne Rich, *Of Woman Born: Motherhood as Experience and Institution* (New York: W.W. Norton, 1976), pp. 186–92.

40. For this dynamic see James B. Nelson, *The Intimate Connection* (Philadelphia: Westminster, 1988), pp. 50–51.

41. Gerda Lerner, *The Creation of Patriarchy* (New York and London: Oxford, 1986), pp. 141–60, Edward E. Barthell, *Gods and Goddesses of Ancient Greece* (Coral Gables, Fla.: University of Miami Press, 1971), and Joan Chambers Engelsman, *The Feminine Dimension of the Divine* (Wilmette, Ind.: Chiron, 1979/1989).

42. See Julian of Norwich, *Revelations of Divine Love*, trans. John Walsh (New York: Harper & Row, 1961), pp. 159–61.

43. Rosemary Radford Ruether, ed., *Womanguides: Readings Toward a Feminist Theology* (Boston: Beacon, 1985), pp. 105–133.

44. On this link, recall again the anthropological studies of gender systems, in Sherry B. Ortner and Harriet Whitehead, eds., *Sexual Meanings* (Cambridge: Cambridge University Press, 1981), and Peggy Reeves Sanday, *Female Power and Male Dominance* (Cambridge: Cambridge University Press, 1981). To say that such subordinationalist language "reinforces" subordinationalist social structures is not to say that it "causes" them.

45. Rita Nakashima Brock, *Journeys by Heart* (New York: Crossroad, 1988), p. 113n.

46. Ibid., pp. 89–104.

47. Penelope Washburn, "Becoming Woman: Menstruation as Spiritual Challenge," in *Womanspirit Rising: A Feminist Reader in Religion*, ed. Carol P. Christ and Judith Plaskow (New York: Harper, 1979), pp. 249–50.

48. Barbara G. Walker, "Menstrual Blood," *The Women's Encyclopedia of Myths and Secrets* (San Francisco: Harper & Row, 1983), pp. 643–44.

49. Washburn, "Becoming Woman," p. 256.

50. Mark Gerzon, *A Choice of Heroes* (Boston: Houghton Mifflin Co., 1982), pp. 20–21.

51. Ibid., p. 18.

52. Lois Paul, "Work and Sex in a Guatemalan Village," in *Women, Culture and Society*, ed. Michelle Zimbalist Rosaldo and Louise Lamphere (Stanford, Calif.: Stanford University Press, 1974), pp. 289–99.

53. Benjamin N. Colby and Lore M. Colby, *The Daykeeper: The Life and Discourse of an Ixil Diviner* (Cambridge, Mass.: Harvard University Press, 1981), pp. 41–42.

54. Numerous studies show that 95–98 percent of Guatemala's land is owned by about 2–4 percent of the population. Landowning elites are predominantly ladino, not the Mayan peoples who make up approximately 60 percent of the population. See, as just one source, Philip Berryman, *Christians in Guatemala's Struggle*

(London: Catholic Institute for International Relations, 1984).

55. See reports on the lives of mothers of the disappeared among GAM, *Grupo de Apoyo Mutuo*, the Mutual Support Group for Families of the "Disappeared" in Jean-Marie Simon, *Guatemala: Eternal Spring, Eternal Tyranny* (New York: W.W. Norton, 1987), pp. 159–61.

56. Jean Bethke Elshtain, *Public Man, Private Woman: Women in Social and Political Thought* (Princeton, N.J.: Princeton University Press, 1981).

57. For discussion of the "separate spheres" approach to women's subordination in Latin America, see Susan C. Bourque and Kay Barbara Warren, *Women of the Andes: Patriarchy and Social Change in Two Peruvian Towns* (Ann Arbor, Mich.: The University of Michigan Press, 1981), pp. 59–65.

58. See not only the earlier summaries in Dinnerstein, but also the more recent studies of how present disproportionate responsibilities for providing maternal functions still limits women's obtaining fulfilling and adequate labor opportunities. Louis Uchitelle, "America's Army of Non-Workers (sic)," *New York Times*, September 27, 1987, sect. 3: pp. 1, 6.

59. For formal statements by men against sexism, see Jon Snodgrass, ed., *A Book of Readings for Men Against Sexism* pp. 135–37.

60. Janice G. Raymond, *A Passion for Friends* (Boston: Beacon Press, 1986), pp. 11–12.

61. Rich, *Of Woman Born*, p. 216.

62. Ibid.

63. Ibid.

64. Adrienne Rich, "Natural Resources," in her *The Fact of a Doorframe* (New York: W. W. Norton, 1984), p. 258.

65. John E. Fortunato, *AIDS and the Spiritual Dilemma* (New York: Harper & Row, 1987), pp. 35–68.

66. Ibid., pp. 61–62.

67. James B. Nelson, *Embodiment* (Minneapolis, Minn.: Augsburg, 1978), pp. 19–36, 70–103. This does not imply a simple continuity between present embodiment and "resurrected bodies."

68. Sallie McFague, *Models of God* (Philadelphia: Fortress, 1987), pp. 127–39.

69. Beverly Wildung Harrison, "Misogyny and Homophobia: The Last Connection," in her *Making the Connections: Essays in Feminist Social Ethics*, Carol S. Robb, ed. (Boston: Beacon Press, 1985), pp. 135–51.

70. Sandra Lee Bartky, "On Psychological Repression," in *Philosophy and Women*, ed. Sharon Bishop and Marjorie Weinsweig (Belmont, Calif.: Wadsworth, 1979), esp. pp. 34ff. on "sexual objectification."

71. See Nancy Hartsock's studies of "shameful sensuality as denial of the body," in her *Money, Sex and Power* (Baltimore: Johns Hopkins University Press, 1983), pp. 172–74, and Susan Griffin, *Pornography and Silence* (New York: Harper, 1981), p. 2: "The bodies of women in pornography, mastered, bound, silenced, beaten, and even murdered, are symbols for natural feeling and the power of nature, which the pornographic mind hates and fears ... 'the woman' in pornography, like the 'Jew' in anti-Semitism and 'the black' in racism, is simply ... that region of being the pornographic mind would forget and deny." These studies do not contravene the need and value of creative erotic art in literature, photography, cinema or other media. See Nelson, *Embodiment*, pp. 163–68, and Beatrice Faust, *Women, Sex and Pornography: A Controversial Study* (New York: Macmillan, 1980), pp. 89–101.

72. For studies of dominance feeling and hostility in pervasive notions of sexuality, see Hartsock, *Money*, pp. 157–66.

73. This in contrast to the explicit affirmation of domination games in Nicholas Davidson, *The Failure of Feminism* (New York: Prometheus Books, 1988), pp. 90–91. On the function of dominance-feeling in sexuality, see A. H. Maslow, "Self-Esteem (Dominance-Feeling) and Sexuality in Women," *Journal of Social Psychology* 16 (1942):291.

74. On the relationships between systemic gender domination in society and the instability built into the institution of heterosexual marriage, see Barbara Ehrenreich, *Hearts of Men* (Garden City, N.Y.: Archor Press, 1983), pp. 14–28.

75. On relations between positive visions of the body, critique of the distortions of sexism, heterosexism, and racism, see Audre Lorde, "The Uses of the Erotic," *Sister Outsider: Essays and Speeches* (Trumansburg, N.Y.: The Crossing Press, 1984), pp. 53–59. Cf. Snodgrass, *A Book of Readings*, pp. 160–96.

76. On the genitalization of sexuality in Western society and as characteristic of sexism, see Snodgrass, *A Book of Readings*, pp. 16–35. See also the discussion of "The Genitalization of Male Sexuality," in James B. Nelson, *The Intimate Connection* (Philadelphia: Westminster, 1988), pp. 34–38.

77. The fear of death and of the body is also linked to white supremacist logic's fantasies of blackness, and all three are operative in the refusal to deal with the AIDS crisis.

78. For historical diversity, consult John Boswell, *Christianity, Social Tolerance and Homosexuality* (Chicago: University of Chicago Press, 1980), pp. 243–68. For the diversity cross-culturally, see ethnologist Walter L. Williams, *The Spirit and the Flesh: Sexual Diversity in American Indian Culture* (Boston: Beacon Press, 1986). Compare this with the detailed expositions in David F. Greenberg, *The Construction of Homosexuality* (Chicago: University of Chicago Press, 1988).

79. Gayraud S. Wilmore, *Black and Presbyterian: The Heritage and the Hope* (Philadelphia: Westminster, 1983), p. 125.

80. Joel Kovell, "Radix Malorum," in his *White Racism* (New York: Columbia University Press, 1970), pp. 86–88. See my discussion of this abstraction in white racism, in chapter 4.

81. Albert B. Cleague, Jr., *The Black Messiah* (New York: Sheed and Ward, 1968); James H. Cone, *God of the Oppressed* (New York: Seabury, 1975); Allan Boesak, *Black and Reformed: Apartheid, Liberation and the Calvinist Tradition* (Maryknoll, N.Y. Orbis, 1984); and Theo Witvliet, *The Way of the Black Messiah: The Hermeneutical Challenge of Black Theology as a Theology of Liberation* (Oak Park, Ill.: Meyer-Stone Books, 1987).

82. Kovell, *White Racism*, pp. xi, 211–30.

83. On romanticization, rejection, and assimilation as three inadequate "traditions" of African American responses to white racism, see Cornel West, *Prophesy Deliverance! An Afro-American Revolutionary Christianity* (Philadelphia: Westminster, 1982), pp. 69–91.

84. Ibid., pp. 91, 85.

85. This and the preceding selection are both from Gwendolyn Brooks, "Primer for Blacks" in Amiri Baraka (LeRoi Jones) and Amina Baraka, eds., *Confirmation: An Anthology of African American Women* (New York: Quill, 1983), pp. 82–83.

86. Margaret Walker, "THIS IS MY CENTURY . . . Black Synthesis of Time," in Baraka and Baraka, *Confirmation*, pp. 361–62, 363.

87. I am indebted, in part, to the work of Ms. Laurie Garrett, who has explored some of these notions in her own work.

88. Brooks, "Primer for Blacks," p. 83.

89. James H. Cone, *For My People: Black Theology and the Black Church* (Maryknoll, N.Y.: Orbis Books, 1984), pp. 78–98.

90. While I see the potential in Cone's work for an emancipatory critique of hetero-realism, I do not yet see that the denial of civil rights to gays and lesbians is a strong item on his theological agenda. A more explicit address of issues pertaining to heterosexism and the other supremacist logics is found in Cornel West's Neo-Gramscian analyses. See Cornel West, "Marxist Theory and the Specificity of Afro-American Oppression," in *Marxism and the Interpretation of Culture*, ed. Cary Nelson and Lawrence Grossberg (Urbana and Chicago: University of Illinois, 1988), pp. 17–33

91. See Gustavo Gutiérrez, *A Theology of Liberation*, trans. and ed. Sister Caridad Inda and John Eagleson, 15th Anniversary Ed. (Maryknoll, N.Y.: Orbis Books, 1988), pp. xxi–xxii.

92. For discussion of how maternalization freed from the sexual division of labor might impact economic modes of organizing production in forms of capitalism, see Chodorow, *The Reproduction of Mothering*, pp. 186–90, 200, 212, esp. the "Afterward: Women's Mothering and Women's Liberation"; and also Hartsock on the relationships between the level of reproduction, the level of production, and the level of capitalist economic exchange, in her *Money*, pp. 231-66.

93. Nicholas Lash, *A Matter of Hope: A Theologian's Reflections on the Thought of Karl Marx* (Notre Dame, Ind.: University of Notre Dame Press, 1981), pp. 88–92, 135-52.

94. On the issues of Marxism and its relation to Christianity, see also Arthur F. McGovern, *Marxism: An American Christian Perspective* (Maryknoll, N.Y.: Orbis, 1987).

95. On the notion of "sustenance rights," see Henry Shue, *Basic Rights: Subsistence, Affluence and U.S. Foreign Policy* (Princeton, N.J.: Princeton University Press, 1980). For discussion of ethical and theological implications of Shue's work, see Nicholas Wolterstorff, *Until Justice and Peace Embrace* (Grand Rapids, Mich.: Eerdmans, 1983), pp. 81–98.

96. For one account of these traditions, note Matthew L. Lamb, "Christian Spirituality and Social Justice," *Horizons* 10/1 (1983):32–49.

97. See above, chapter 4.

98. Johanne Baptist Metz, *The Emergent Church: The Future of Christianity in a Postbourgeois World* (New York: Crossroad, 1981), pp. 14–16.

99. Ibid., p. 15.

100. Ibid., pp. 15–16.

101. The actual Christ title used in this passage is "son of man," the transcendent, apocalyptic figure frequently linked by the synoptic gospels to Jesus. This figure, this Christ, was frequently presented as the one in whom Jesus' life-praxis for all humanity would come to fruition. On the New Testament literature on "Son of Man," see S. E. Johnson, *The Interpreter's Dictionary of the Bible*, 4 vols. (Nashville, Tenn.: Abingdon, 1962), 4:413–20.

102. M. H. Shepherd, Jr., "Lord's Supper," *The Interpreter's Dictionary of the Bible*, 3:159.

103. Ibid., 3:160.

104. Marvin Harris, *Cannibals and Kings: The Origins of Cultures* (New York: Random House, 1977), p. 158.

105. Mary Daly, *Pure Lust: Elemental Feminist Philosophy* (Boston: Beacon Press, 1984), p. 51.

106. "Declaracion de la segunda convencion nacional de presbiterios del Ecuador," NADOC, no. 204 (May 1971), p. 169, cited in Gutiérrez, *A Theology of Liberation*, p. 247 n.

107. John Paul II, *The Holy Eucharist* (Vatican: Polygrot Press, 1980), a. 6.

108. See Clodovis Boff, "The Lord's Supper Like That of St. Paul in Troas," in *Feet-On-The-Ground Theology: A Brazilian Journey* (Maryknoll, N.Y.: Orbis Books, 1987), pp. 132–34.

109. For additional sources developing a theology of the sacraments in relation to the material needs of the earth's peoples, see David Hollenbach, "A Prophetic Church and the Catholic Sacramental Imagination" in *The Faith That Does Justice: Examining the Christian Sources for Social Change*, John C. Haughey, ed. (New York: Paulist Press, 1977), pp. 234–63; Tissa Balasuriya, *The Eucharist and Human Liberation* (Maryknoll, N.Y.: Orbis Books, 1979); and Dermot A. Lane, "The Eucharist and the Praxis of Social Justice" in *Foundations for a Social Theology: Praxis, Process and Salvation* (New York: Paulist Press, 1984), pp. 141–69.

110. See Gayatri Chakravorty Spivak, "The Politics of Interpretation," in *The Politics of Interpretation*, ed. W. J. T. Mitchell (Chicago: University of Chicago Press, 1982), p. 366.

111. For one summary of issues in the conversation between cultural anthropology and Marxist analyses, see Maurice Godelier, *Perspectives in Marxist Anthropology* (London: Cambridge University Press, 1973).

EPILOGUE: RE-MEMBERING ESPERANZA

1. This phrase and the following stanzas are from Julia Esquivel, "They Have Threatened Us with Resurrection," in her *Threatened with Resurrection (Amenazado de Resurrecion): Prayers and Poems from an Exiled Guatemalan* (Elgin, Ill.: The Brethren Press, 1982), pp. 59–63.

2. I am indebted to Ms. Lauren J. McFeaters for calling my attention in her own studies to this poem by Frances Croake Frank in J. Morley and H. Ward, eds., *Celebrating Women* (Women in Theology and the Movement for the Ordination of Women, 1976).

INDEX